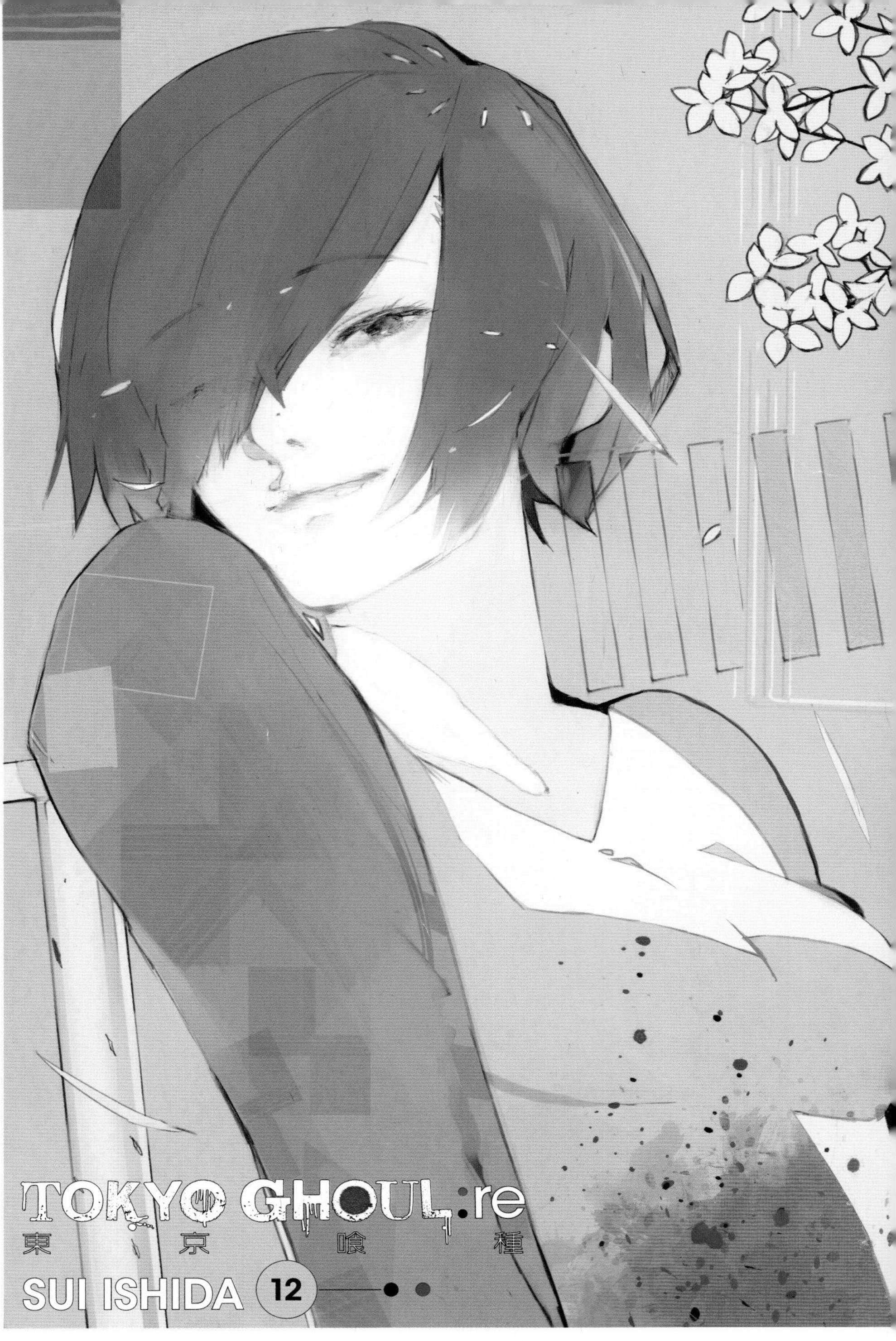
TOKYO GHOUL:re
東京喰種
SUI ISHIDA
12

CONTENTS

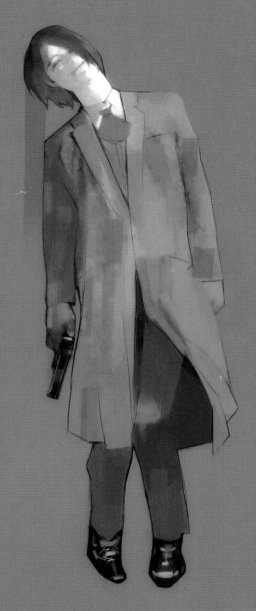

T O K Y O G H O U L

CCG Ghoul Investigators / Tokyo Ghoul:re

The CCG is the only organization in the world that investigates and solves Ghoul-related crimes. Founded by the Washu Family, the CCG developed and evolved Quinques, a type of weapon derived from Ghouls' Kagune. Quinx, an advanced, next-generation technology where humans are implanted with Quinques is currently under development.

Mado Squad

Qs (Quinx): Investigators implanted with Quinques. They all live together in a house called the Chateau along with Investigator Sasaki.

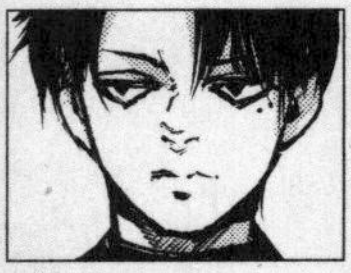

Kuki Urie
瓜江久生
Senior Investigator
New Quinx Squad leader and most talented fighter in the squad. Demonstrating leadership after the death of Shirazu. Appointed head of S2 Squad.

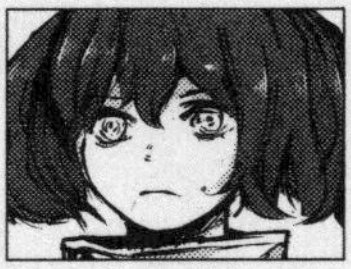

Saiko Yonebayashi
米林才子
Rank 2 Investigator
Supporting Urie as Deputy Squad Leader while playing with her subordinates. Very bad at time management and a sucker for games and snacks.

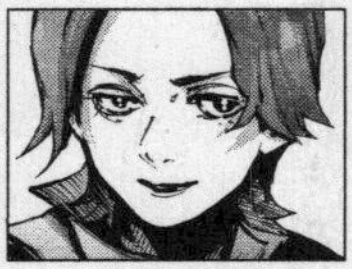

Toma Higemaru
髯丸トウマ
Rank 3 Investigator
Discovered his Quinx aptitude before enrolling in the academy. Looks up to Urie. Comes from a wealthy family.

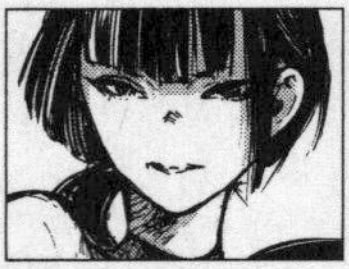

Ching-li Hsiao
小静麗
Rank 1 Investigator
From Hakubi Garden like Hairu Ihei. Skilled in hand-to-hand combat. Came to Japan from Taiwan as a child.

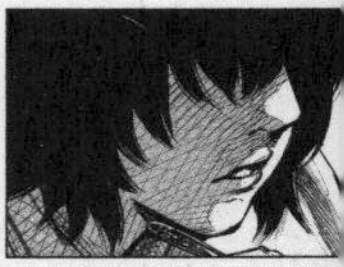

Shinsanpei Aura
安浦晋三平
Rank 2 Investigator
Nephew of Special Investigator Kiyoko Aura. Unlike his aunt, who graduated at the top of her class, his grades were not that great.

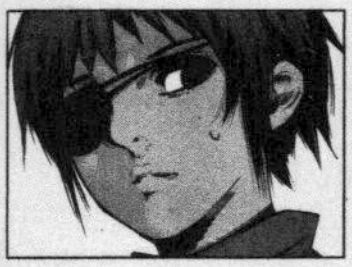

Toru Mutsuki
六月 透
Rank 1 Investigator
Assigned female at birth, he transitioned after the Quinx procedure. Struggling with the lie he has been living with...

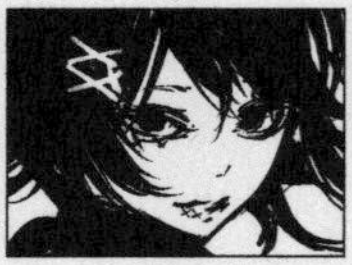

Juzo Suzuya
鈴屋什造
Special Investigator
Promoted to special investigator at 22, a feat previously only accomplished by Kisho Arima. A maverick who fights with knives hidden in his prosthetic leg. Appointed head of S3 Squad.

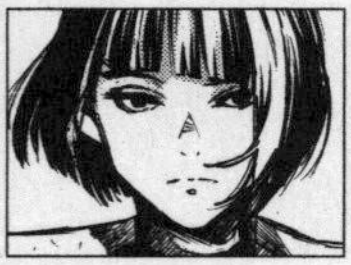

Kori Ui
宇井 郡
Special Investigator
Promising investigator formerly with the Arima Squad. Became a special investigator at a young age, but has a stubborn side. Assistant to the new bureau chief.

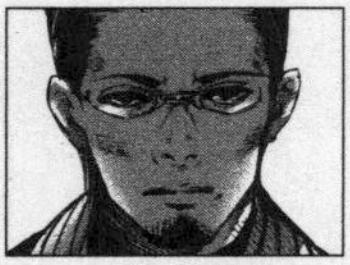

Matsuri Washu
和修 政
Special Investitgator
Yoshitoki's son. A Washu supremacist. Is skeptical of Quinxes. The only surviving member of the Washu family after the Rushima Operation. Current whereabouts unknown.

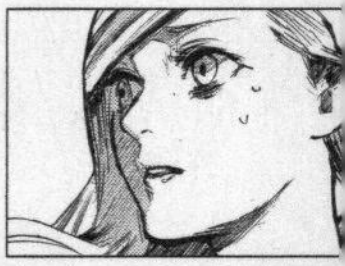

Akira Mado
真戸 暁
Assistant Special Investigator
Mentor to Haise. Determined to eradicate Ghouls. In hiding with the Goat after aiding a Ghoul during the Rushima operation.

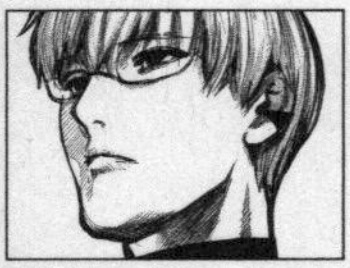

Kisho Arima
有馬貴将
Special Investigator
An undefeated investigator respected by many at the CCG. Killed at Cochlea by the One-Eyed King.

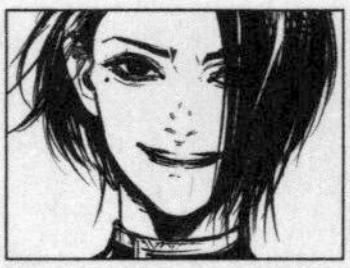

Kichimura Washu
和修吉福
CCG Bureau Chief
Mysterious investigator related to the Washu family. Developed the Oggai for Tokyo Dissolution, a plan to eradicate all Ghouls.

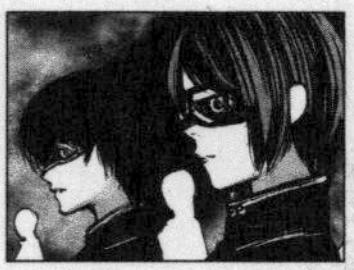

The Oggai
殀

A new Qs Squad solely composed of children. They locate Ghouls with their heightened sense of smell.

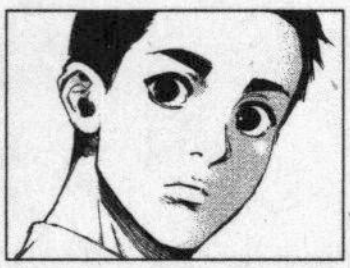

Takeomi Kuroiwa
黒磐武臣
Rank 1 Investigator
Son of Special Investigator Iwao Kuroiwa. Has a strong sense of justice and has restrained Ghouls with his bare hands.

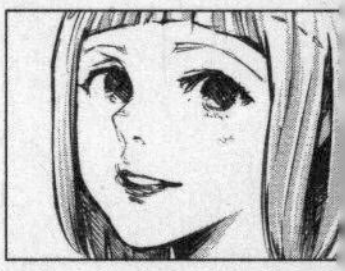

Yoriko Kosaka
小坂依子

Touka's high school friend. Works at a bakery. Accepted Takeomi Kuroiwa's marriage proposal.

T ● K Y ● G H ● U L

Tokyo Ghoul :re

Ghouls

They appear human, but have a unique predation organ called Kagune and can only survive by feeding on human flesh. They are the nemesis of humanity. Besides human flesh, the only other thing they can ingest is coffee. Ghouls can only be wounded by a Kagune or a Quinque made from a Kagune.

Goat

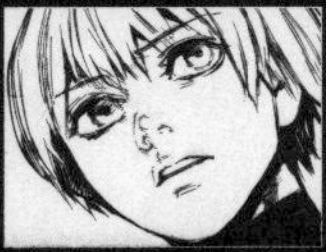

Ken Kaneki
金木 研
Served as the Qs Squad mentor as Haise Sasaki. A half-Ghoul who has succeeded Kisho Arima as the One-Eyed King. Living at Café:re and leading the anti-human group Goat.

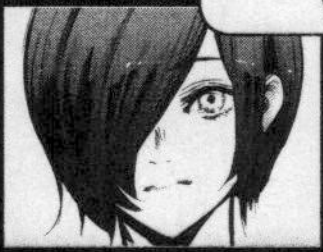

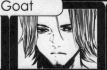

Touka Kirishima
霧嶋董香
Manager of Café :re. Wants to carry on the traditions of Anteiku.

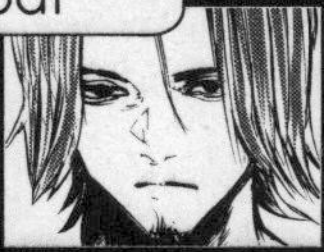

Renji Yomo
四方蓮示
Café :re barista. Touka and Ayato's uncle.

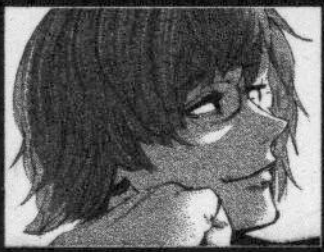

Nishiki Nishio
西尾 錦
The Ghoul known as Orochi. Tracking the Aogiri Tree.

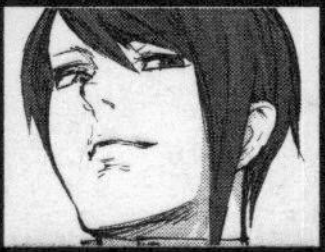

Shu Tsukiyama
月山 習
A gourmet Ghoul. Continues to follow Kaneki after the dissolution of his family's conglomerate.

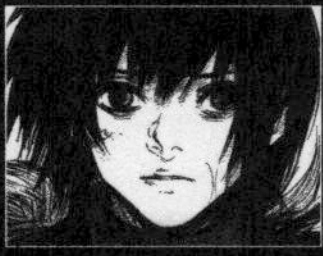

Ayato
霧嶋絢都
Touka's younger brother. A Rate SS Ghoul known as the Rabbit.

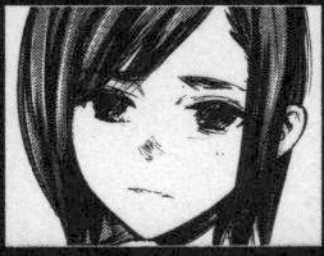

Hinami Fueguchi
笛口雛実
Freed from Cochlea by Kaneki.

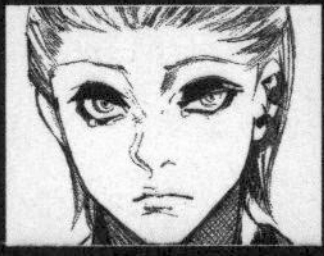

Naki
ナキ
Current leader of the White Suits. A Rate S, but frequently loses control.

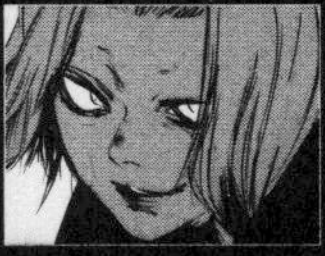

The Owl
オウル
The current incarnation of investigator Seido Takizawa after Dr. Kano implanted him with a Kakuho. Over-whelmingly powerful.

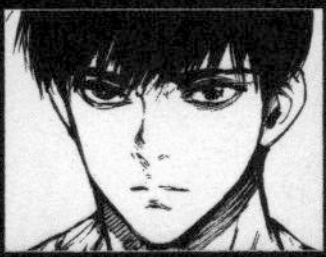

Kotaro Amon
亜門鋼太朗
Considered a Floppy after undergoing Kano's Kakuho transplant procedure, but after receiving Rc suppressant, he made a miraculous recovery. In hiding with the Goat.

Clown Masks

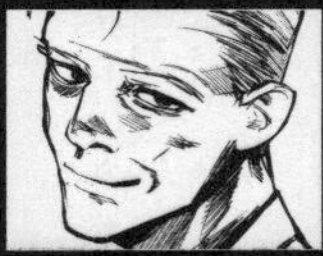

Akihiro Kano
嘉納明博
Medical examiner for the Aogiri Tree. Researching Kakuho transplants to create artificial half-Ghouls.

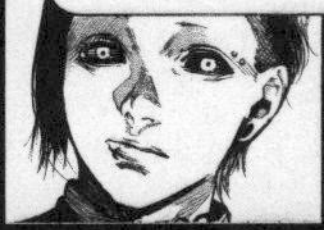

Uta
ウタ
Owner of HySy Artmask Studio. Made Kaneki and the Qs' masks.

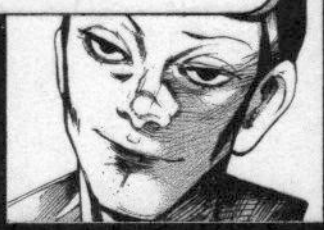

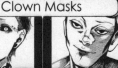

Nico
ニコ
A gay man in love.

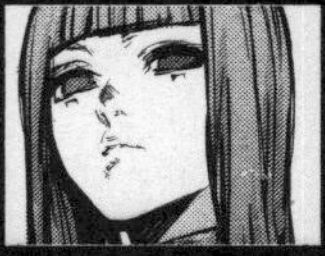

Kuro
クロ
Like Ken Kaneki, she underwent Kano's Ghoulification Procedure. Absorbed her twin sister Shiro.

So far in :re

T ● K Y ● G H ● U L

Ken Kaneki succeeded Kisho Arima as the One-Eyed King and formed the anti-human organization the Goat after conflicts at Cochlea and Rushima, hoping to create a world where Ghouls and humans can coexist peacefully. Meanwhile, the Washu family's dark side has been made public and Nimura Furuta, now known as Kichimura Washu, has been appointed the new bureau chief of the CCG. He hopes to completely eradicate and displace all Ghouls from Tokyo with the Oggai. Just as the Goat decides to flee Café :re due to the threat of these dark children, Mutsuki arrives on their doorstep...

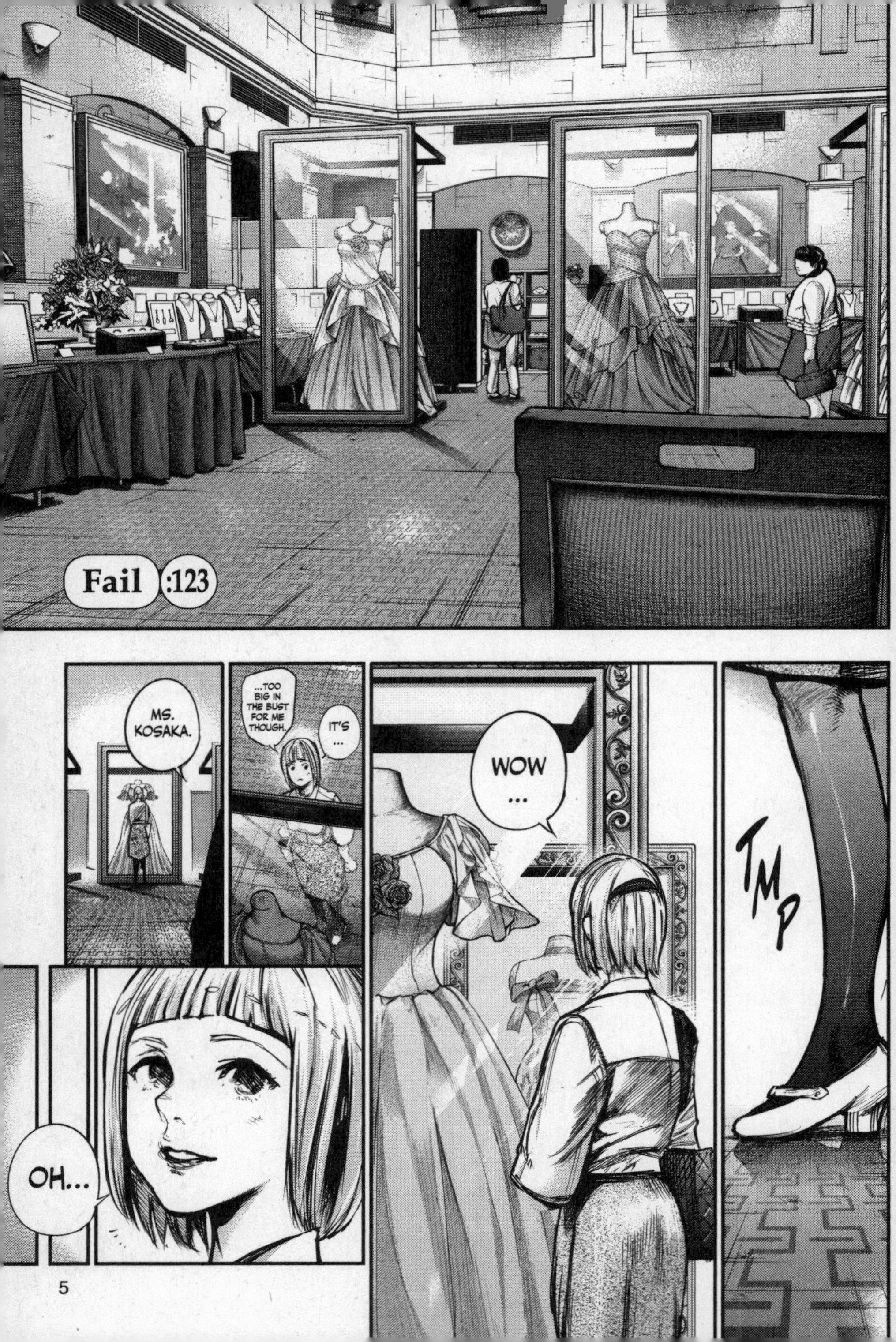
Fail :123
TMP
WOW ...
IT'S ...
...TOO BIG IN THE BUST FOR ME THOUGH.
MS. KOSAKA.
OH...

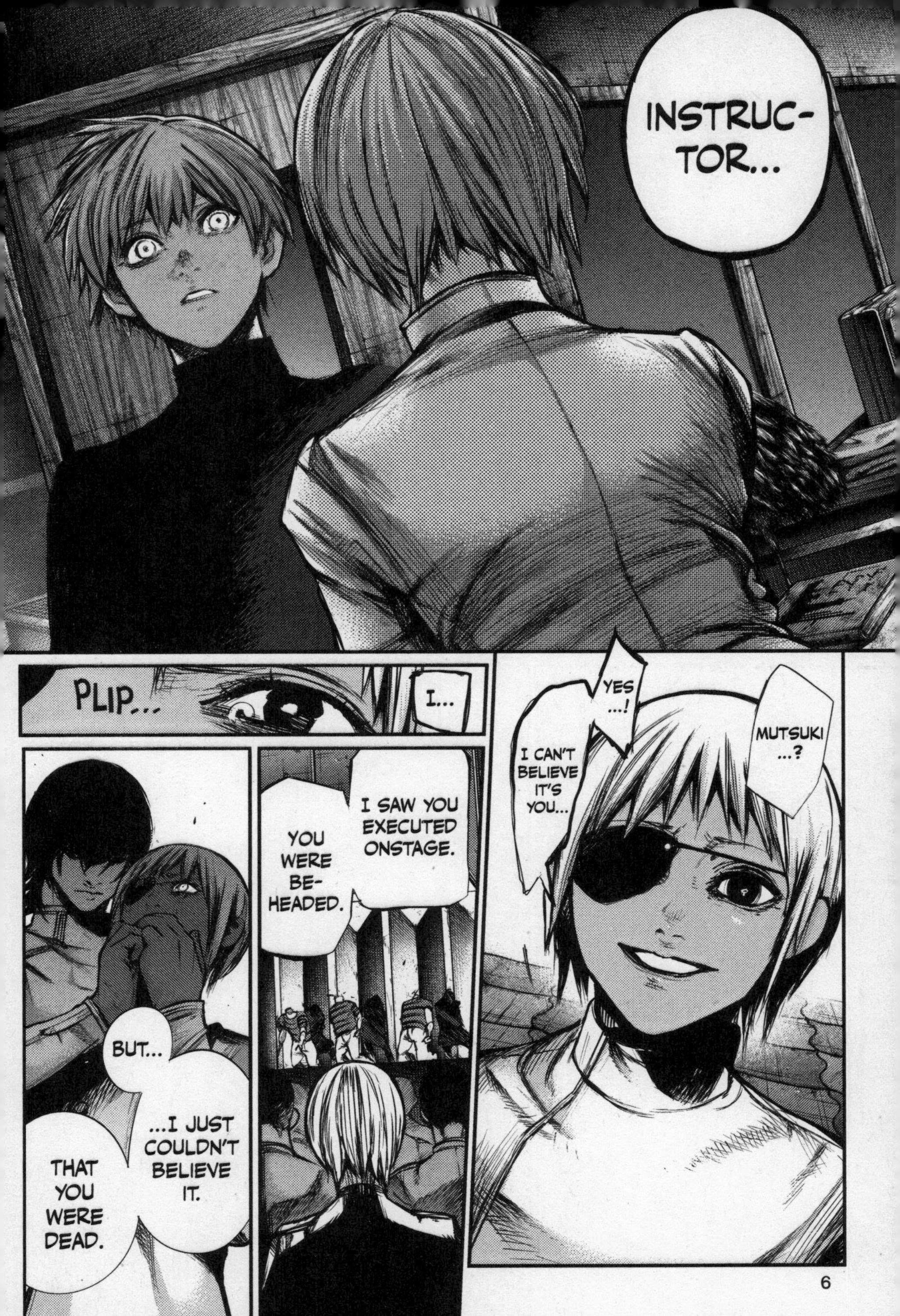
INSTRUC-
TOR...
MUTSUKI
...?
YES
...!
I CAN'T
BELIEVE
IT'S
YOU...
I...
PLIP...
I SAW YOU
EXECUTED
ONSTAGE.
YOU
WERE
BE-
HEADED.
BUT...
...I JUST
COULDN'T
BELIEVE
IT.
THAT
YOU
WERE
DEAD.

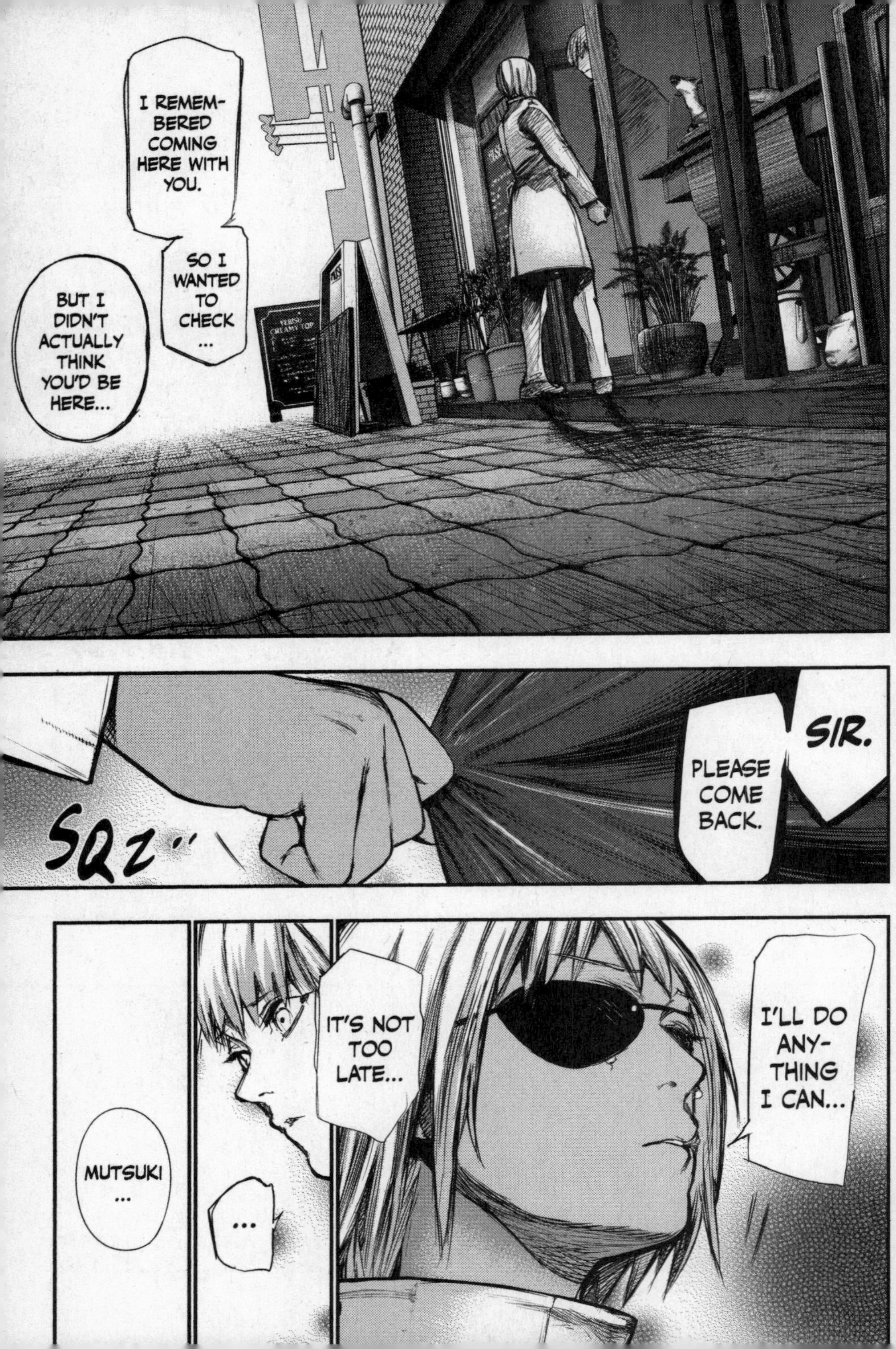
I REMEMBERED COMING HERE WITH YOU.
SO I WANTED TO CHECK...
BUT I DIDN'T ACTUALLY THINK YOU'D BE HERE...
YEBISU CREAMY TOP
SIR.
PLEASE COME BACK.
SQZ
I'LL DO ANYTHING I CAN...
IT'S NOT TOO LATE...
...
MUTSUKI...

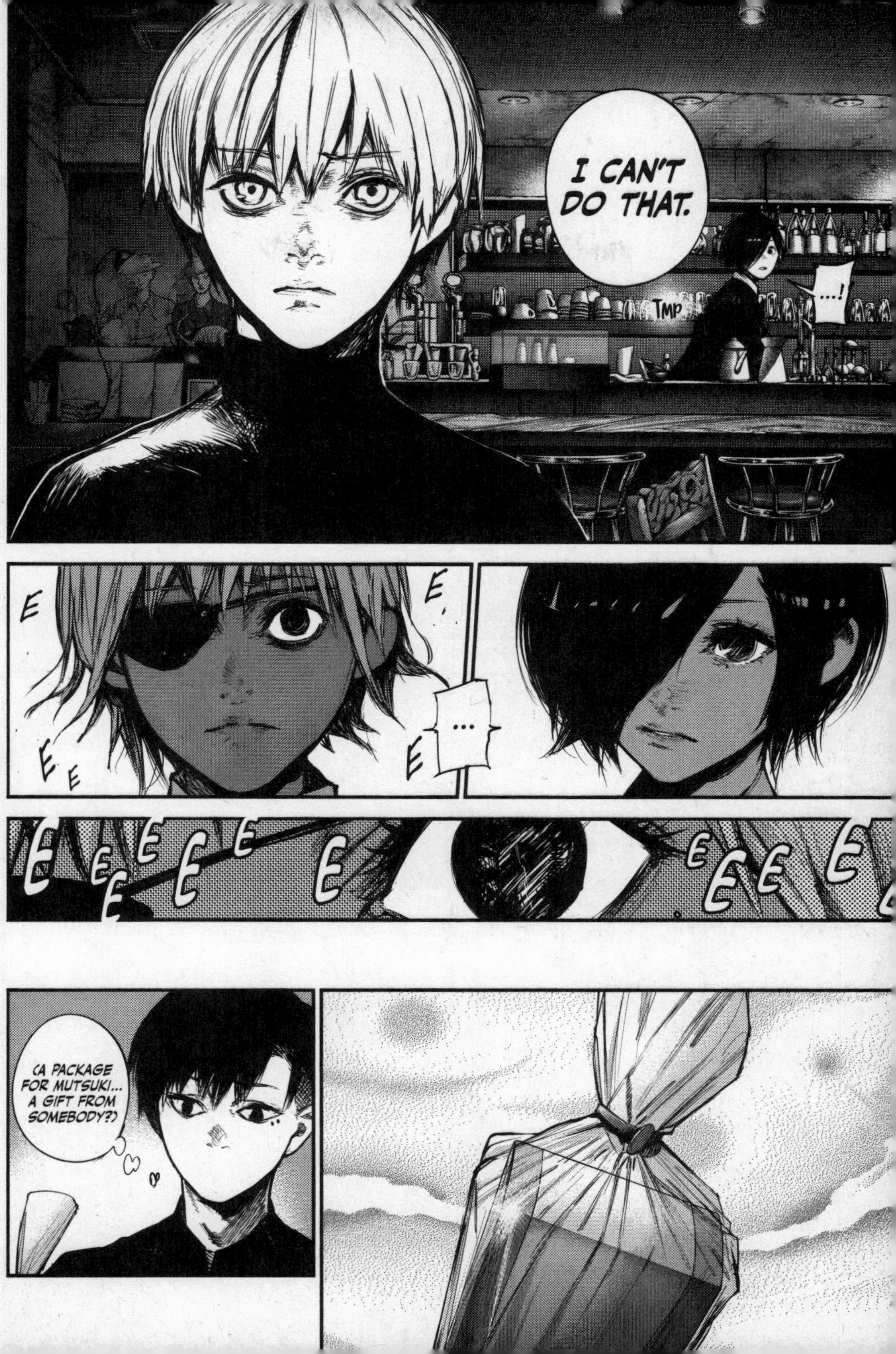
I CAN'T DO THAT.
...!
TMP
...
(A PACKAGE FOR MUTSUKI... A GIFT FROM SOMEBODY?)

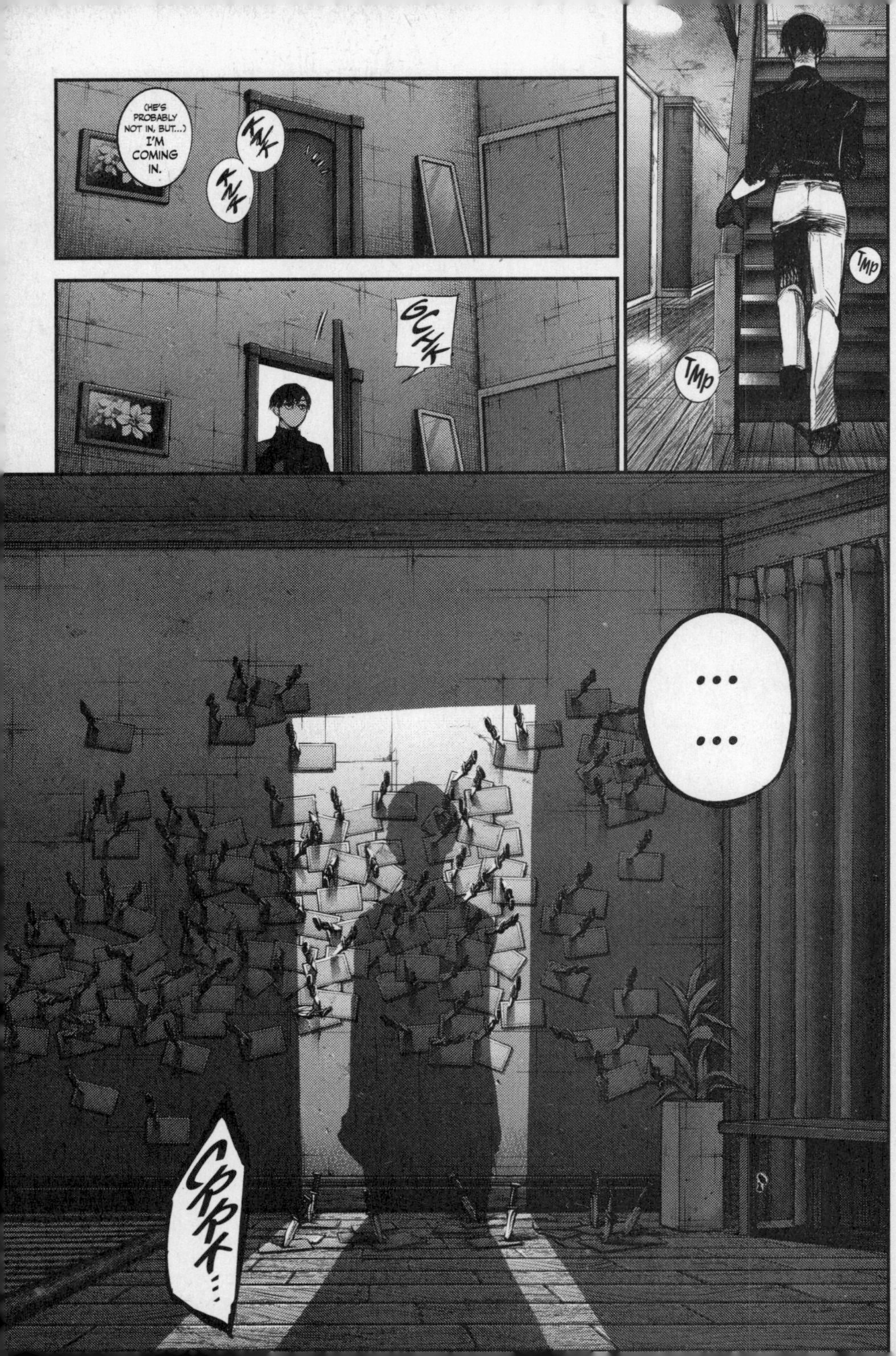
TMp
TMp
(HE'S PROBABLY NOT IN, BUT...) I'M COMING IN.
KNK
KNK
GCHK
...
...
CRRK...

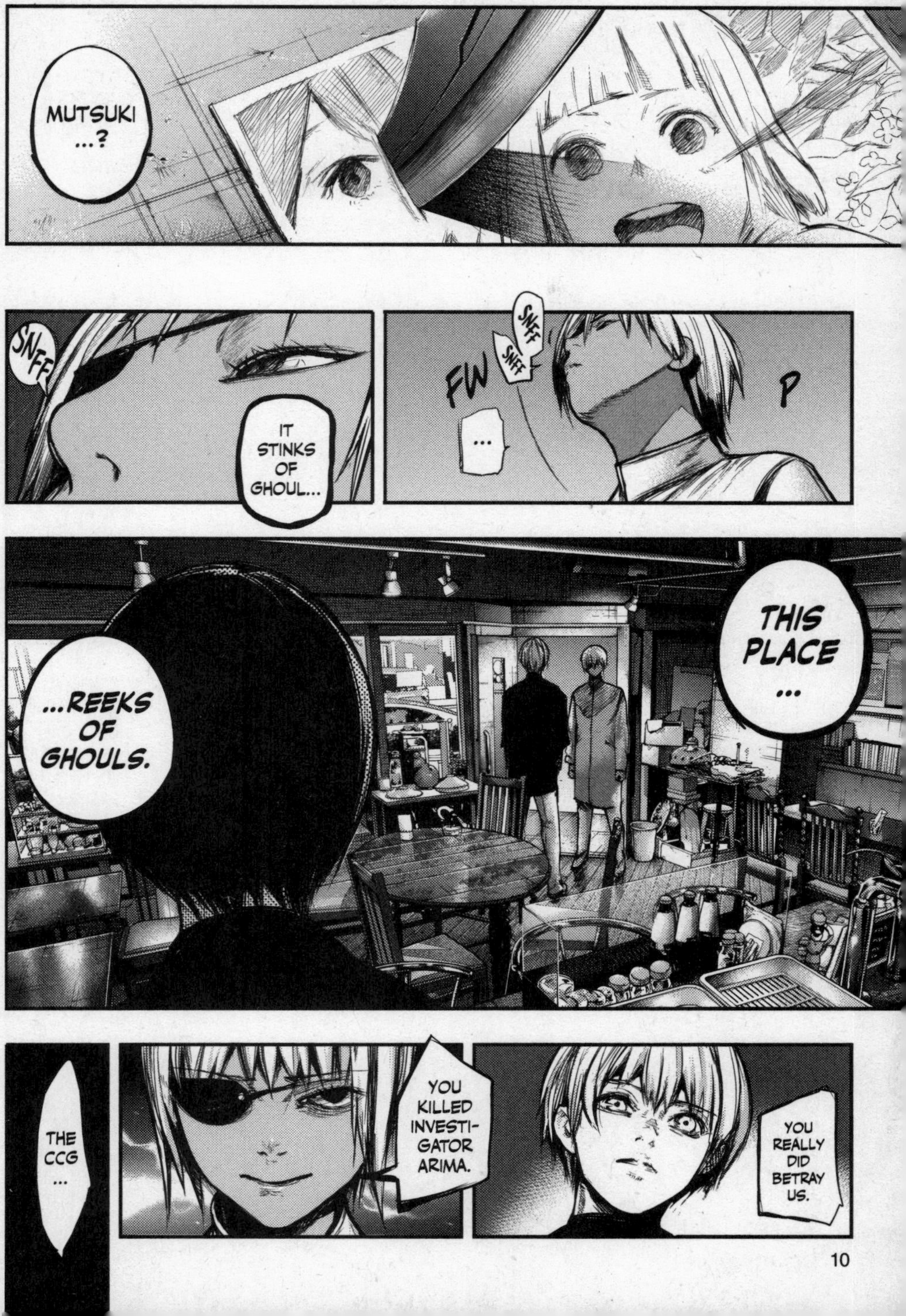
MUTSUKI ...?
SNFF
SNFF
FW
P
...
SNFF
IT STINKS OF GHOUL...
THIS PLACE ...
...REEKS OF GHOULS.
YOU REALLY DID BETRAY US.
YOU KILLED INVESTI-GATOR ARIMA.
THE CCG ...

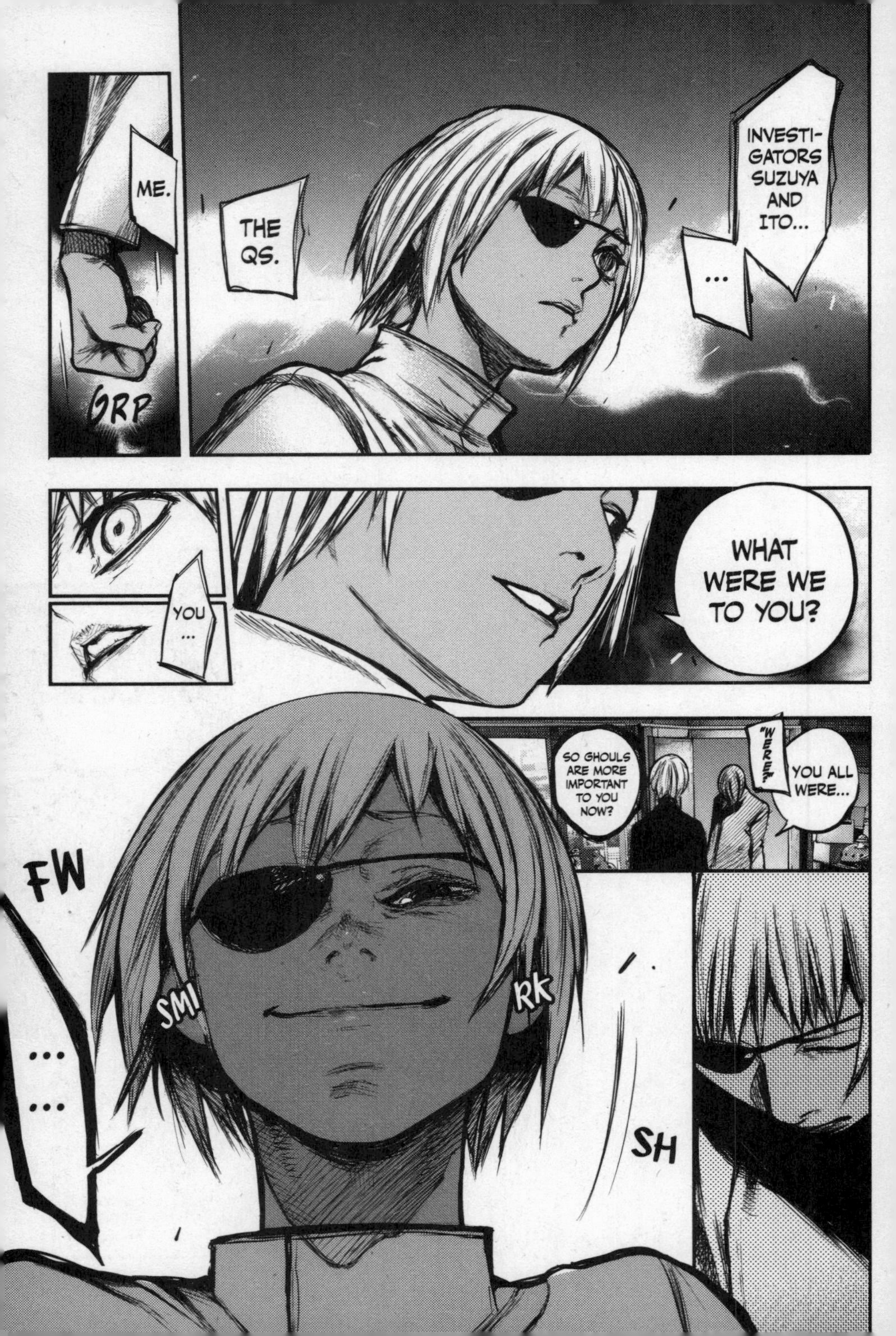
INVESTIGATORS SUZUYA AND ITO...
...
THE QS.
ME.
GRP
WHAT WERE WE TO YOU?
YOU ...
YOU ALL WERE...
"WERE"
SO GHOULS ARE MORE IMPORTANT TO YOU NOW?
SH
SMIRK
FW
...
...

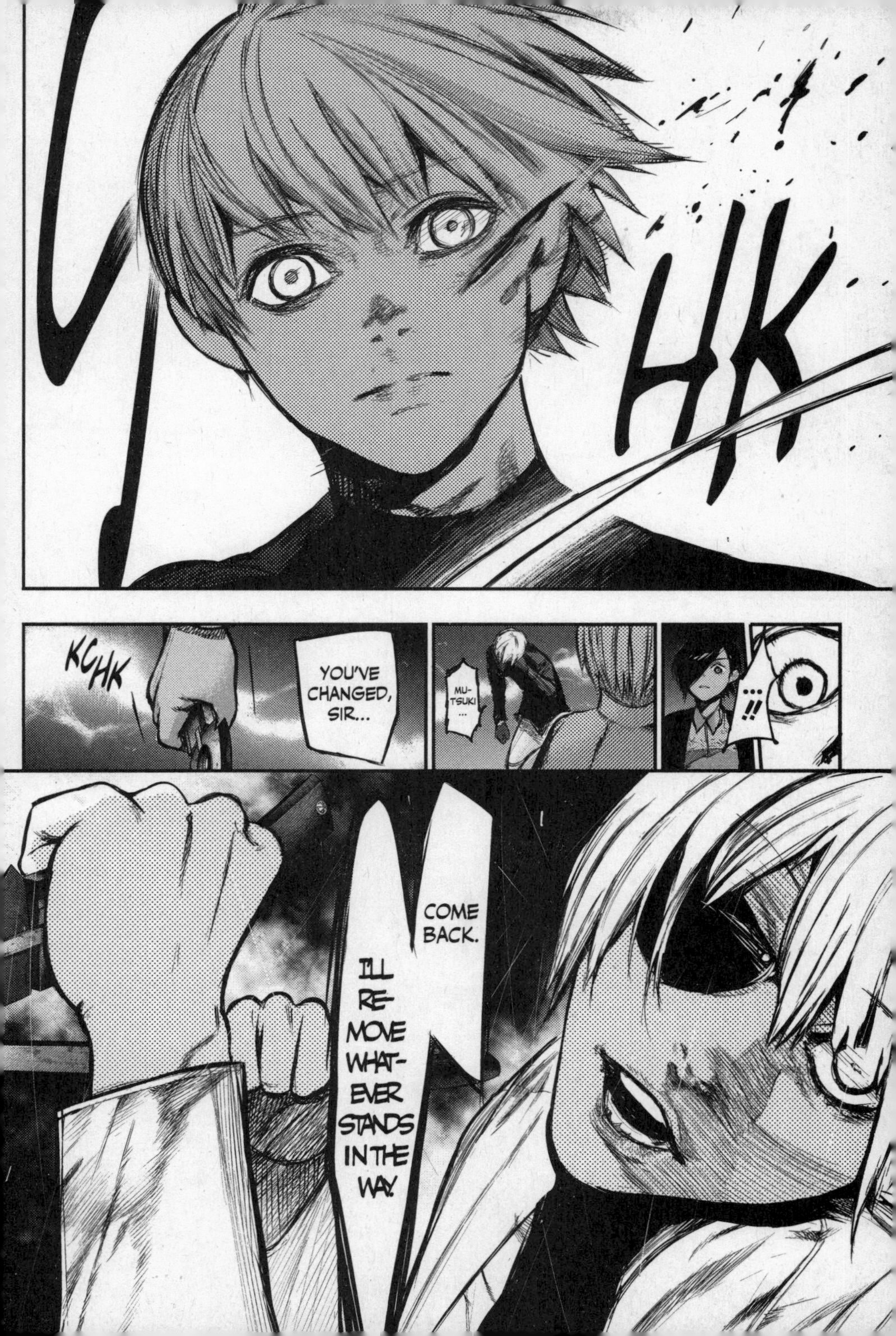
HK
...!!
MU-TSUKI...
YOU'VE CHANGED, SIR...
KCHK
COME BACK.
I'LL RE-MOVE WHAT-EVER STANDS IN THE WAY.

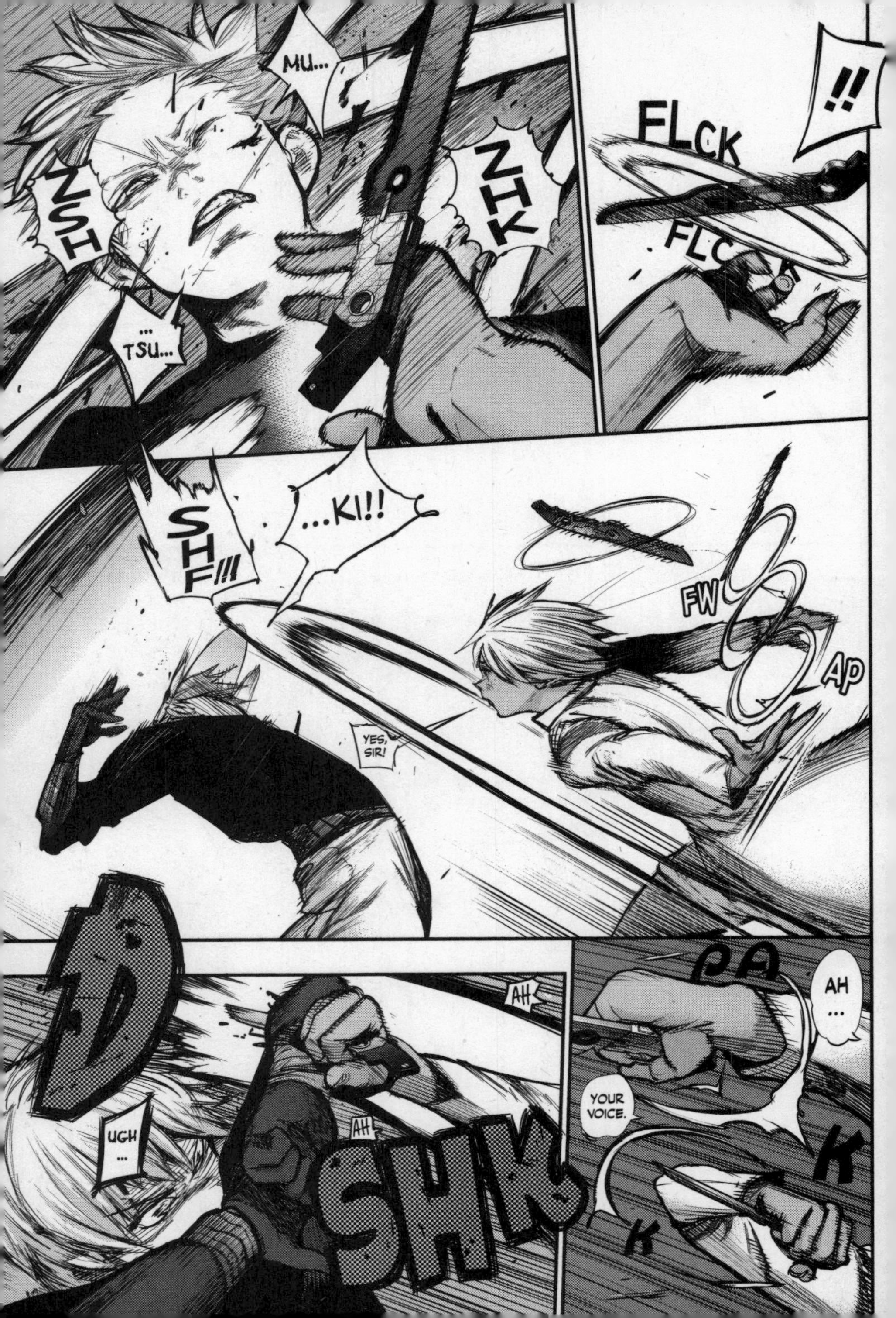
!!
FLCK
FLCK
MU...
ZHK
ZSH
... TSU...
...KI!!
SHF!!!
FWAP
YES, SIR!
PA
AH ...
YOUR VOICE.
K
K
AH
D
AH
SHK
UGH ...

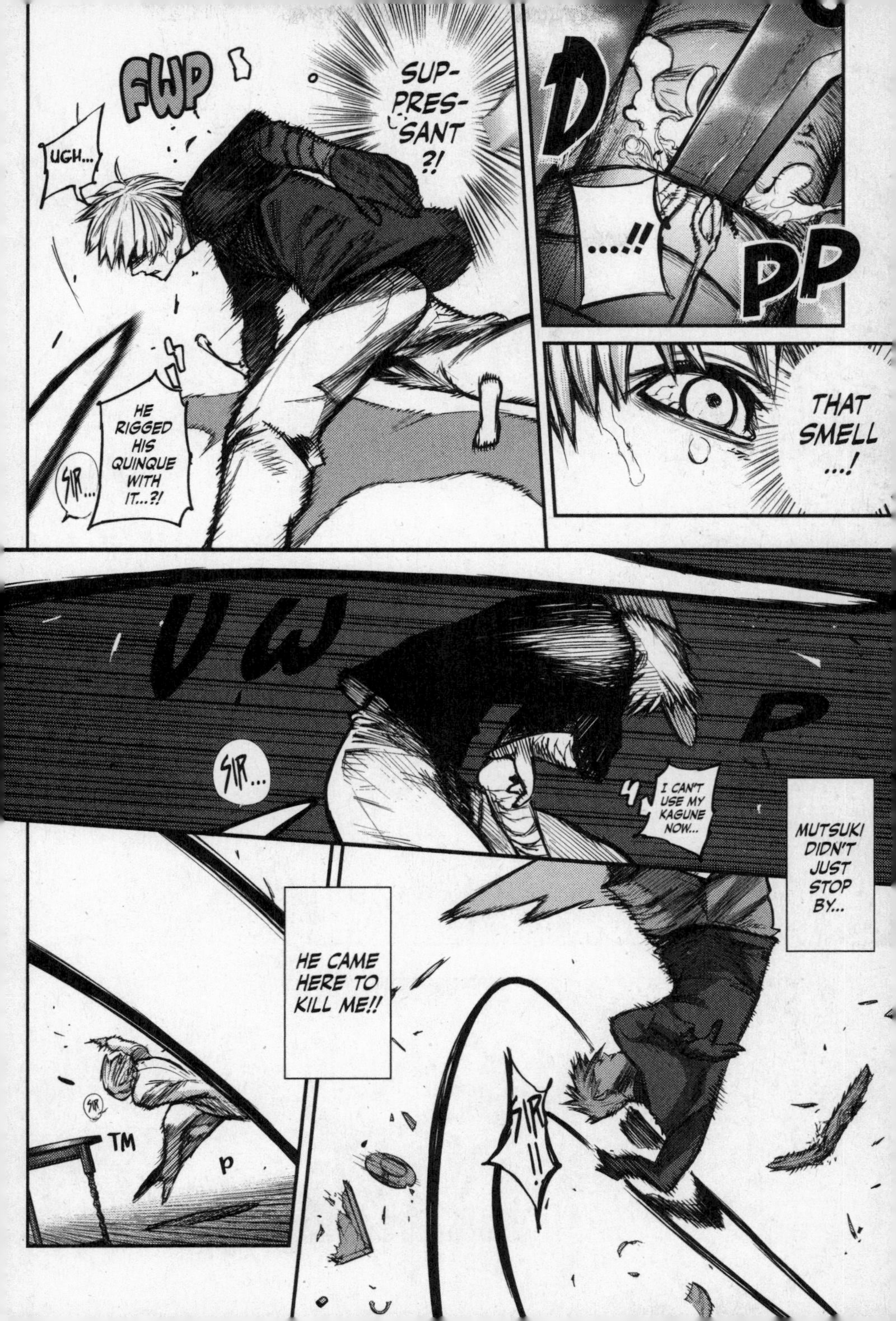
D
....!!
PP
THAT SMELL ...!
SUP-PRES-SANT ?!
FWP
UGH...
HE RIGGED HIS QUINQUE WITH IT...?!
SIR...
V W
P
MUTSUKI DIDN'T JUST STOP BY...
I CAN'T USE MY KAGUNE NOW...
SIR...
HE CAME HERE TO KILL ME!!
SIR!!
SIR
TM
p

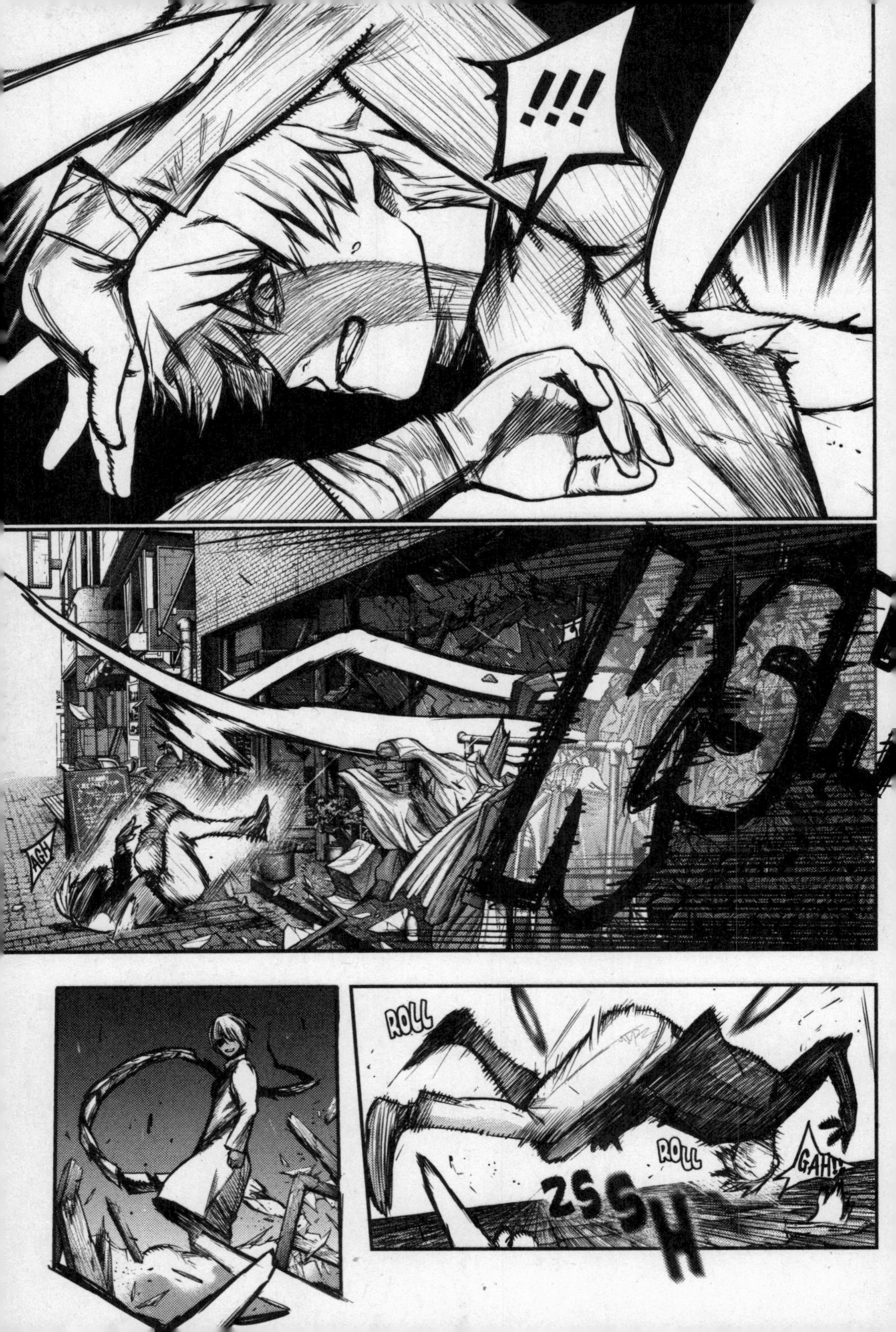
!!!
AGH
ROLL
ROLL
GAH!!
ZSSH

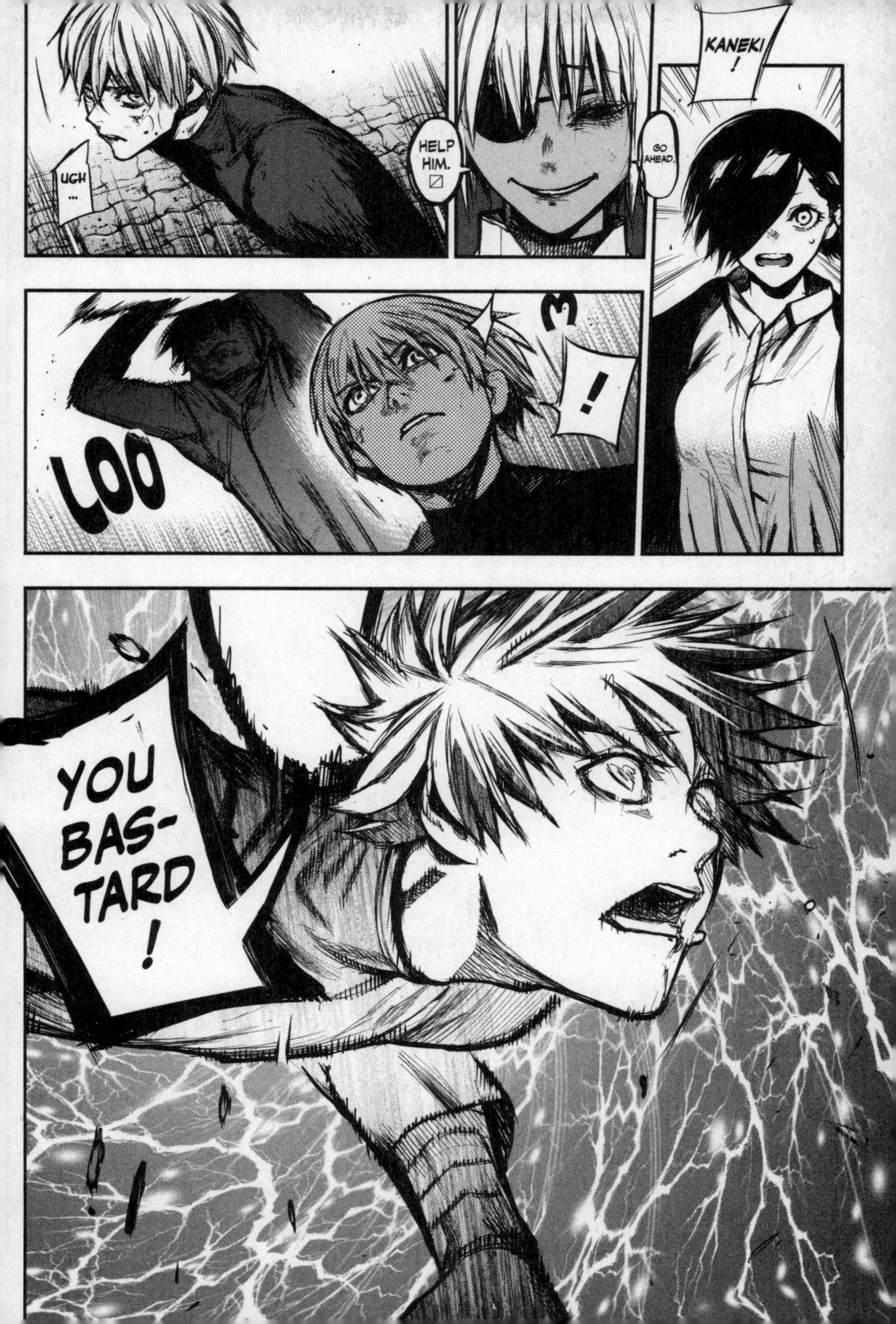
KANEKI!
GO AHEAD.
HELP HIM.
UGH ...
M
!
LOO
YOU BAS-TARD!

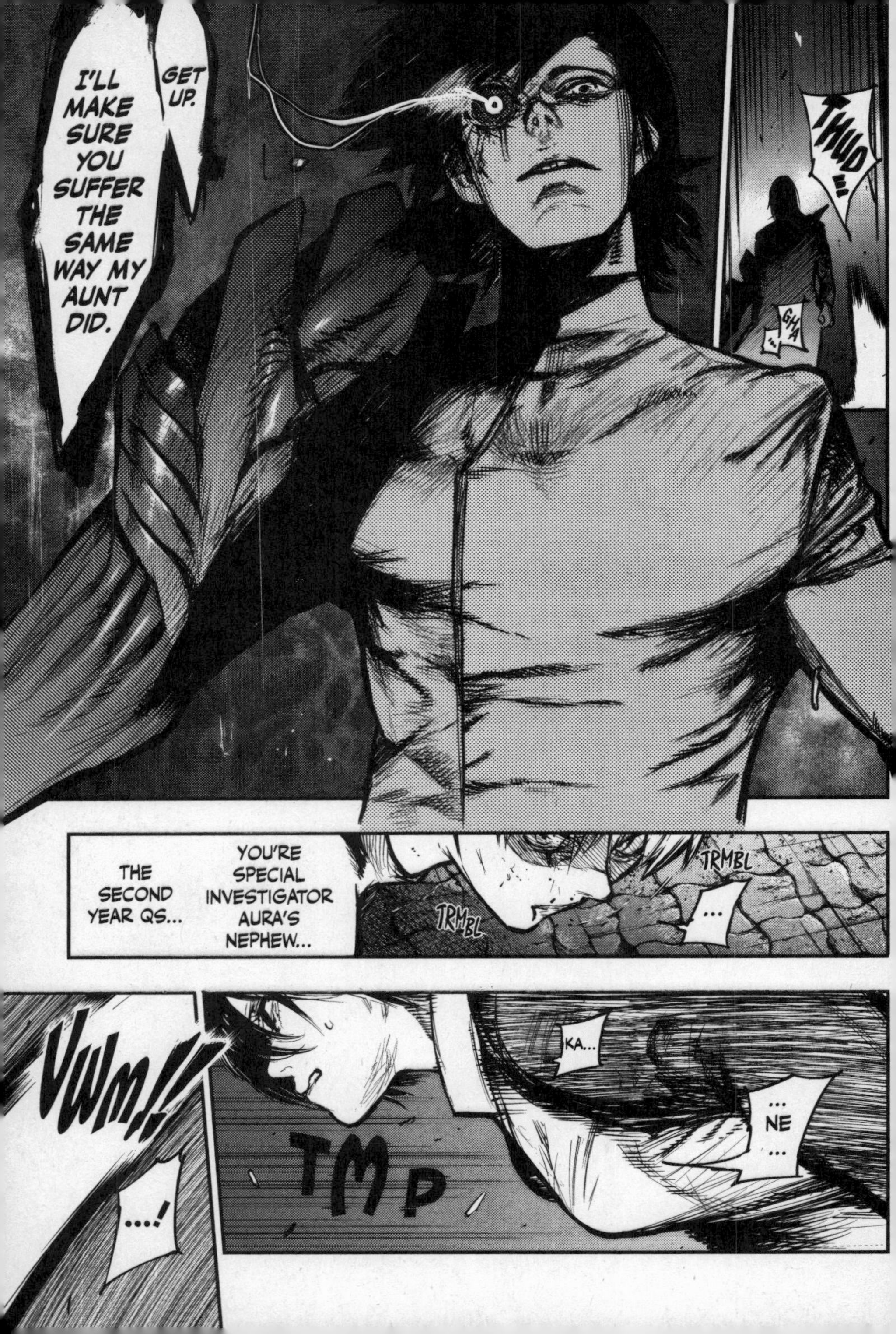
THUD!!
GHA...
GET UP.
I'LL MAKE SURE YOU SUFFER THE SAME WAY MY AUNT DID.
TRMBL
...
TRMBL
YOU'RE SPECIAL INVESTIGATOR AURA'S NEPHEW...
THE SECOND YEAR QS...
KA...
...NE...
TMP
VWM!!
...!

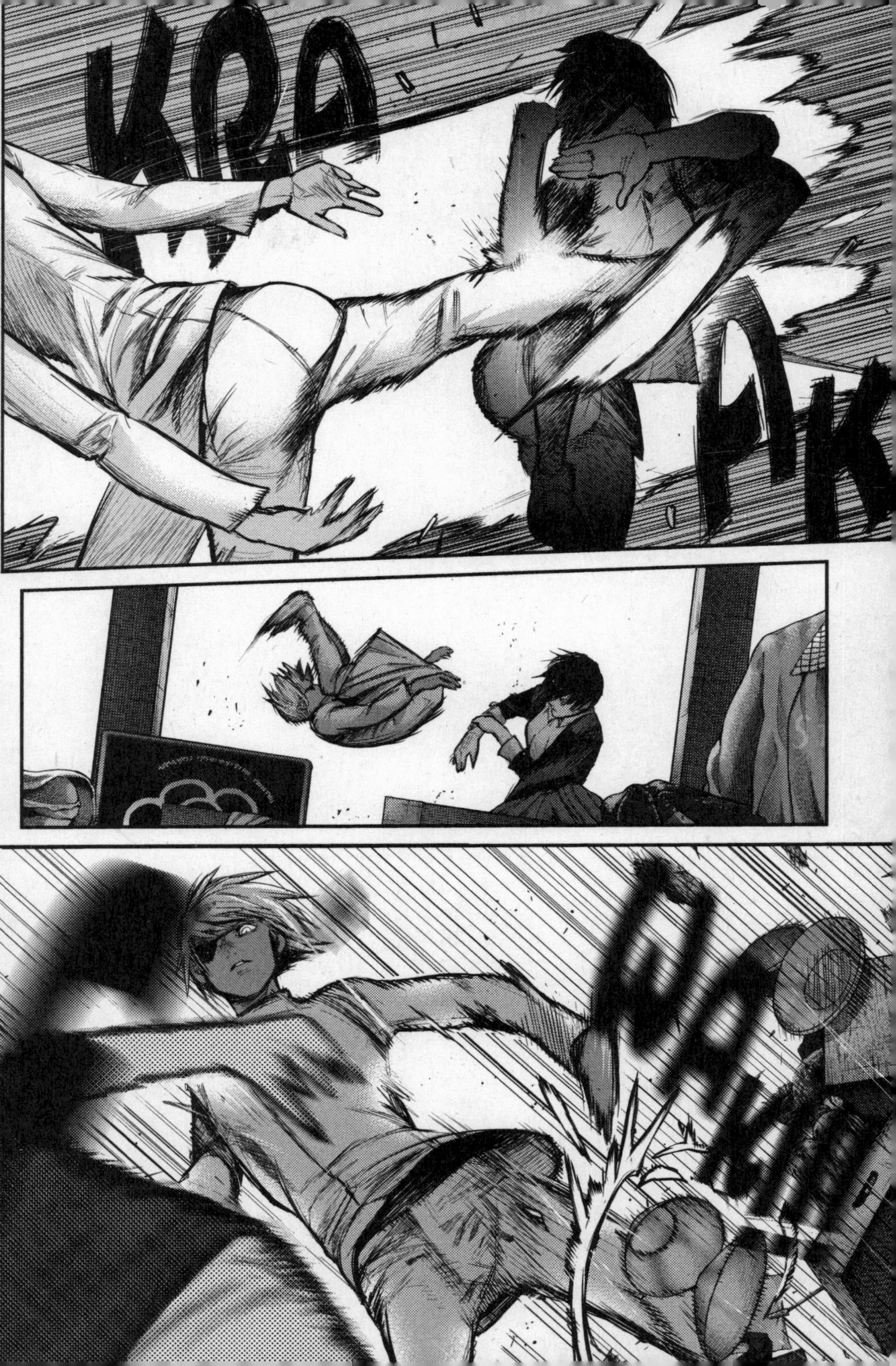
KRA
AK

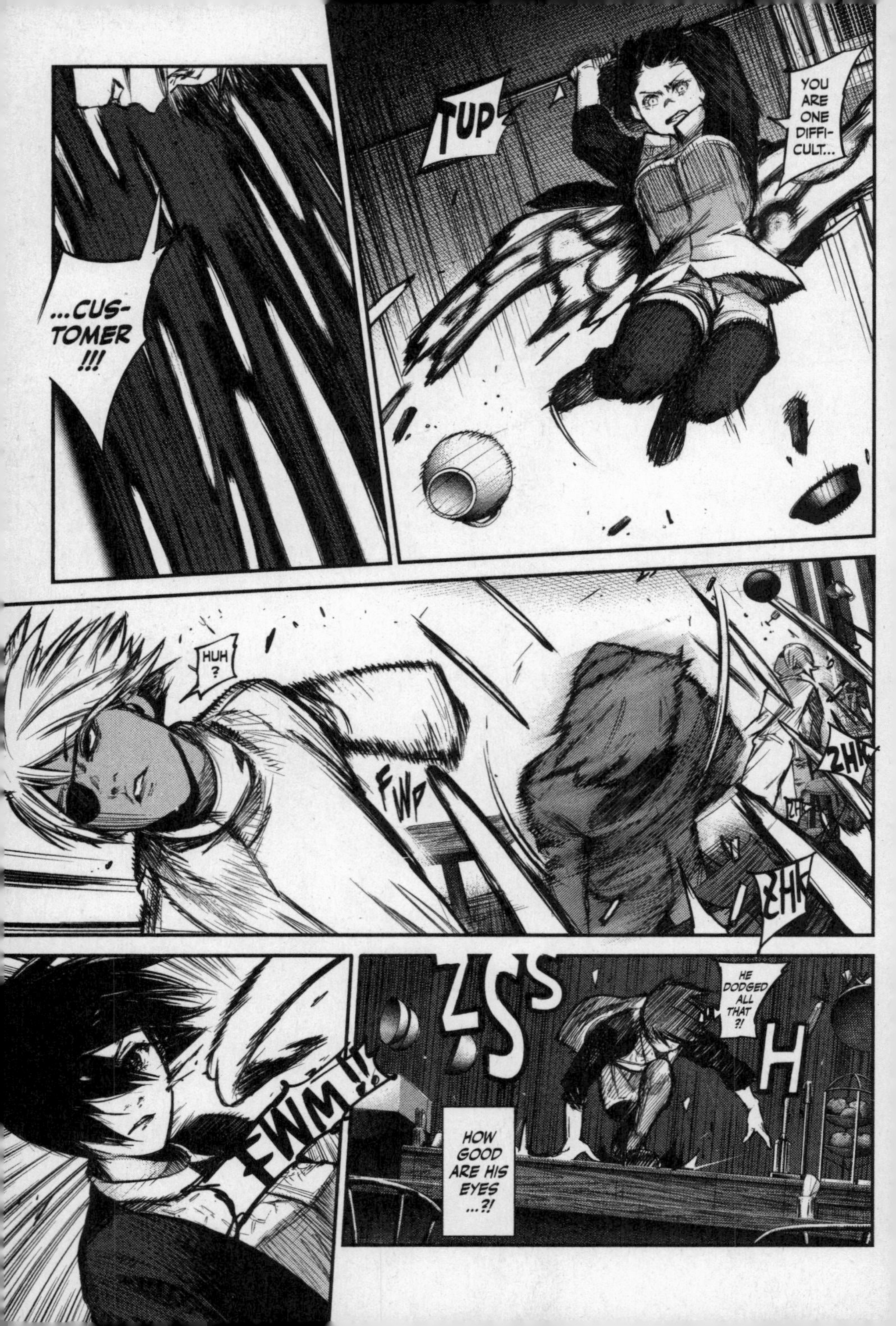
YOU ARE ONE DIFFI-CULT...
TUP
...CUS-TOMER!!!
ZHK
HUH?
FWP
ZHK
HE DODGED ALL THAT?!
ZSSH
HOW GOOD ARE HIS EYES...?!
FWM!!

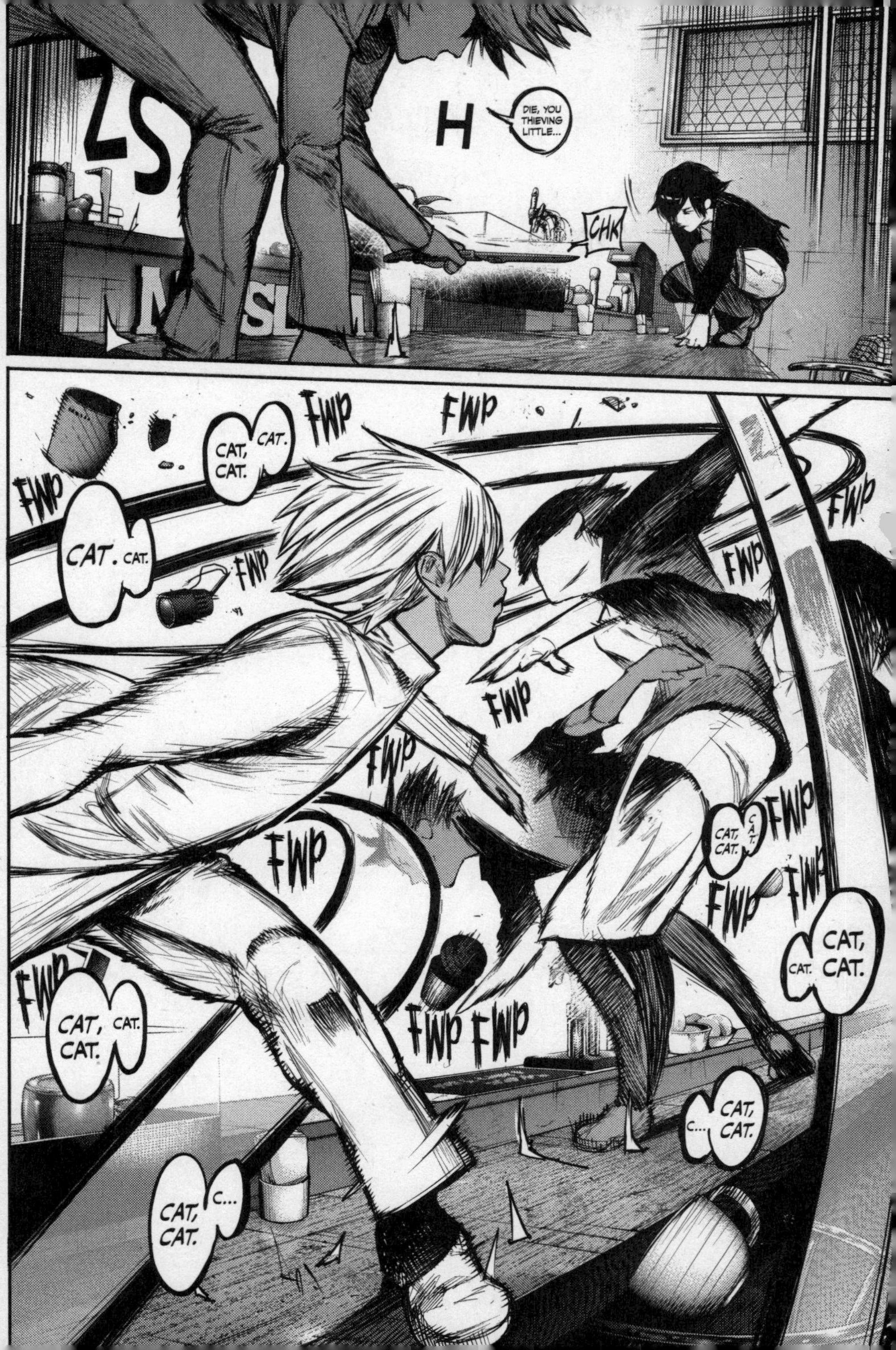
DIE, YOU THIEVING LITTLE...
CHK
ZS
H
FWP
FWP
CAT, CAT. CAT.
FWP
FWP
CAT. CAT.
FWP
FWP
FWP
CAT, CAT. CAT.
FWP
FWP
FWP
FWP
FWP
CAT, CAT. CAT.
FWP
CAT, CAT. CAT.
FWP FWP
C... CAT, CAT.
CAT, CAT. C...

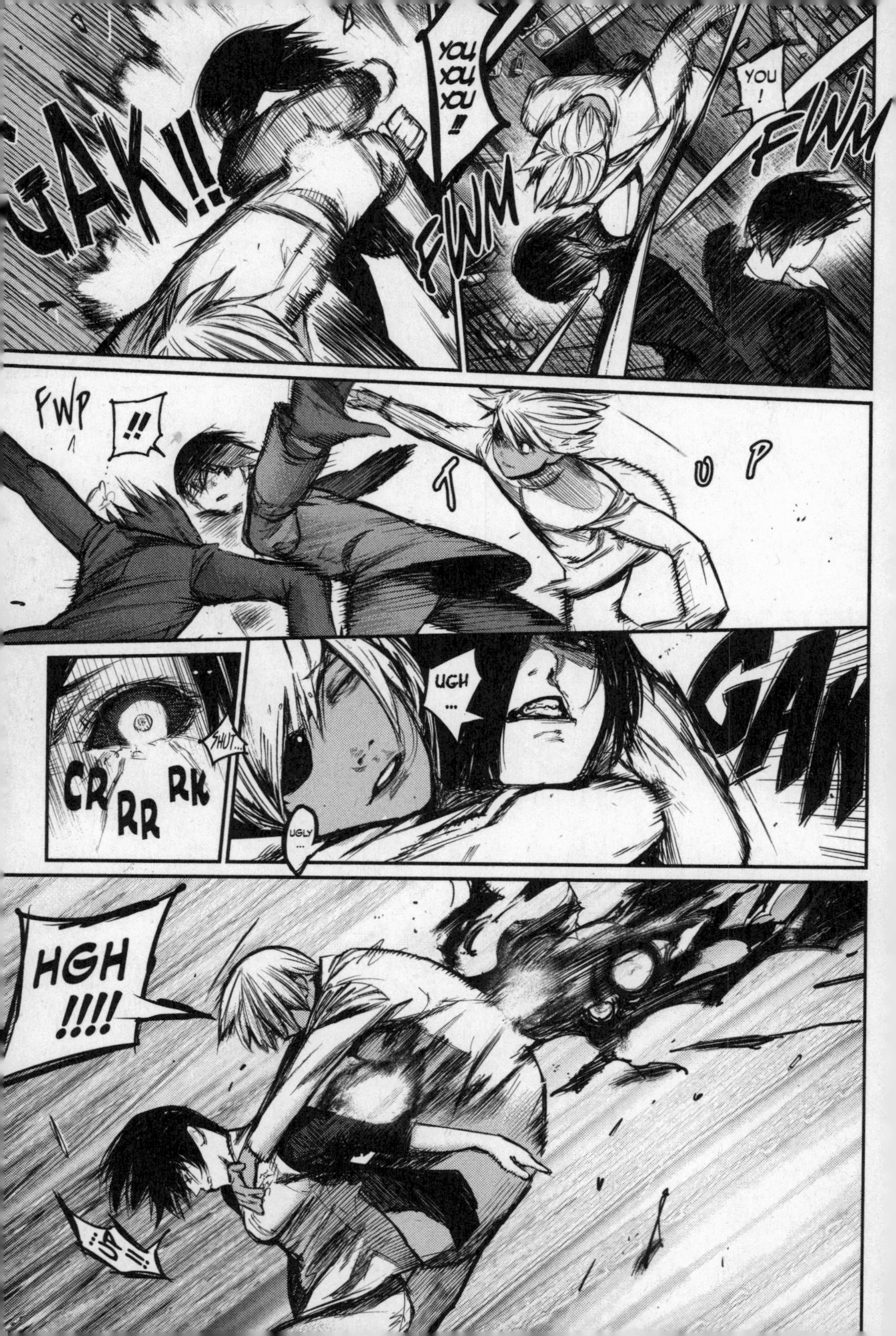
YOU !
FWM
YOU YOU YOU !!
FWM
GAK!!
T U P
FWP
!!
GAK
UGH ...
UGLY ...
SHUT...
CRRRRRK
HGH !!!!

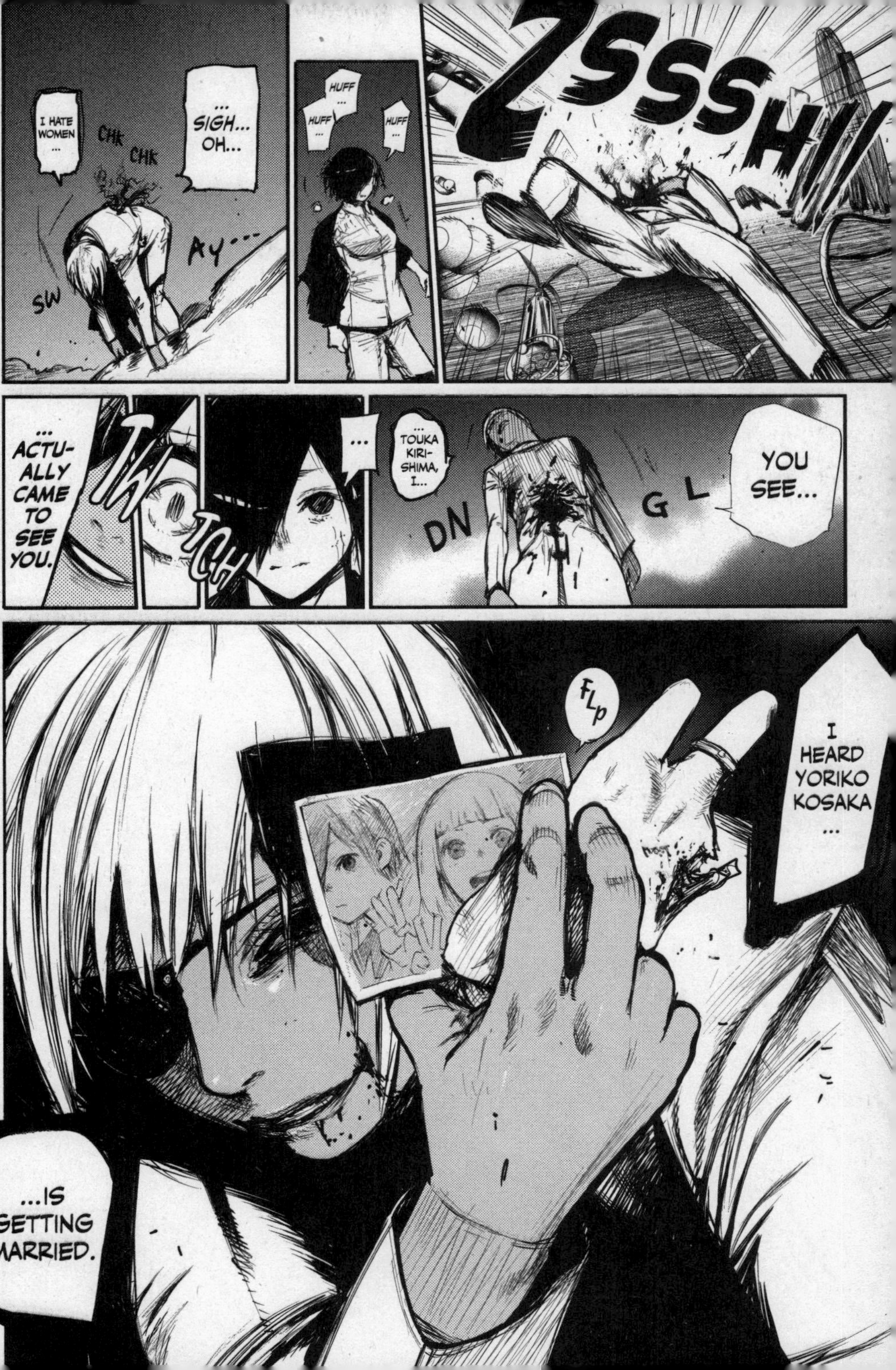
ZSSSHH
HUFF ...
HUFF ...
HUFF ...
... SIGH... OH...
I HATE WOMEN ...
CHK CHK
AY...
SW
YOU SEE...
DN G L
... TOUKA KIRI-SHIMA, I...
...
TWITCH
... ACTU-ALLY CAME TO SEE YOU.
I HEARD YORIKO KOSAKA ...
FLp
...IS GETTING MARRIED.

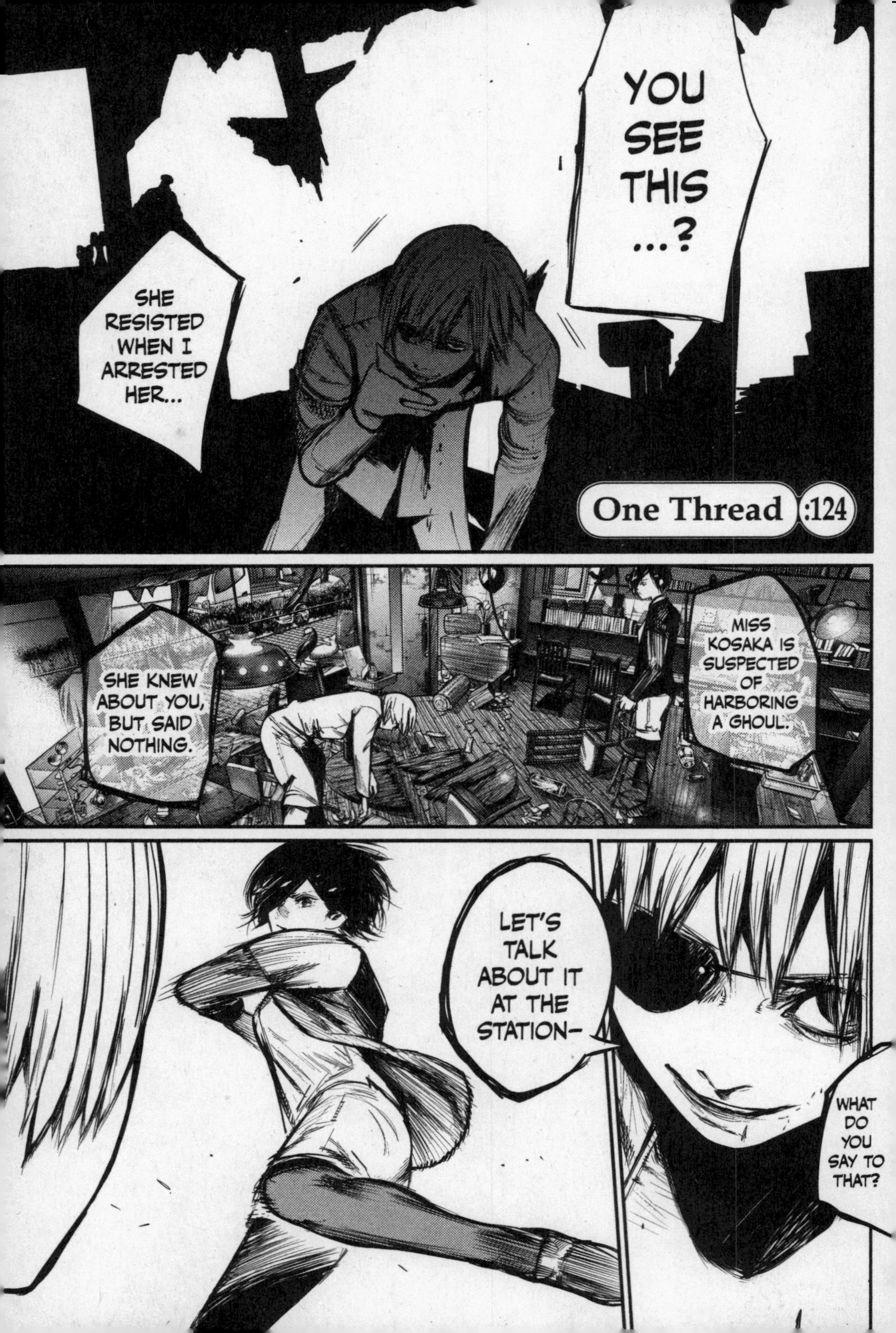
YOU SEE THIS ...?
SHE RESISTED WHEN I ARRESTED HER...
One Thread :124
MISS KOSAKA IS SUSPECTED OF HARBORING A GHOUL.
SHE KNEW ABOUT YOU, BUT SAID NOTHING.
LET'S TALK ABOUT IT AT THE STATION-
WHAT DO YOU SAY TO THAT?

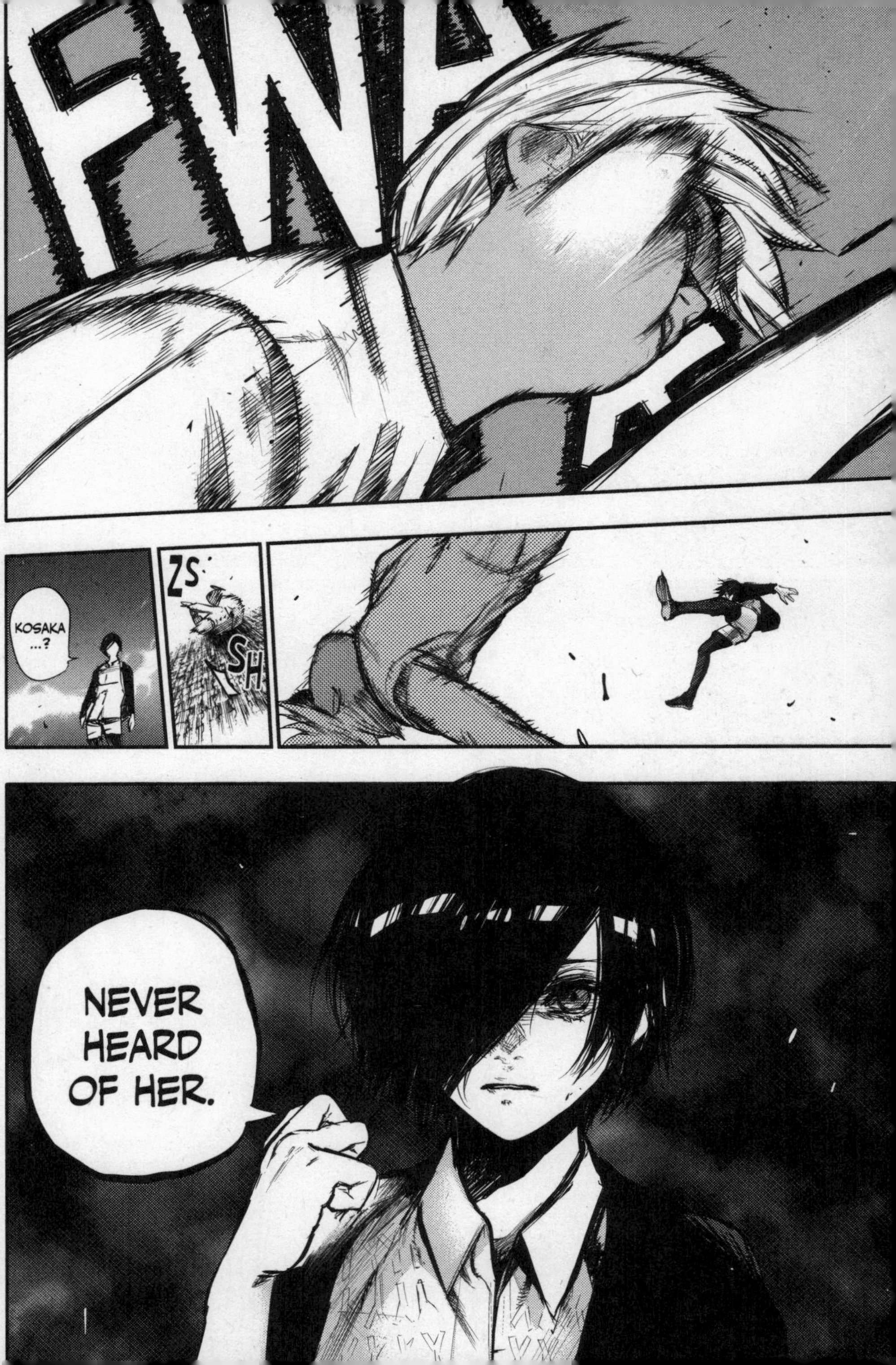
ZS
SH
KOSAKA ...?
NEVER HEARD OF HER.

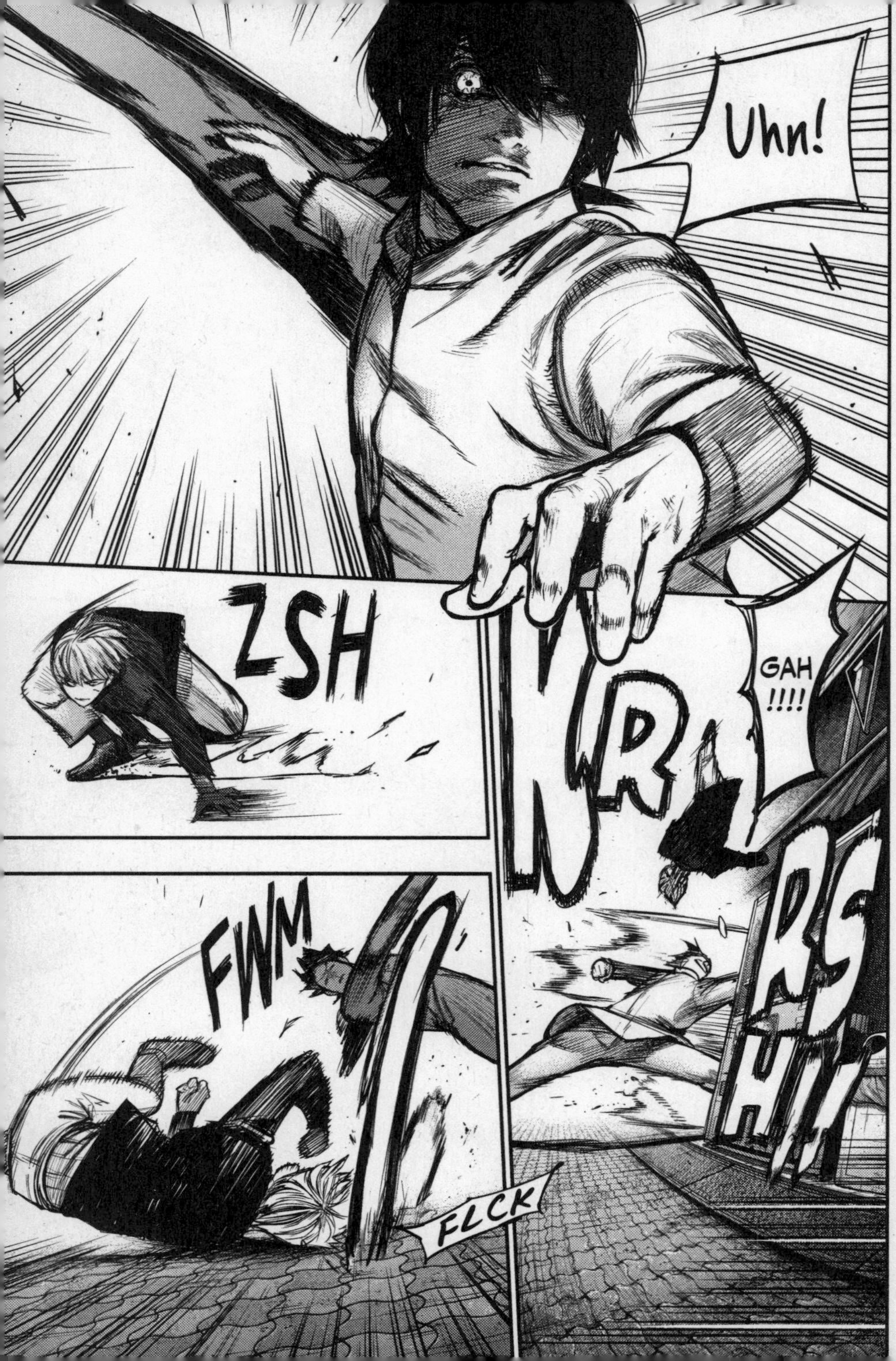
Uhn!
GAH!!!!
ZSH
FWM
FLCK

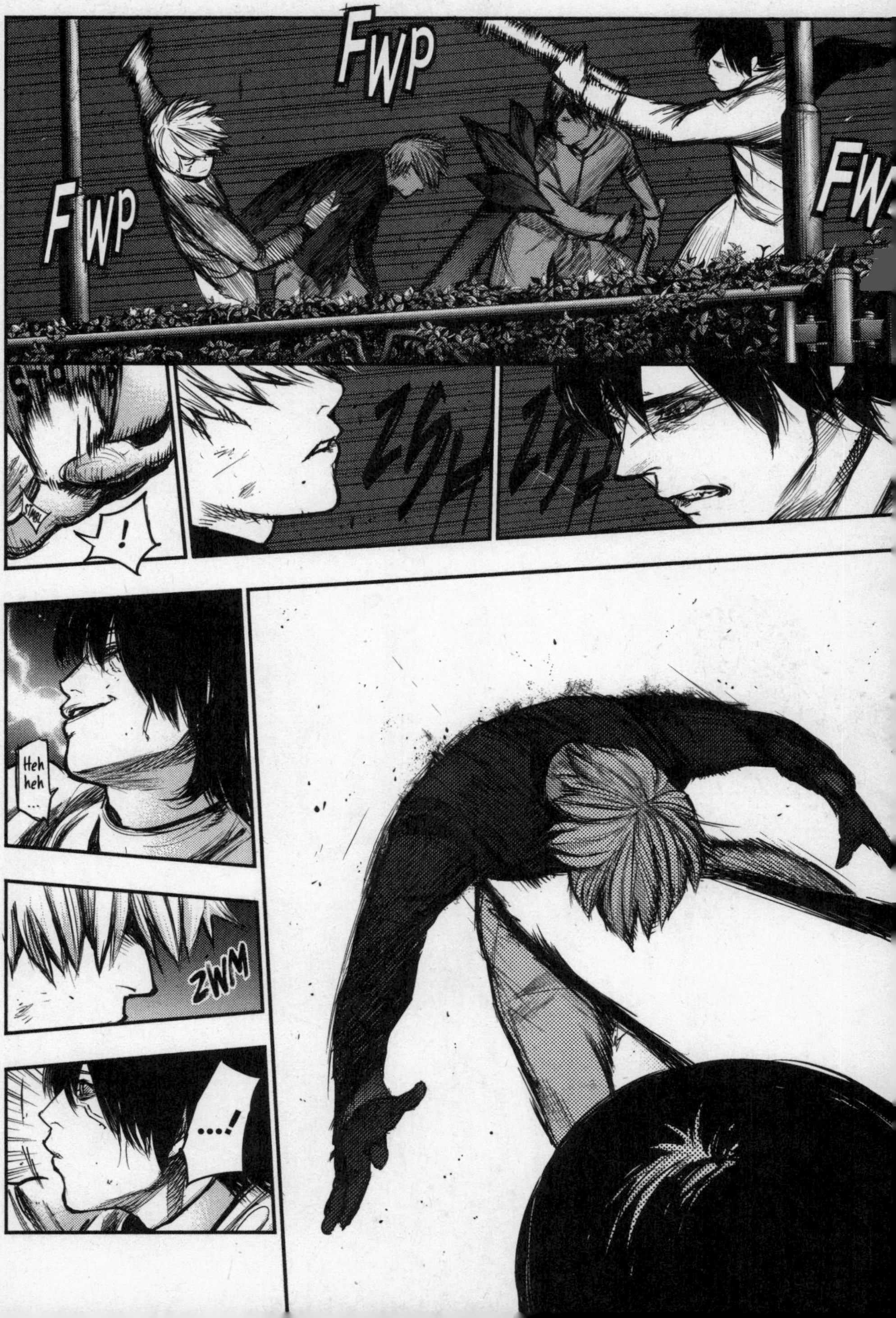
Fwp
Fwp
Fw
!
Heh heh ...
ZWM
...!

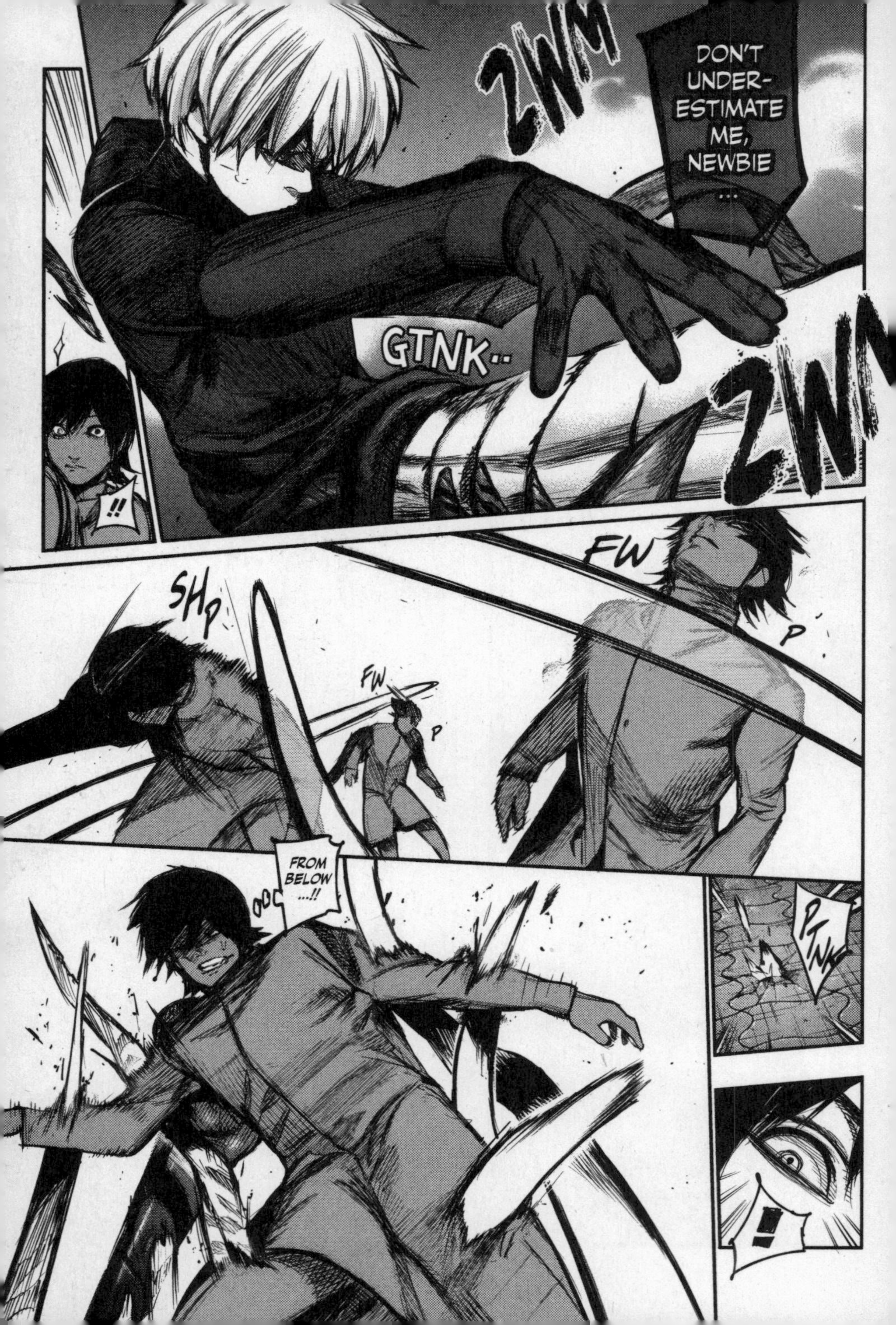

ZWM
DON'T UNDER-ESTIMATE ME, NEWBIE ...
ZWM
GTNK..
!!
FW
P
SHP
FW
P
FROM BELOW ...!!
PTNK
ODC
!

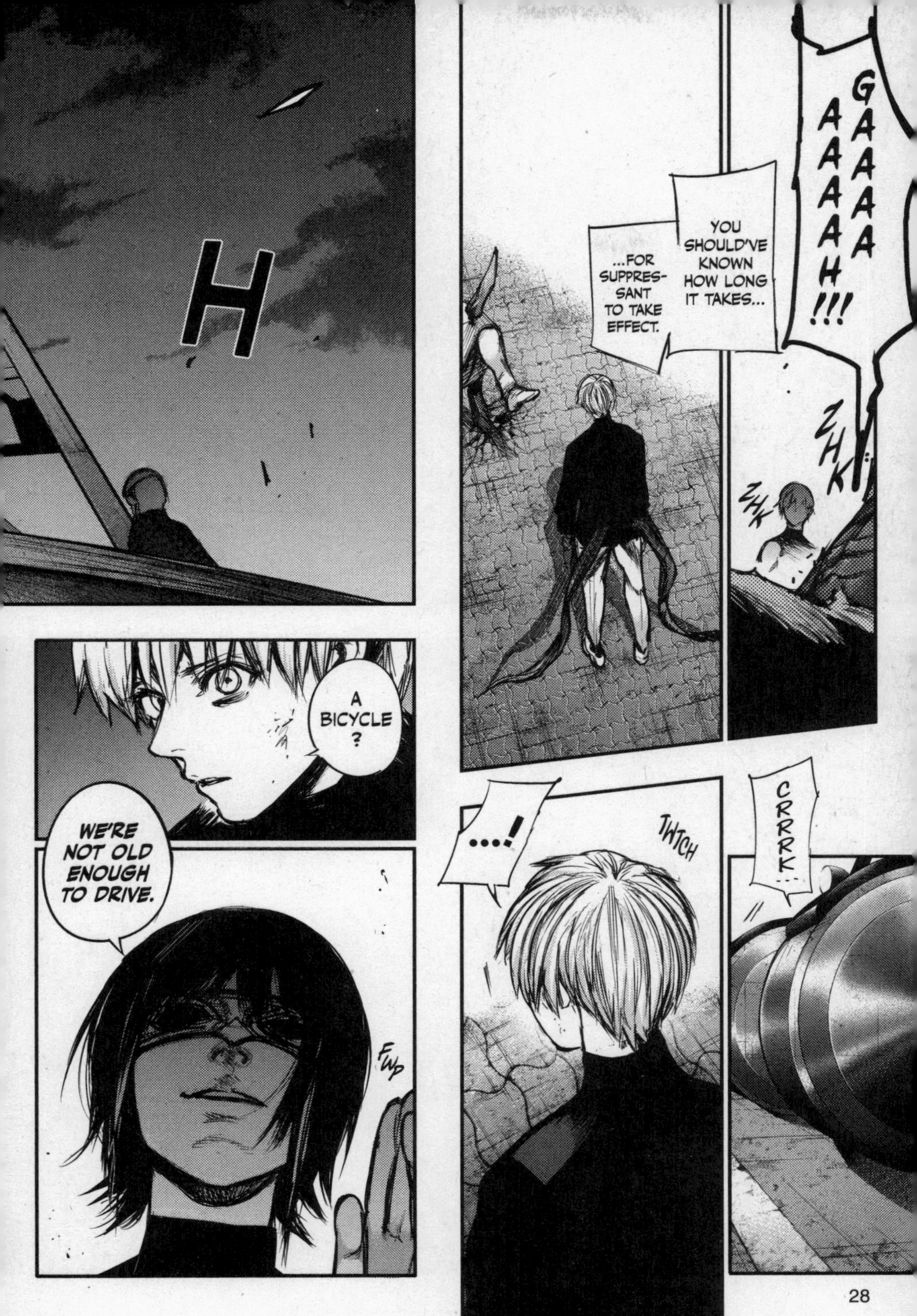
GAAAAAAAAAH!!!
ZHK
ZHK
YOU SHOULD'VE KNOWN HOW LONG IT TAKES...
...FOR SUPPRESSANT TO TAKE EFFECT.
CRRRK
...!
TWITCH
H
A BICYCLE?
WE'RE NOT OLD ENOUGH TO DRIVE.
FWP

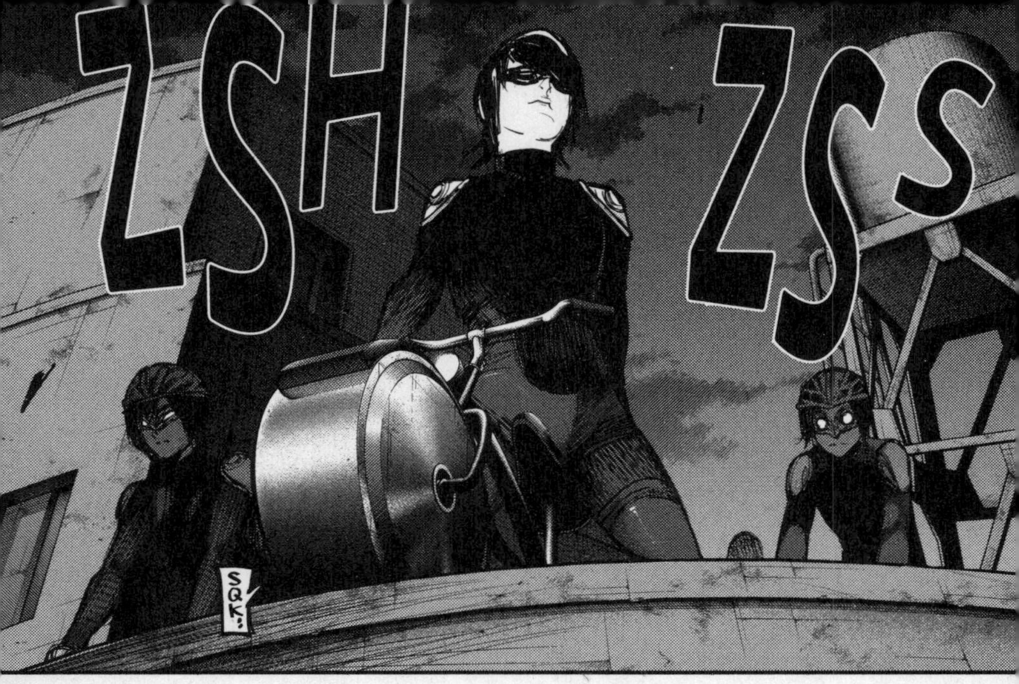
ZSS
ZSH
SQK!
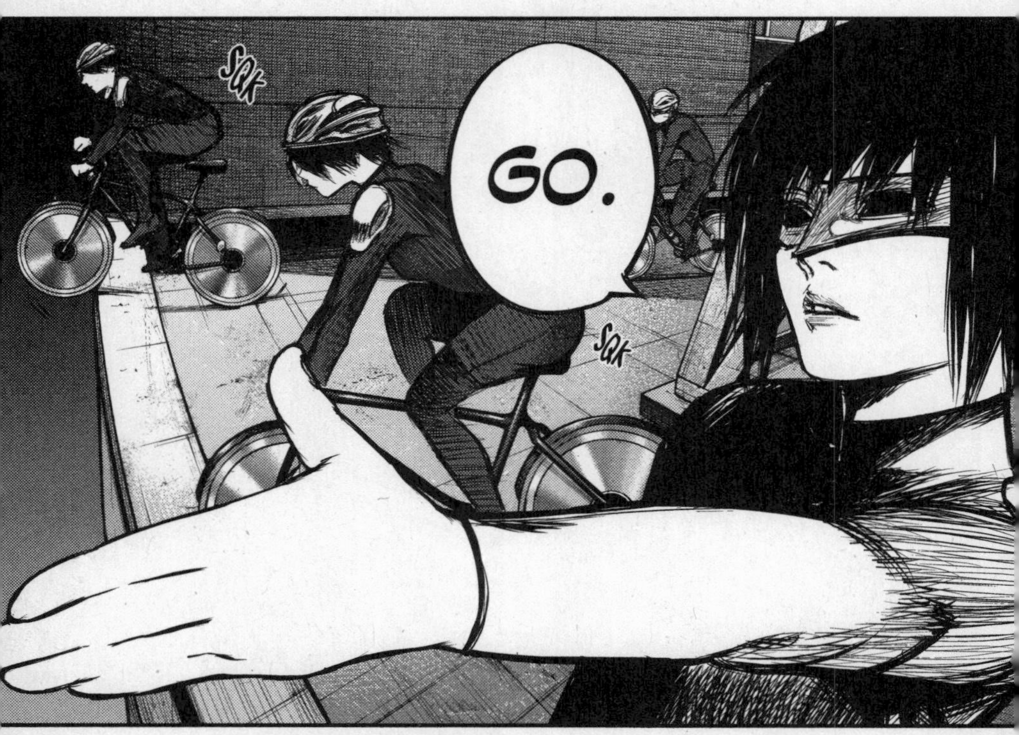
GO.
SQK
SQK

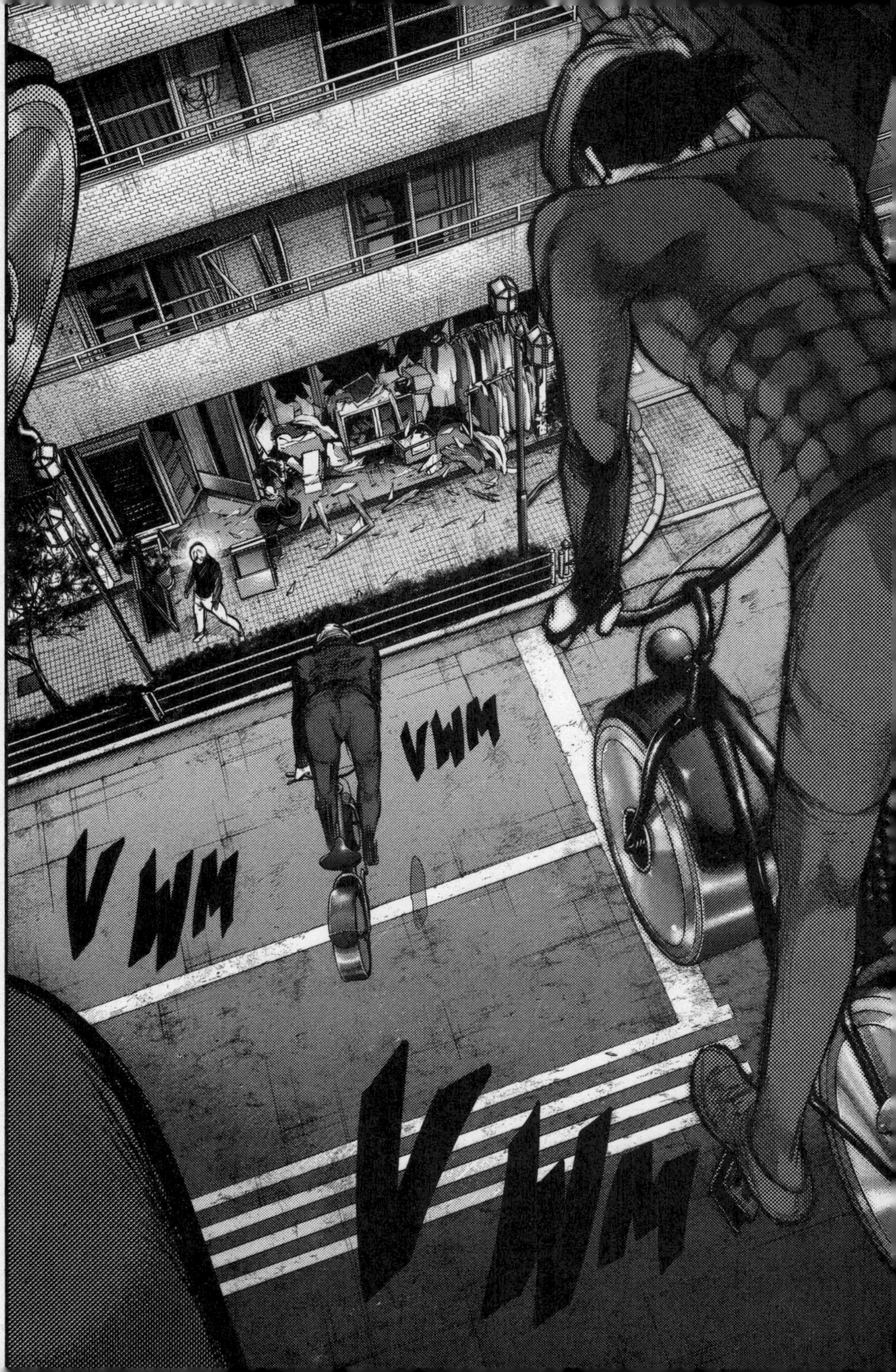
VWM
VWM
VWM

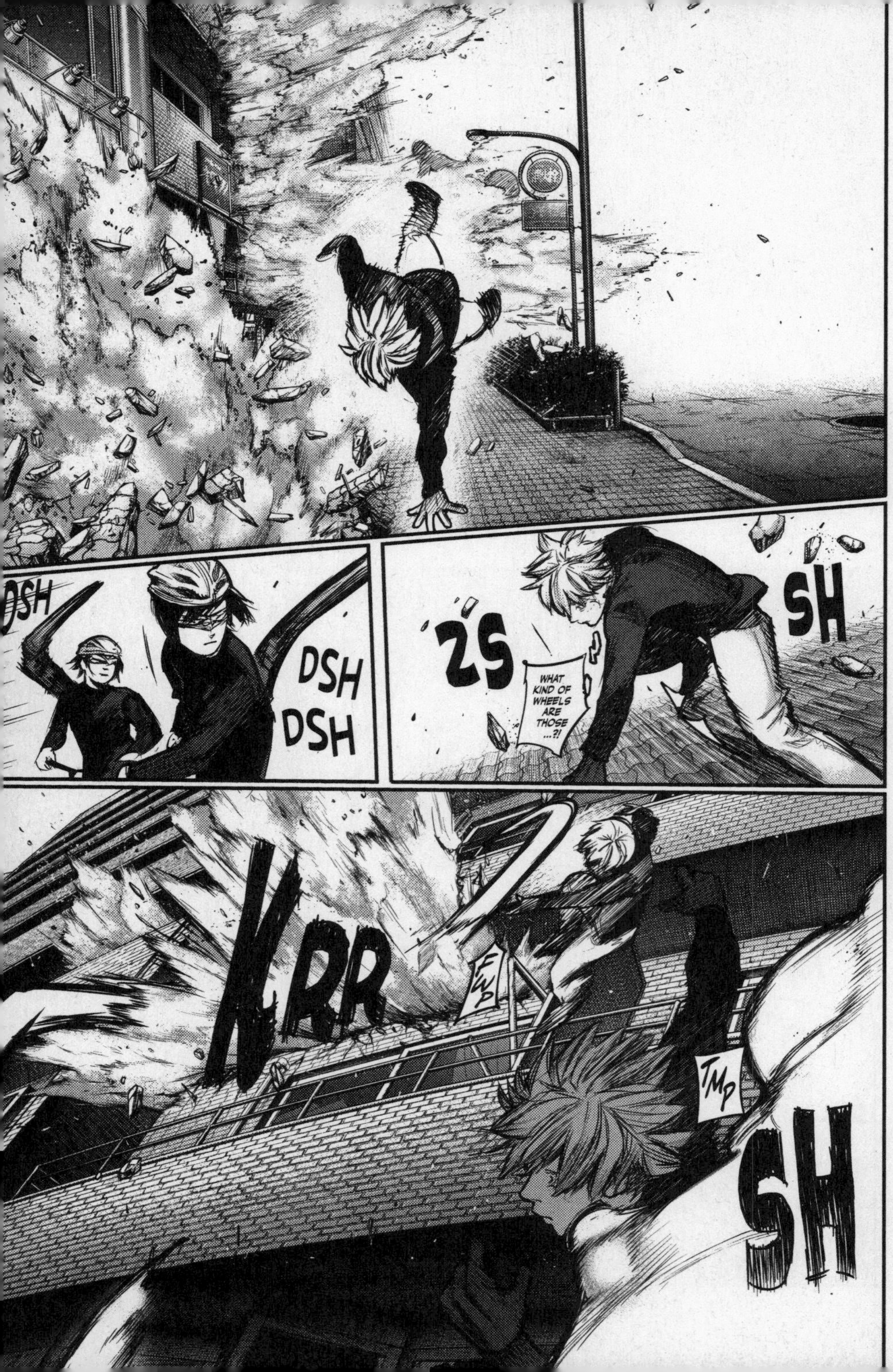
SH
ZS
WHAT KIND OF WHEELS ARE THOSE ...?!
DSH DSH
DSH
FWP
TMP
SH
KRR

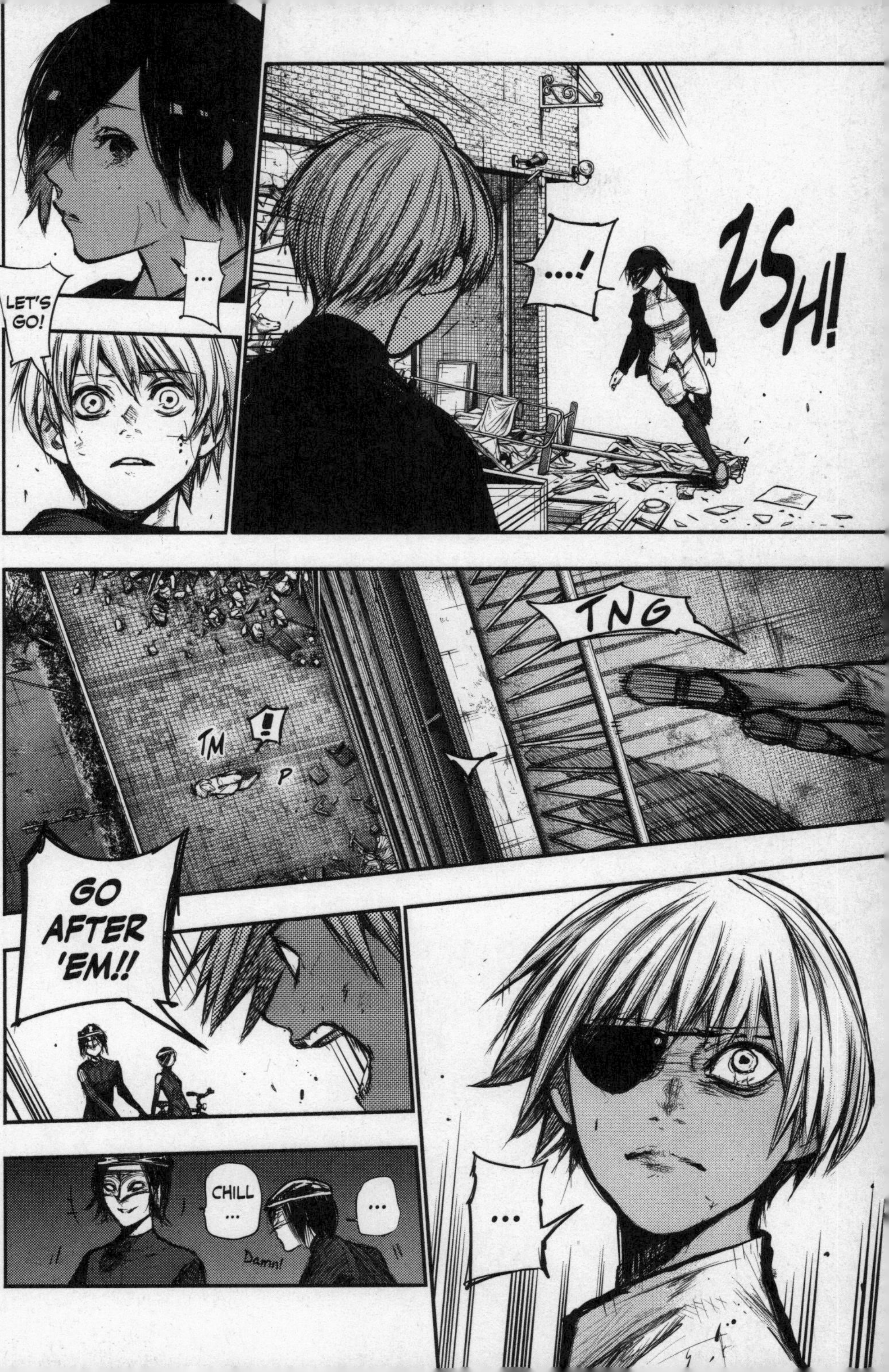

...!
ZSH!
...
LET'S GO!
TNG
!
TMP
...
GO AFTER 'EM!!
CHILL ...
...
Damn!

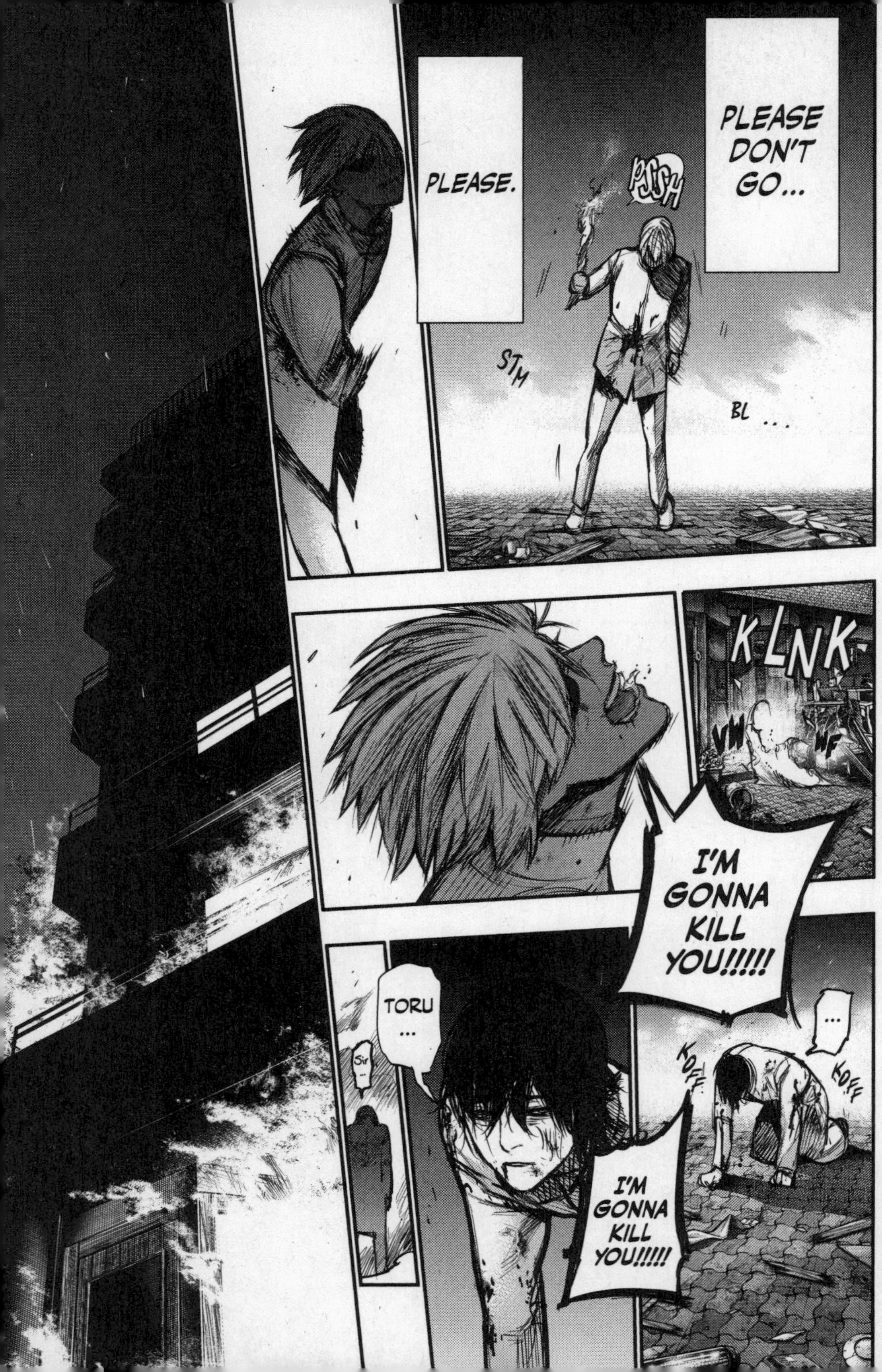
PLEASE DON'T GO...
PSSH
STM
BL...
PLEASE.
KLNK
VW
WF
I'M GONNA KILL YOU!!!!!
...
KOFF
KOFF
I'M GONNA KILL YOU!!!!!
TORU ...
Sir ...

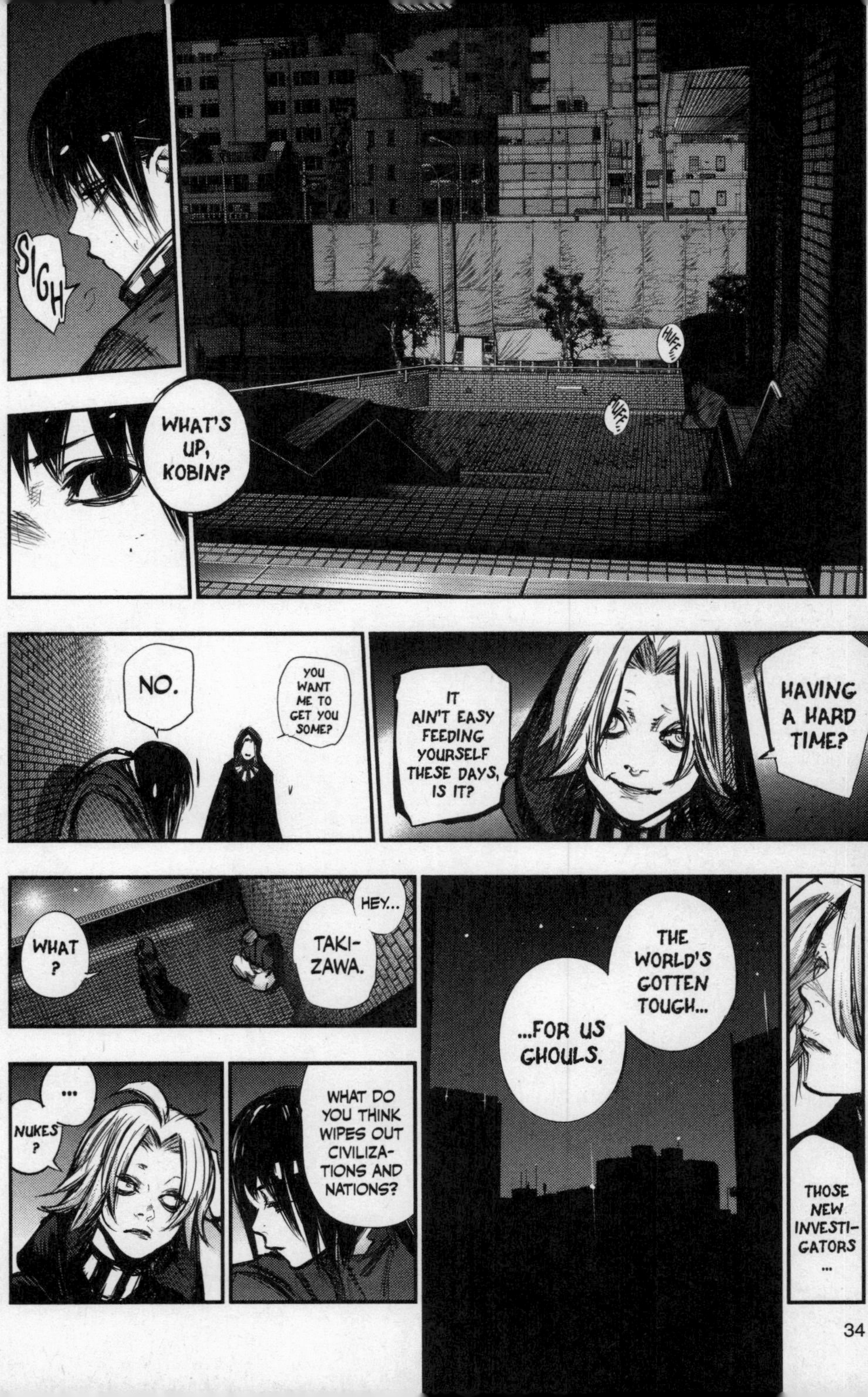
HUFF...
HUFF...
SIGH
WHAT'S UP, KOBIN?
HAVING A HARD TIME?
IT AIN'T EASY FEEDING YOURSELF THESE DAYS, IS IT?
YOU WANT ME TO GET YOU SOME?
NO.
THOSE NEW INVESTIGATORS...
THE WORLD'S GOTTEN TOUGH...
...FOR US GHOULS.
HEY...
TAKIZAWA.
WHAT?
WHAT DO YOU THINK WIPES OUT CIVILIZATIONS AND NATIONS?
...
NUKES?

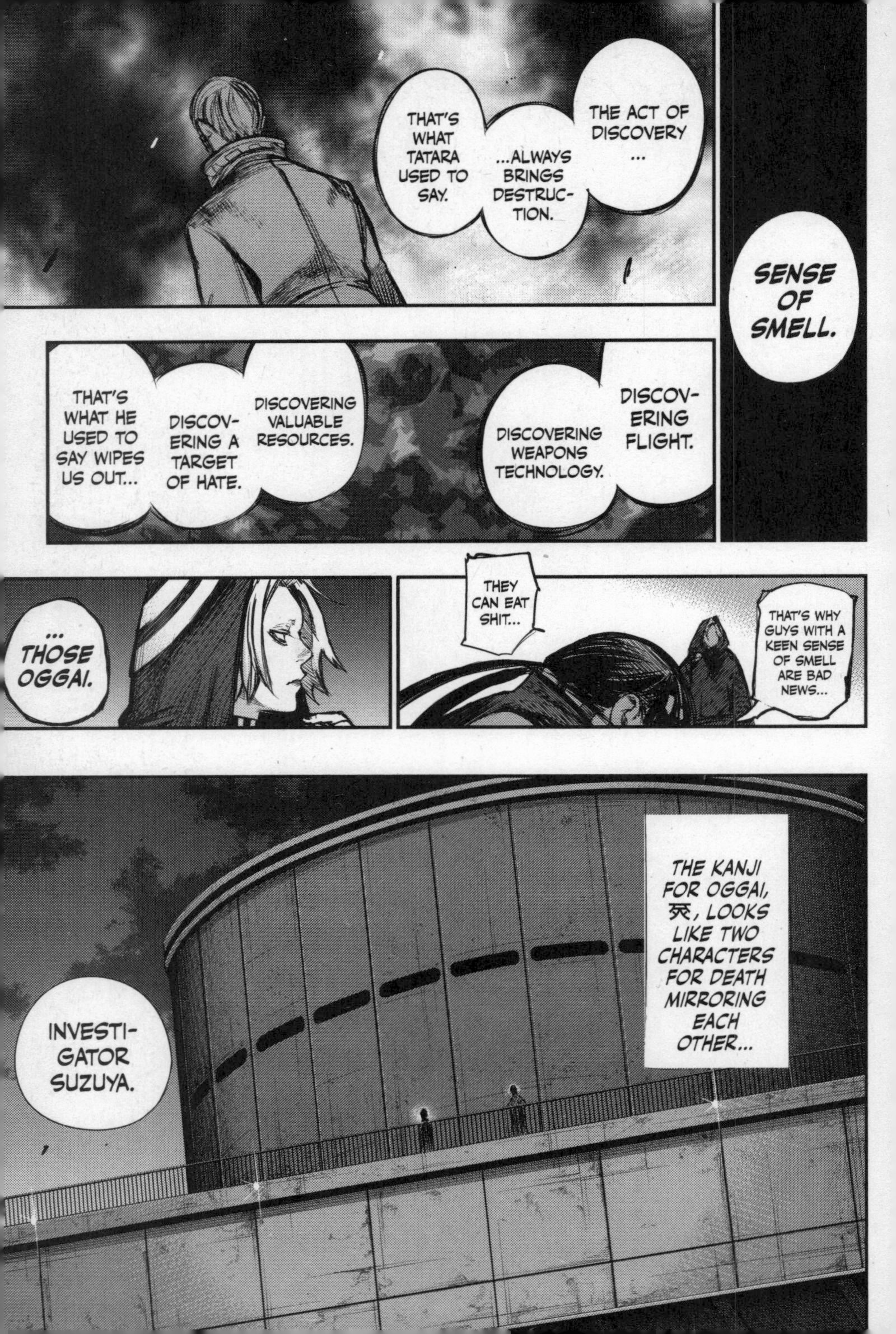
SENSE OF SMELL.
THE ACT OF DISCOVERY ...
...ALWAYS BRINGS DESTRUC-TION.
THAT'S WHAT TATARA USED TO SAY.
DISCOV-ERING FLIGHT.
DISCOVERING WEAPONS TECHNOLOGY.
DISCOVERING VALUABLE RESOURCES.
DISCOV-ERING A TARGET OF HATE.
THAT'S WHAT HE USED TO SAY WIPES US OUT...
THAT'S WHY GUYS WITH A KEEN SENSE OF SMELL ARE BAD NEWS...
THEY CAN EAT SHIT...
... THOSE OGGAI.
THE KANJI FOR OGGAI, 㱚, LOOKS LIKE TWO CHARACTERS FOR DEATH MIRRORING EACH OTHER...
INVESTI-GATOR SUZUYA.

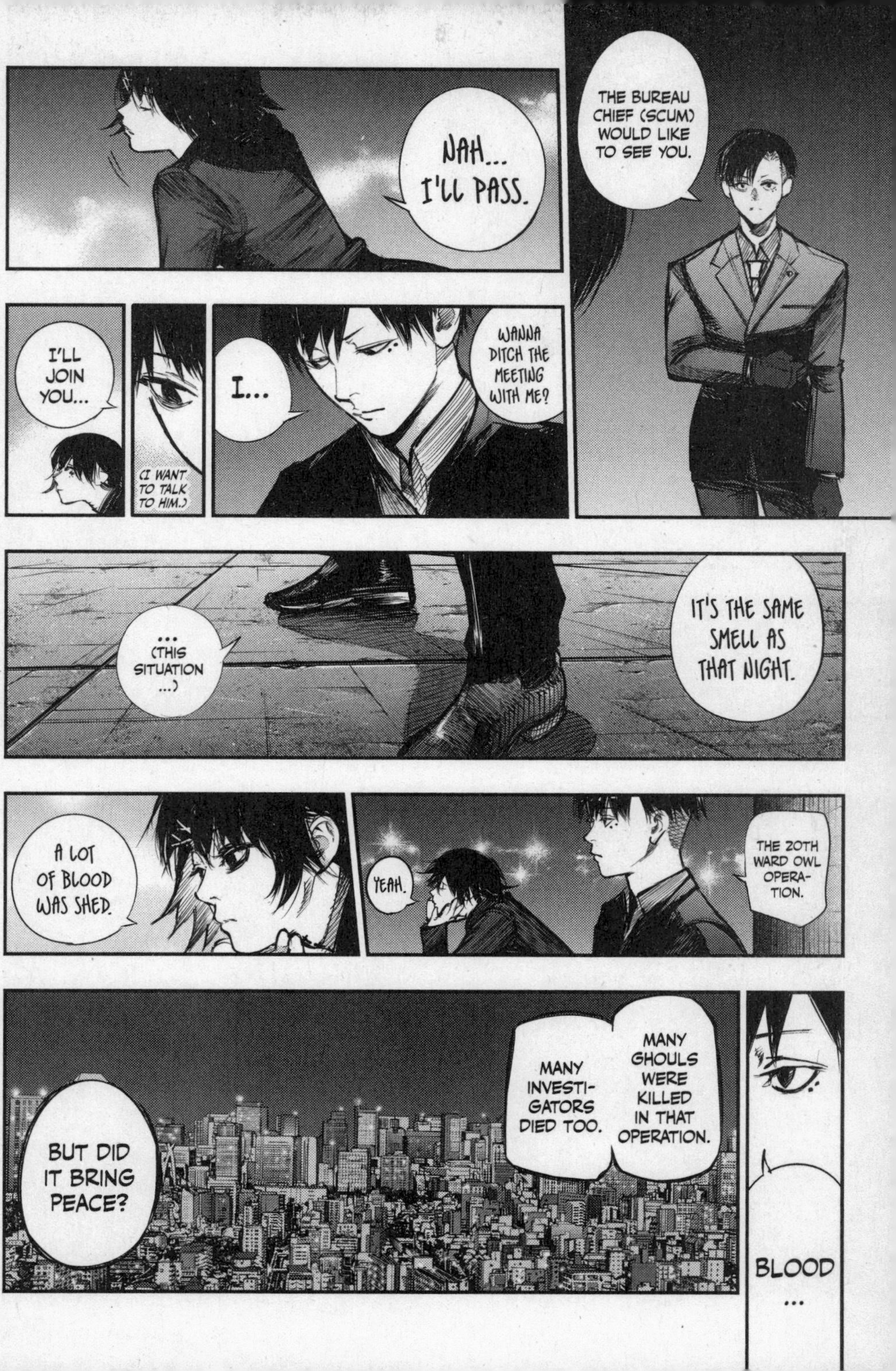
THE BUREAU CHIEF (SCUM) WOULD LIKE TO SEE YOU.
NAH... I'LL PASS.
WANNA DITCH THE MEETING WITH ME?
I...
(I WANT TO TALK TO HIM.)
I'LL JOIN YOU...
IT'S THE SAME SMELL AS THAT NIGHT.
... (THIS SITUATION ...)
THE 20TH WARD OWL OPERATION.
YEAH.
A LOT OF BLOOD WAS SHED.
BLOOD ...
MANY GHOULS WERE KILLED IN THAT OPERATION.
MANY INVESTIGATORS DIED TOO.
BUT DID IT BRING PEACE?

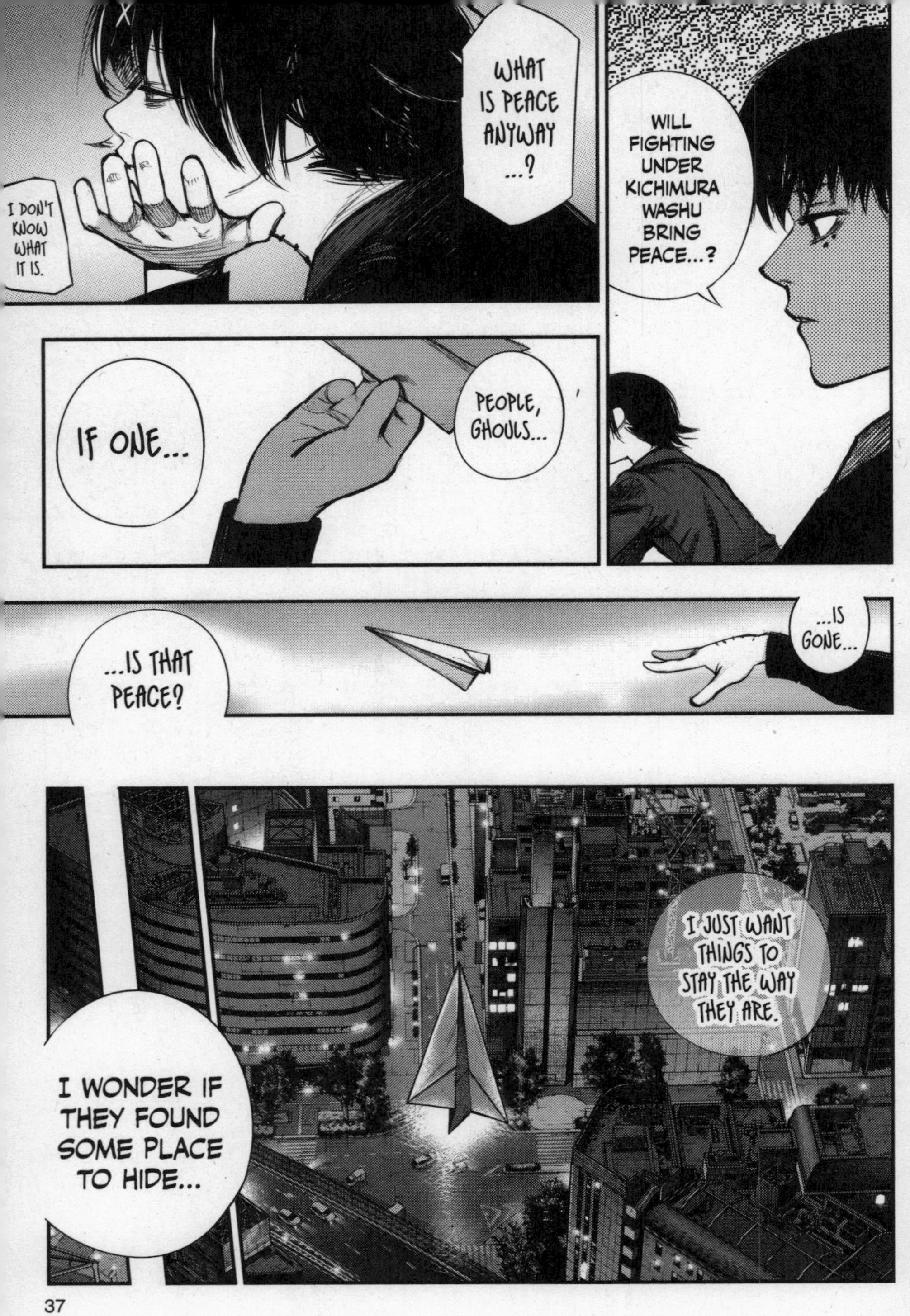
WILL FIGHTING UNDER KICHIMURA WASHU BRING PEACE...?
WHAT IS PEACE ANYWAY ...?
I DON'T KNOW WHAT IT IS.
PEOPLE, GHOULS...
IF ONE...
...IS GONE...
...IS THAT PEACE?
I JUST WANT THINGS TO STAY THE WAY THEY ARE.
I WONDER IF THEY FOUND SOME PLACE TO HIDE...

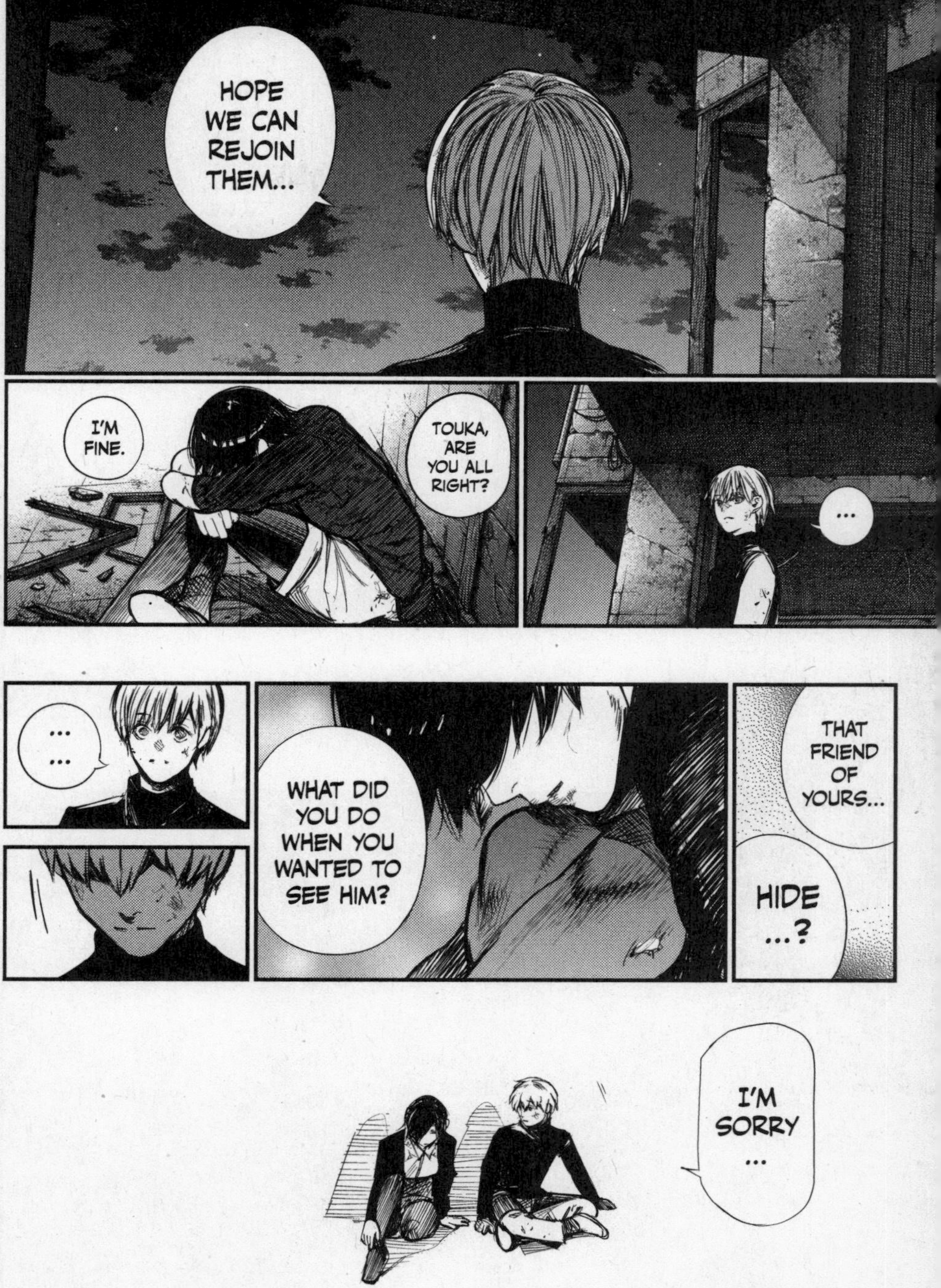
HOPE WE CAN REJOIN THEM...
...
TOUKA, ARE YOU ALL RIGHT?
I'M FINE.
THAT FRIEND OF YOURS...
HIDE ...?
WHAT DID YOU DO WHEN YOU WANTED TO SEE HIM?
... ...
I'M SORRY ...

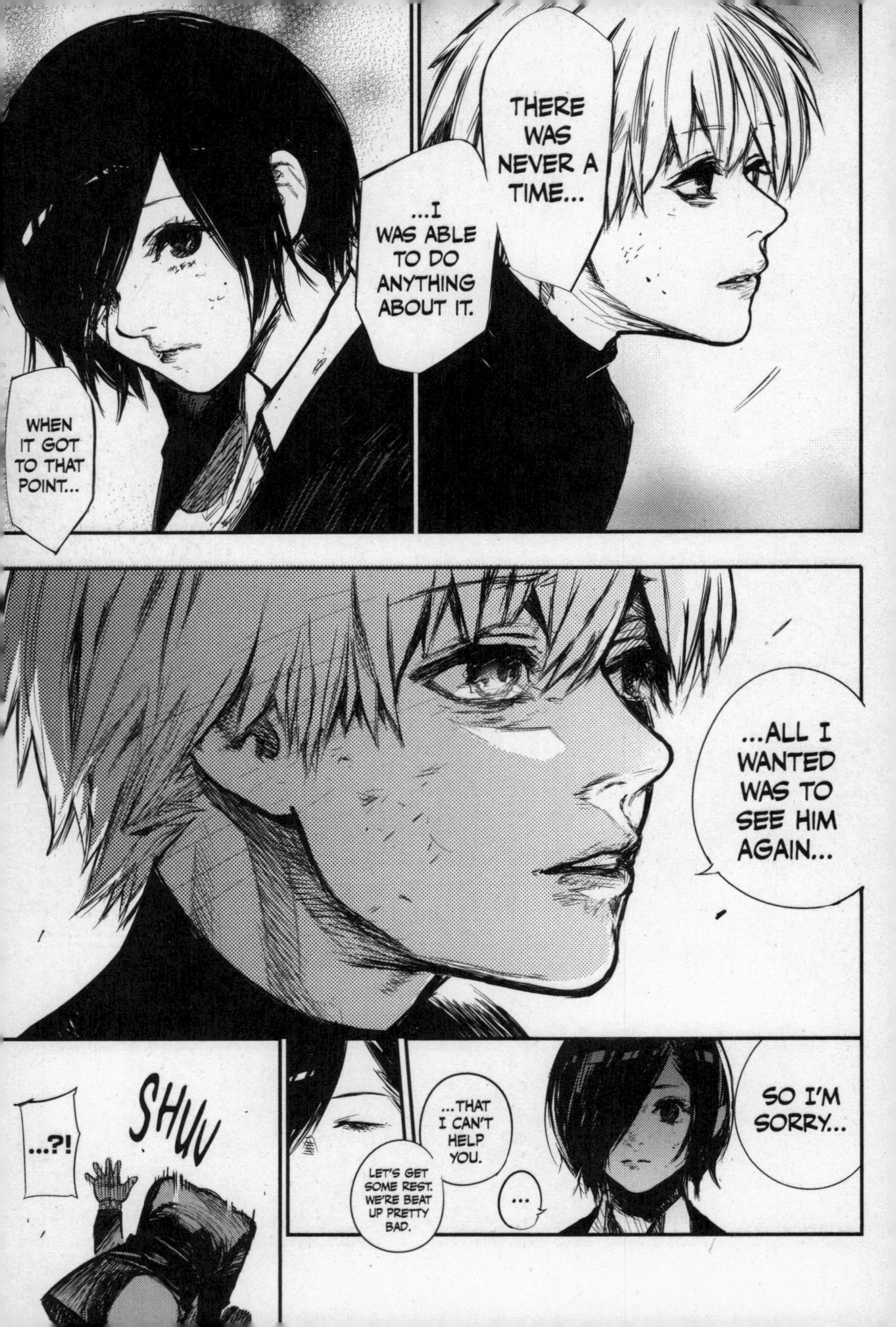
THERE WAS NEVER A TIME...
...I WAS ABLE TO DO ANYTHING ABOUT IT.
WHEN IT GOT TO THAT POINT...
...ALL I WANTED WAS TO SEE HIM AGAIN...
SO I'M SORRY...
...THAT I CAN'T HELP YOU.
...
LET'S GET SOME REST. WE'RE BEAT UP PRETTY BAD.
SHUU
...?!

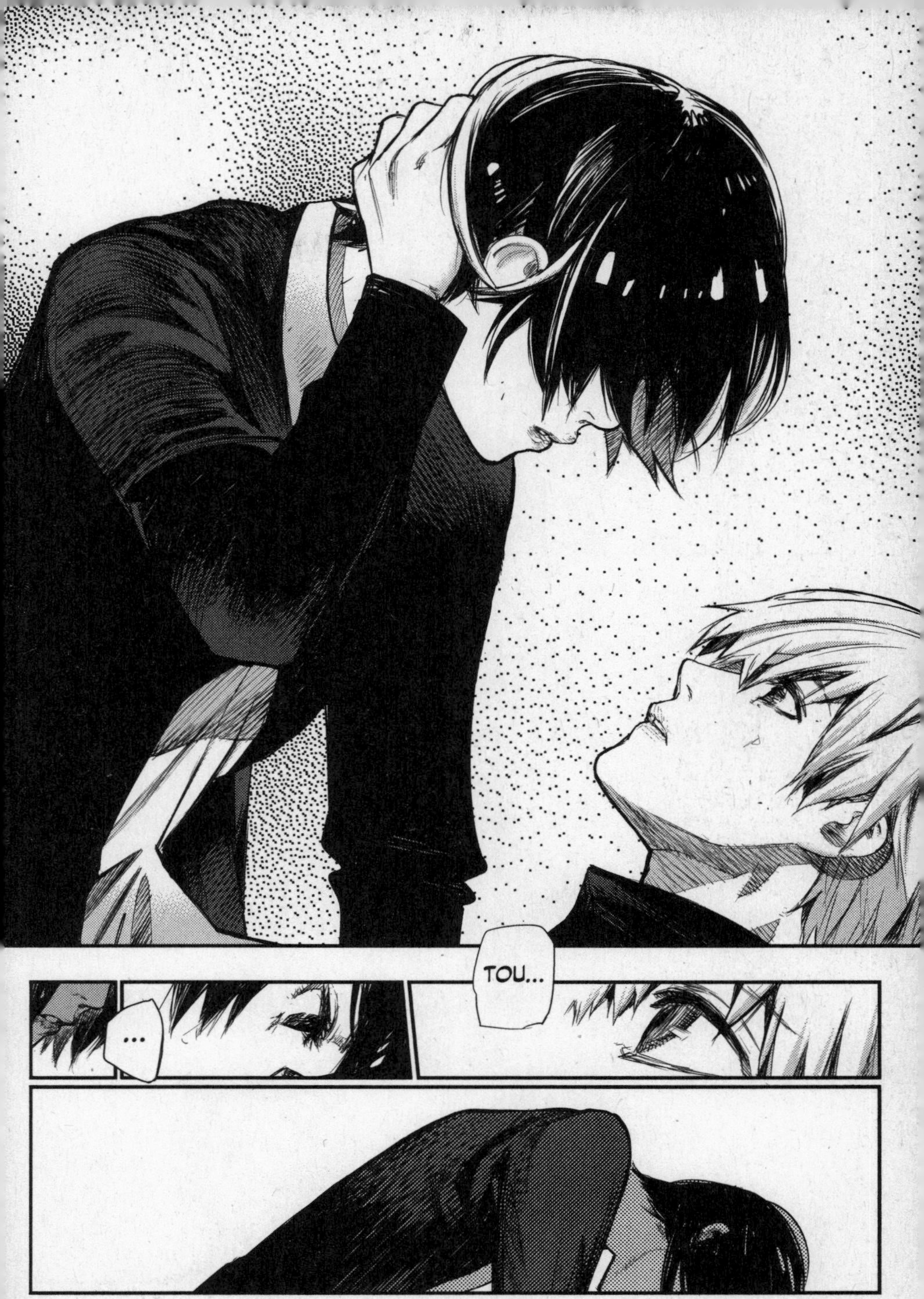
TOU...
...

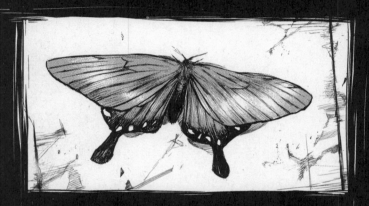

x:125 Sui Ishida

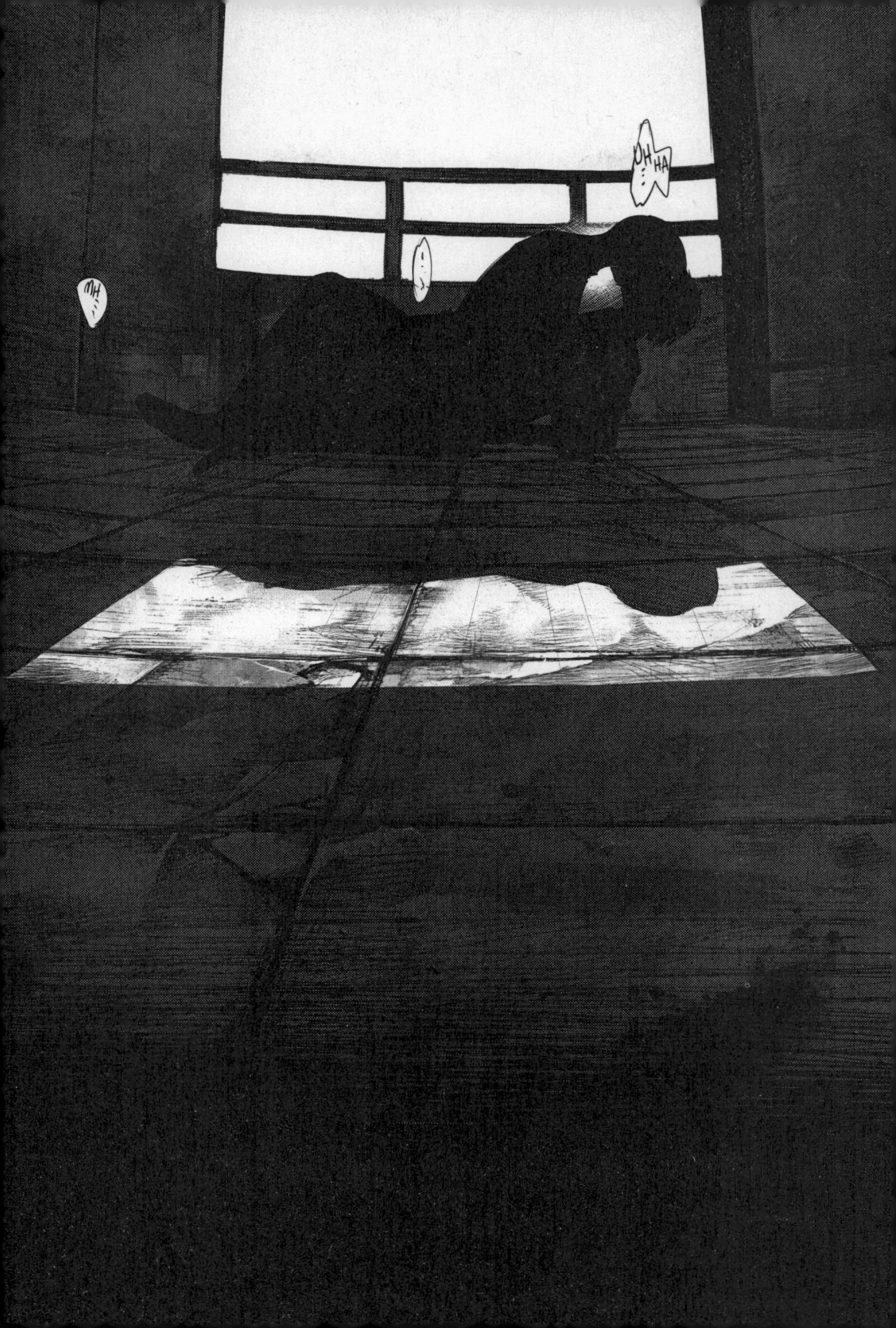
UH... HA
...
MH...

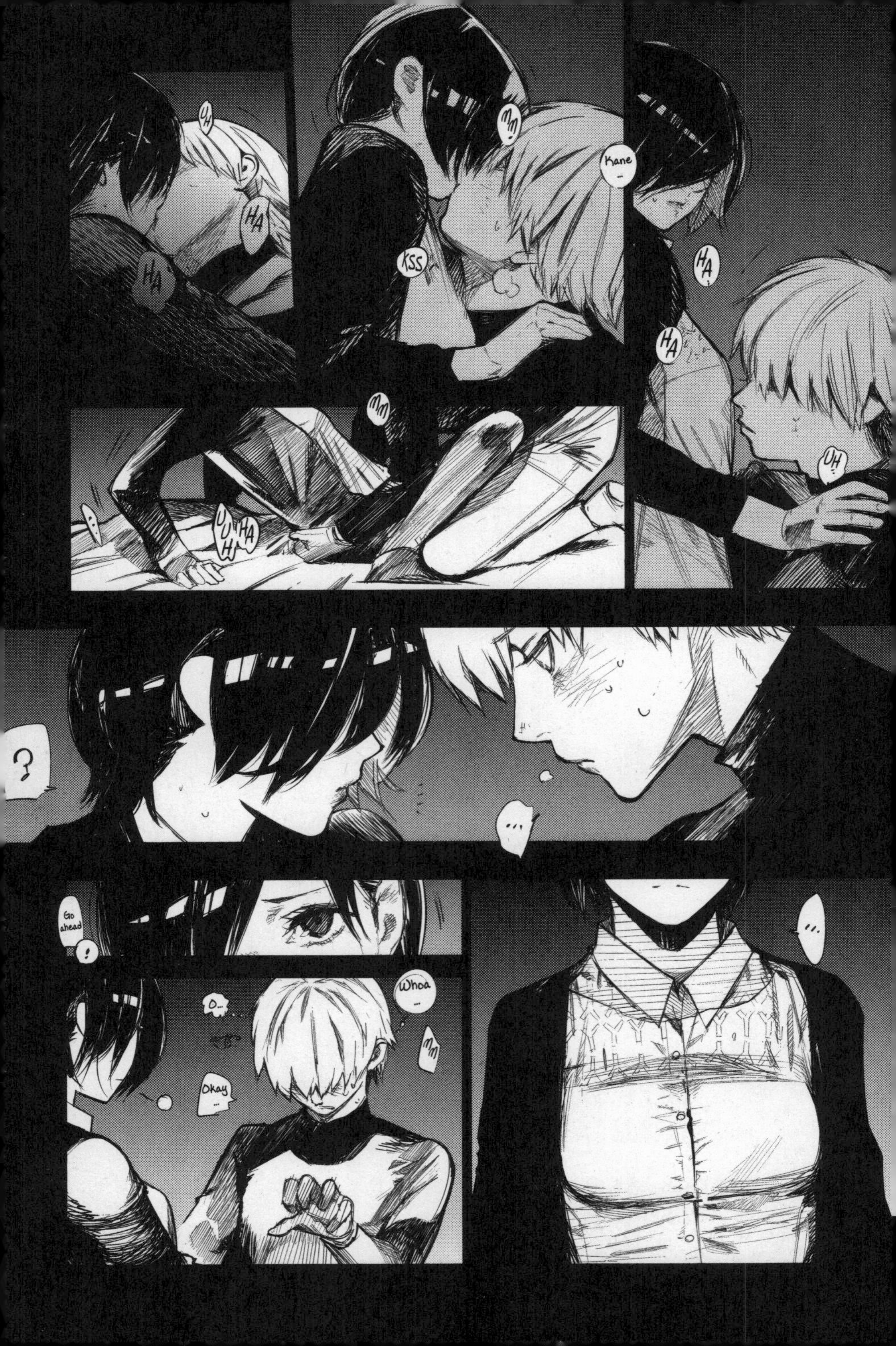
Kane...
HA
HA
UH!
MM
KSS
UH
HA
HA
MM
UH
HA
!
...
?
...
Go ahead!
Whoa...
MM
O...
Okay...

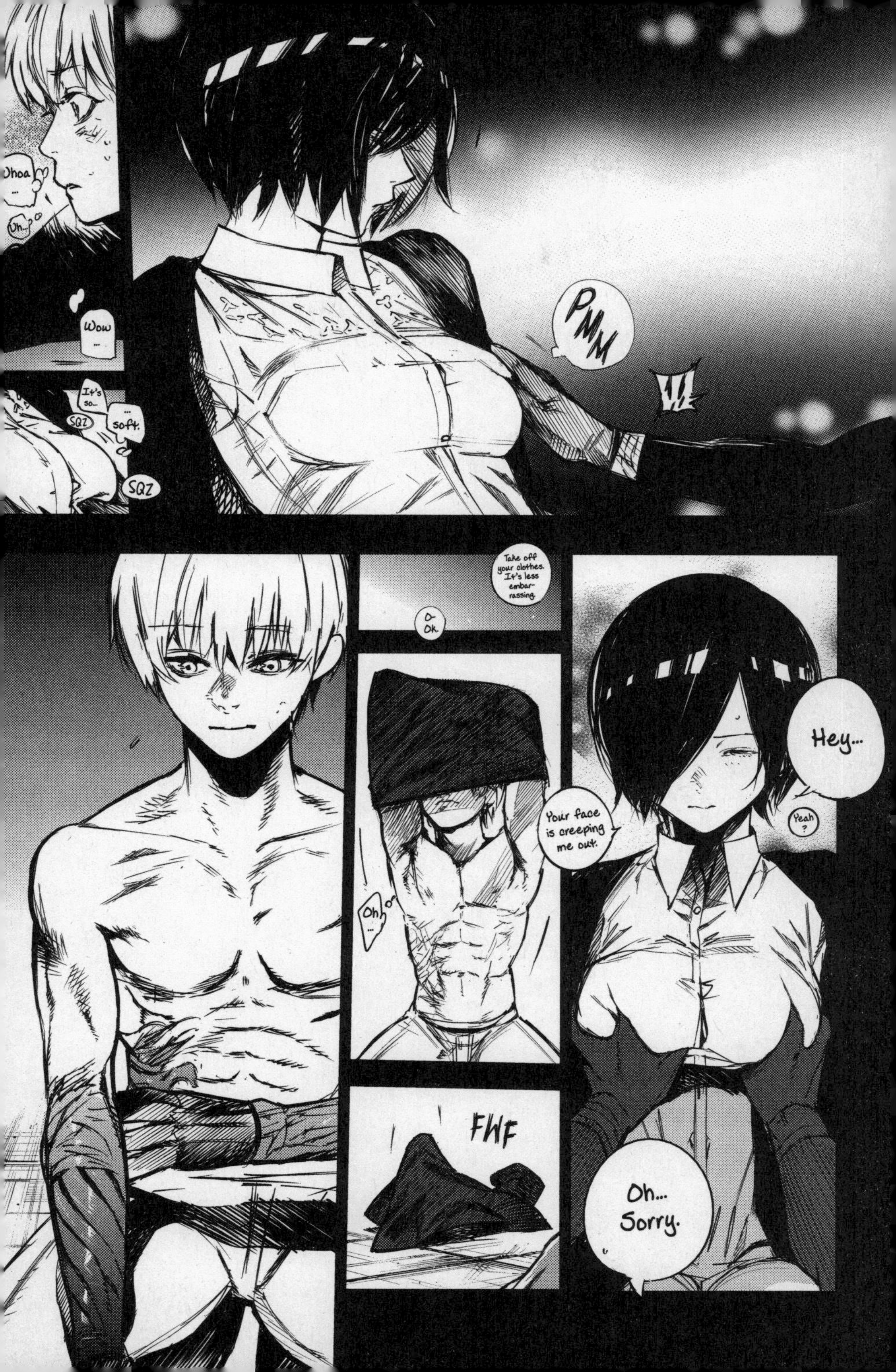
PMM
!!
Whoa...
Oh...
Wow...
It's so...
...soft.
SQZ
SQZ
Hey...
Yeah?
Your face is creeping me out.
Oh... Sorry.
Take off your clothes. It's less embarrassing.
O-Ok.
Oh...
FWF

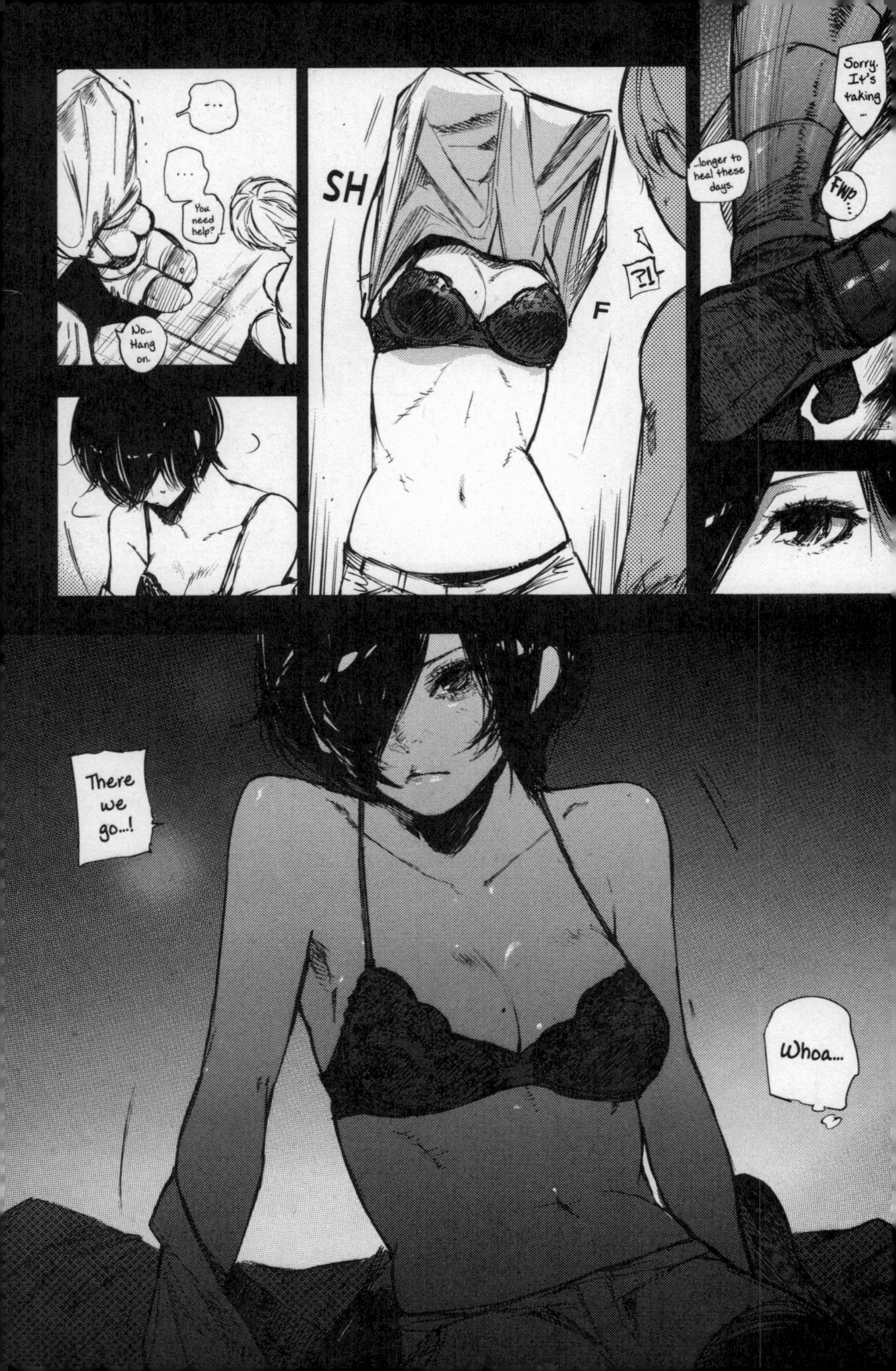
Sorry. It's taking...
...longer to heal these days.
Fwp...
SH
F
?!
...
...
You need help?
No... Hang on.
There we go...!
Whoa...

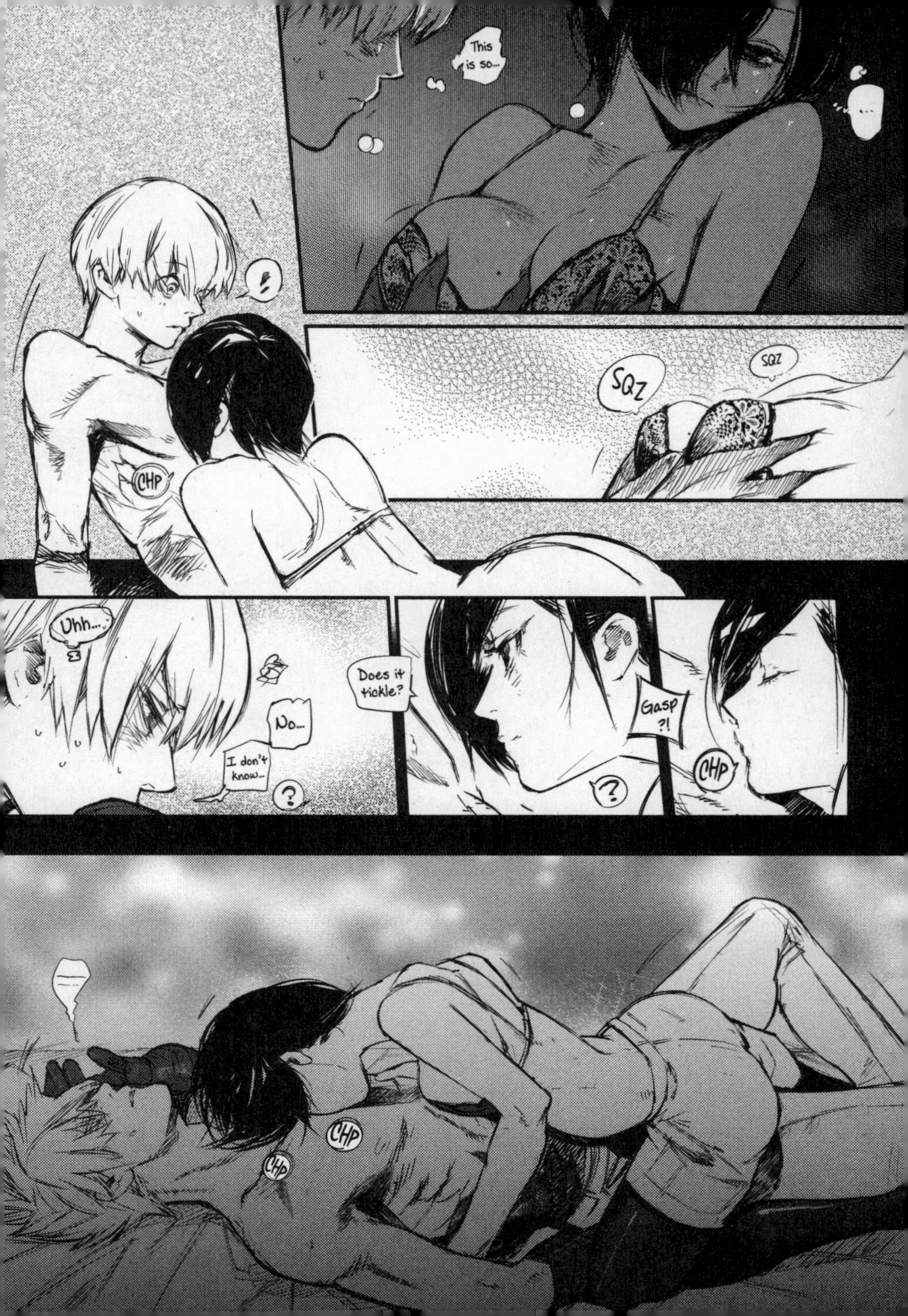
...
This is so...
SQZ
SQZ
!
CHP
Gasp ?!
CHP
?
Does it tickle?
No...
I don't know...
?
Uhh...
—
CHP
CHP

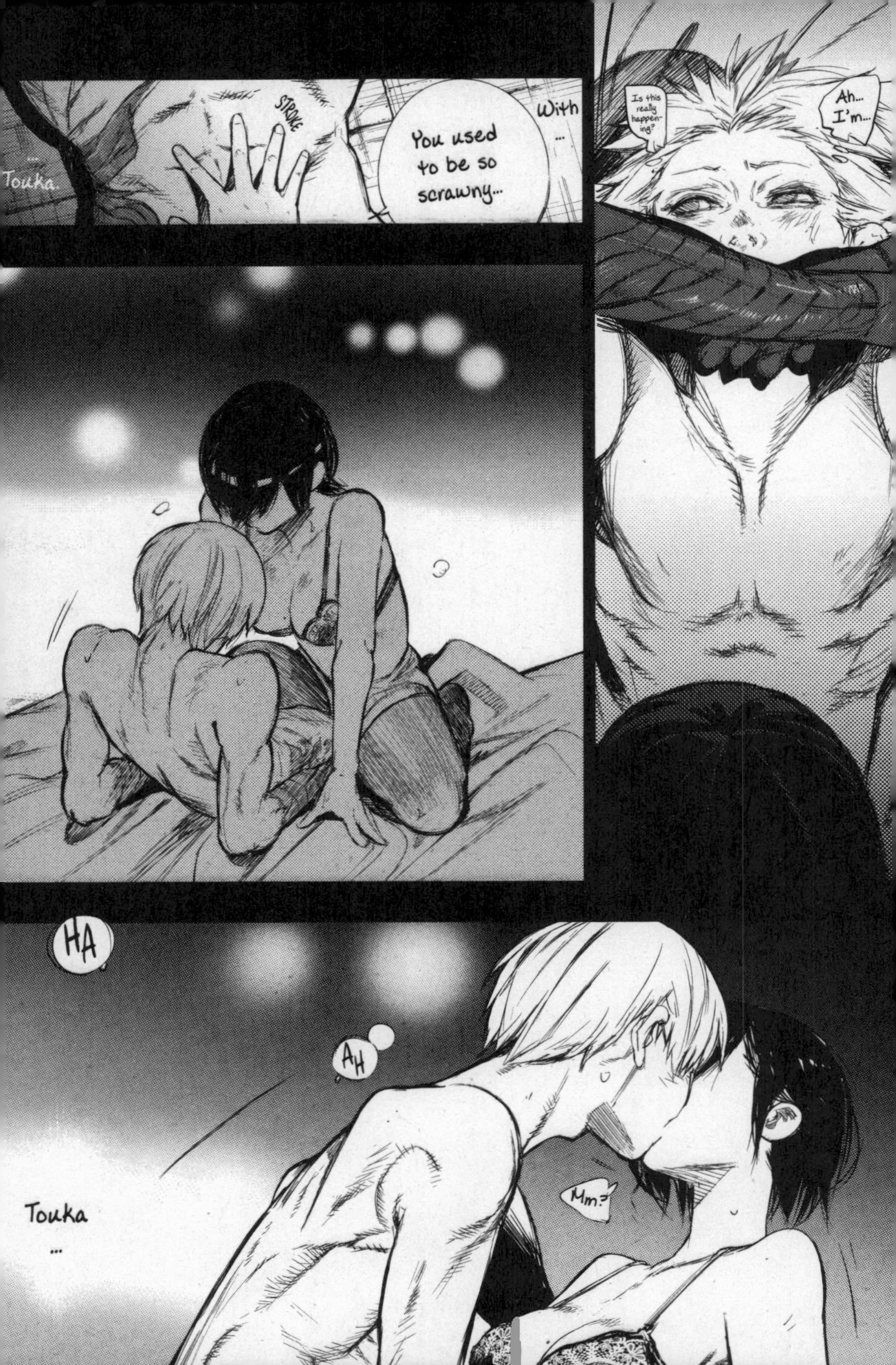
Ah... I'm...
Is this really happening?
With ...
You used to be so scrawny...
STROKE
... Touka.
HA
AH
Mm?
Touka ...

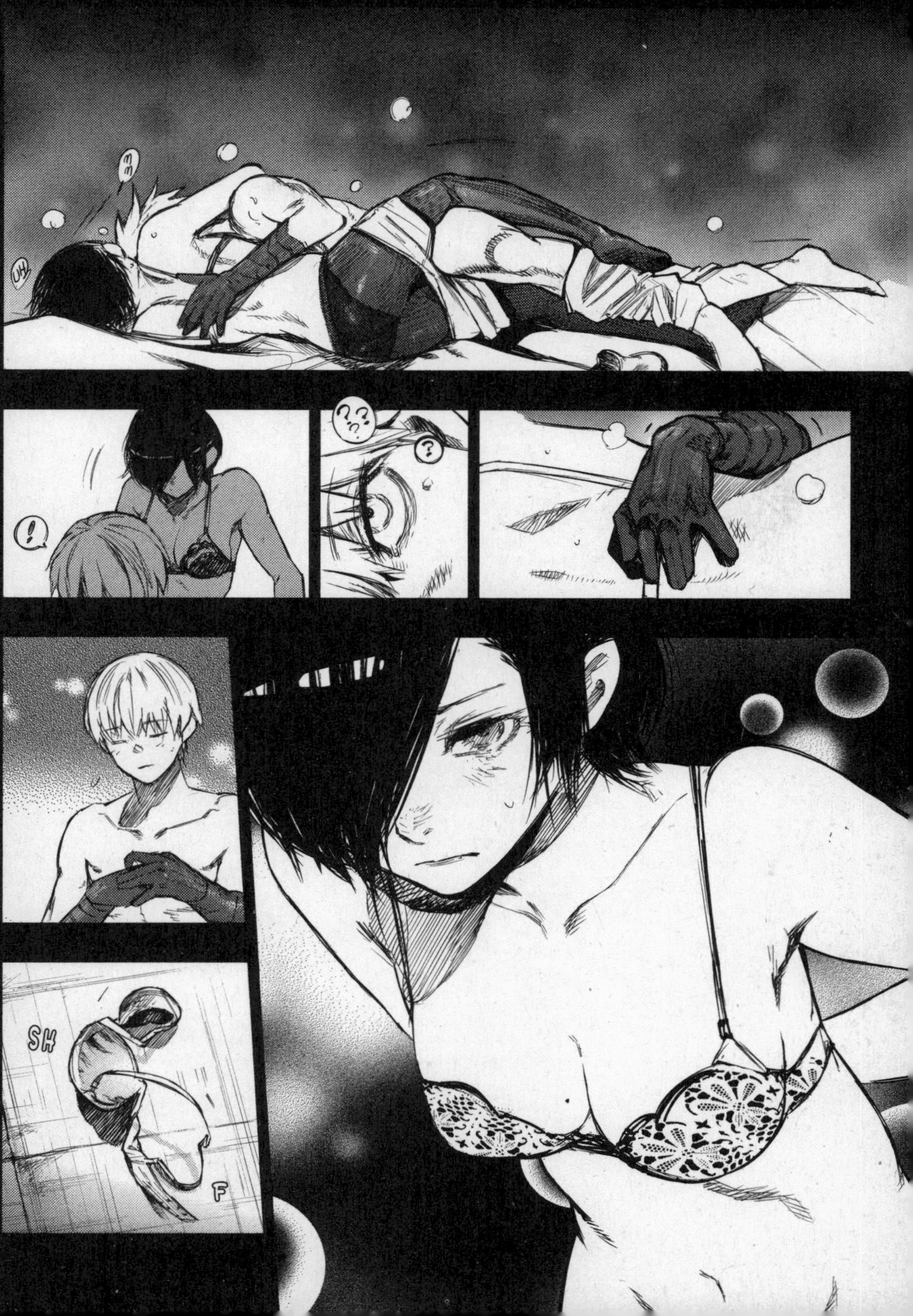
UH
??
?
!
SH
F

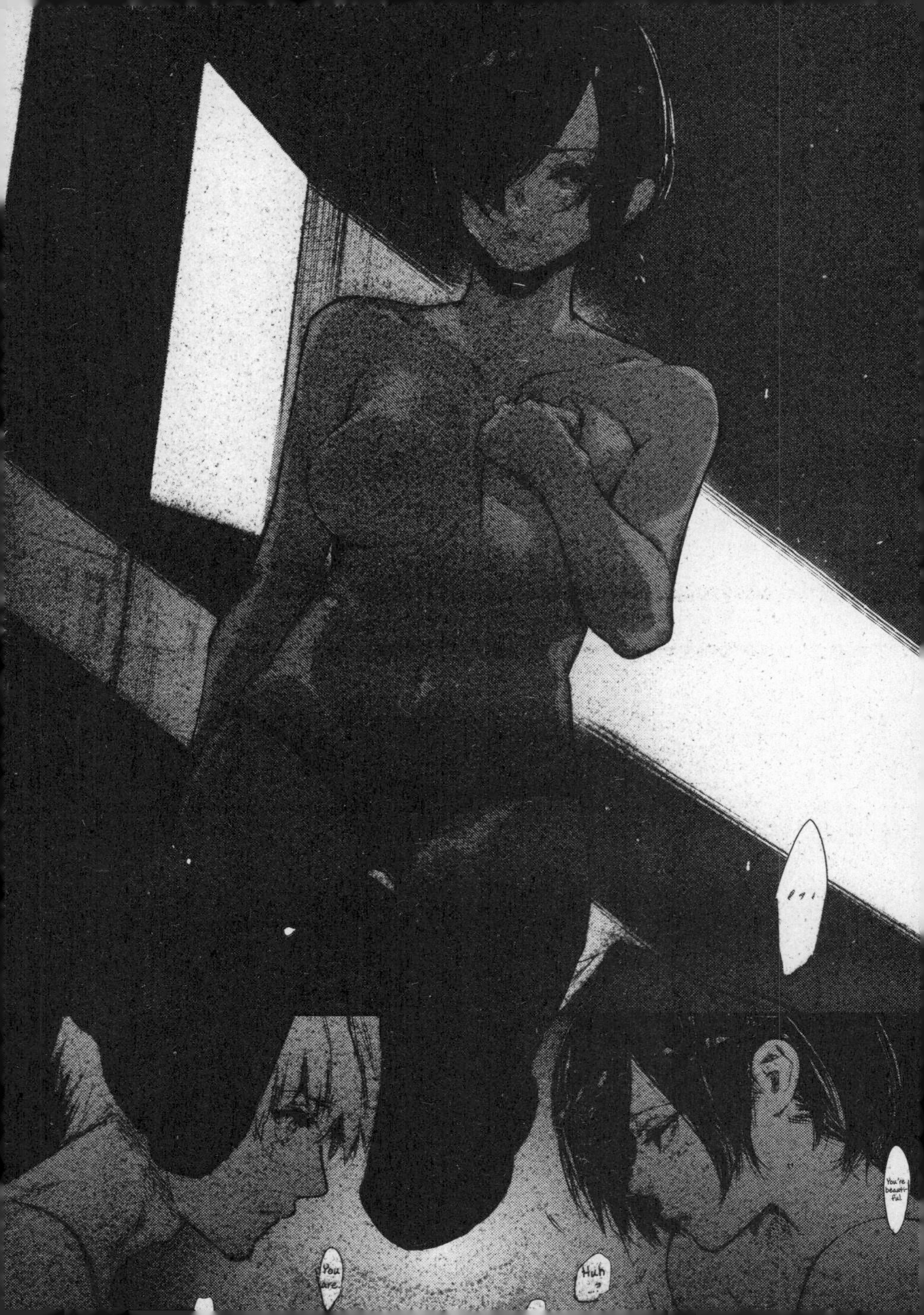

You're beautiful.
Huh...?
You are.

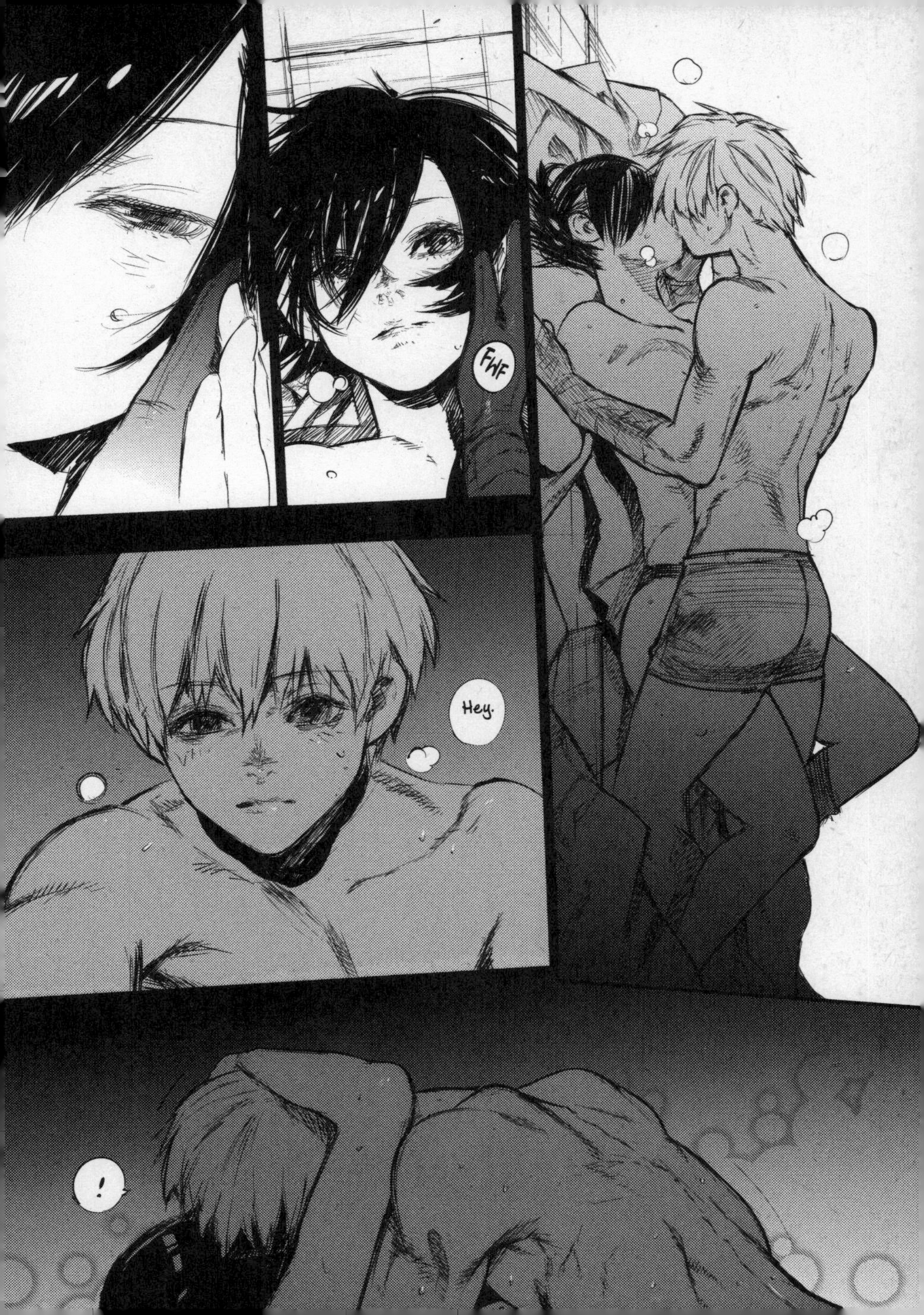
FWF
Hey.
!

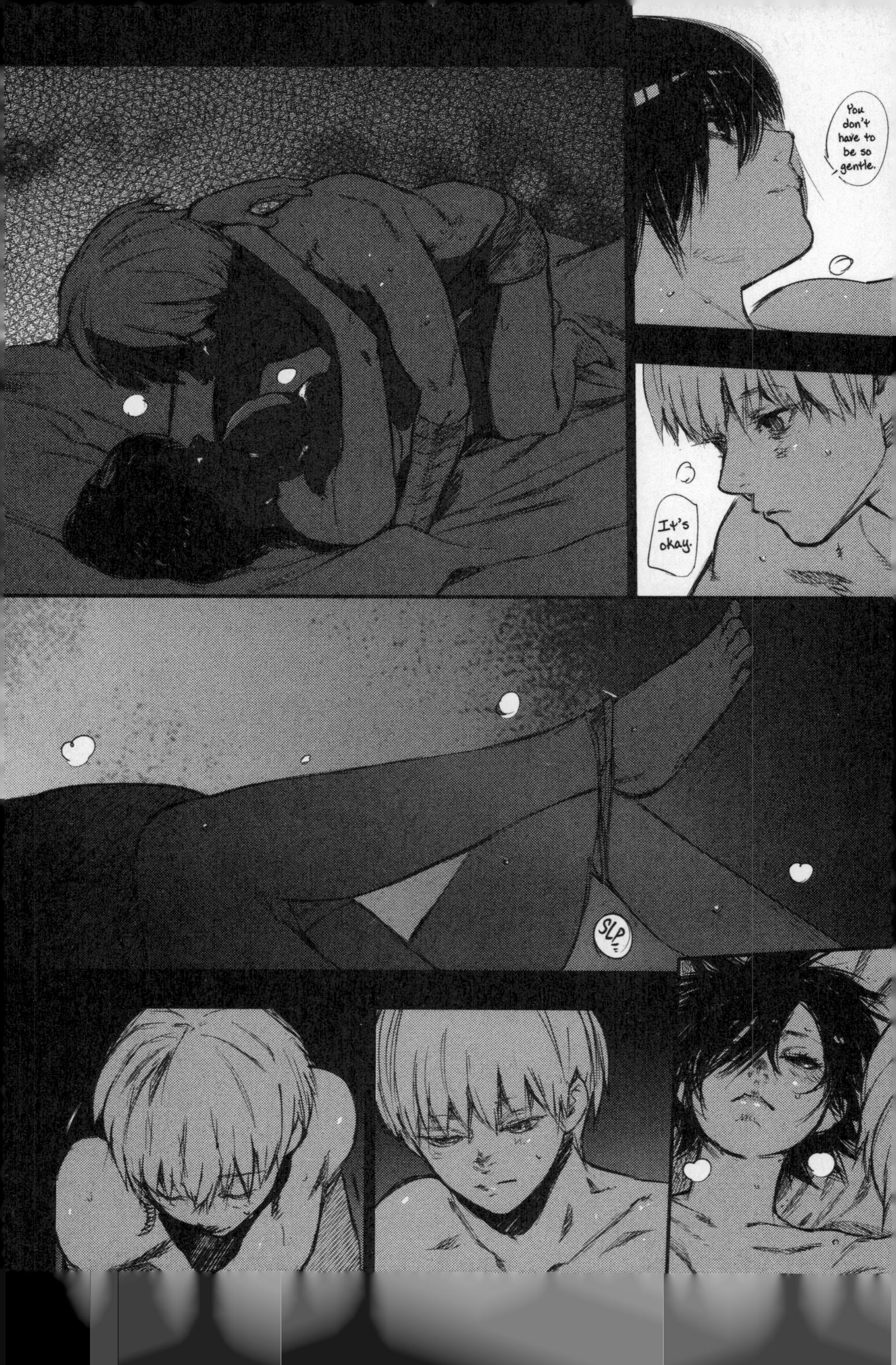
You don't have to be so gentle.
It's okay.
SLP

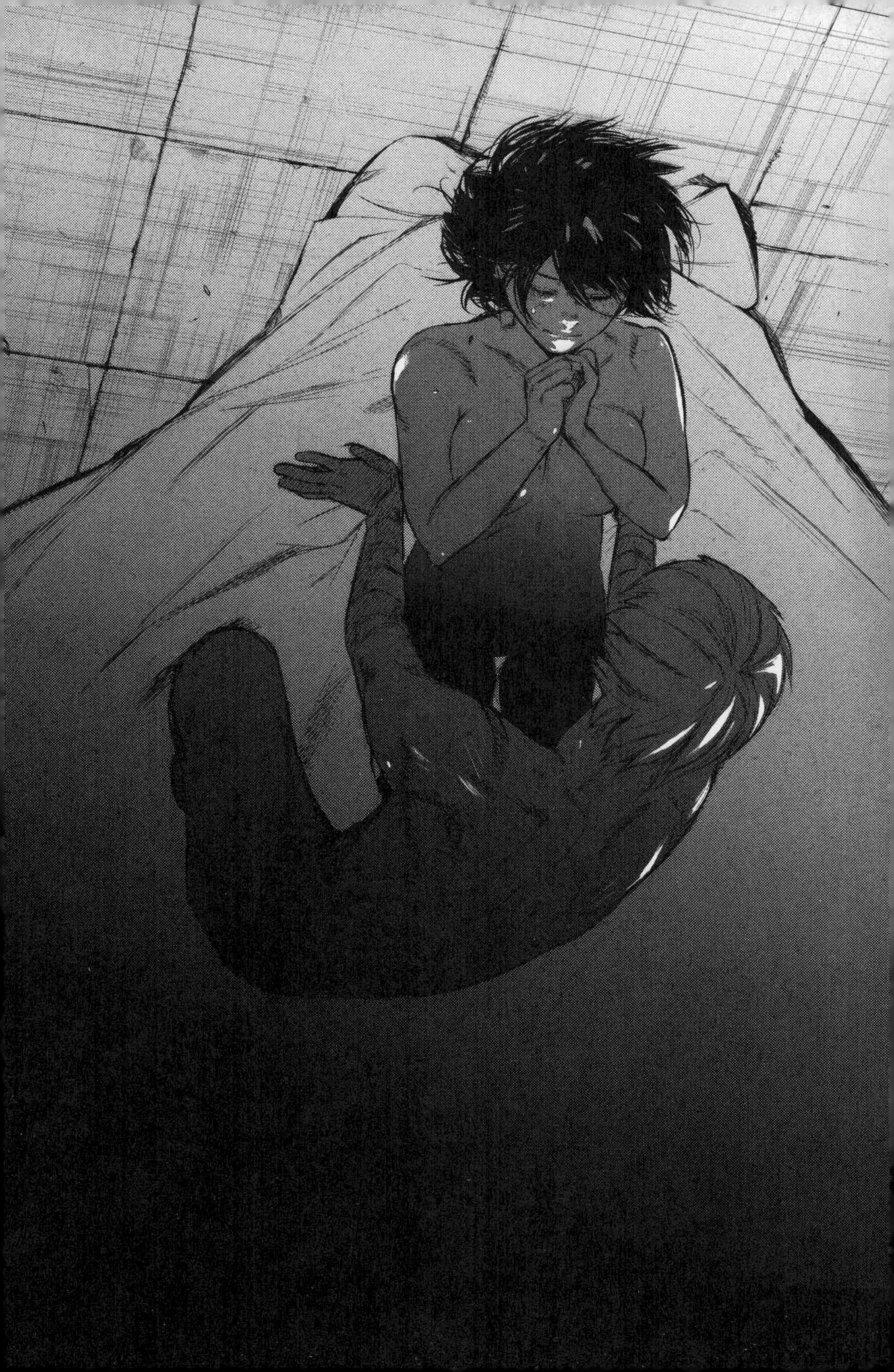

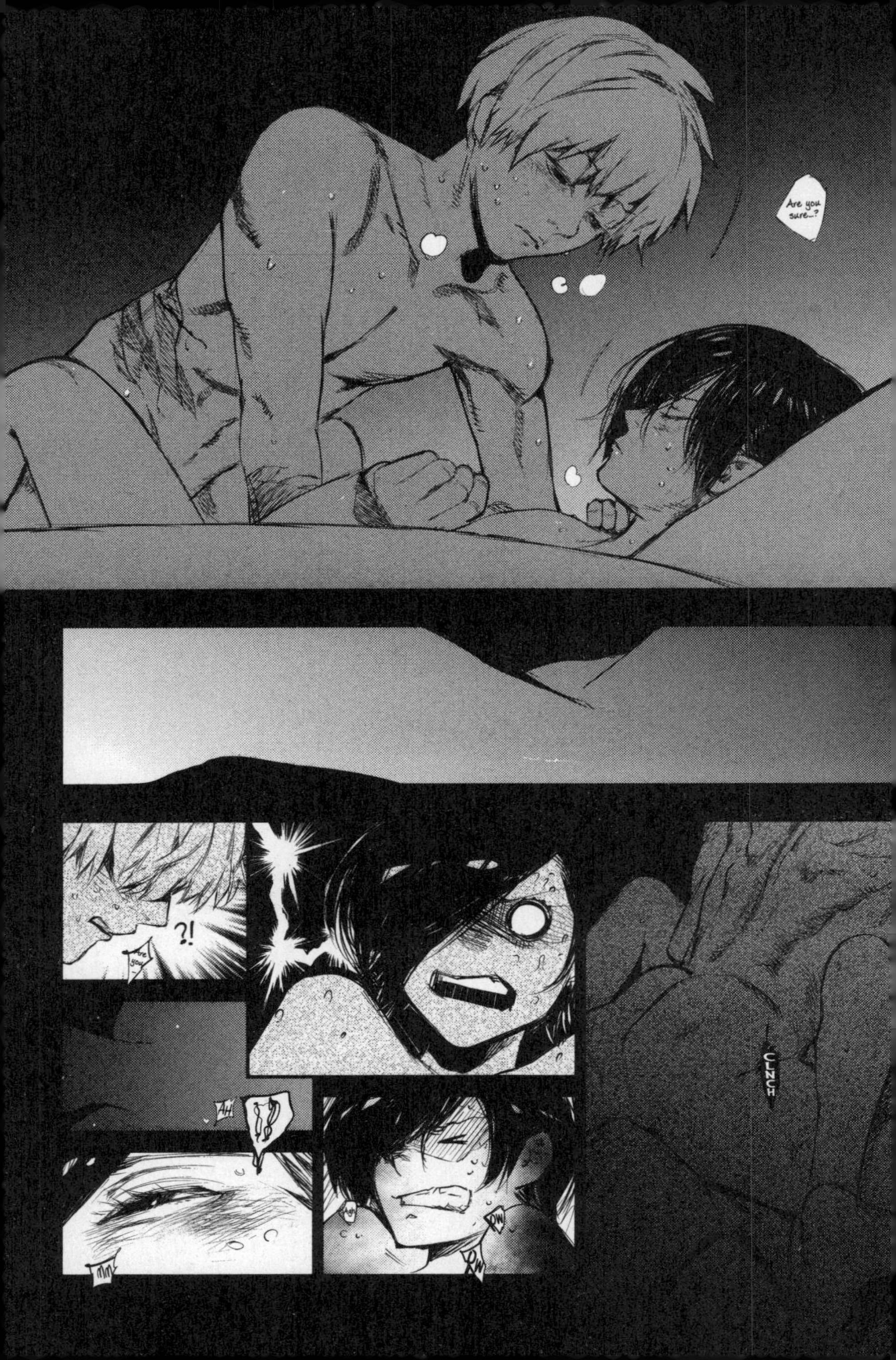

Are you sure...?
CLNCH
?!
Are you
OW
OW
AH
MN

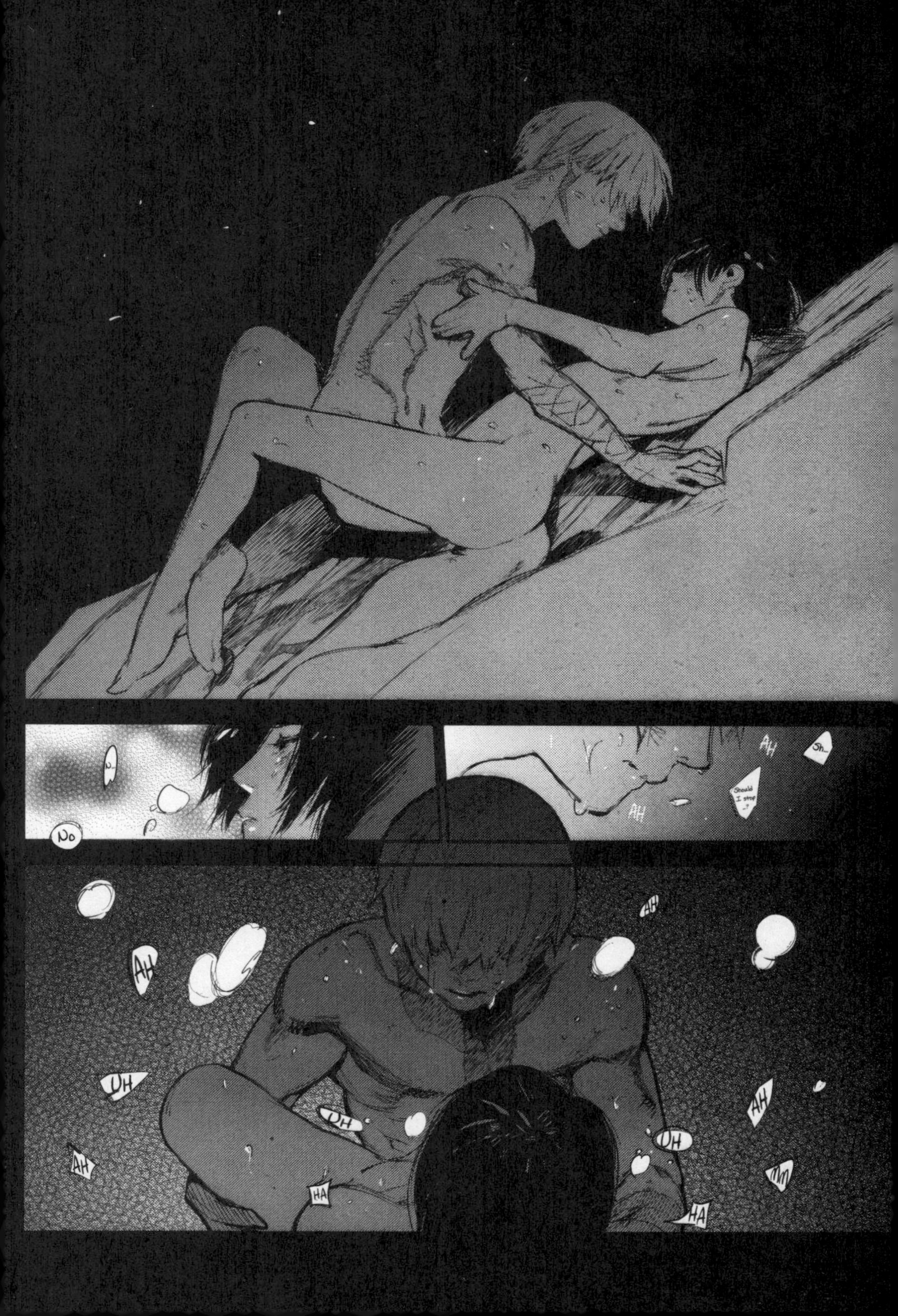
Sh...
AH
Should I stop...?
AH
N...
No
AH
AH
UH
UH
AH
UH
AH
HA
Mn
HA

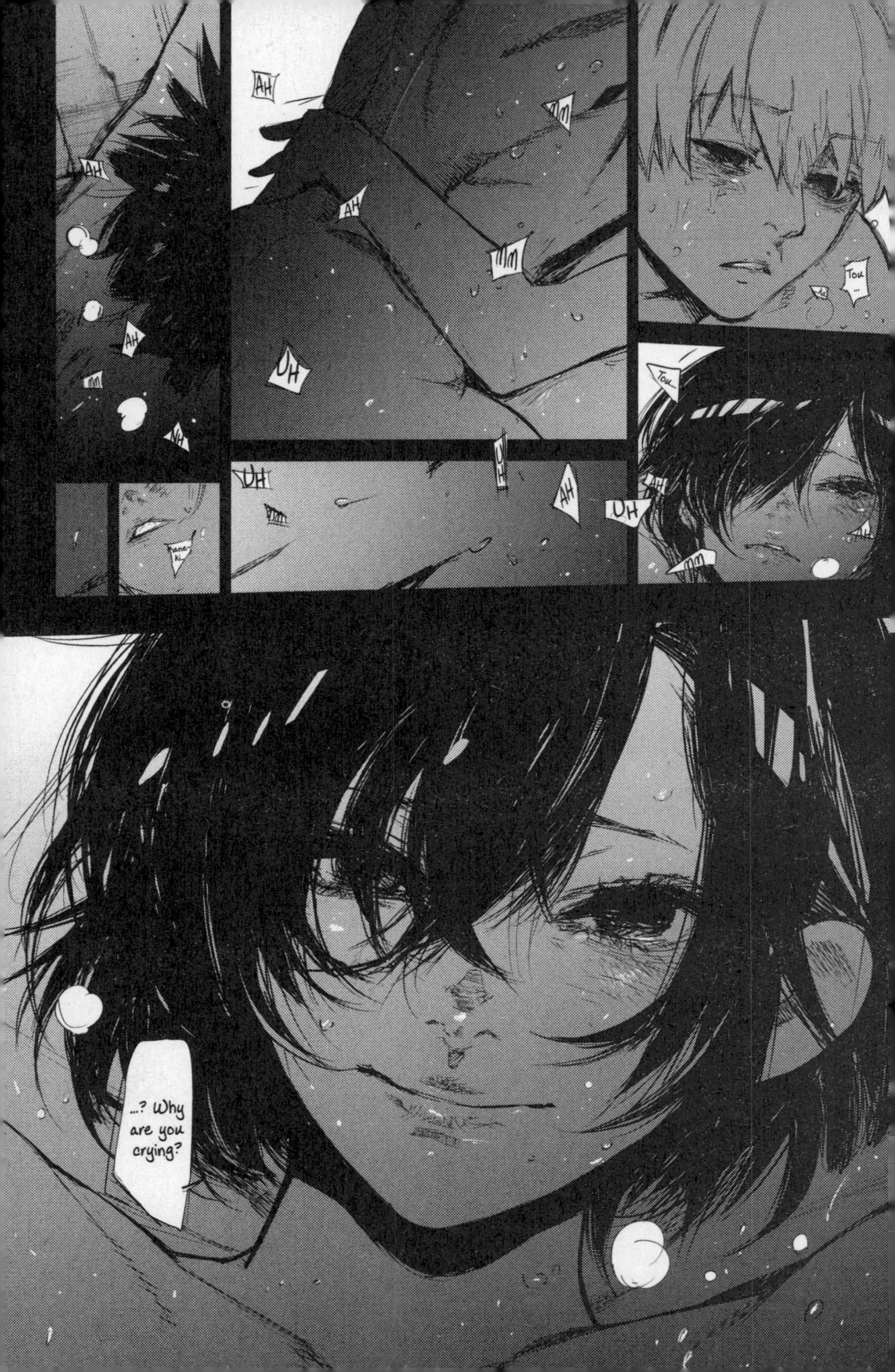
Tou
...
Tou...
AH
UH
MM
AH
MM
AH
MM
UH
AH
AH
MM
NH
UH
MM
UH
AH
Kane-
ki...
...? Why are you crying?

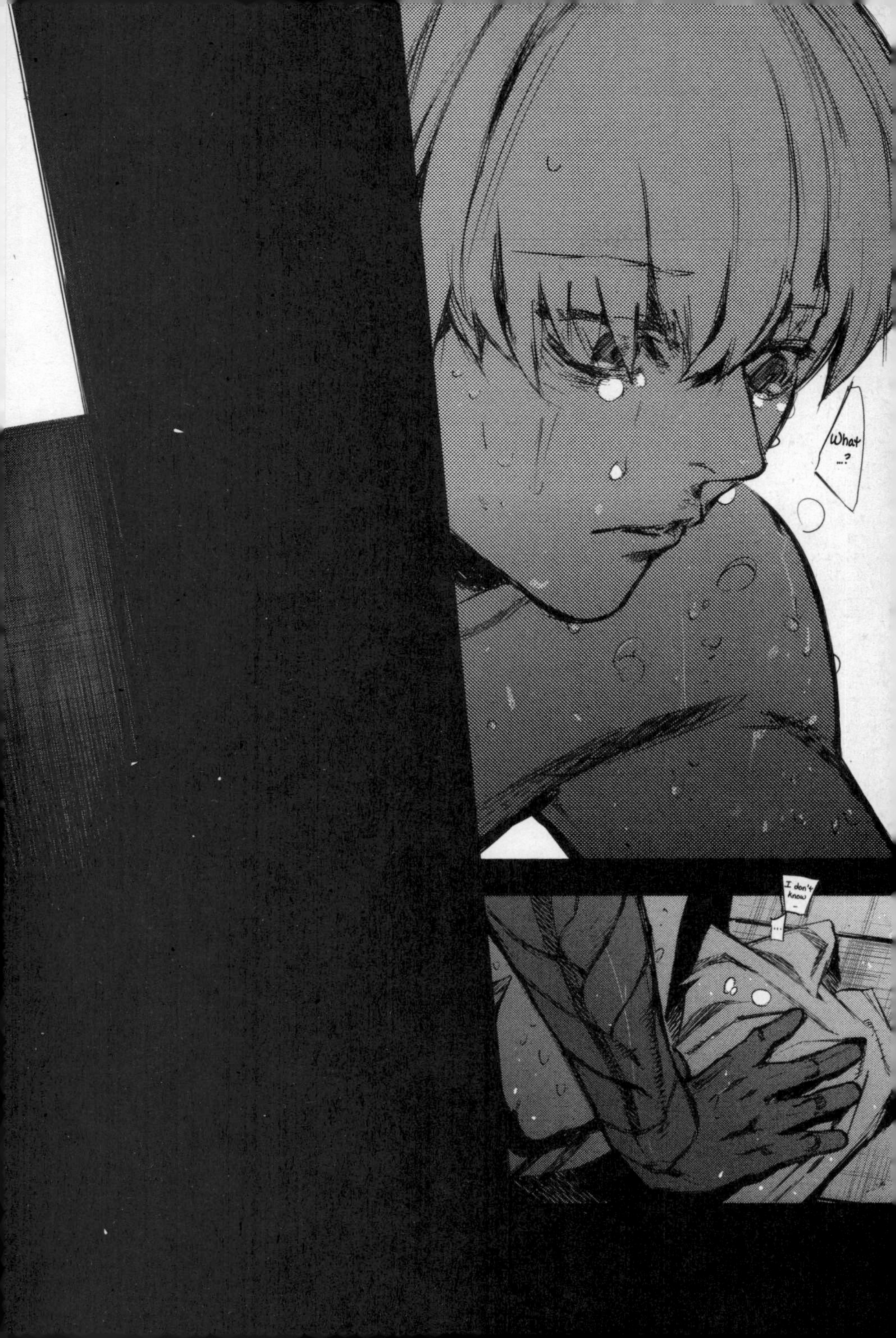
What ...?
I don't know –
...

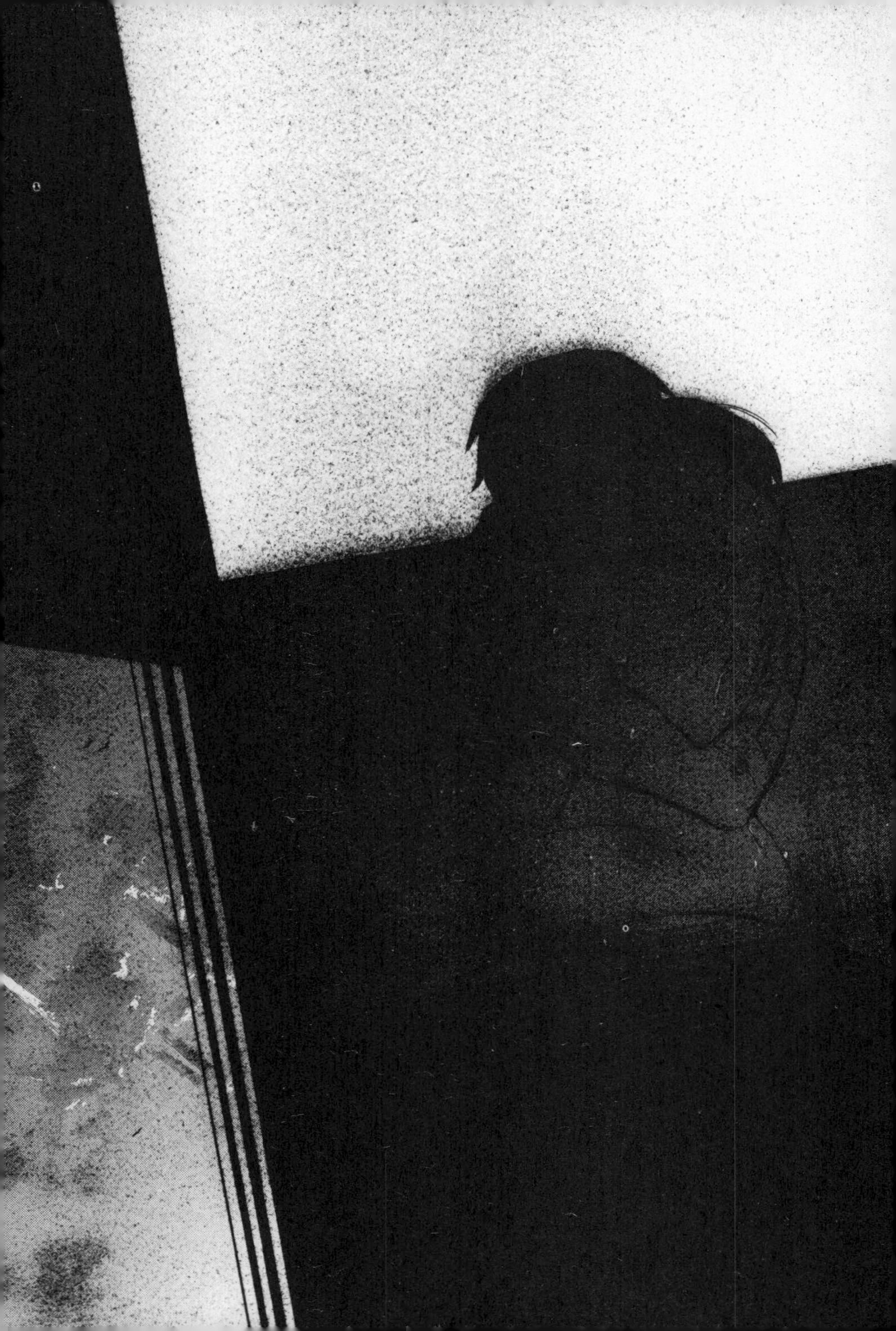

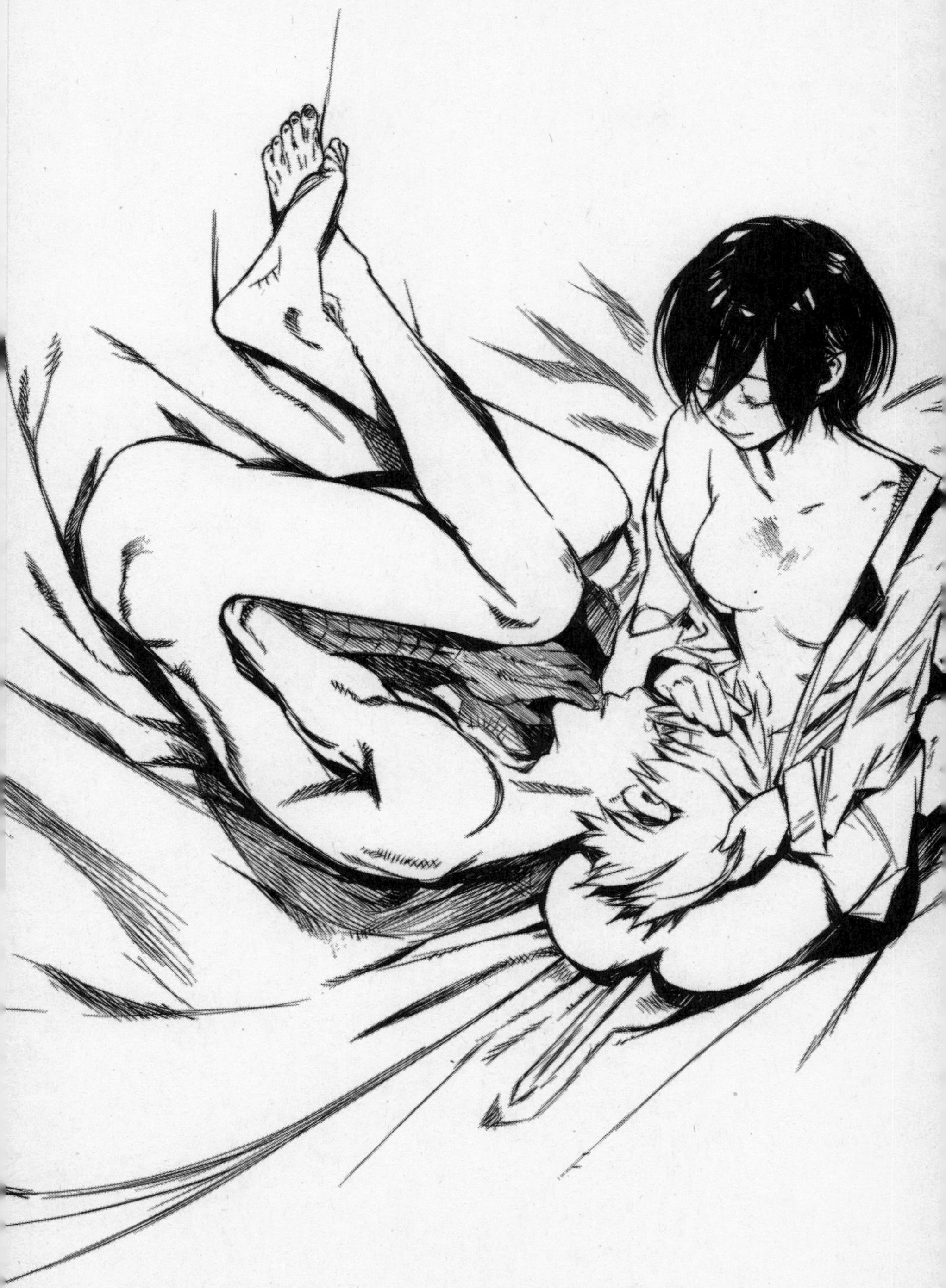

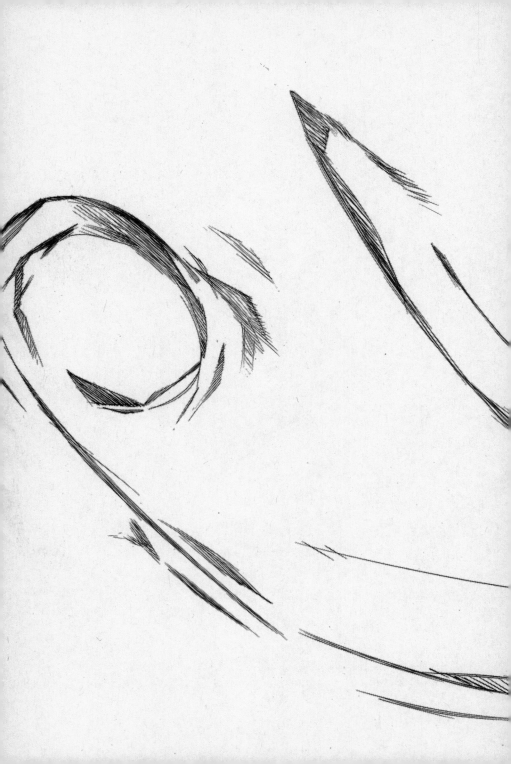

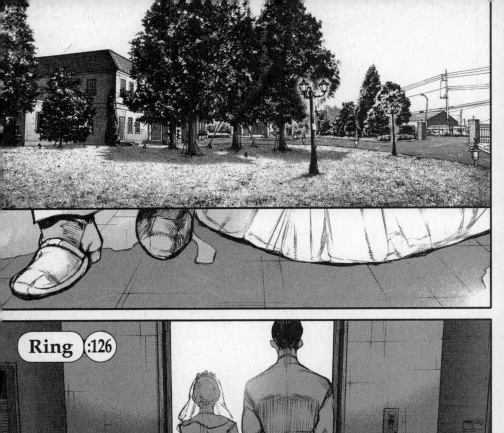

Ring :126

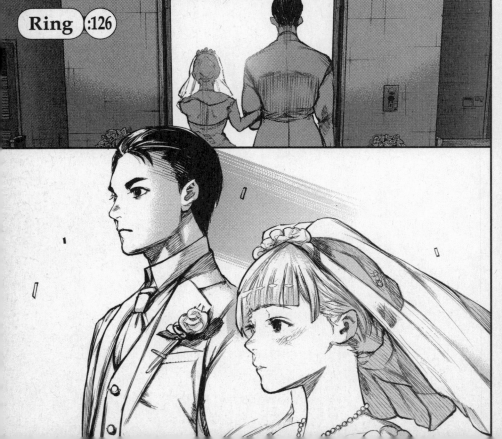

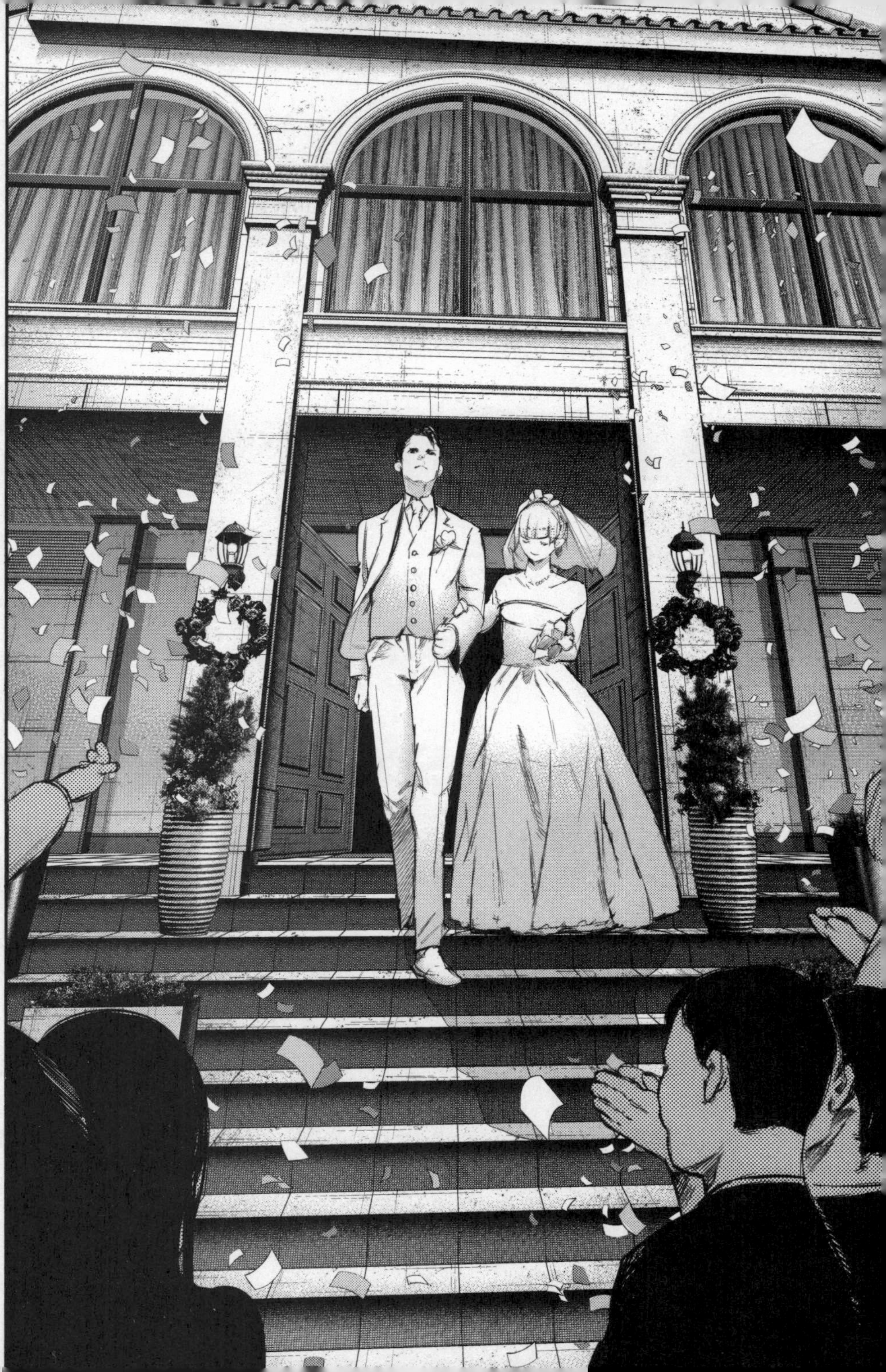

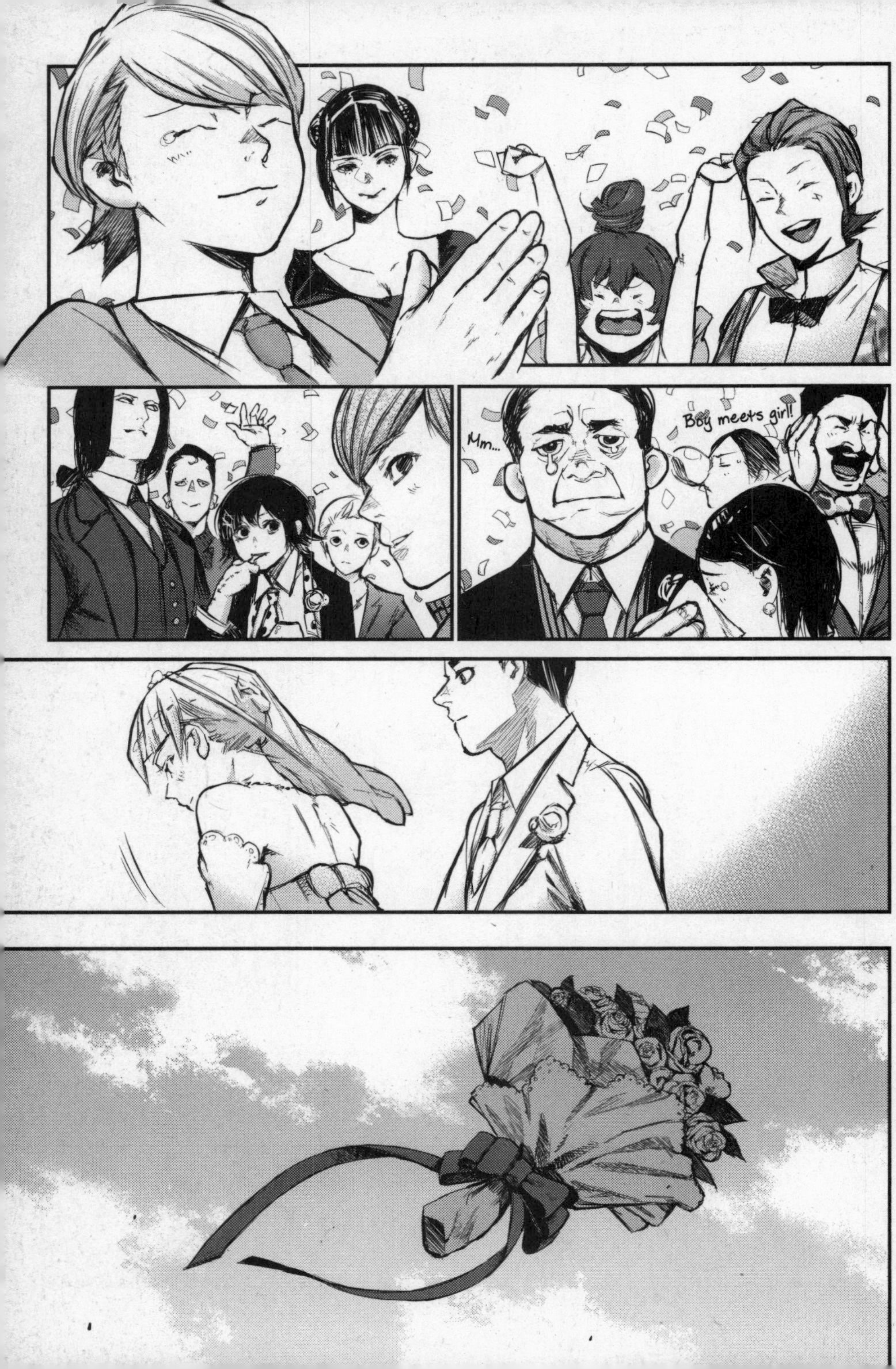
Boy meets girl!
Mm...

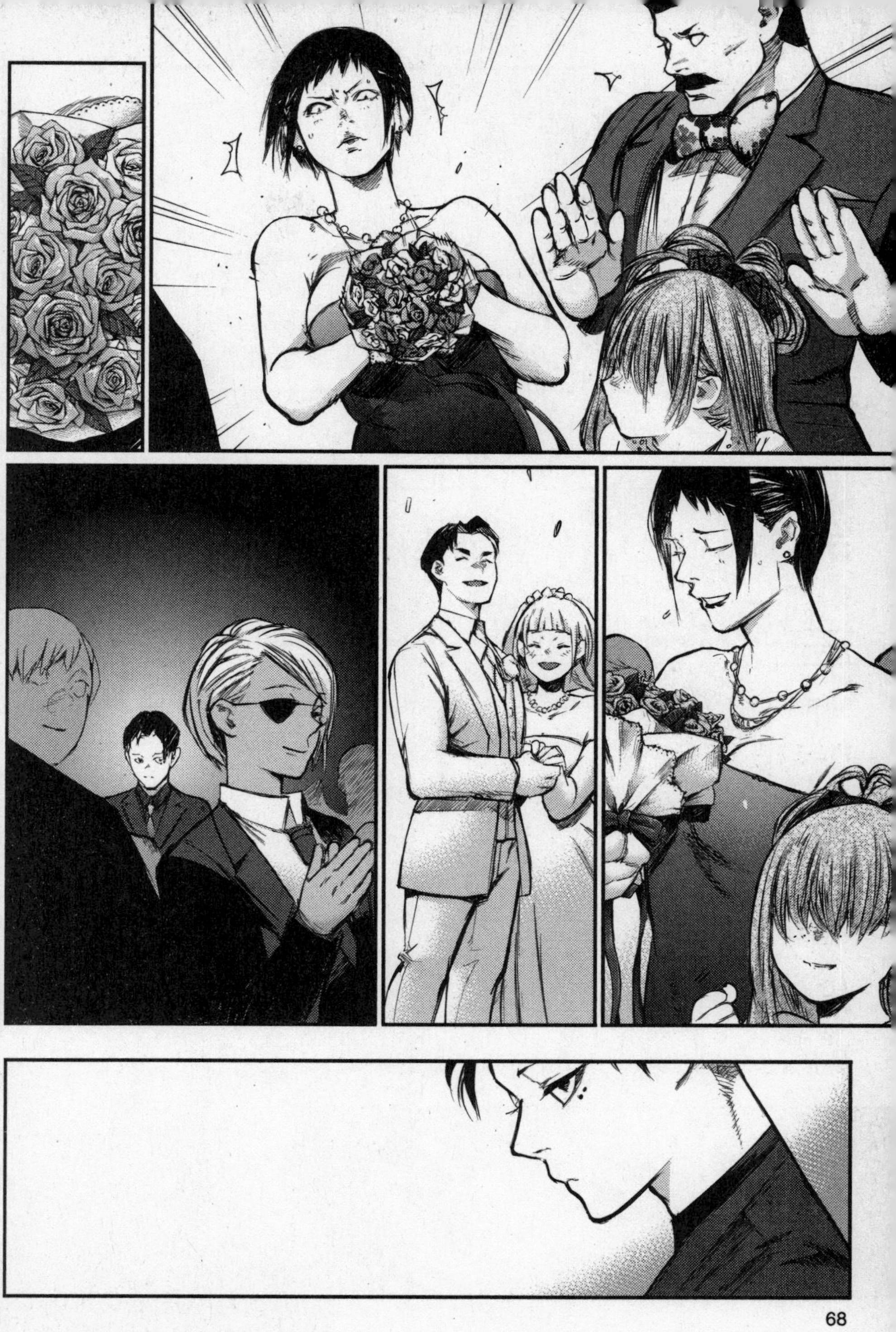

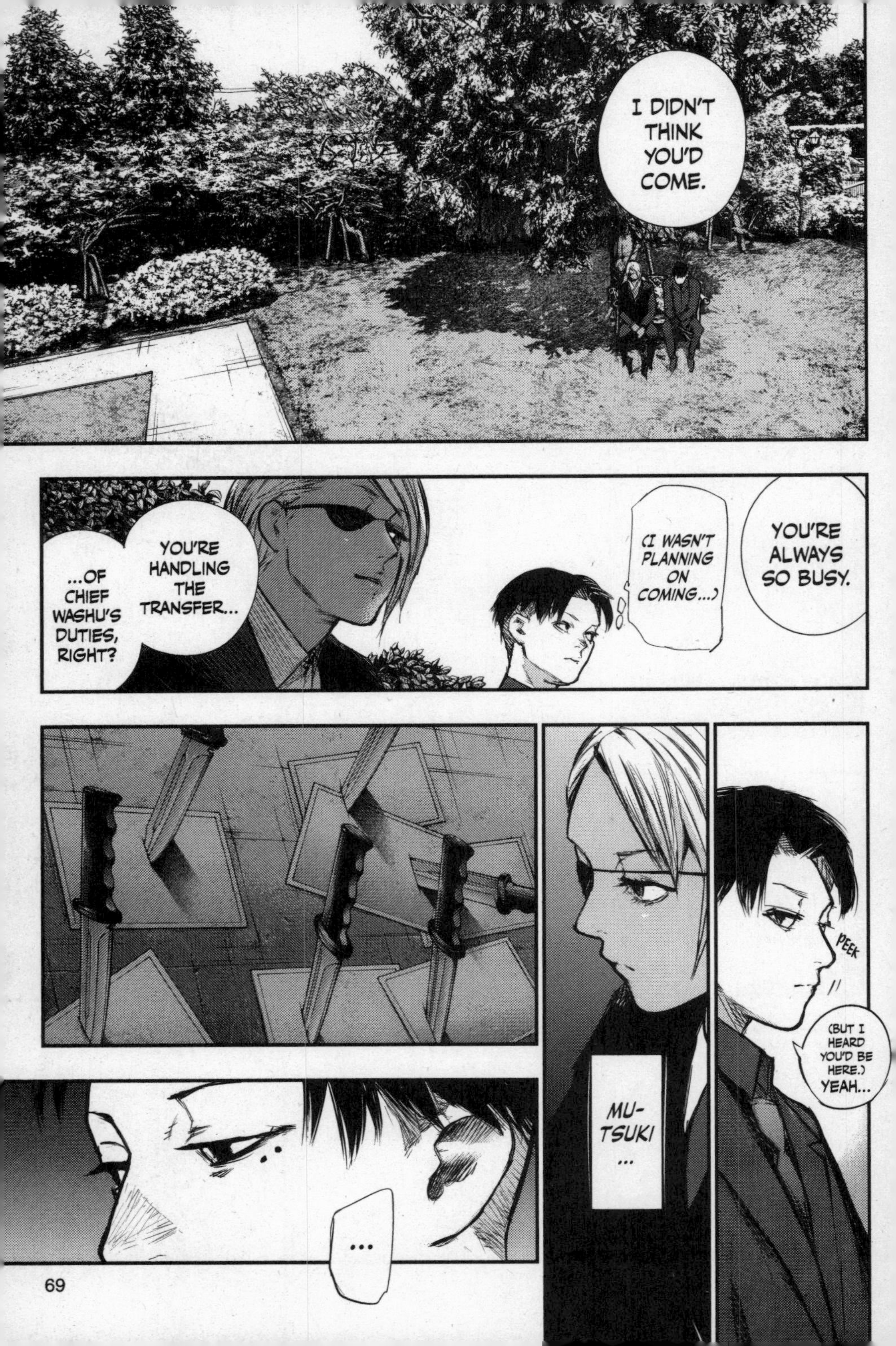
I DIDN'T THINK YOU'D COME.
YOU'RE ALWAYS SO BUSY.
(I WASN'T PLANNING ON COMING...)
YOU'RE HANDLING THE TRANSFER...
...OF CHIEF WASHU'S DUTIES, RIGHT?
PEEK
(BUT I HEARD YOU'D BE HERE.) YEAH...
MU-TSUKI ...
...

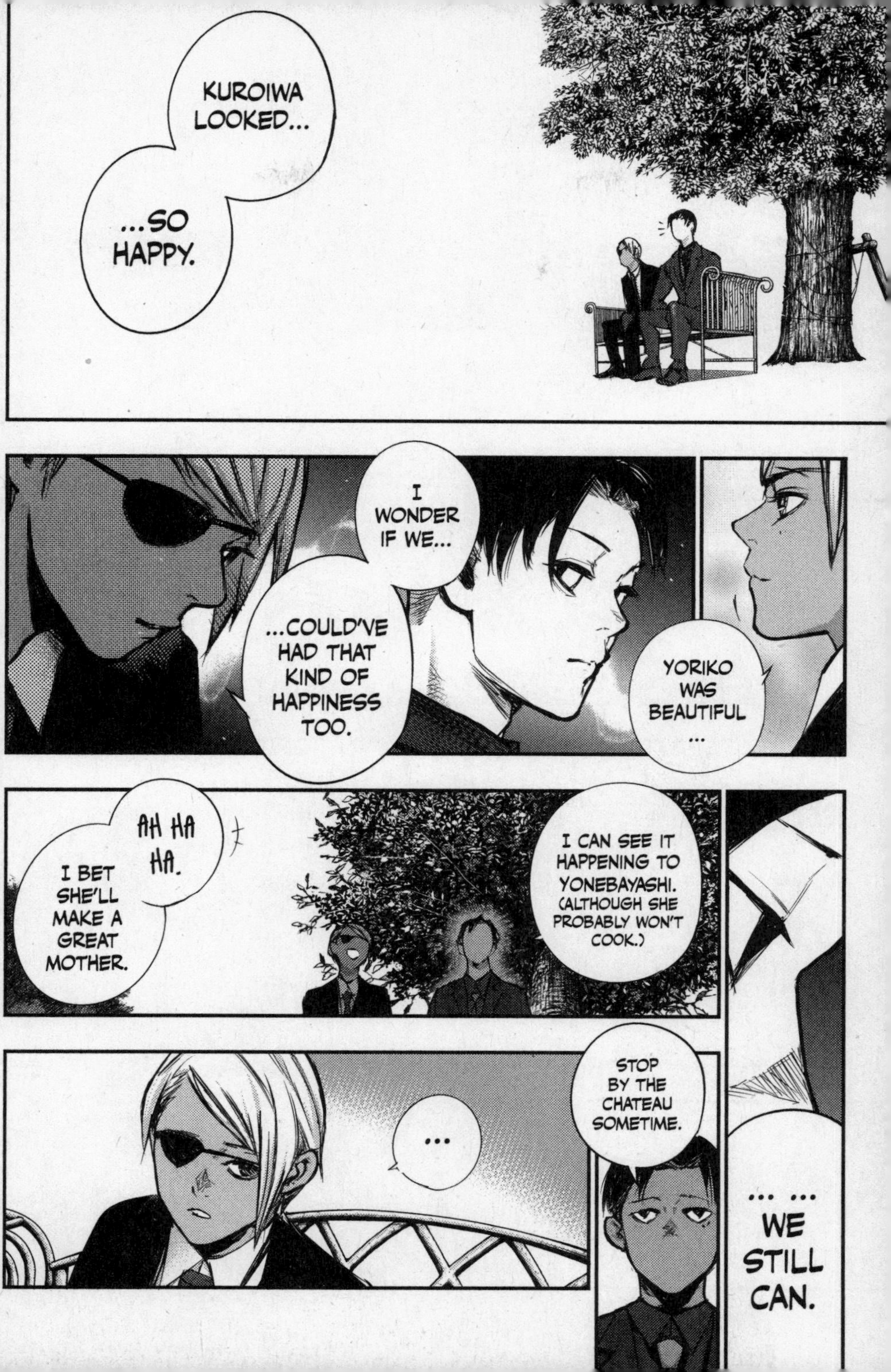
KUROIWA LOOKED...
...SO HAPPY.
YORIKO WAS BEAUTIFUL ...
I WONDER IF WE...
...COULD'VE HAD THAT KIND OF HAPPINESS TOO.
... ... WE STILL CAN.
I CAN SEE IT HAPPENING TO YONEBAYASHI. (ALTHOUGH SHE PROBABLY WON'T COOK.)
AH HA HA.
I BET SHE'LL MAKE A GREAT MOTHER.
STOP BY THE CHATEAU SOMETIME.
...

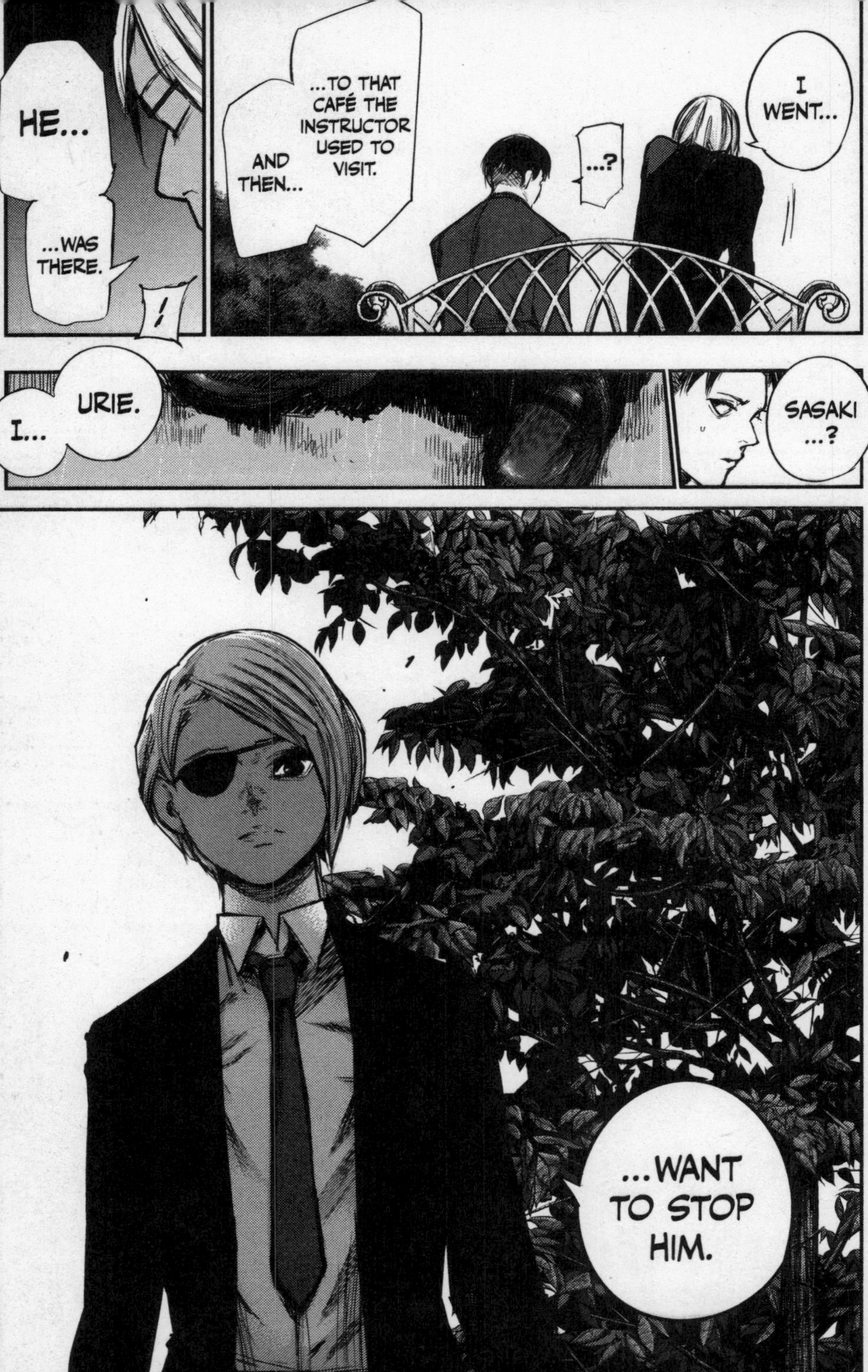
I WENT...
...?
...TO THAT CAFÉ THE INSTRUCTOR USED TO VISIT.
AND THEN...
HE...
...WAS THERE.
!
SASAKI ...?
URIE.
I...
...WANT TO STOP HIM.

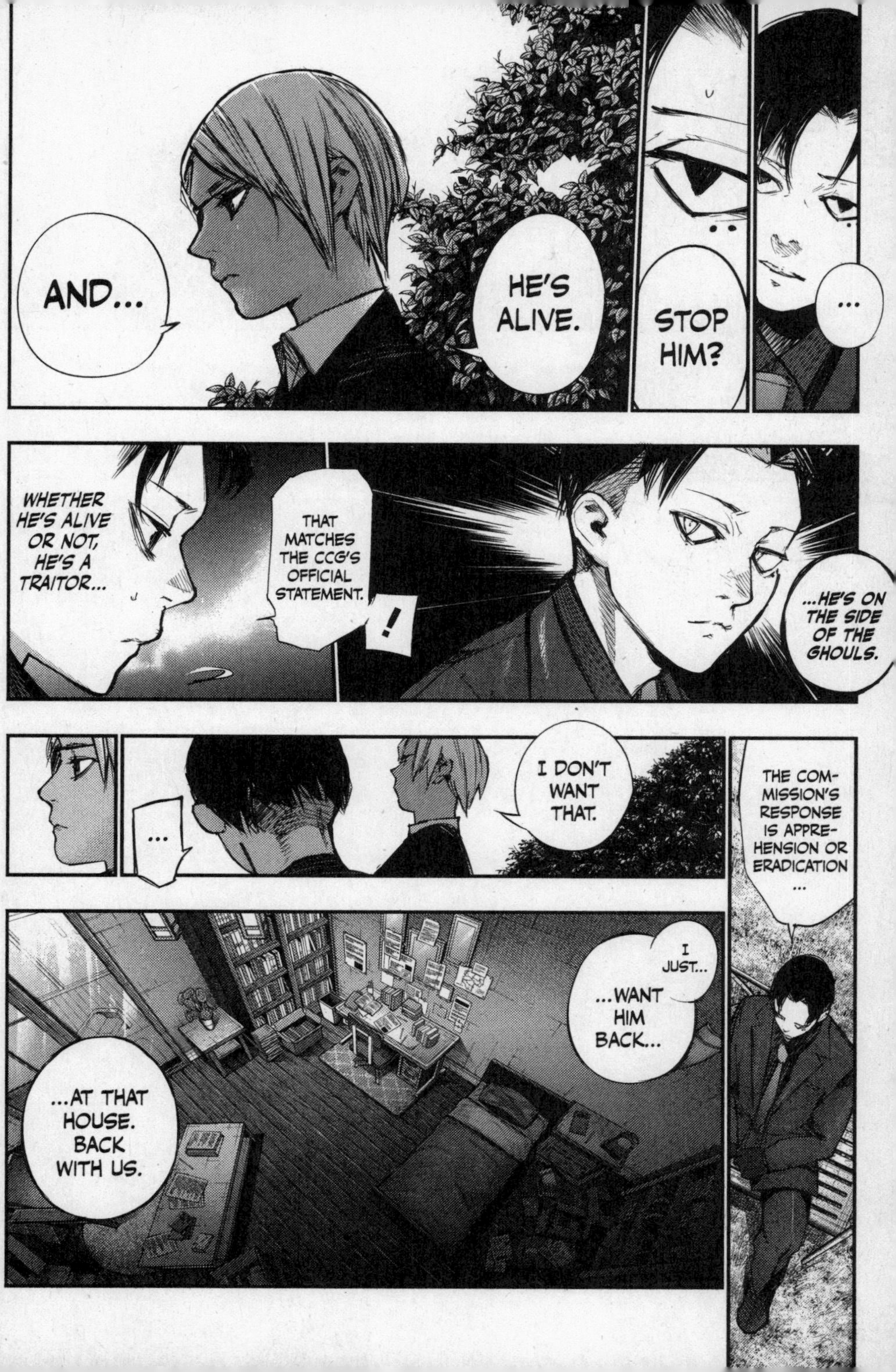
...
STOP HIM?
HE'S ALIVE.
AND...
...HE'S ON THE SIDE OF THE GHOULS.
!
THAT MATCHES THE CCG'S OFFICIAL STATEMENT.
WHETHER HE'S ALIVE OR NOT, HE'S A TRAITOR...
THE COMMISSION'S RESPONSE IS APPREHENSION OR ERADICATION...
I DON'T WANT THAT.
...
I JUST...
...WANT HIM BACK...
...AT THAT HOUSE. BACK WITH US.

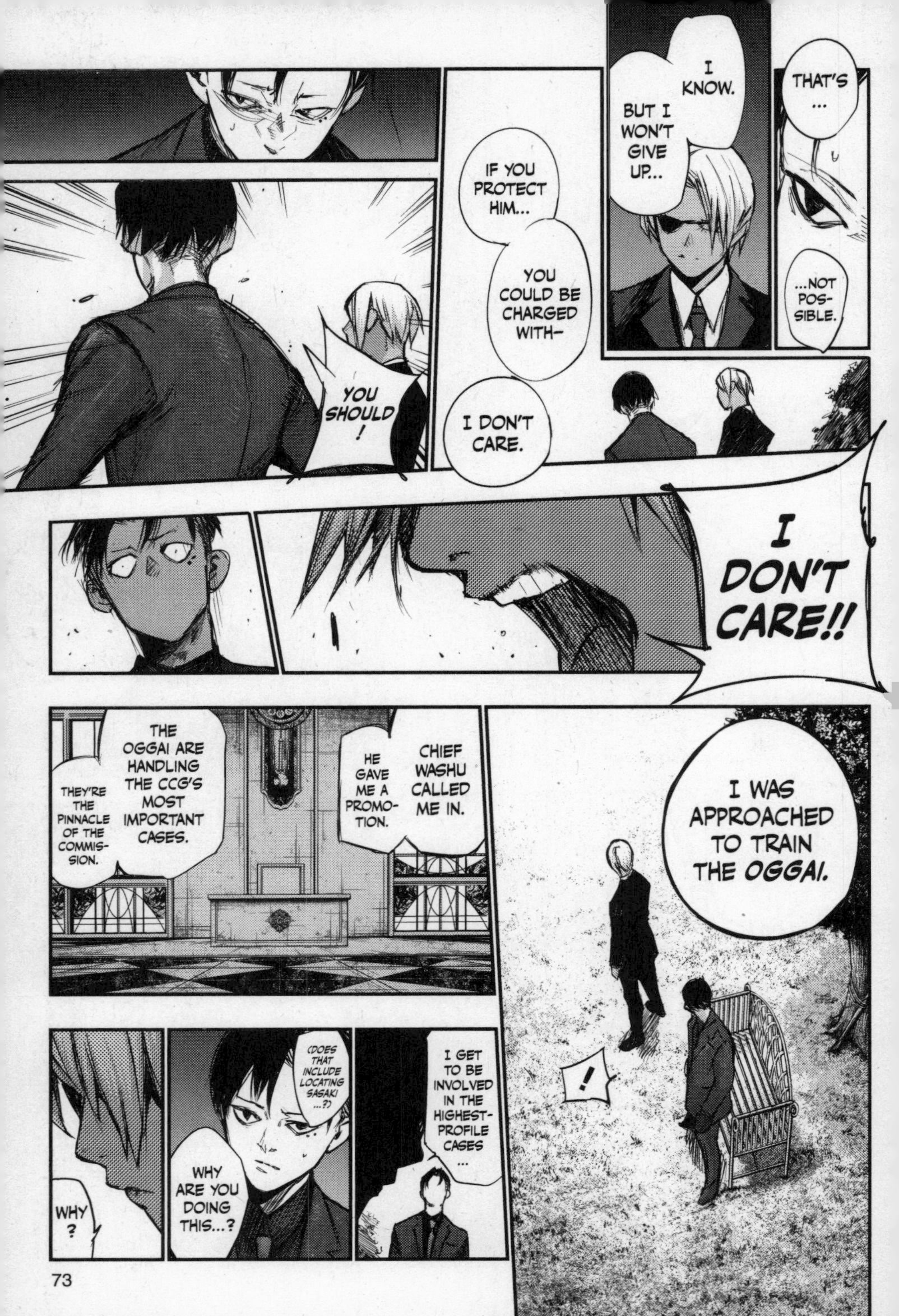
THAT'S...
...NOT POS-SIBLE.
I KNOW.
BUT I WON'T GIVE UP...
IF YOU PROTECT HIM...
YOU COULD BE CHARGED WITH-
I DON'T CARE.
YOU SHOULD!
I DON'T CARE!!
I WAS APPROACHED TO TRAIN THE OGGAI.
!
CHIEF WASHU CALLED ME IN.
HE GAVE ME A PROMO-TION.
THE OGGAI ARE HANDLING THE CCG'S MOST IMPORTANT CASES.
THEY'RE THE PINNACLE OF THE COMMIS-SION.
I GET TO BE INVOLVED IN THE HIGHEST-PROFILE CASES...
(DOES THAT INCLUDE LOCATING SASAKI...?)
WHY ARE YOU DOING THIS...?
WHY?

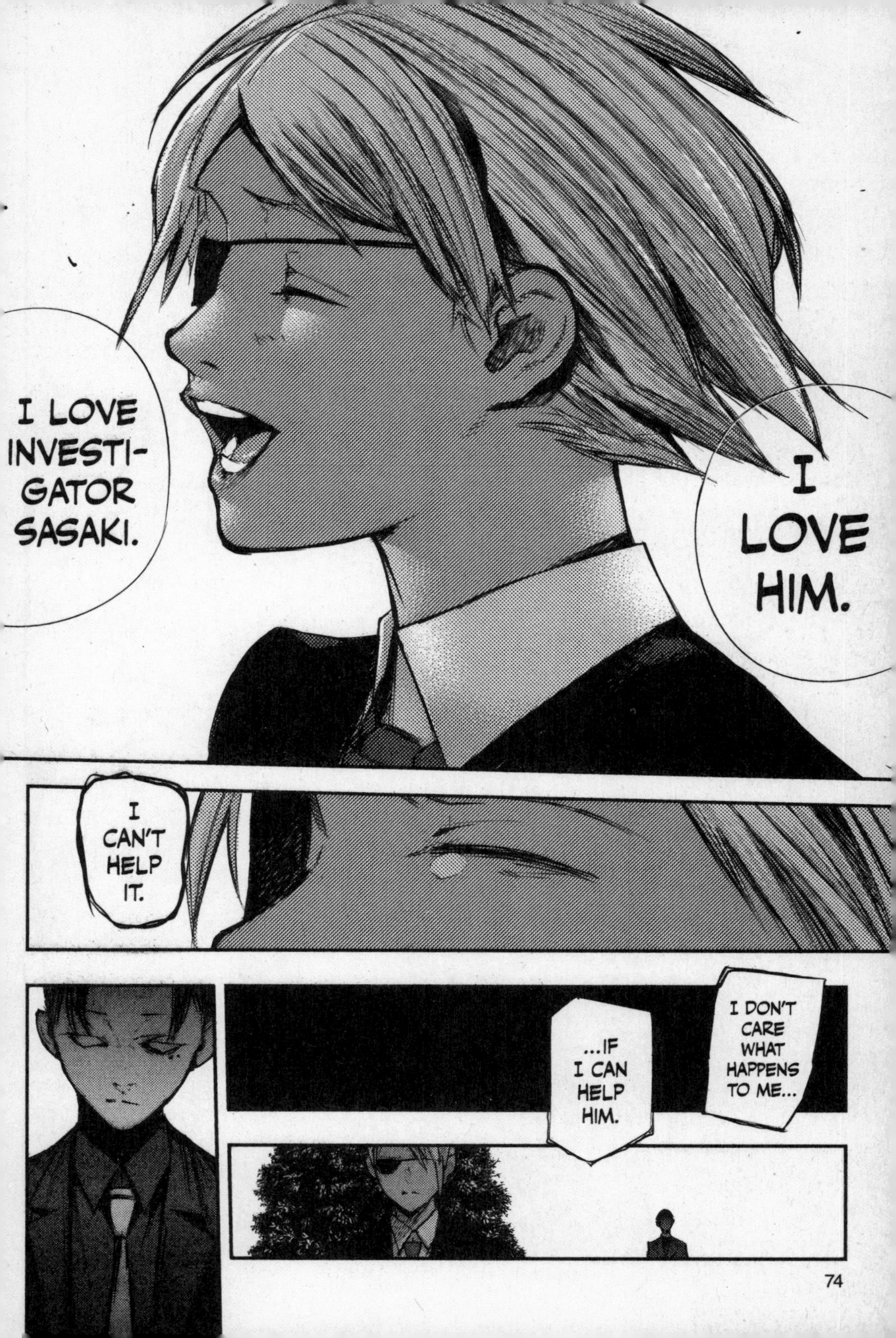
I LOVE INVESTI-GATOR SASAKI.
I LOVE HIM.
I CAN'T HELP IT.
I DON'T CARE WHAT HAPPENS TO ME...
...IF I CAN HELP HIM.

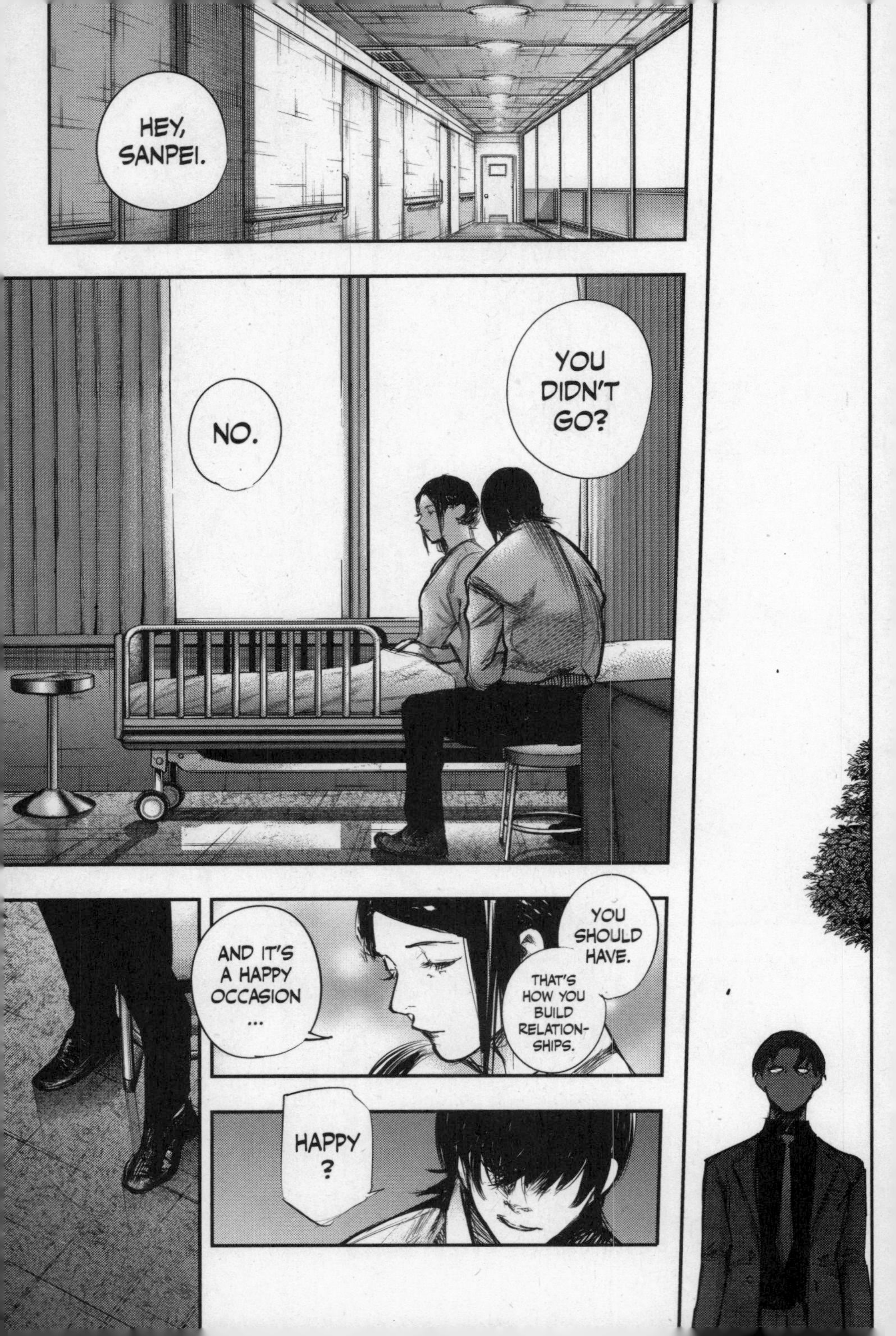
HEY, SANPEI.
YOU DIDN'T GO?
NO.
YOU SHOULD HAVE.
THAT'S HOW YOU BUILD RELATION-SHIPS.
AND IT'S A HAPPY OCCASION ...
HAPPY ?

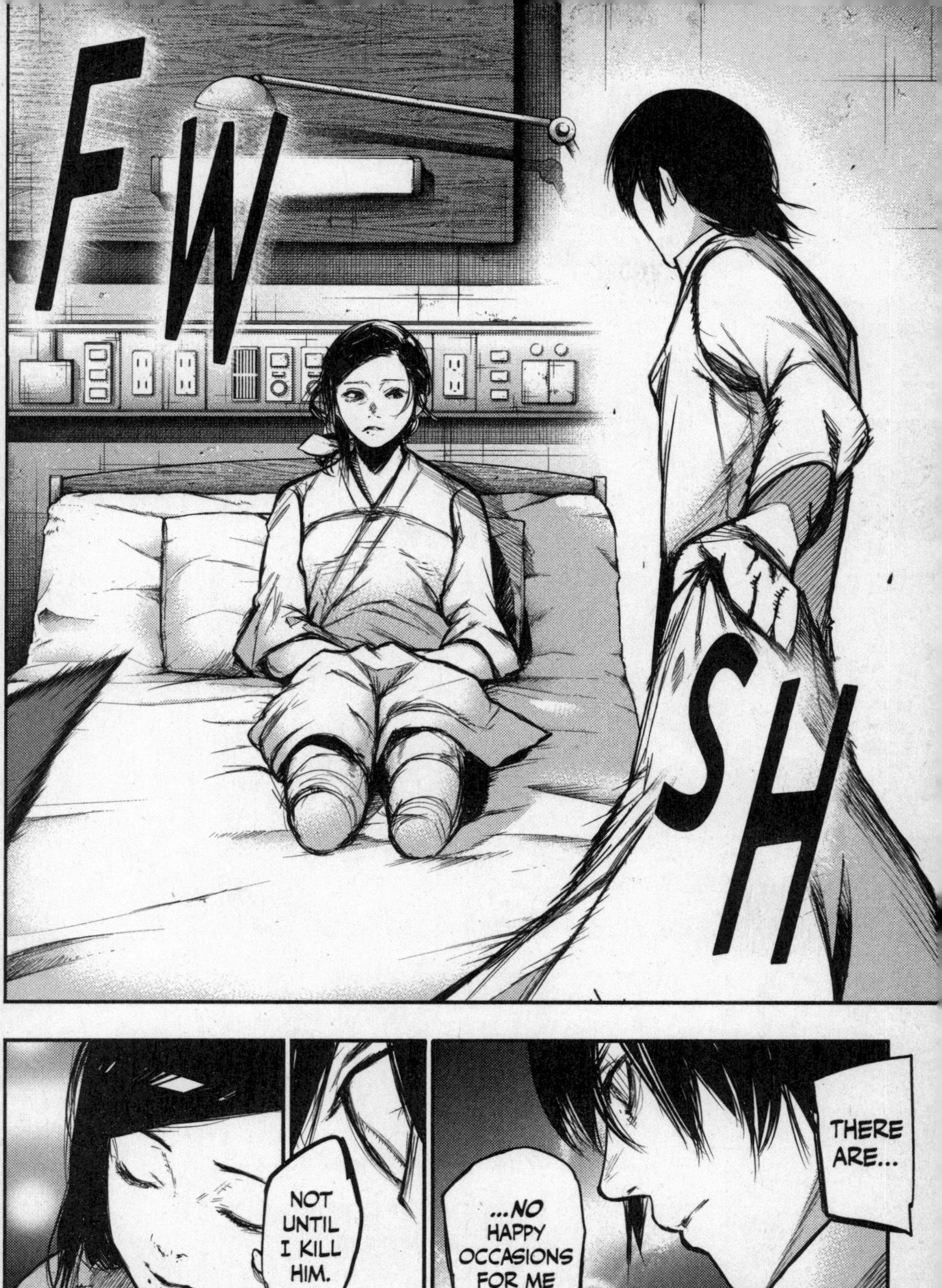
FW
SH
THERE ARE...
...NO HAPPY OCCASIONS FOR ME NOW.
NOT UNTIL I KILL HIM.

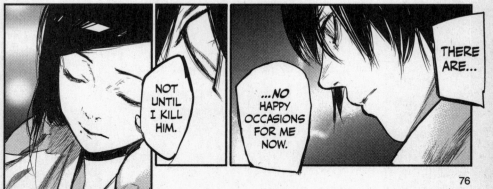

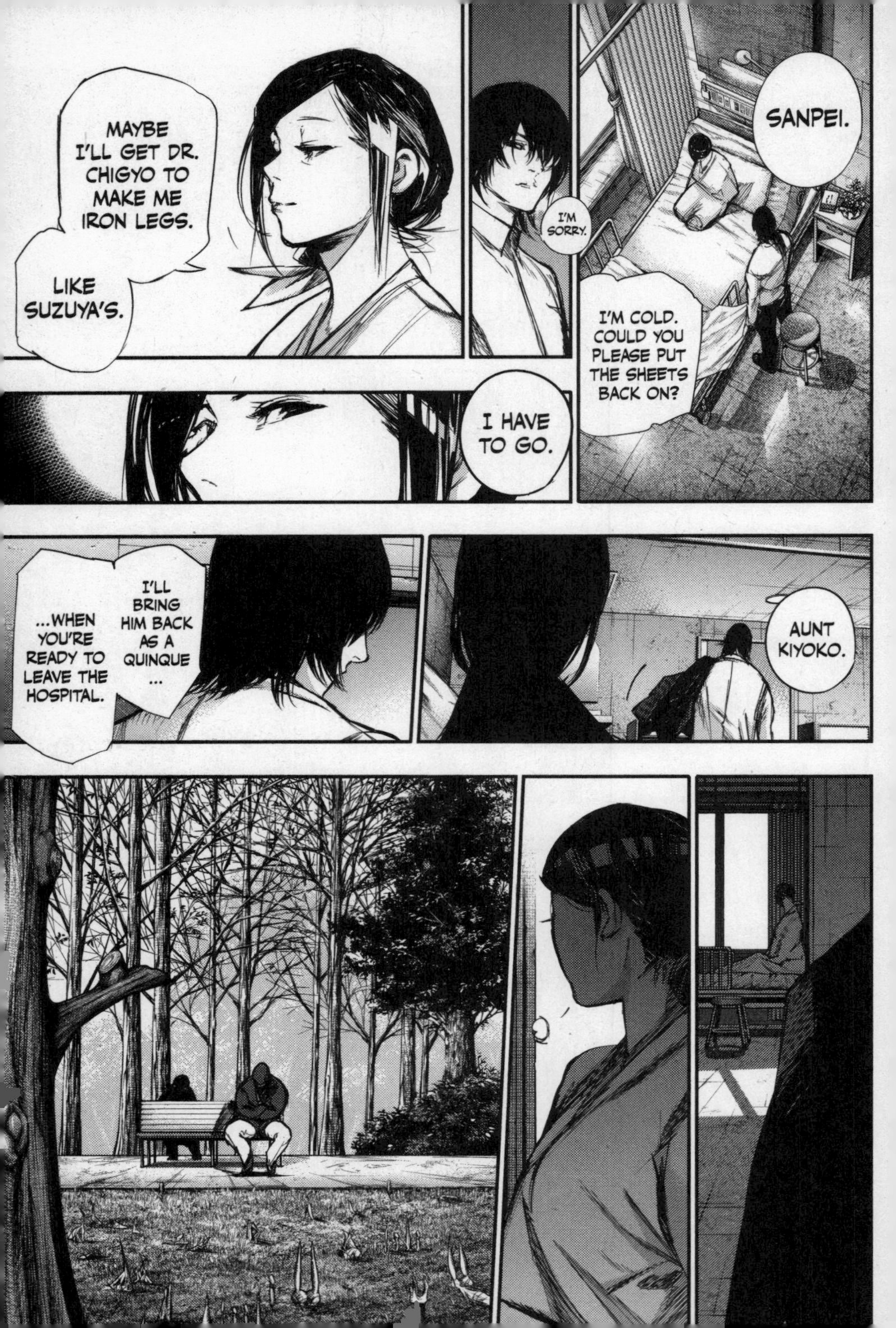
SANPEI.
I'M COLD. COULD YOU PLEASE PUT THE SHEETS BACK ON?
I'M SORRY.
MAYBE I'LL GET DR. CHIGYO TO MAKE ME IRON LEGS.
LIKE SUZUYA'S.
I HAVE TO GO.
AUNT KIYOKO.
I'LL BRING HIM BACK AS A QUINQUE ...
...WHEN YOU'RE READY TO LEAVE THE HOSPITAL.

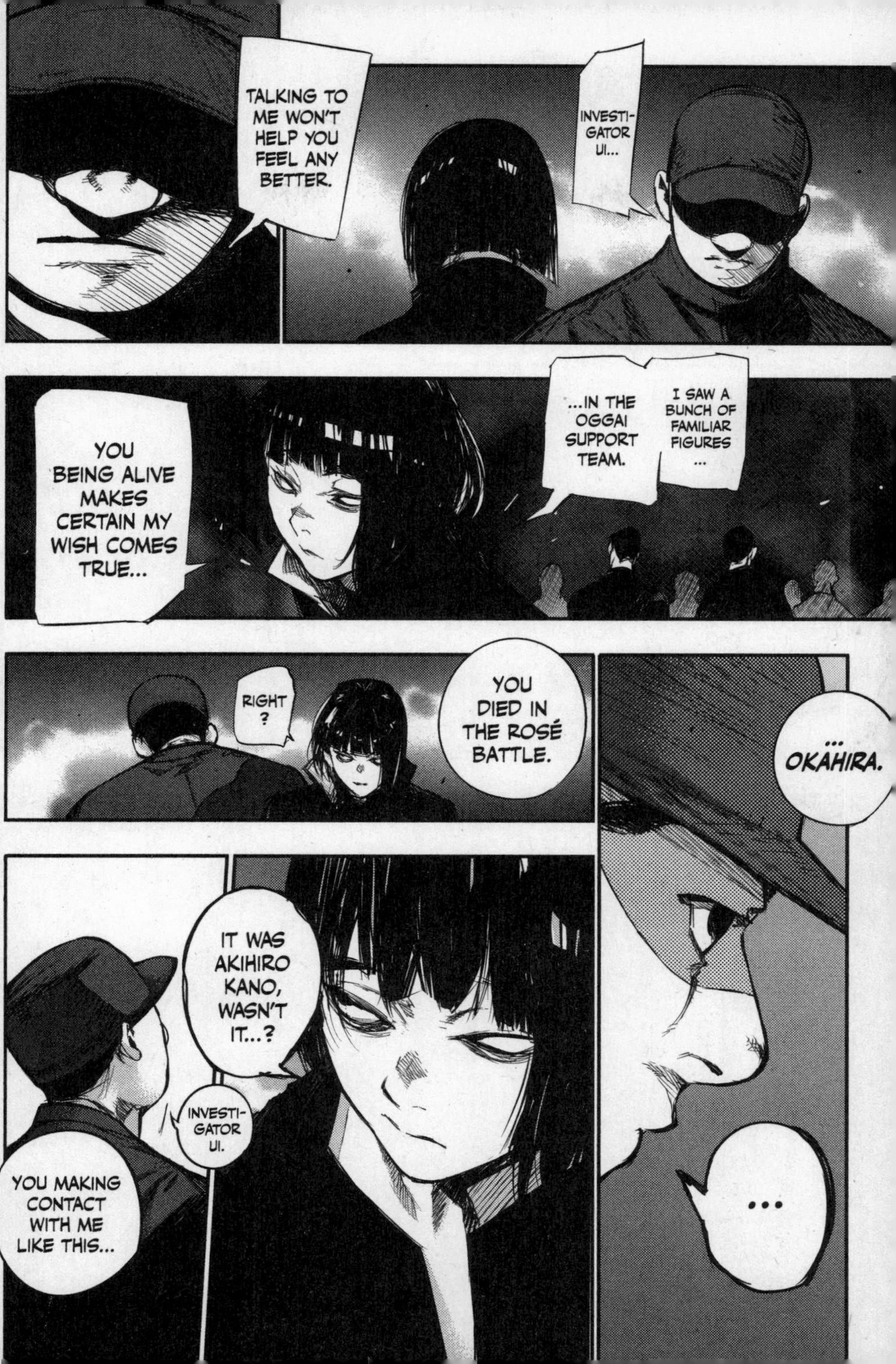
INVESTIGATOR UI...
TALKING TO ME WON'T HELP YOU FEEL ANY BETTER.
I SAW A BUNCH OF FAMILIAR FIGURES ...
...IN THE OGGAI SUPPORT TEAM.
YOU BEING ALIVE MAKES CERTAIN MY WISH COMES TRUE...
... OKAHIRA.
...
YOU DIED IN THE ROSÉ BATTLE.
RIGHT?
IT WAS AKIHIRO KANO, WASN'T IT...?
INVESTIGATOR UI.
YOU MAKING CONTACT WITH ME LIKE THIS...

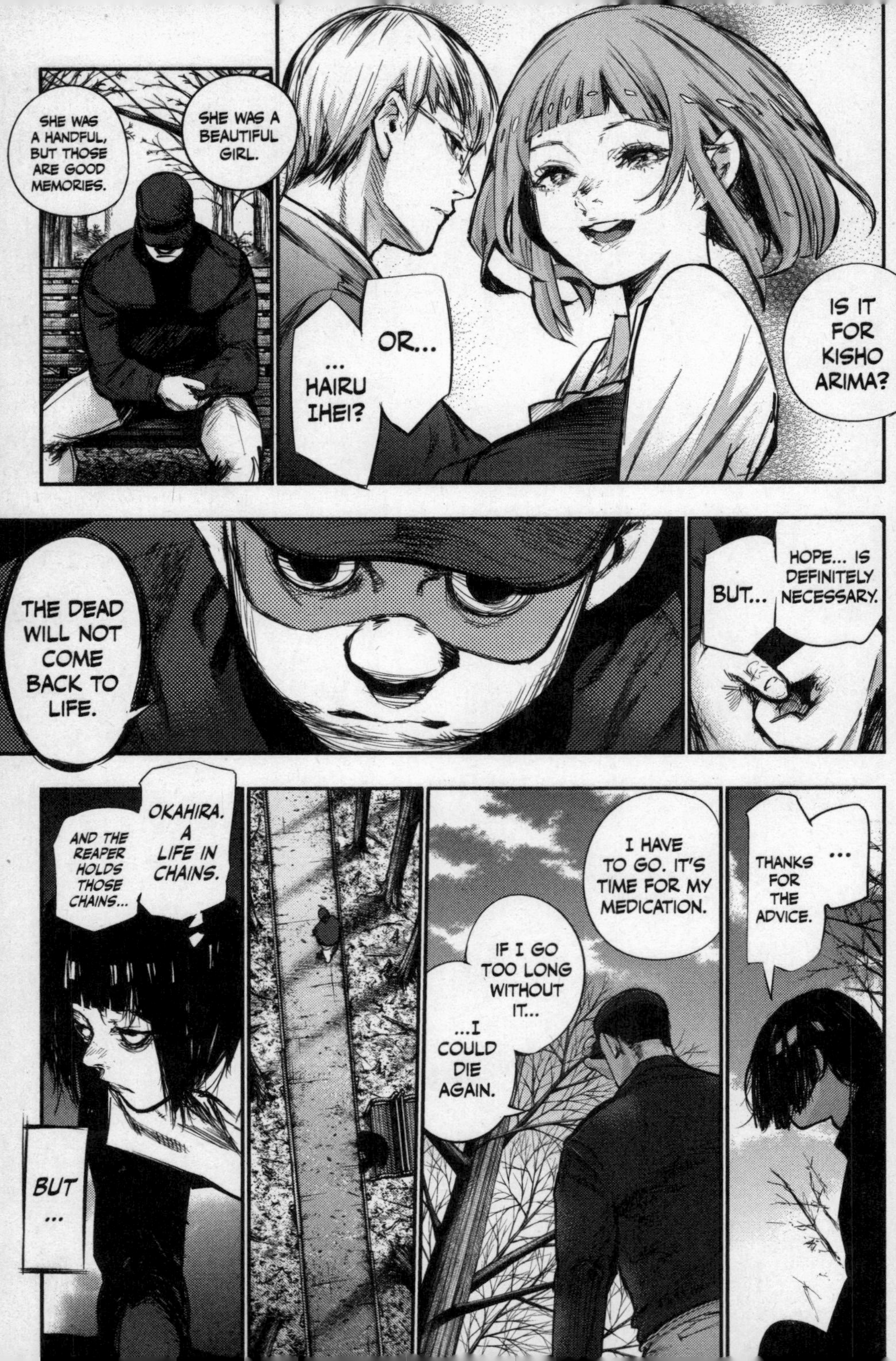
IS IT FOR KISHO ARIMA?
OR... ...HAIRU IHEI?
SHE WAS A BEAUTIFUL GIRL.
SHE WAS A HANDFUL, BUT THOSE ARE GOOD MEMORIES.
HOPE... IS DEFINITELY NECESSARY.
BUT...
THE DEAD WILL NOT COME BACK TO LIFE.
...
THANKS FOR THE ADVICE.
I HAVE TO GO. IT'S TIME FOR MY MEDICATION.
IF I GO TOO LONG WITHOUT IT...
...I COULD DIE AGAIN.
OKAHIRA. A LIFE IN CHAINS.
AND THE REAPER HOLDS THOSE CHAINS...
BUT ...

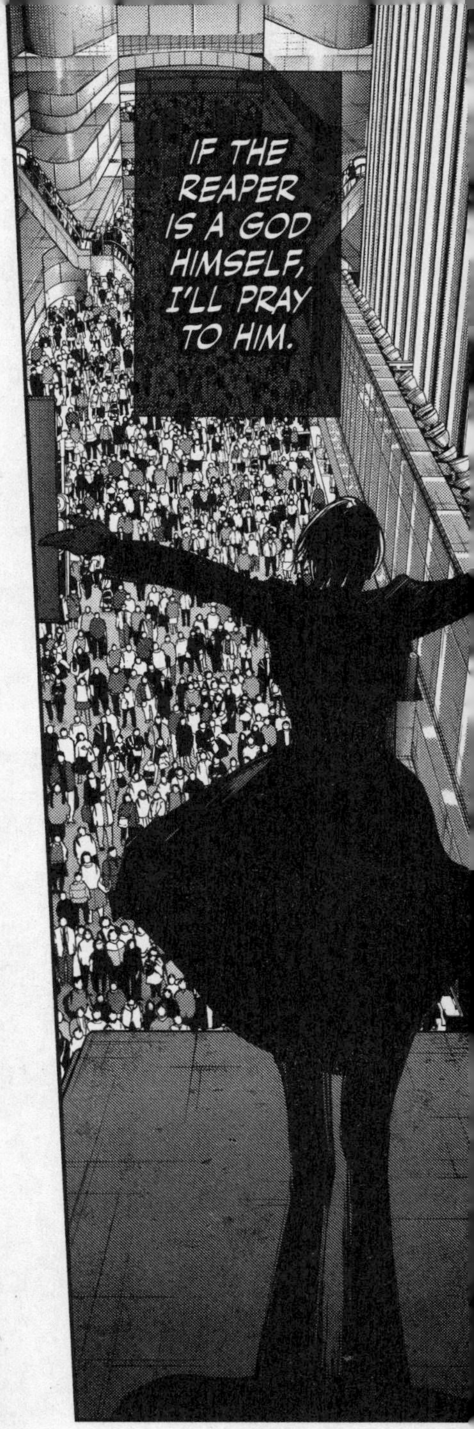
IF THE REAPER IS A GOD HIMSELF, I'LL PRAY TO HIM.
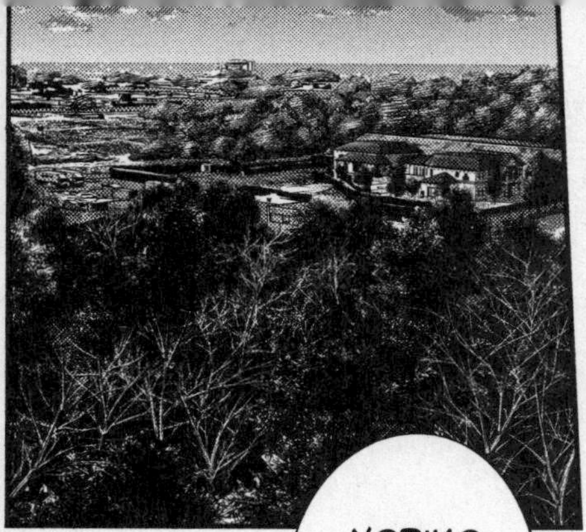
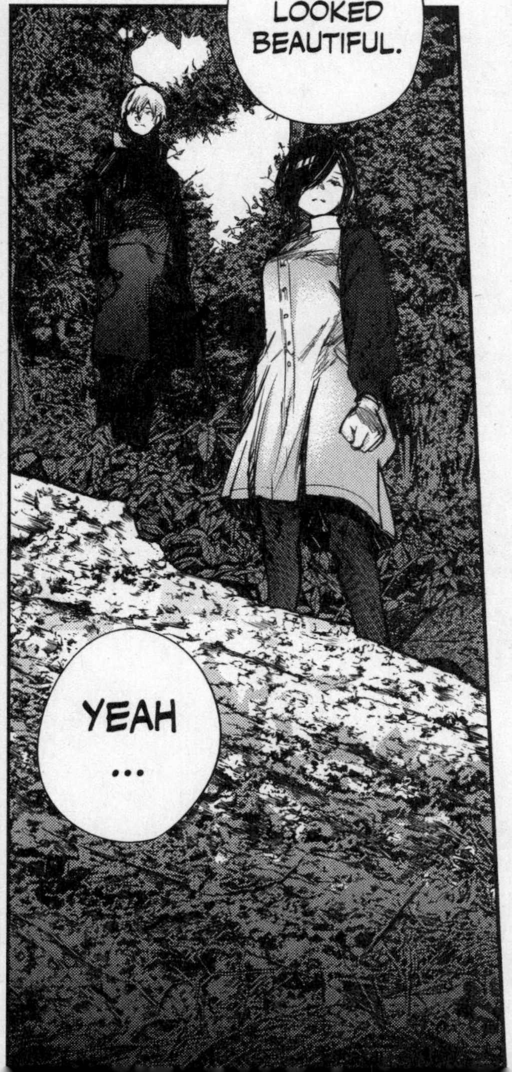
YORIKO LOOKED BEAUTIFUL.
YEAH ...

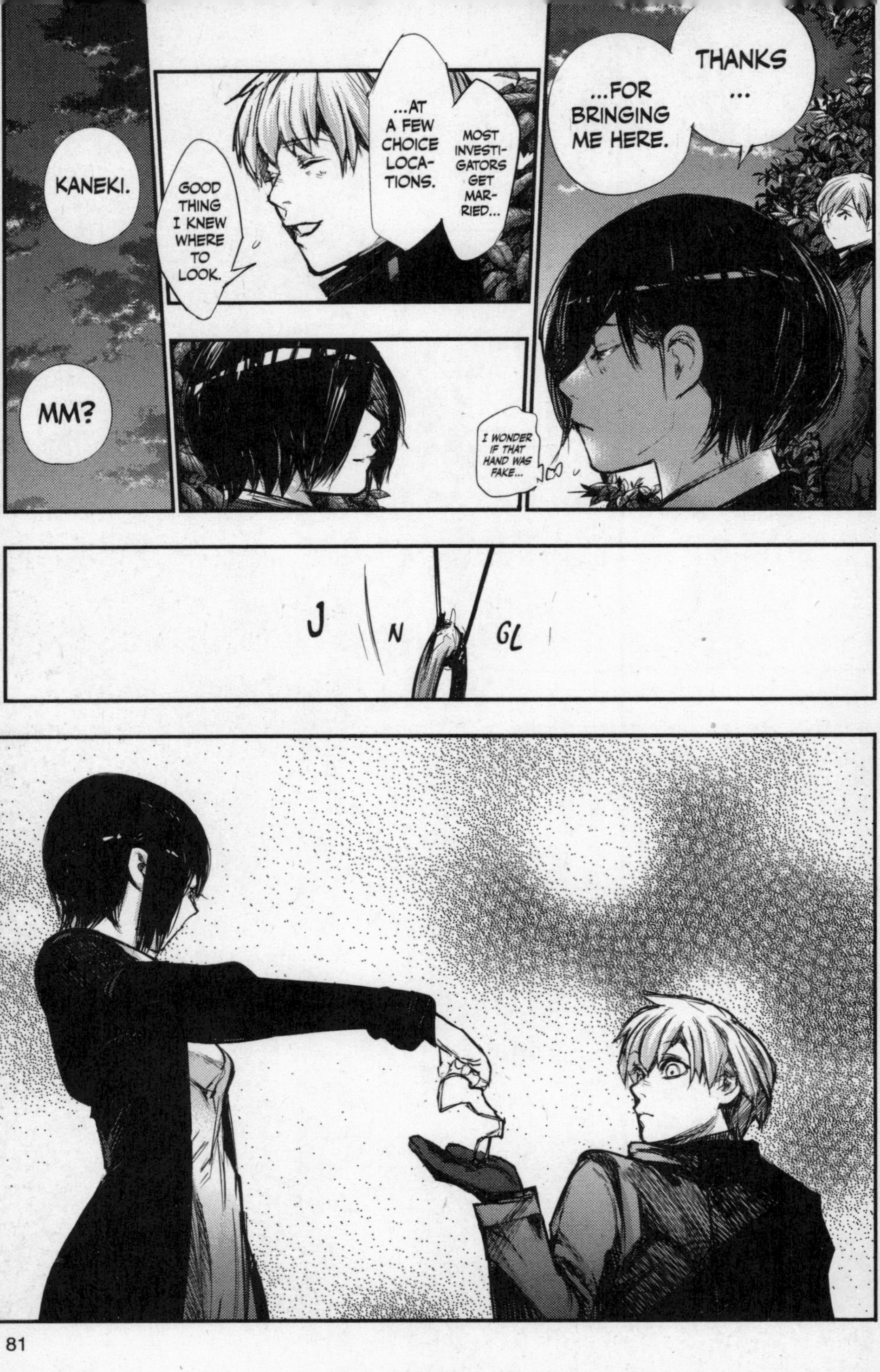
THANKS ...
...FOR BRINGING ME HERE.
I WONDER IF THAT HAND WAS FAKE...
MOST INVESTIGATORS GET MARRIED...
...AT A FEW CHOICE LOCATIONS.
GOOD THING I KNEW WHERE TO LOOK.
KANEKI.
MM?
J N GL

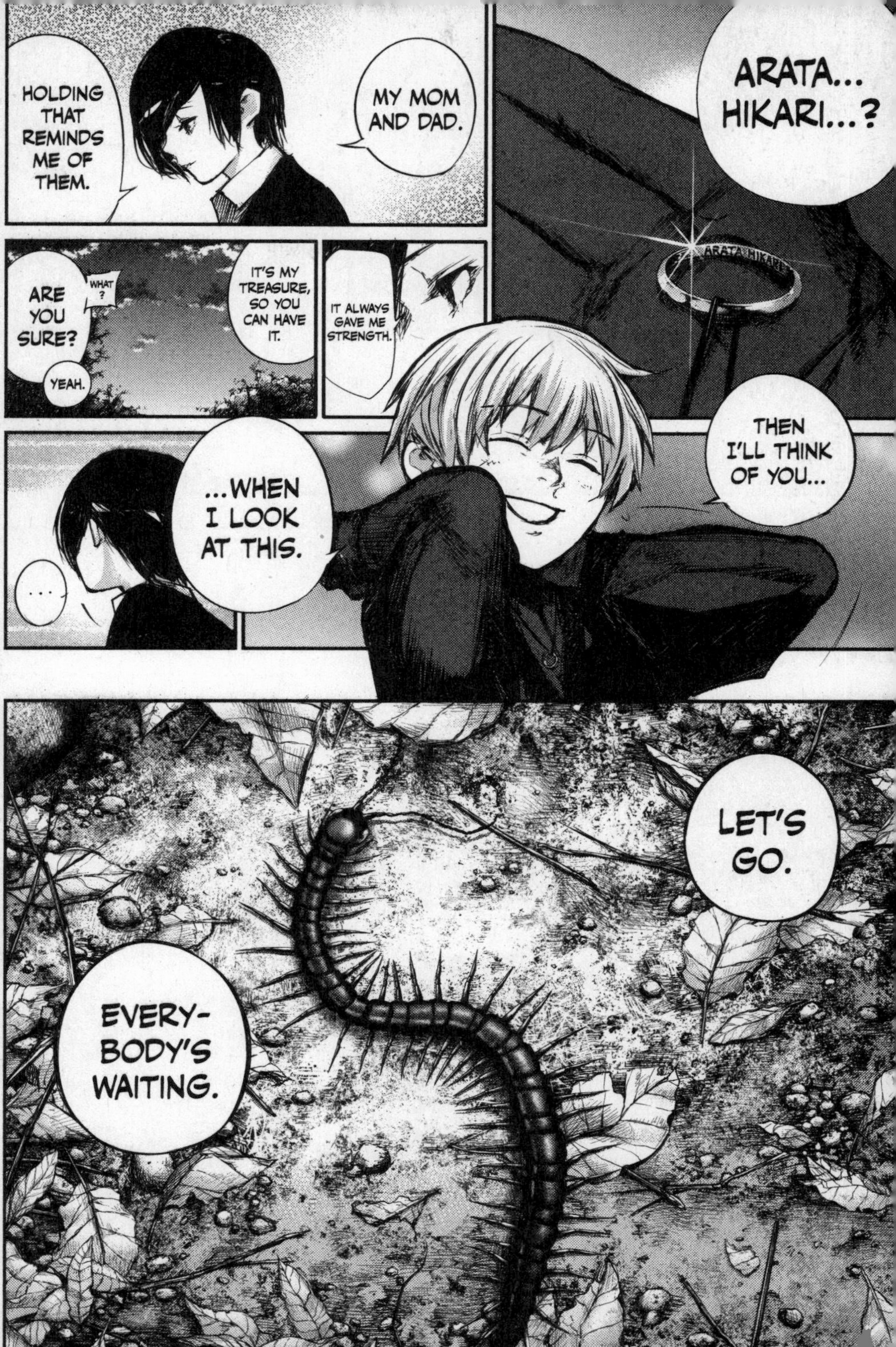
ARATA... HIKARI...?
ARATA HIKARI
MY MOM AND DAD.
HOLDING THAT REMINDS ME OF THEM.
IT ALWAYS GAVE ME STRENGTH.
IT'S MY TREASURE, SO YOU CAN HAVE IT.
WHAT?
ARE YOU SURE?
YEAH.
THEN I'LL THINK OF YOU...
...WHEN I LOOK AT THIS.
...
LET'S GO.
EVERY-BODY'S WAITING.

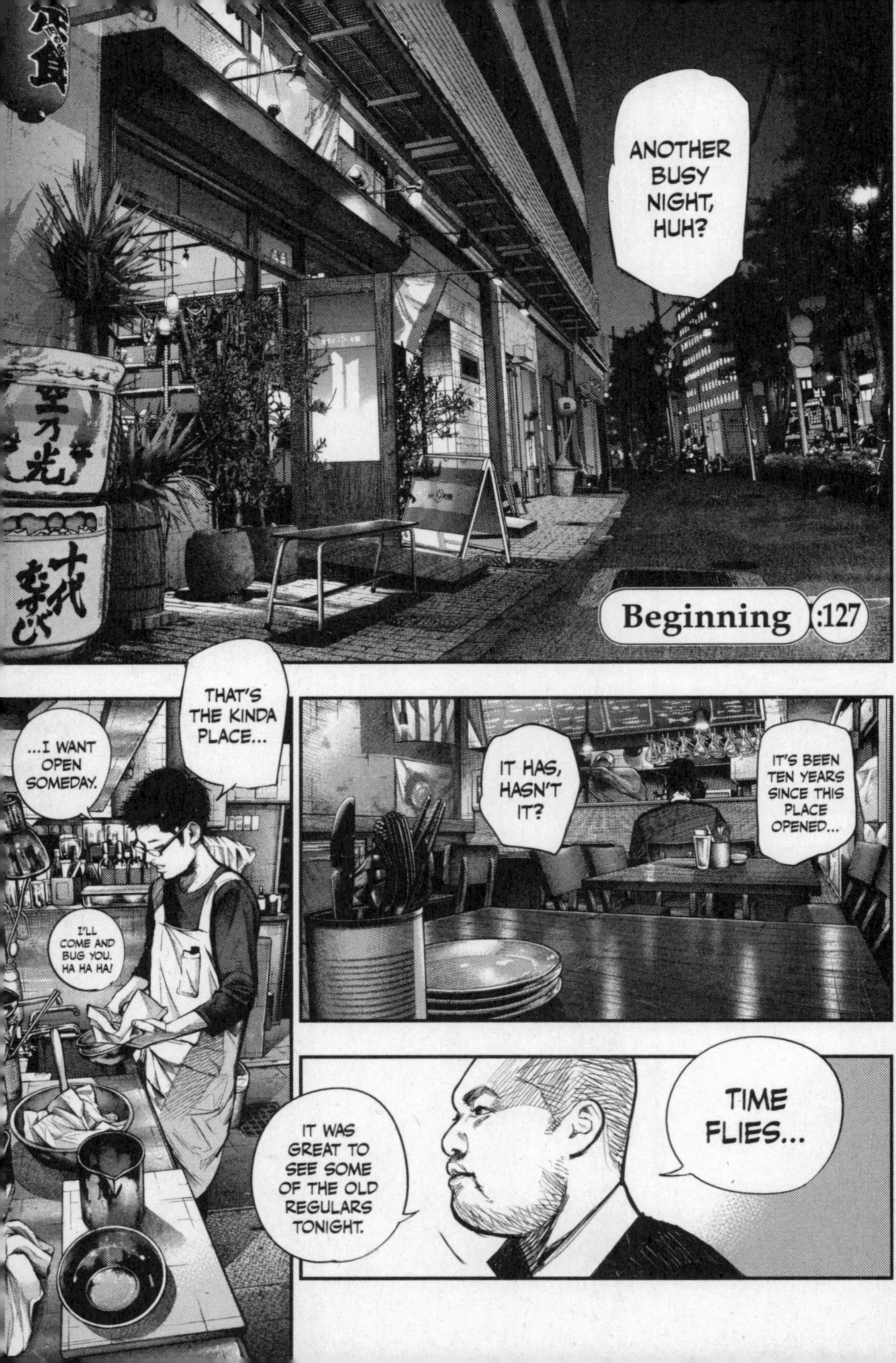
ANOTHER BUSY NIGHT, HUH?
Beginning :127
IT'S BEEN TEN YEARS SINCE THIS PLACE OPENED...
IT HAS, HASN'T IT?
TIME FLIES...
IT WAS GREAT TO SEE SOME OF THE OLD REGULARS TONIGHT.
THAT'S THE KINDA PLACE...
...I WANT OPEN SOMEDAY.
I'LL COME AND BUG YOU. HA HA HA!

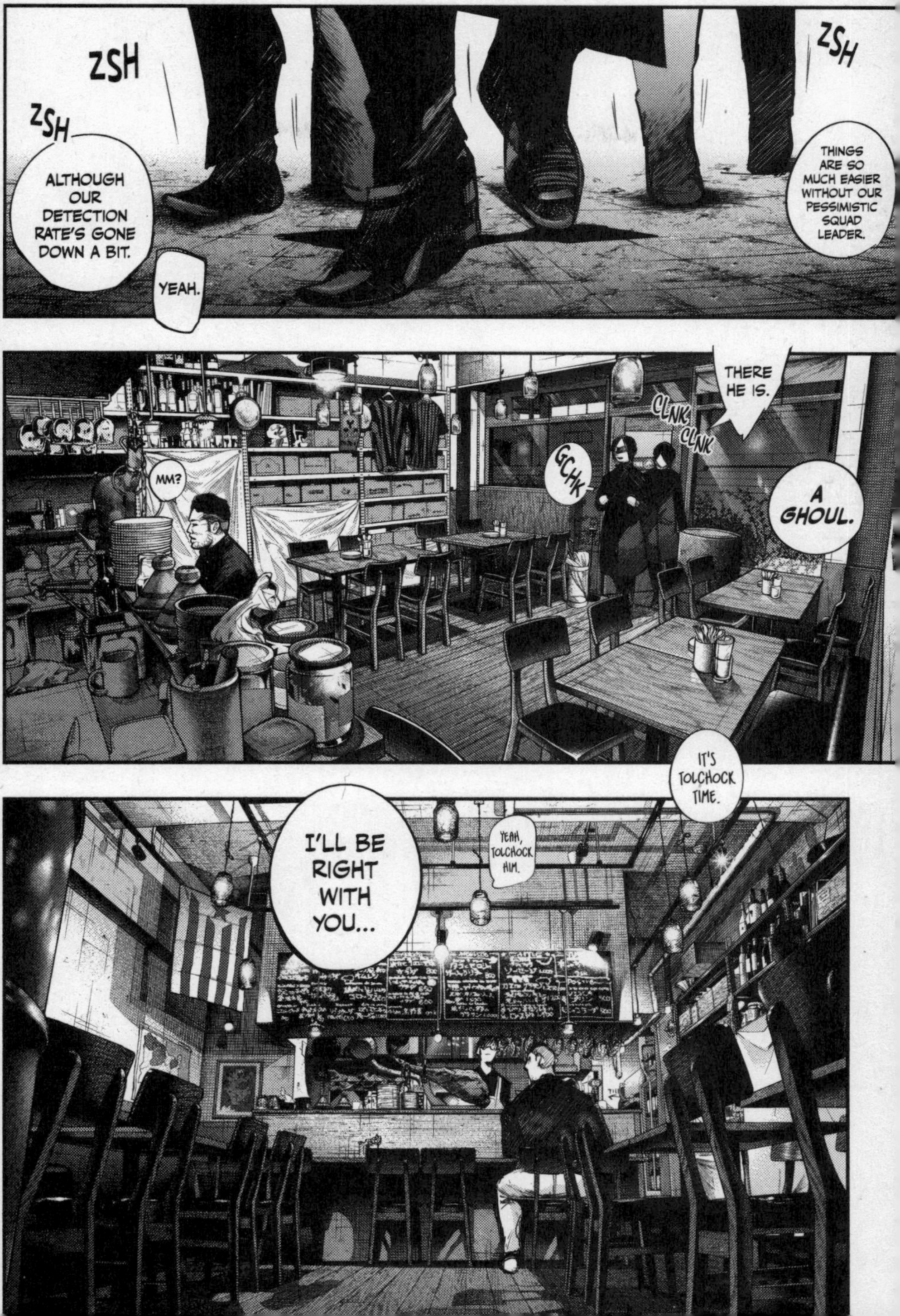
ZSH
THINGS ARE SO MUCH EASIER WITHOUT OUR PESSIMISTIC SQUAD LEADER.
ZSH
ZSH
ALTHOUGH OUR DETECTION RATE'S GONE DOWN A BIT.
YEAH.
THERE HE IS.
CLNK CLNK
A GHOUL.
GCHK
MM?
IT'S TOLCHOCK TIME.
YEAH, TOLCHOCK HIM.
I'LL BE RIGHT WITH YOU...

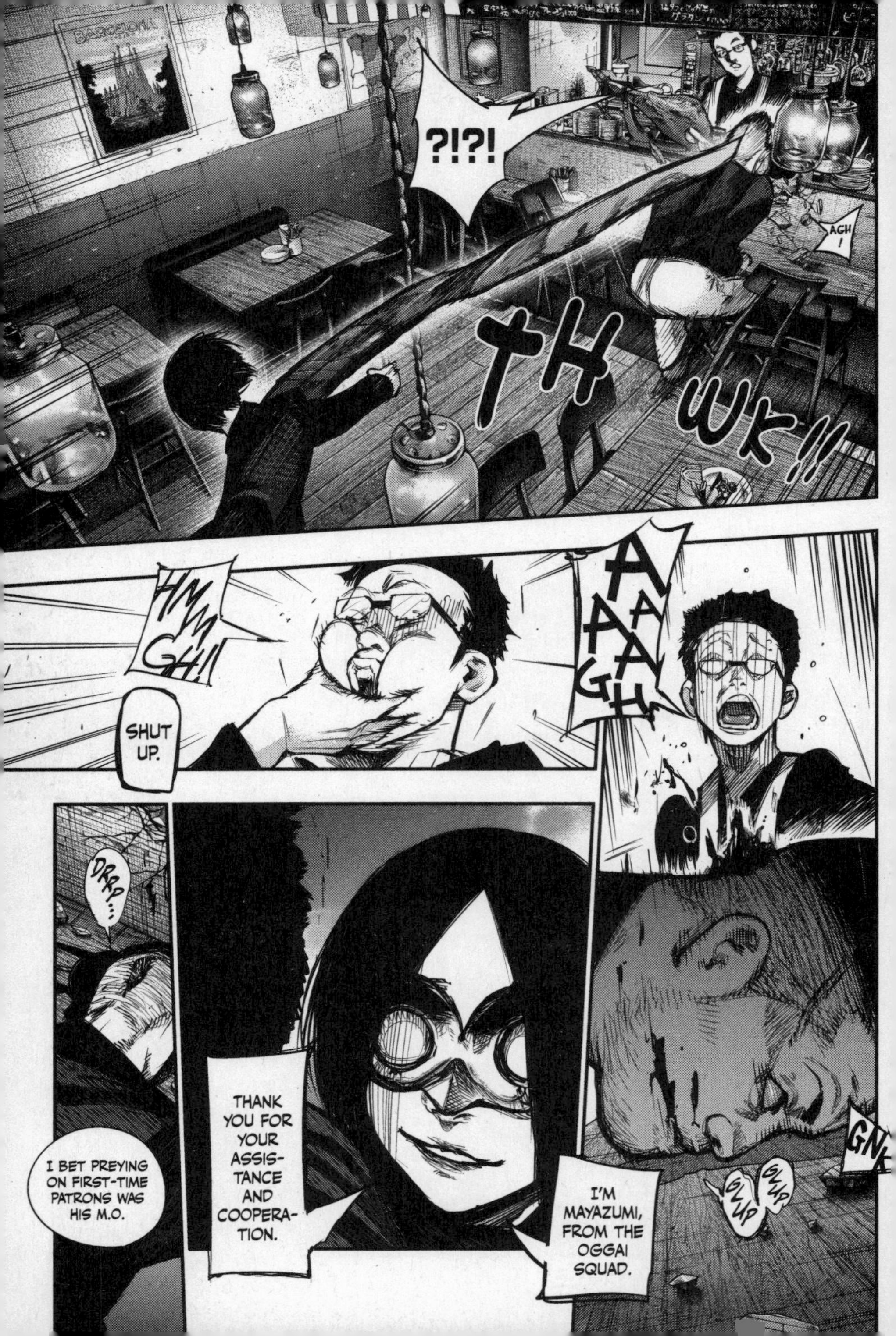

?!?!
ACH!
THWK!!
AAAAGH!
HMMGH!!
SHUT UP.
GNK
GLUP GLUP GLUP
I'M MAYAZUMI, FROM THE OGGAI SQUAD.
THANK YOU FOR YOUR ASSIS-TANCE AND COOPERA-TION.
DRRP...
I BET PREYING ON FIRST-TIME PATRONS WAS HIS M.O.

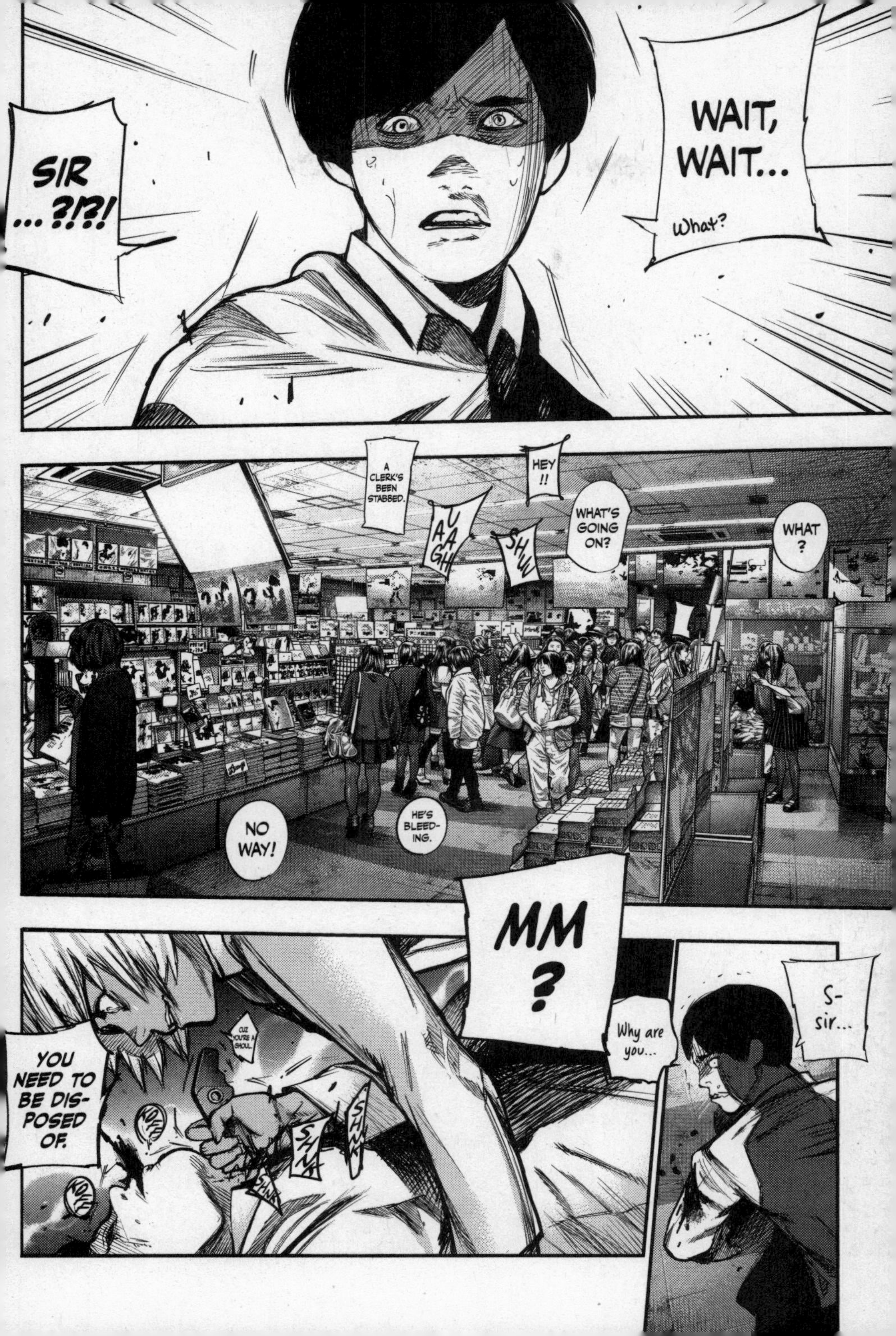
WAIT, WAIT...
What?
SIR ...?!?!
WHAT?
WHAT'S GOING ON?
HEY !!
SHUU
UAAGH
A CLERK'S BEEN STABBED.
HE'S BLEED-ING.
NO WAY!
S-sir...
Why are you...
MM?
CUZ YOU'RE A GHOUL.
YOU NEED TO BE DIS-POSED OF.
SHNK
SHNK
SHNK
KOFF
KOFF

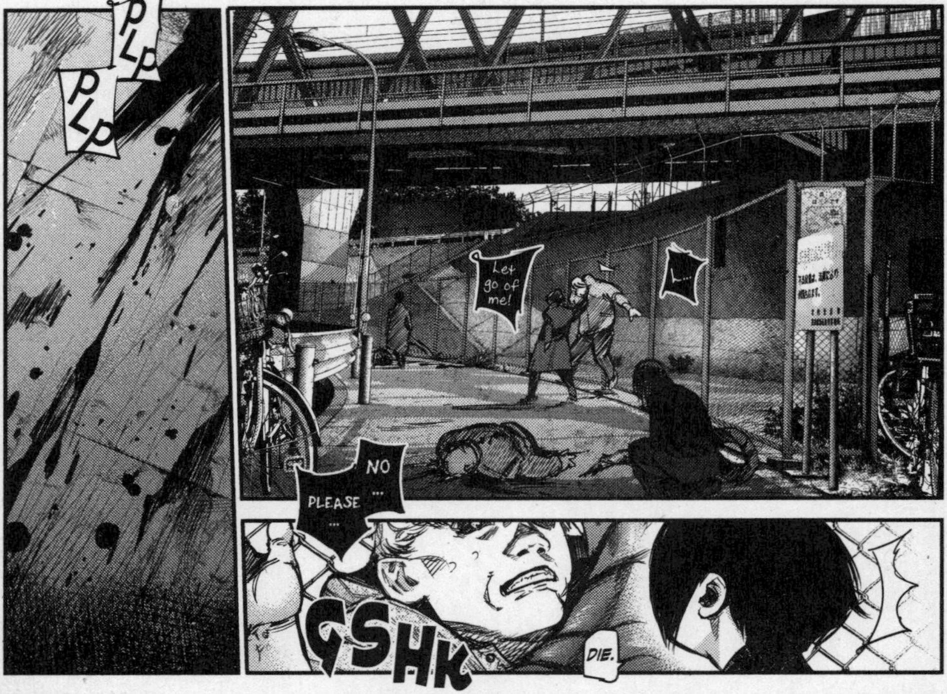
I...
Let go of me!
NO... PLEASE...
DIE.
GSHK
PLP
PLP

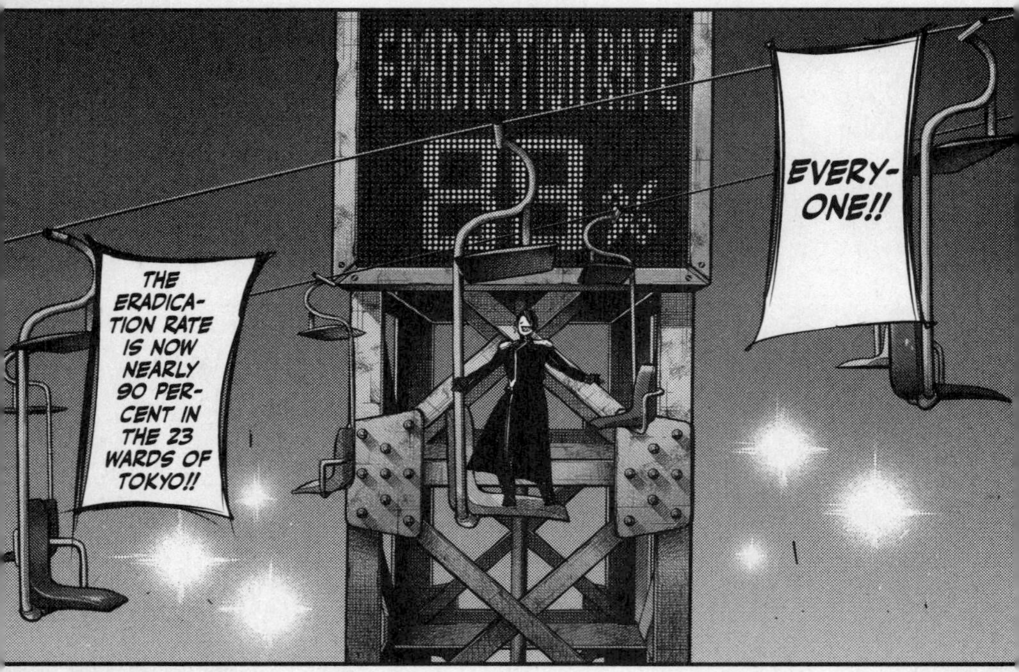
EVERY-ONE!!
THE ERADICATION RATE IS NOW NEARLY 90 PERCENT IN THE 23 WARDS OF TOKYO!!

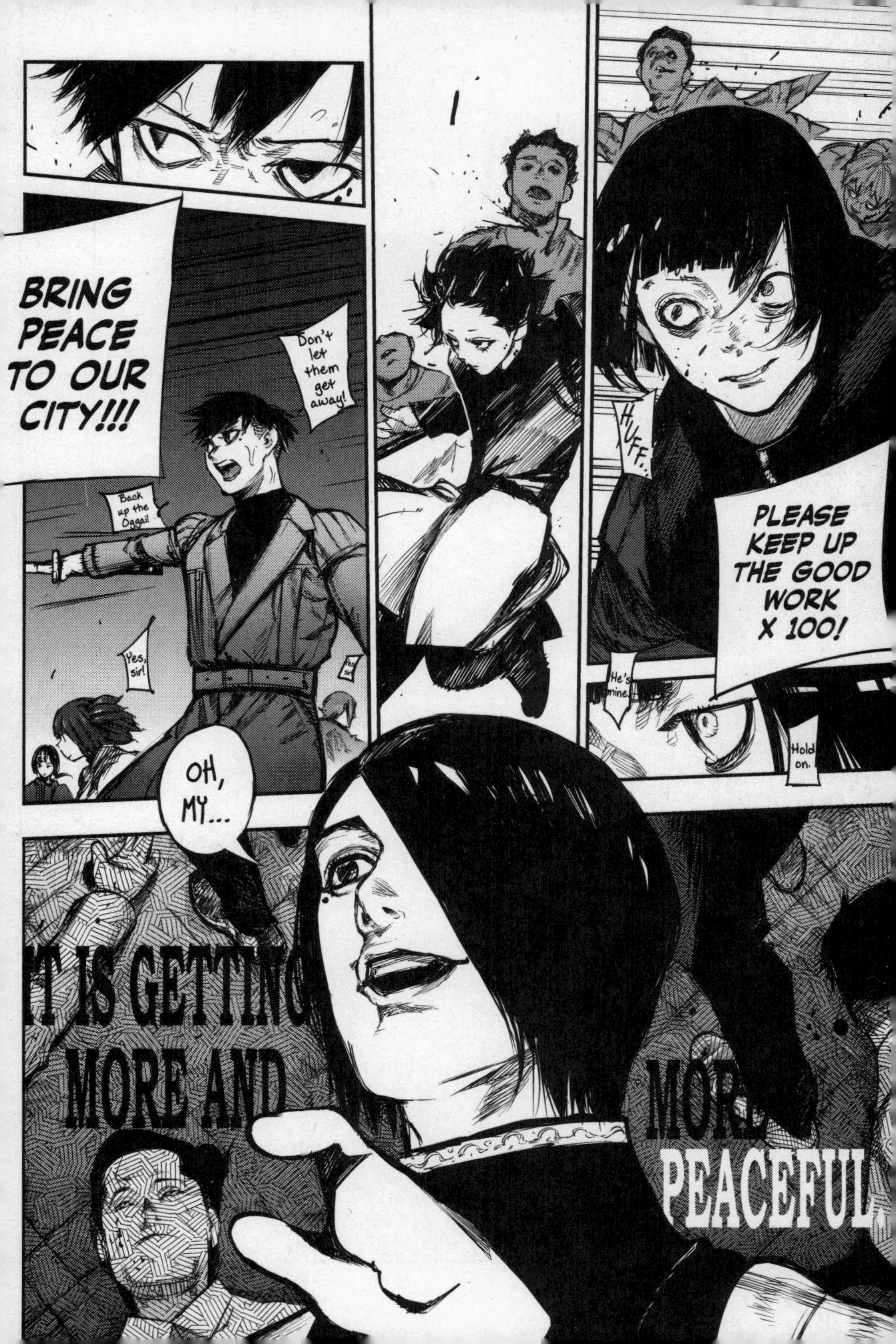
HUFF...
PLEASE KEEP UP THE GOOD WORK X 100!
He's mine.
Hold on.
Don't let them get away!
BRING PEACE TO OUR CITY!!!
Back up the Oggai!
Yes, sir!
OH, MY...
IT IS GETTING MORE AND MORE PEACEFUL.

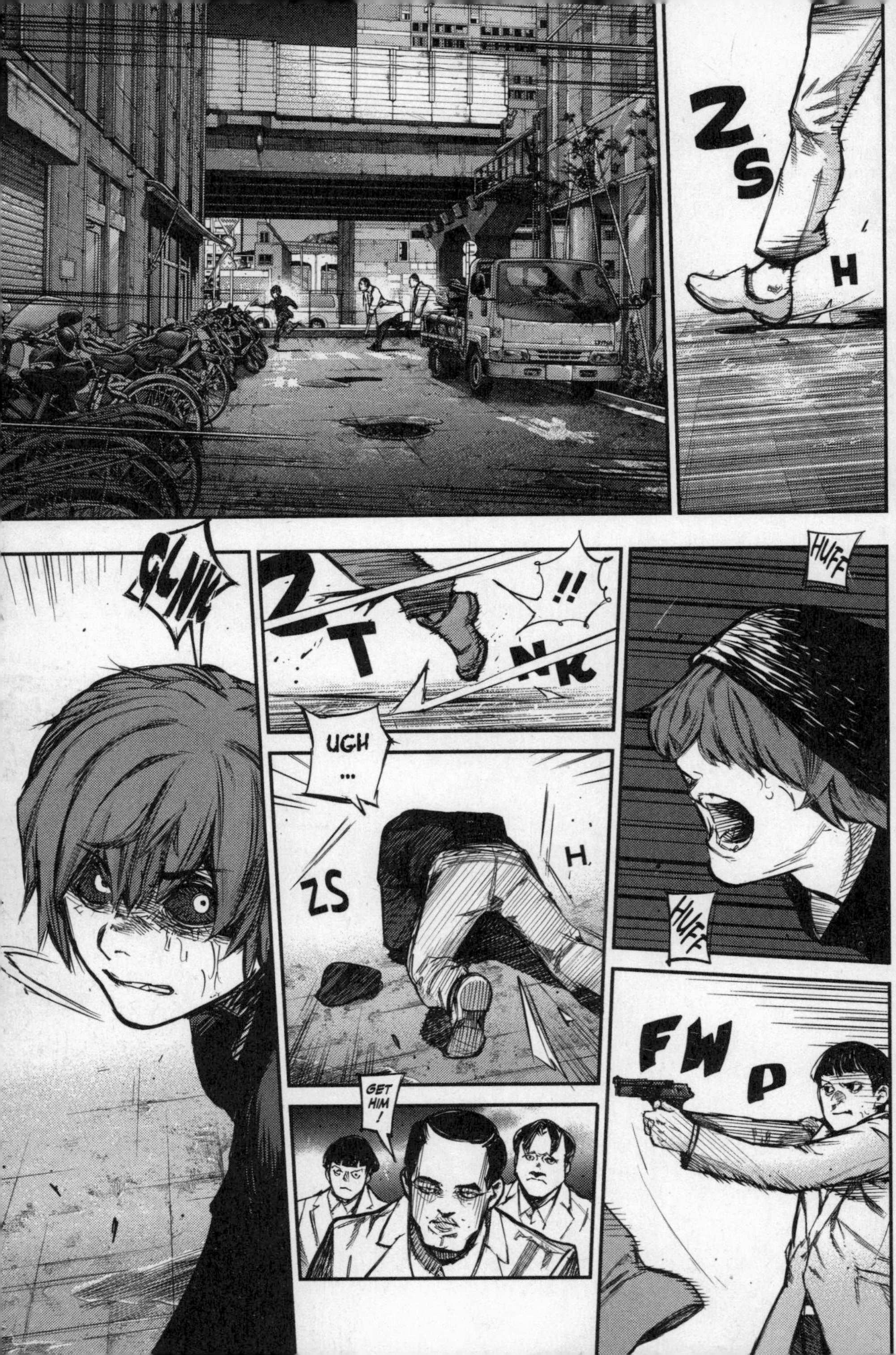
ZSH
HUFF
HUFF
FWP
!!
ZTNK
UGH ...
ZSH
GET HIM!
GLNK

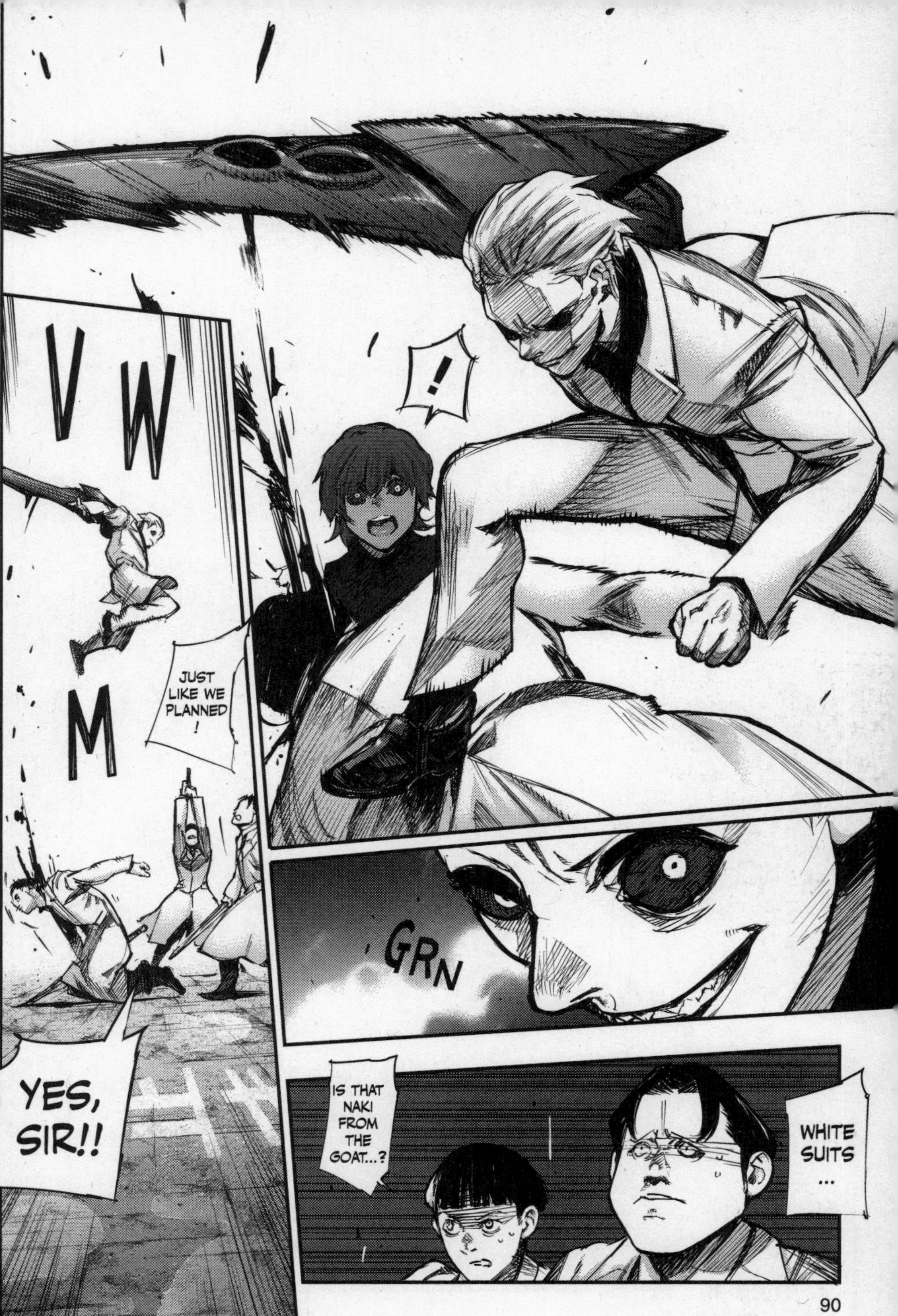
!
GRN
WHITE SUITS ...
IS THAT NAKI FROM THE GOAT...?
VWM
JUST LIKE WE PLANNED !
YES, SIR!!

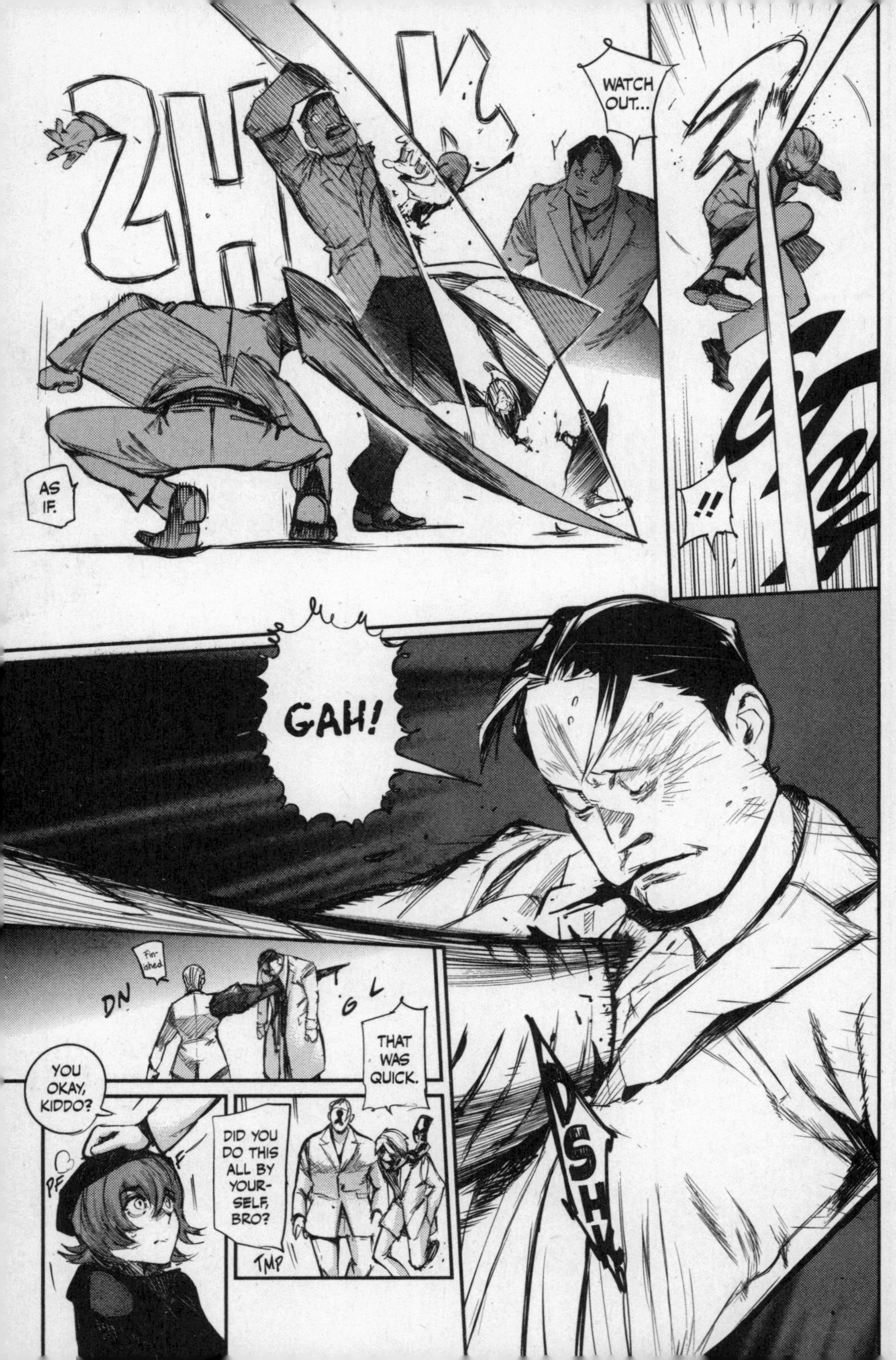
!!
WATCH OUT...
AS IF.
GAH!
DSHH
Fin-ished.
DN
THAT WAS QUICK.
DID YOU DO THIS ALL BY YOURSELF, BRO?
TMP
YOU OKAY, KIDDO?
PF

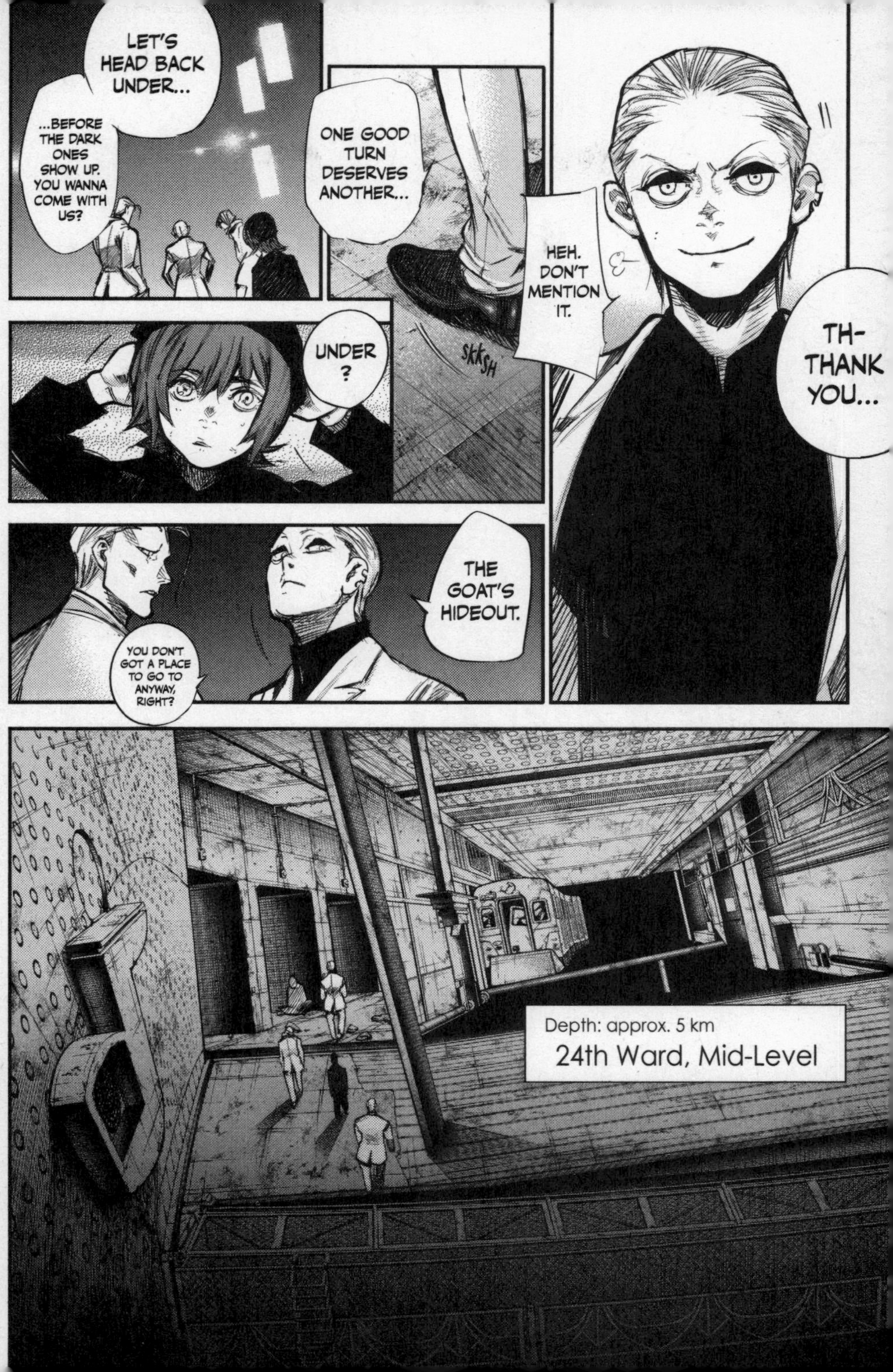
TH-THANK YOU...
HEH. DON'T MENTION IT.
ONE GOOD TURN DESERVES ANOTHER...
LET'S HEAD BACK UNDER...
...BEFORE THE DARK ONES SHOW UP. YOU WANNA COME WITH US?
SKKSH
UNDER?
THE GOAT'S HIDEOUT.
YOU DON'T GOT A PLACE TO GO TO ANYWAY, RIGHT?
Depth: approx. 5 km
24th Ward, Mid-Level

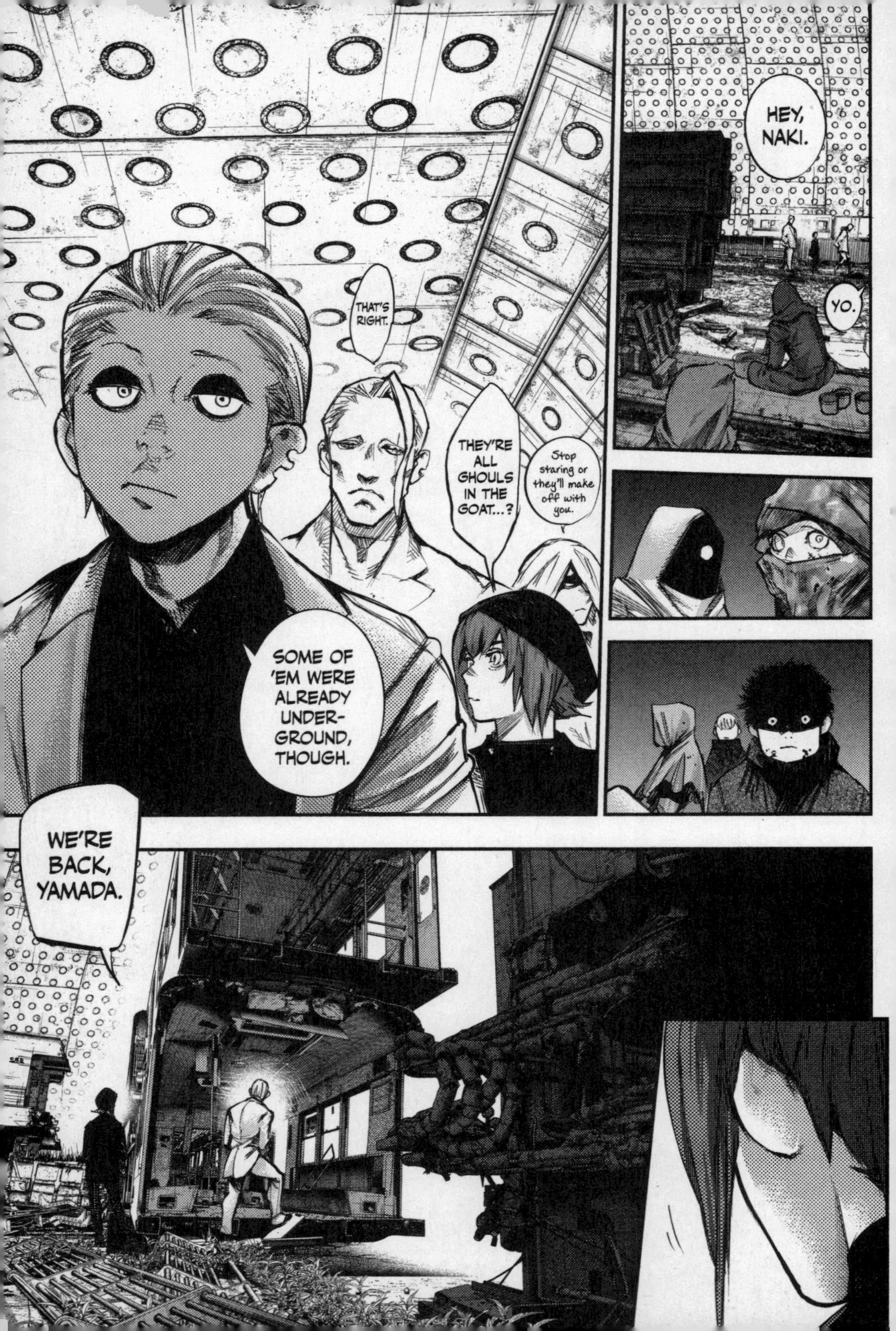
HEY, NAKI.
YO.
THEY'RE ALL GHOULS IN THE GOAT...?
THAT'S RIGHT.
Stop staring or they'll make off with you.
SOME OF 'EM WERE ALREADY UNDER-GROUND, THOUGH.
WE'RE BACK, YAMADA.

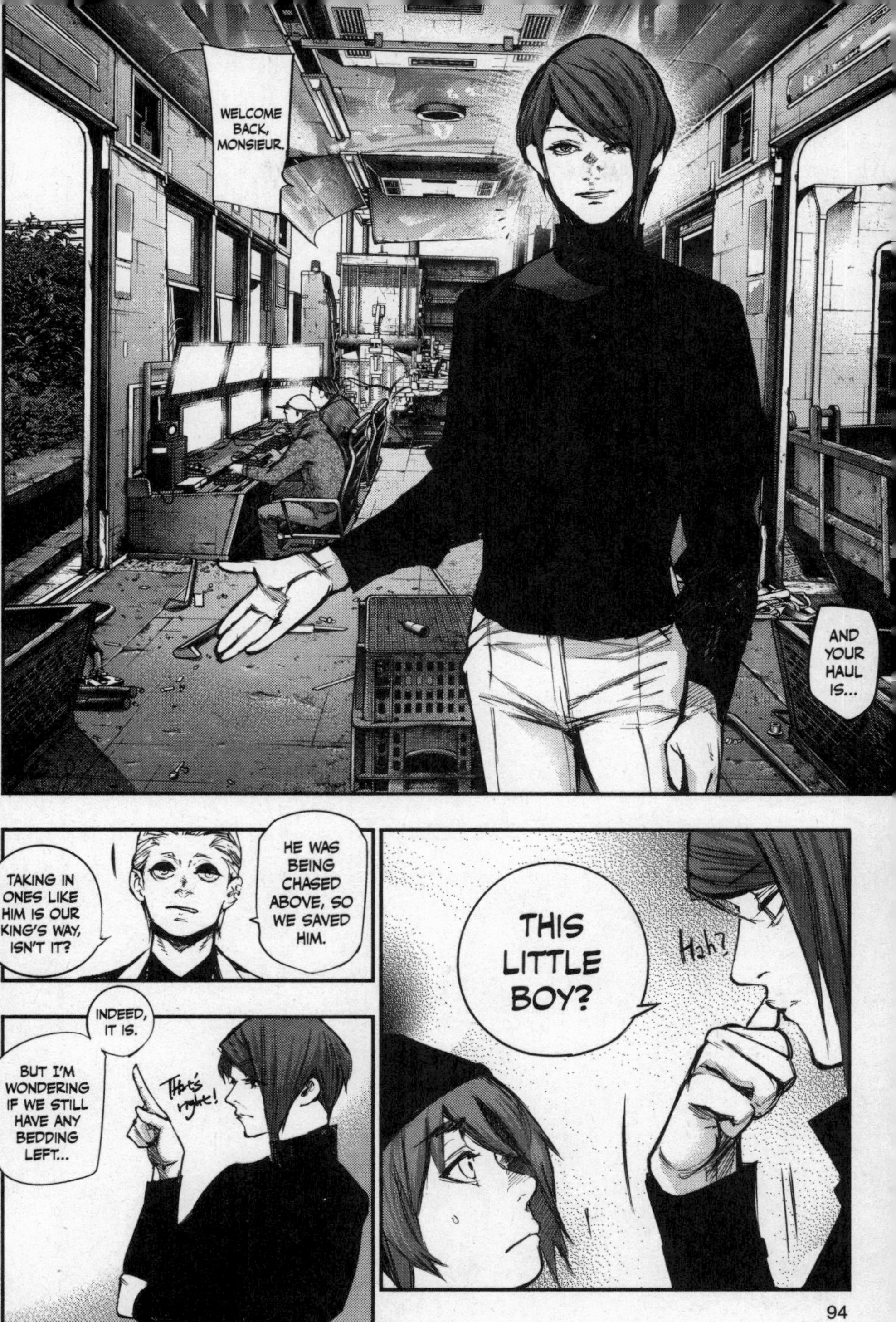
WELCOME BACK, MONSIEUR.
AND YOUR HAUL IS...
THIS LITTLE BOY?
Hah?
HE WAS BEING CHASED ABOVE, SO WE SAVED HIM.
TAKING IN ONES LIKE HIM IS OUR KING'S WAY, ISN'T IT?
INDEED, IT IS.
That's right!
BUT I'M WONDERING IF WE STILL HAVE ANY BEDDING LEFT...

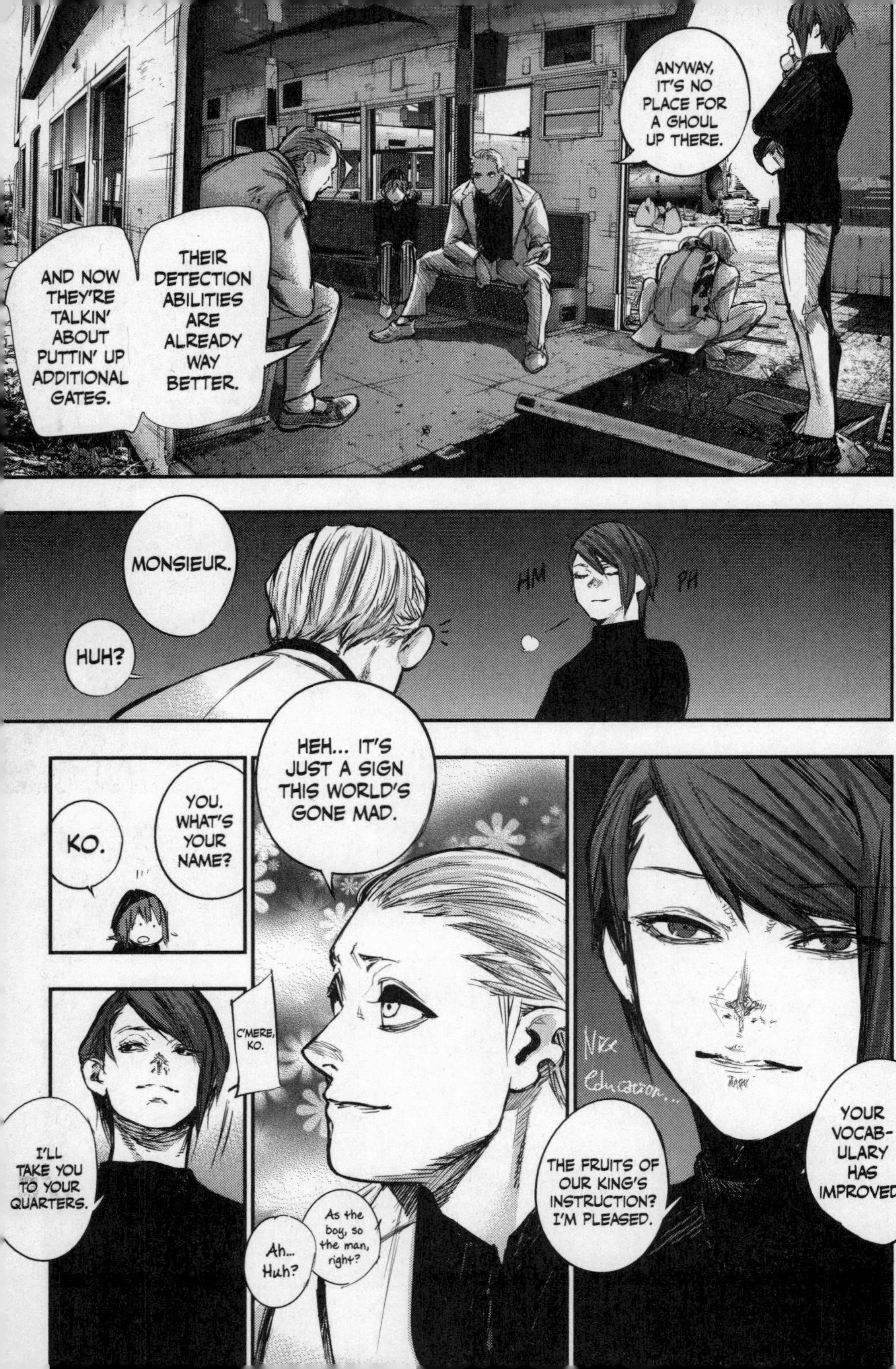

ANYWAY, IT'S NO PLACE FOR A GHOUL UP THERE.
THEIR DETECTION ABILITIES ARE ALREADY WAY BETTER.
AND NOW THEY'RE TALKIN' ABOUT PUTTIN' UP ADDITIONAL GATES.
HM PH
MONSIEUR.
HUH?
Nice Education...
YOUR VOCAB-ULARY HAS IMPROVED.
THE FRUITS OF OUR KING'S INSTRUCTION? I'M PLEASED.
HEH... IT'S JUST A SIGN THIS WORLD'S GONE MAD.
As the boy, so the man, right?
Ah... Huh?
YOU. WHAT'S YOUR NAME?
KO.
C'MERE, KO.
I'LL TAKE YOU TO YOUR QUARTERS.

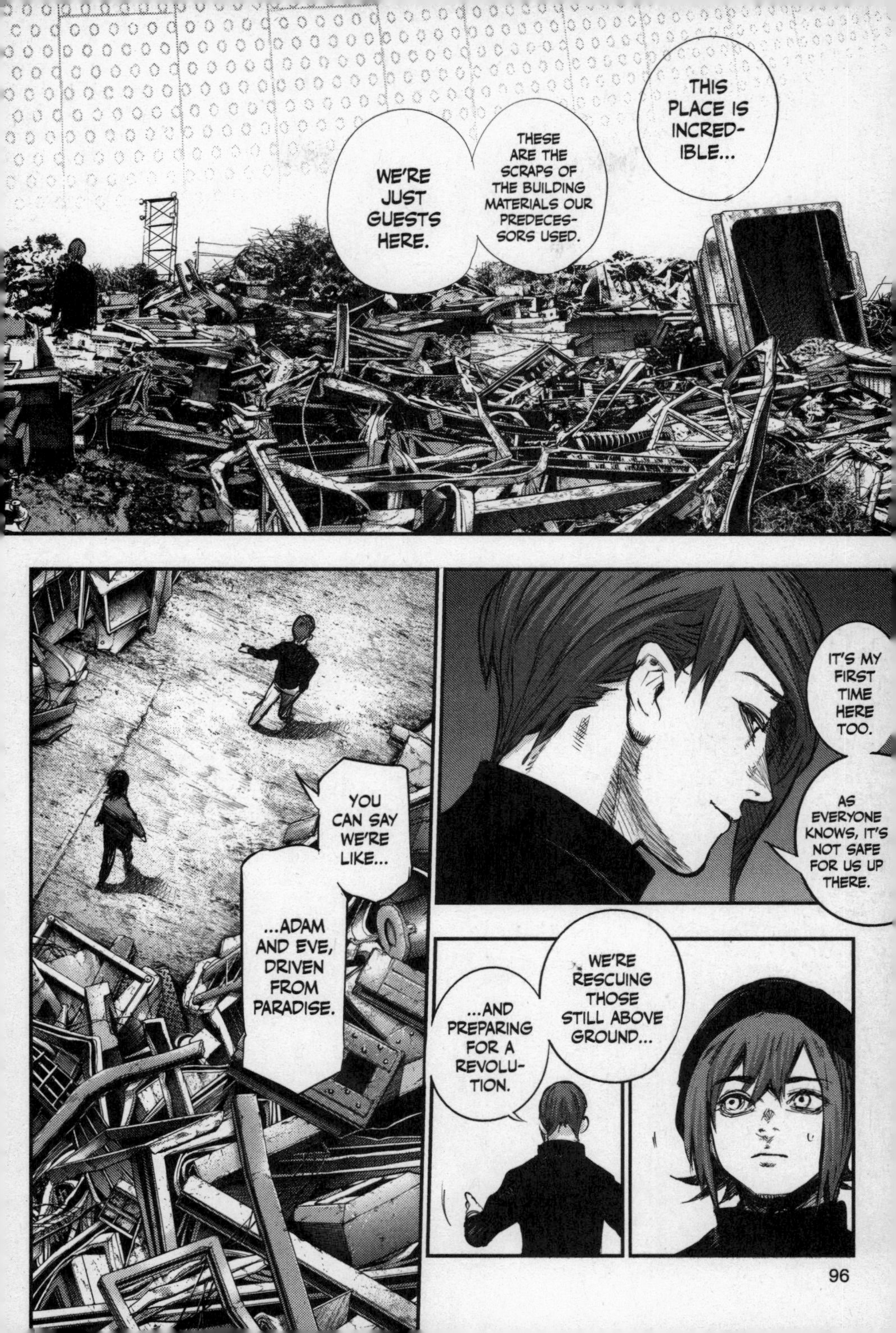
THIS PLACE IS INCRED-IBLE...
THESE ARE THE SCRAPS OF THE BUILDING MATERIALS OUR PREDECES-SORS USED.
WE'RE JUST GUESTS HERE.
IT'S MY FIRST TIME HERE TOO.
AS EVERYONE KNOWS, IT'S NOT SAFE FOR US UP THERE.
WE'RE RESCUING THOSE STILL ABOVE GROUND...
...AND PREPARING FOR A REVOLU-TION.
YOU CAN SAY WE'RE LIKE...
...ADAM AND EVE, DRIVEN FROM PARADISE.

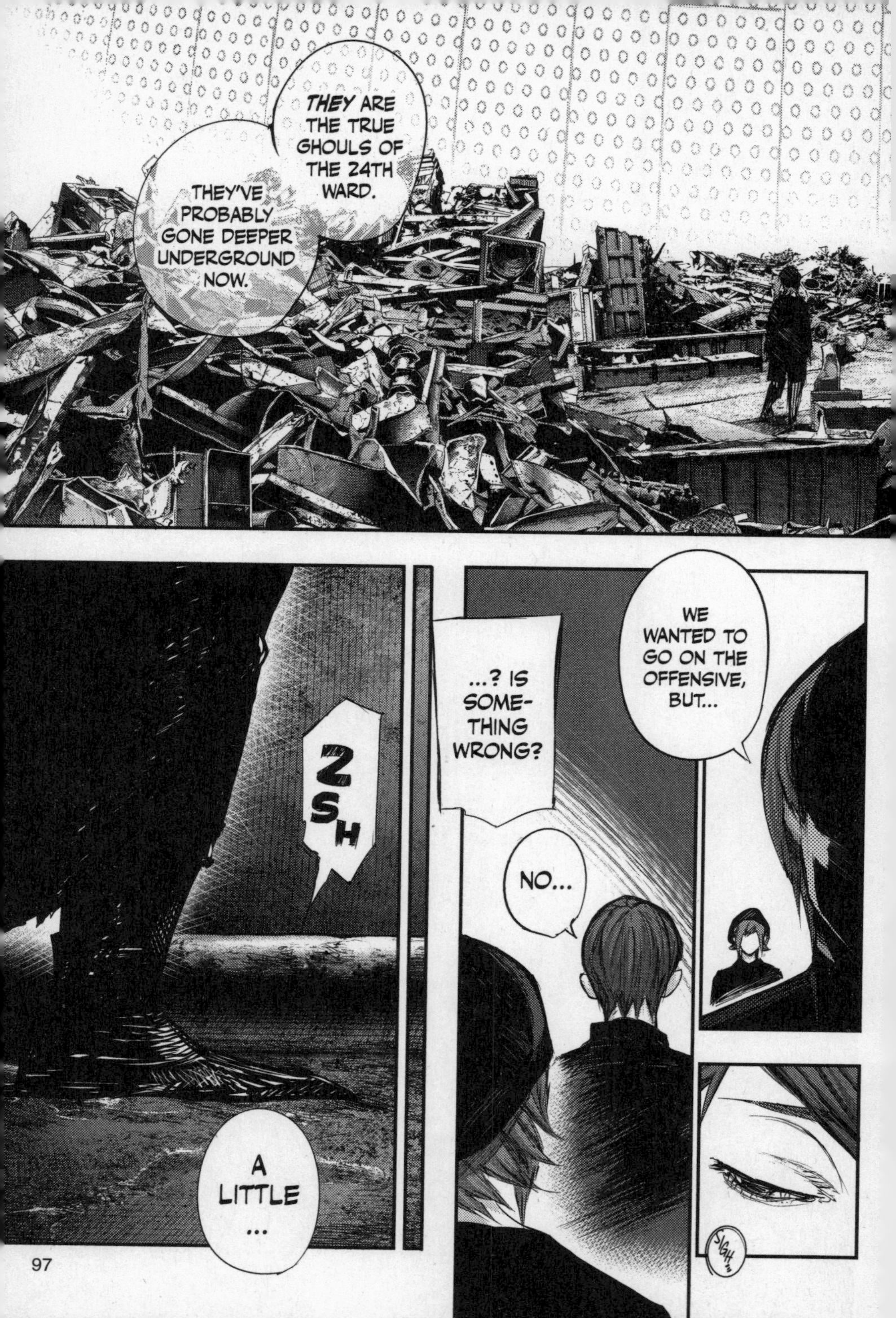
THEY ARE THE TRUE GHOULS OF THE 24TH WARD.
THEY'VE PROBABLY GONE DEEPER UNDERGROUND NOW.
WE WANTED TO GO ON THE OFFENSIVE, BUT...
SIGH
...? IS SOME-THING WRONG?
NO...
ZSH
A LITTLE ...

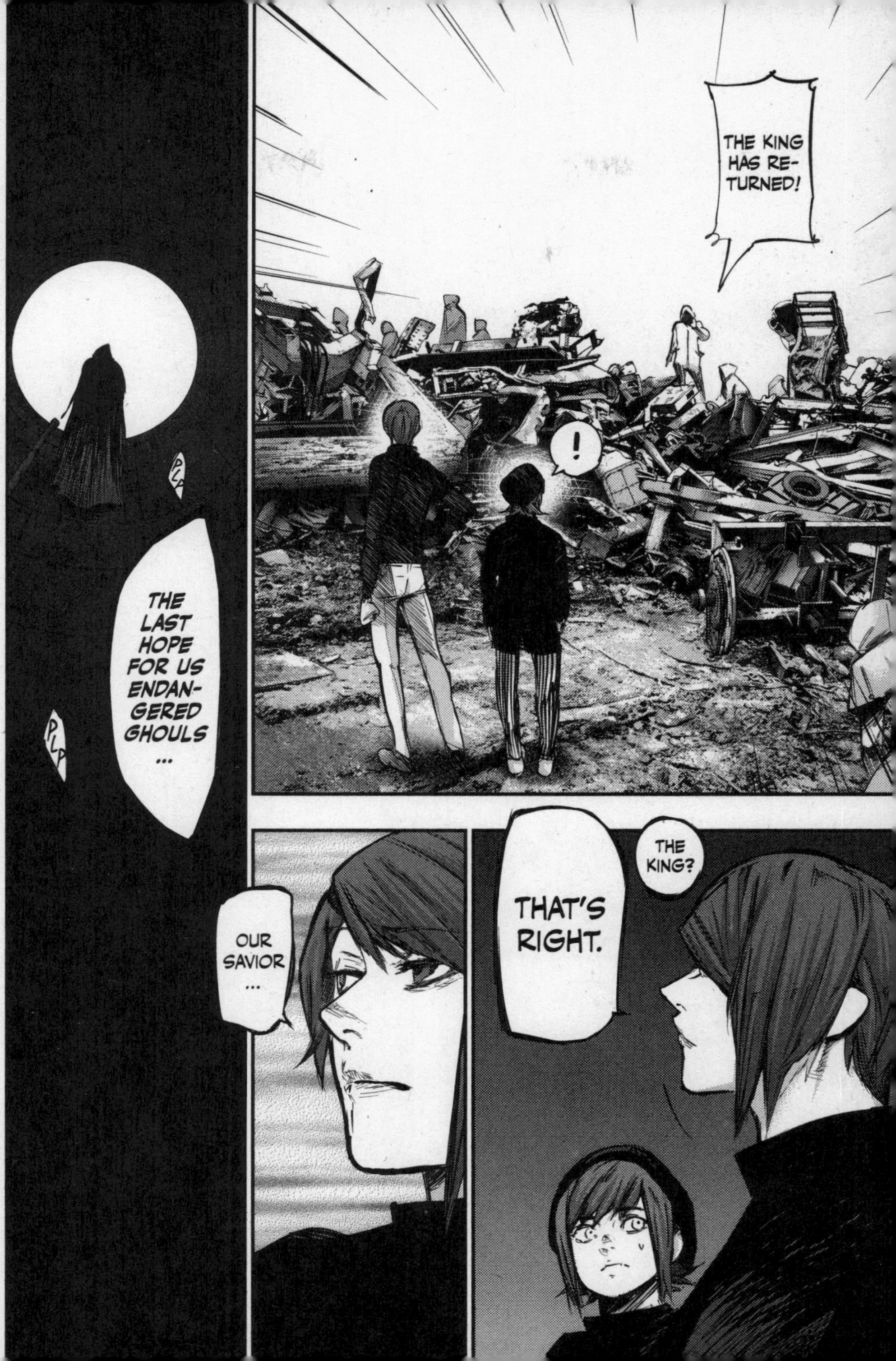
THE KING HAS RE-TURNED!
!
THE KING?
THAT'S RIGHT.
OUR SAVIOR...
PLP
THE LAST HOPE FOR US ENDANGERED GHOULS...
PLP

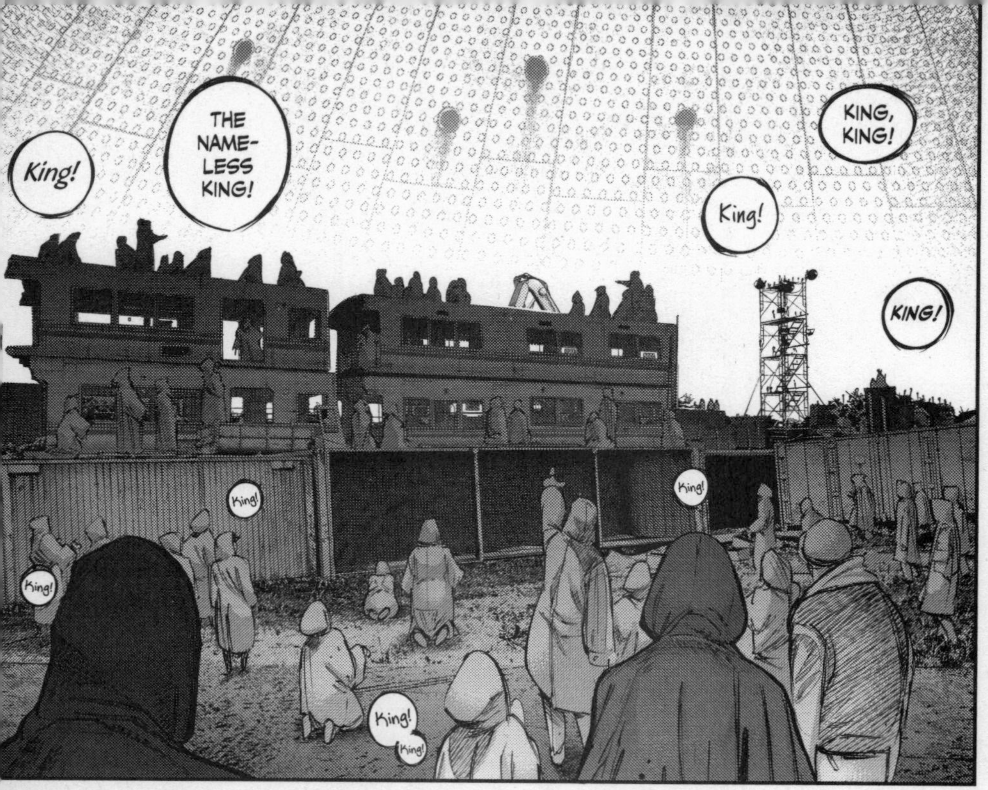
KING, KING!
THE NAME-LESS KING!
King!
King!
KING!
King!
King!
King!
King!
King!
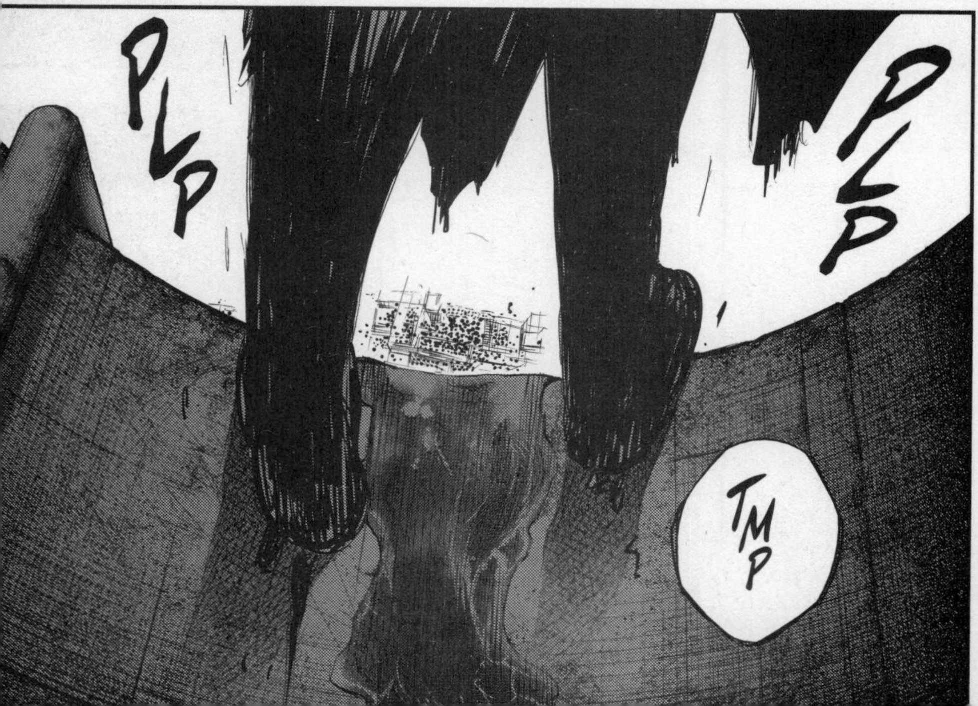
PLP
PLP
TMP

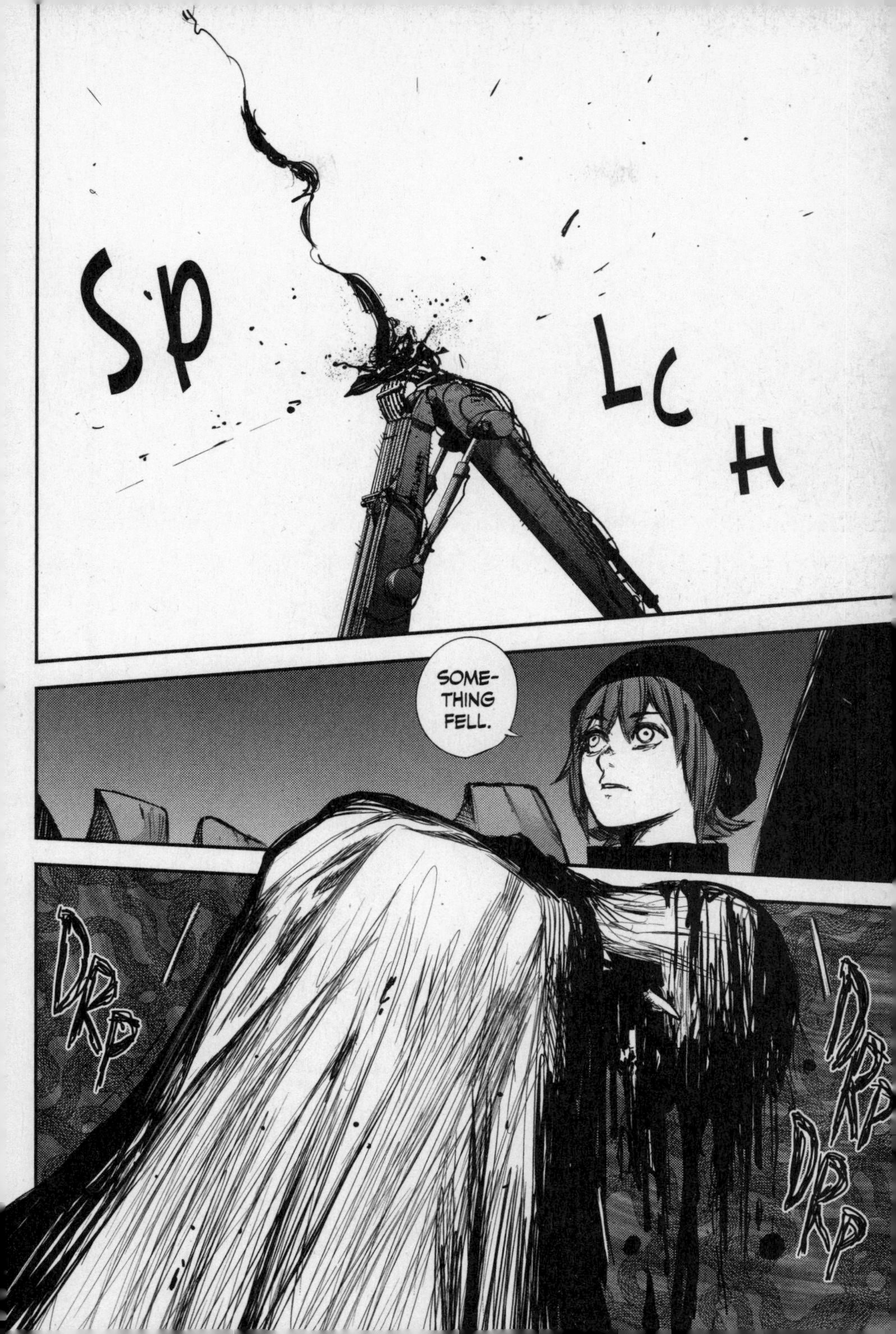
SPLCH
SOME-THING FELL.
DRP DRP
DRP DRP

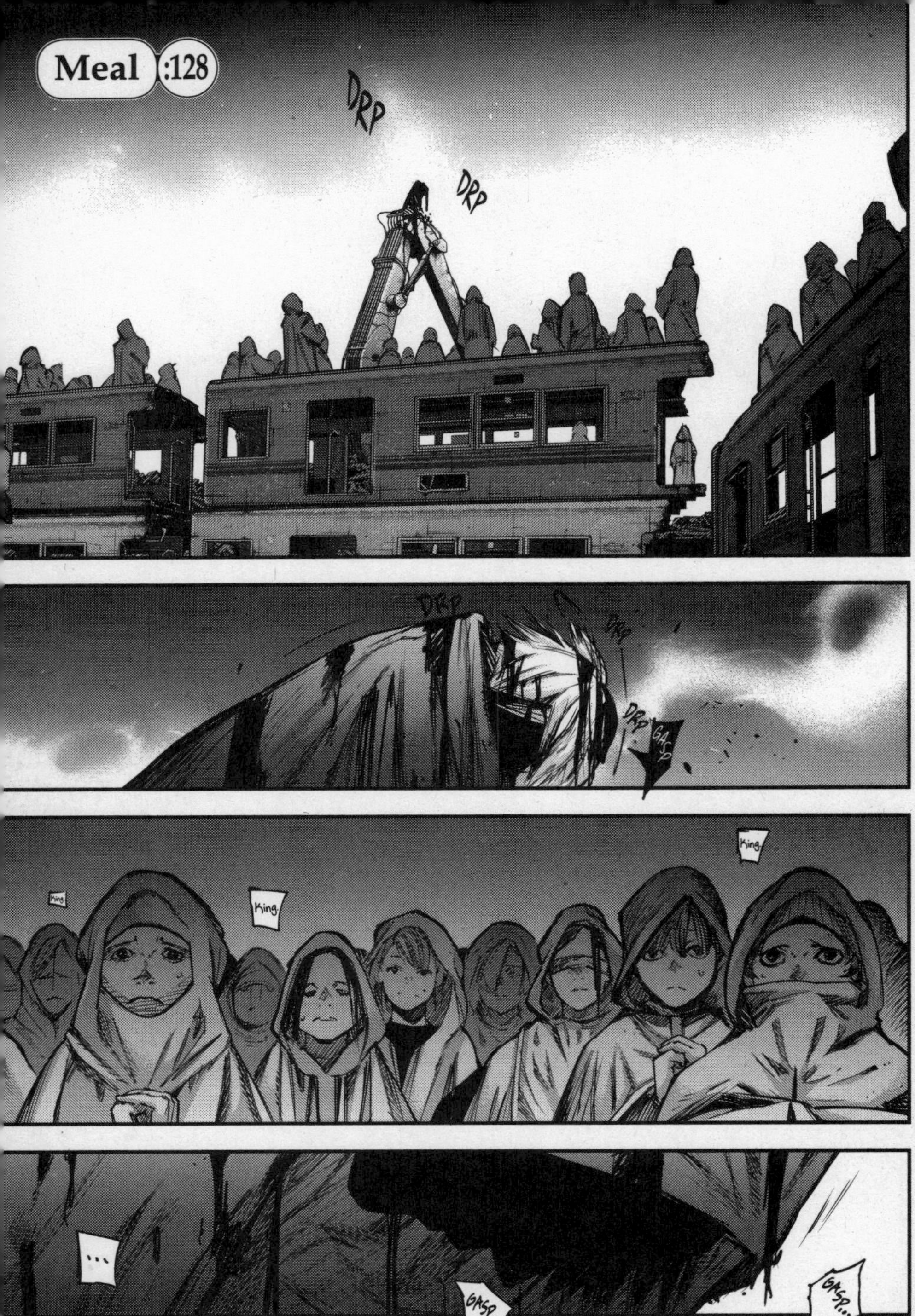

Meal :128
DRP
DRP
DRP
DRP
DRP
GASP
King.
King.
King.
GASP...
GASP...
...

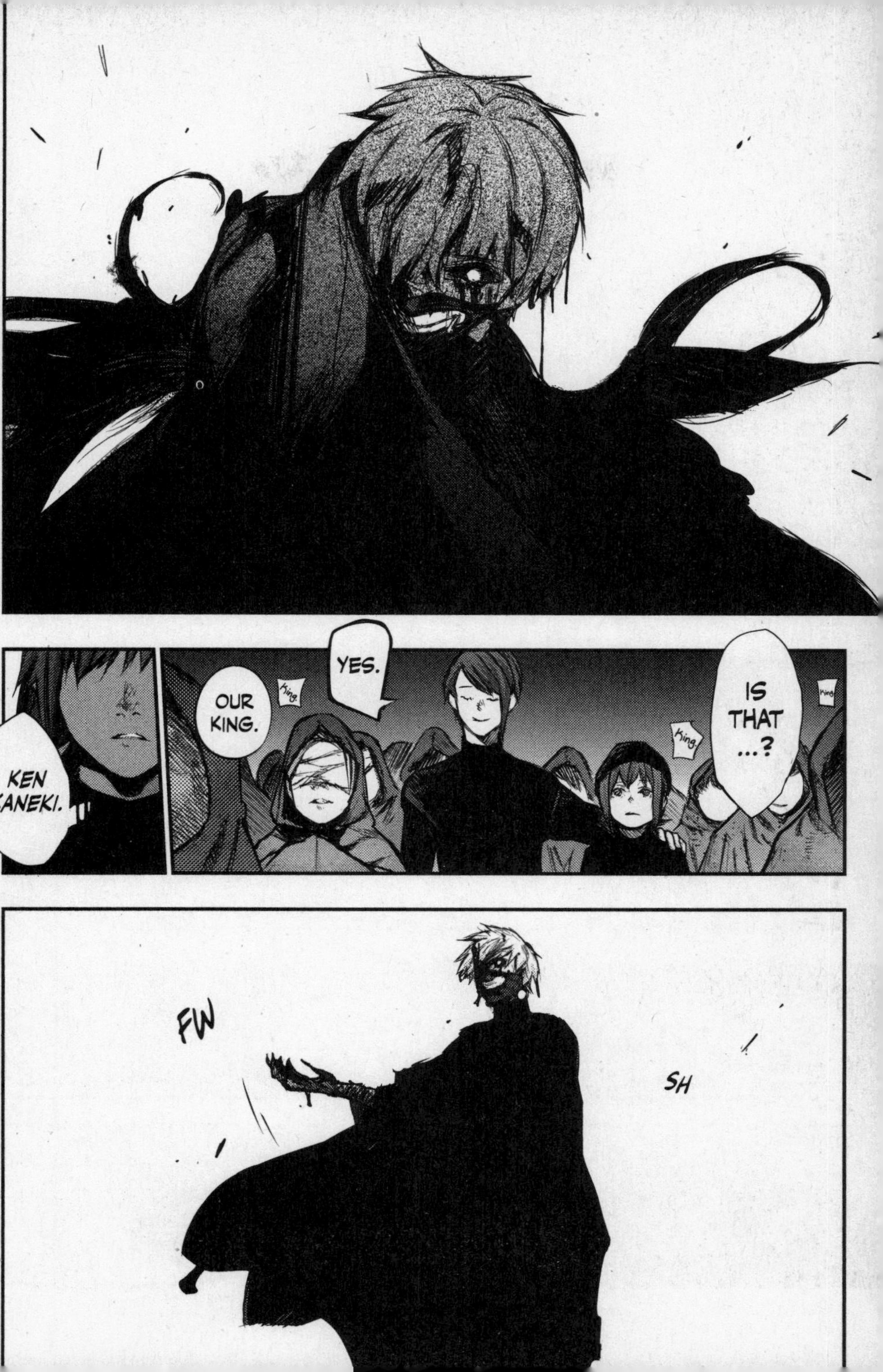
IS THAT ...?
King.
King.
YES.
OUR KING.
King.
KEN KANEKI.
SH
FW

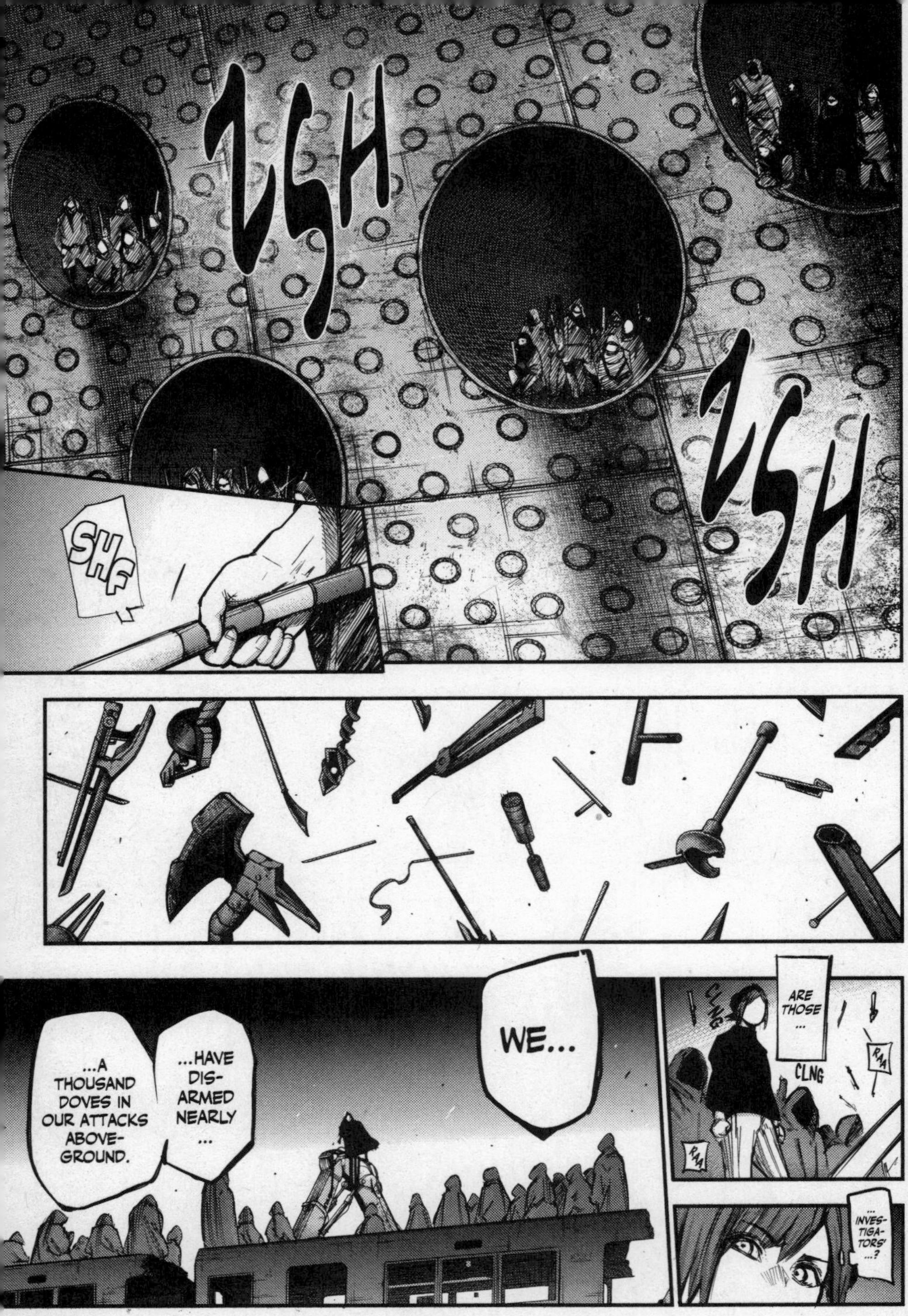
ZSH
ZSH
SHF
ARE THOSE ...
CLNG
CLNG
RAA
RAA
... INVESTIGATORS' ...?
WE...
...HAVE DISARMED NEARLY ...
...A THOUSAND DOVES IN OUR ATTACKS ABOVEGROUND.

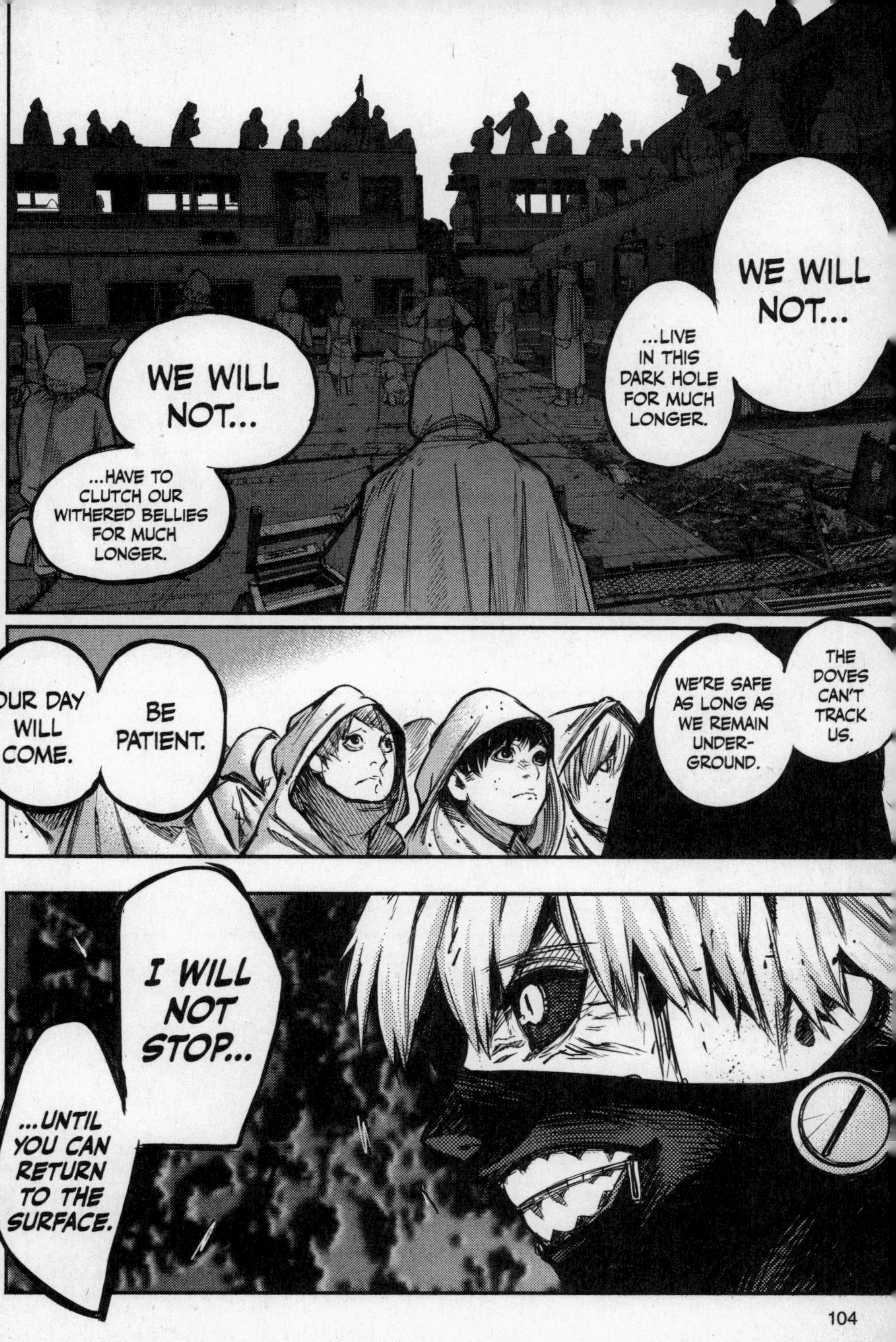
WE WILL NOT...
...LIVE IN THIS DARK HOLE FOR MUCH LONGER.
WE WILL NOT...
...HAVE TO CLUTCH OUR WITHERED BELLIES FOR MUCH LONGER.
THE DOVES CAN'T TRACK US.
WE'RE SAFE AS LONG AS WE REMAIN UNDER-GROUND.
BE PATIENT.
OUR DAY WILL COME.
I WILL NOT STOP...
...UNTIL YOU CAN RETURN TO THE SURFACE.

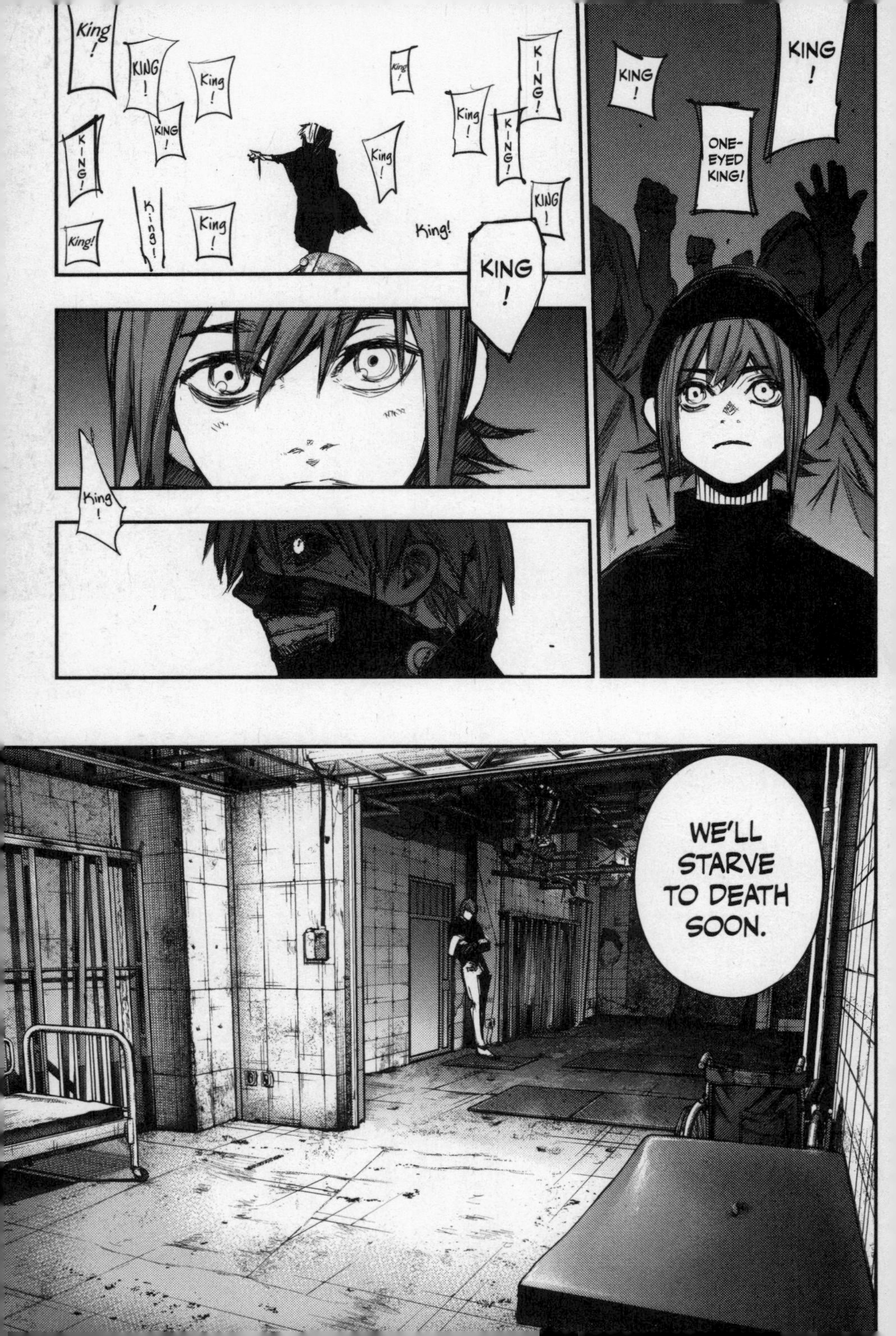
KING!
KING!
ONE-EYED KING!
KING!
KING!
King!
KING!
King!
King!
KING!
King!
KING!
King!
KING!
King!
King!
KING!
King!
King!
KING!
King!
WE'LL STARVE TO DEATH SOON.

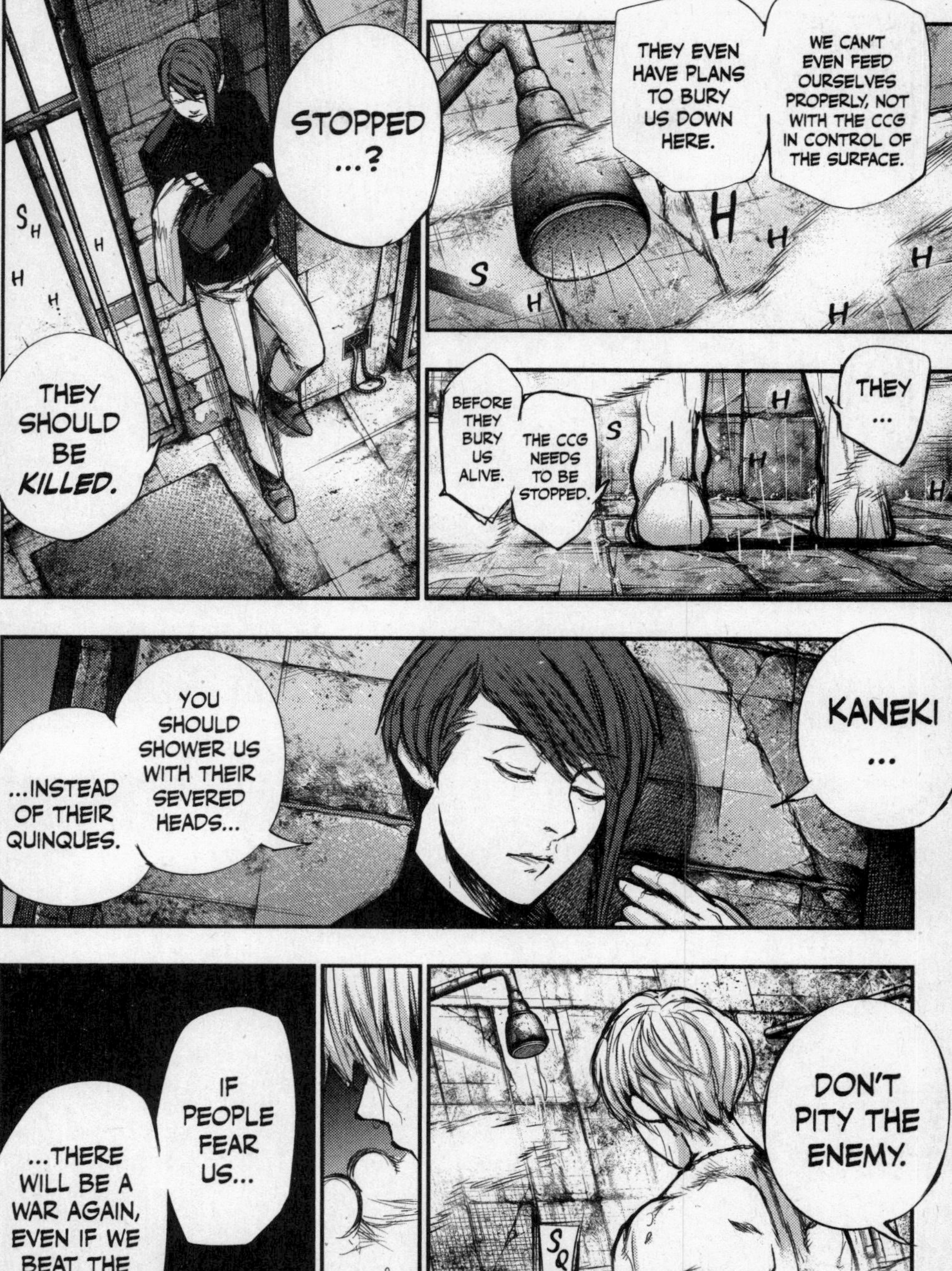
WE CAN'T EVEN FEED OURSELVES PROPERLY, NOT WITH THE CCG IN CONTROL OF THE SURFACE.
THEY EVEN HAVE PLANS TO BURY US DOWN HERE.
SHHHHH
THEY ...
SHHH
THE CCG NEEDS TO BE STOPPED.
BEFORE THEY BURY US ALIVE.
STOPPED ...?
SHHHH
THEY SHOULD BE *KILLED.*
KANEKI ...
YOU SHOULD SHOWER US WITH THEIR SEVERED HEADS...
...INSTEAD OF THEIR QUINQUES.
DON'T PITY THE ENEMY.
SQK
IF PEOPLE FEAR US...
...THERE WILL BE A WAR AGAIN, EVEN IF WE BEAT THE CCG.

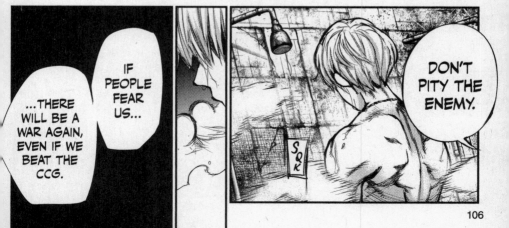

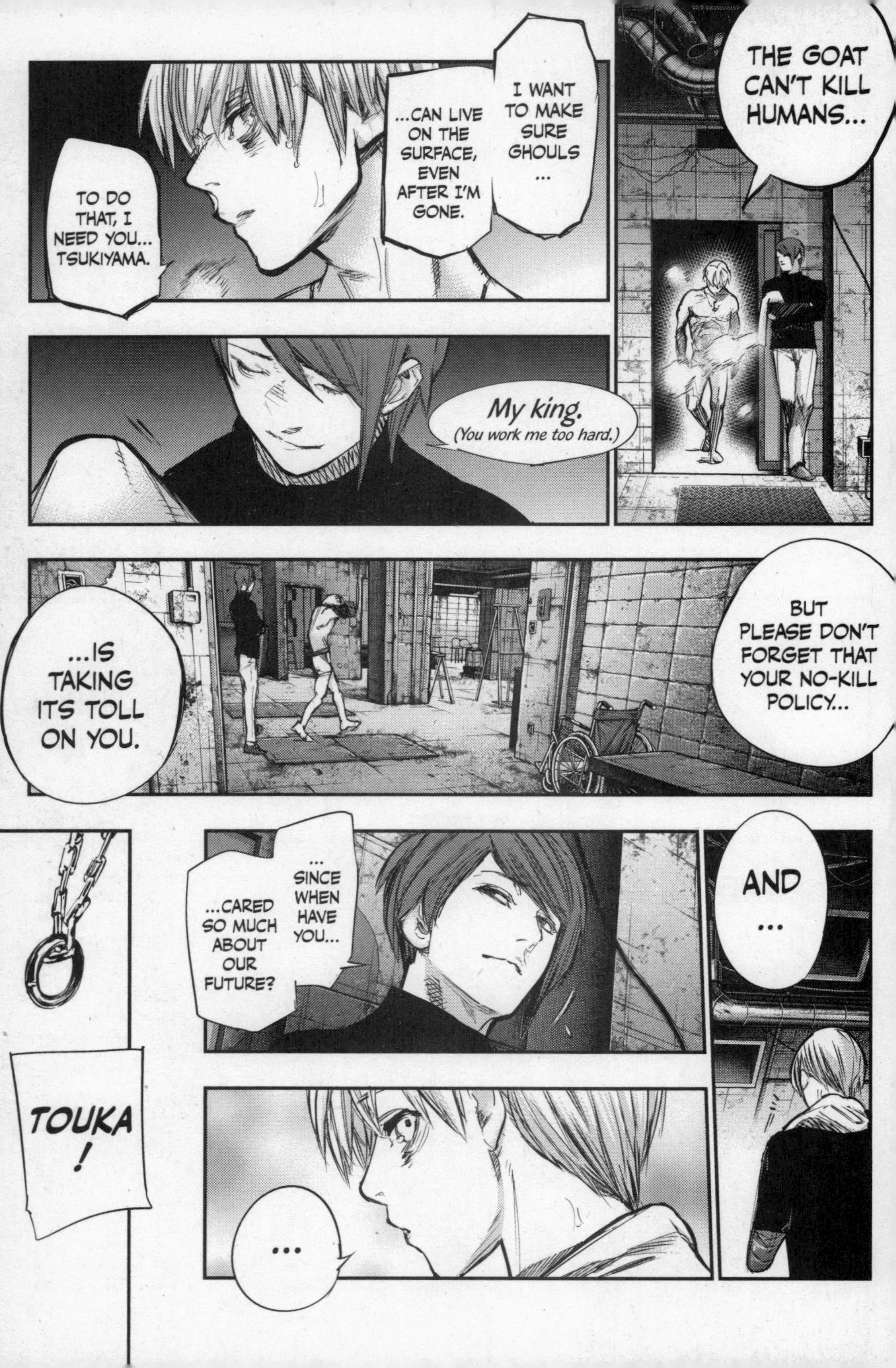
THE GOAT CAN'T KILL HUMANS...
I WANT TO MAKE SURE GHOULS ...
...CAN LIVE ON THE SURFACE, EVEN AFTER I'M GONE.
TO DO THAT, I NEED YOU... TSUKIYAMA.
My king.
(You work me too hard.)
BUT PLEASE DON'T FORGET THAT YOUR NO-KILL POLICY...
...IS TAKING ITS TOLL ON YOU.
AND ...
... SINCE WHEN HAVE YOU...
...CARED SO MUCH ABOUT OUR FUTURE?
...
TOUKA!

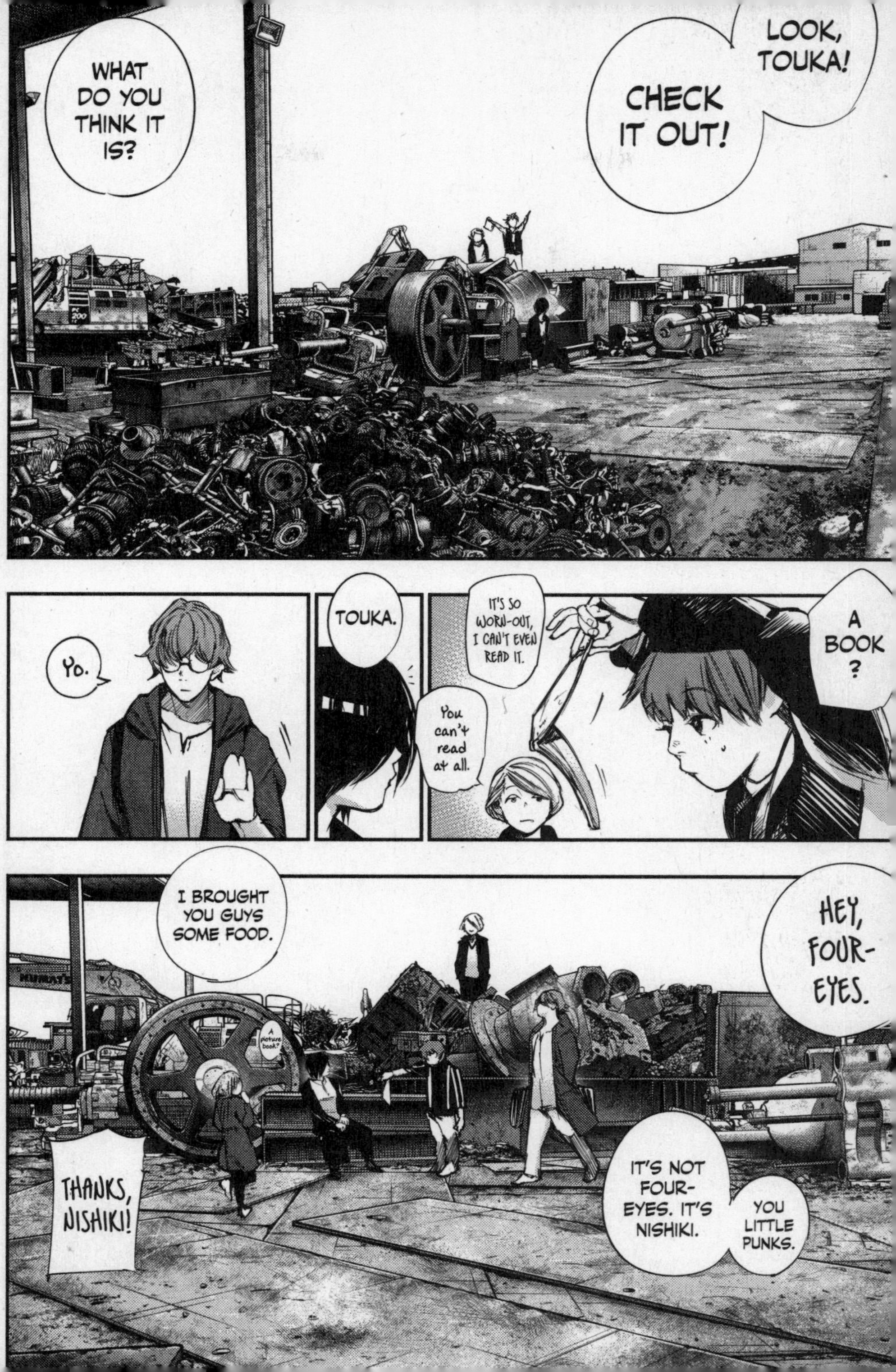
LOOK, TOUKA!
CHECK IT OUT!
WHAT DO YOU THINK IT IS?
A BOOK?
IT'S SO WORN-OUT, I CAN'T EVEN READ IT.
You can't read at all.
TOUKA.
Yo.
HEY, FOUR-EYES.
I BROUGHT YOU GUYS SOME FOOD.
A picture book?
IT'S NOT FOUR-EYES. IT'S NISHIKI.
YOU LITTLE PUNKS.
THANKS, NISHIKI!

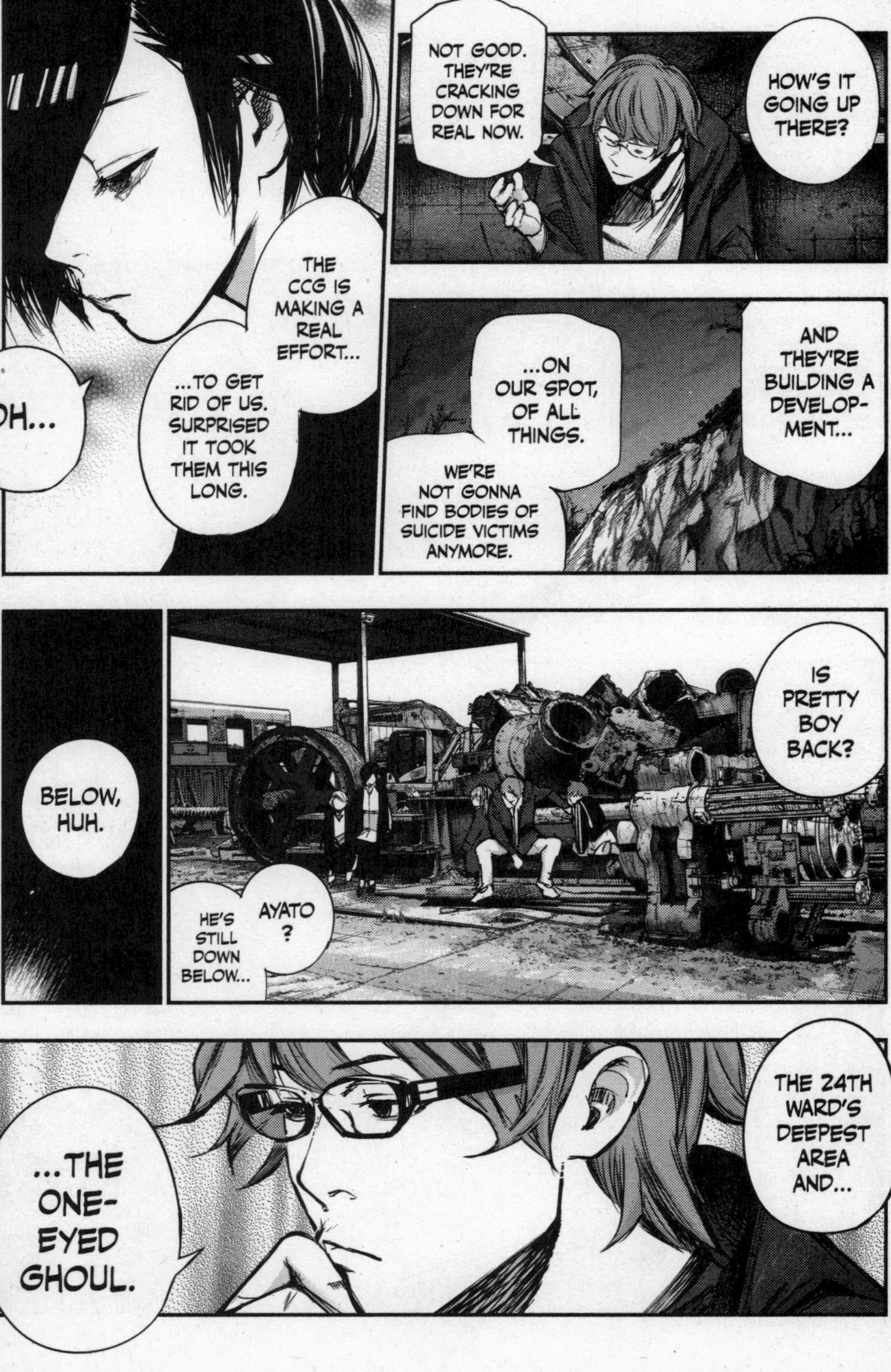
HOW'S IT GOING UP THERE?
NOT GOOD. THEY'RE CRACKING DOWN FOR REAL NOW.
AND THEY'RE BUILDING A DEVELOPMENT...
...ON OUR SPOT, OF ALL THINGS.
WE'RE NOT GONNA FIND BODIES OF SUICIDE VICTIMS ANYMORE.
THE CCG IS MAKING A REAL EFFORT...
...TO GET RID OF US. SURPRISED IT TOOK THEM THIS LONG.
OH...
IS PRETTY BOY BACK?
AYATO?
HE'S STILL DOWN BELOW...
BELOW, HUH.
THE 24TH WARD'S DEEPEST AREA AND...
...THE ONE-EYED GHOUL.

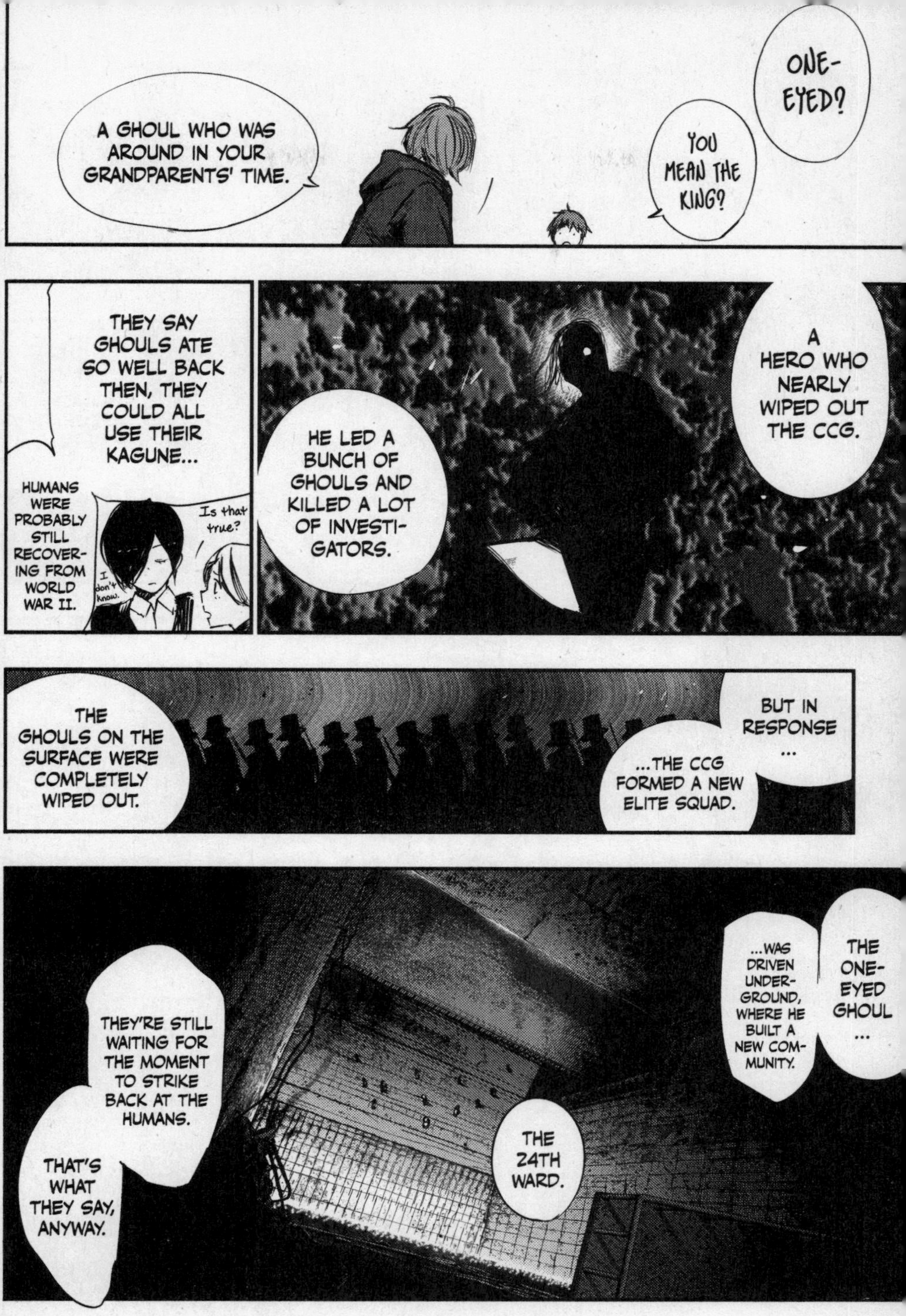
ONE-EYED?
YOU MEAN THE KING?
A GHOUL WHO WAS AROUND IN YOUR GRANDPARENTS' TIME.
A HERO WHO NEARLY WIPED OUT THE CCG.
HE LED A BUNCH OF GHOULS AND KILLED A LOT OF INVESTI-GATORS.
THEY SAY GHOULS ATE SO WELL BACK THEN, THEY COULD ALL USE THEIR KAGUNE...
Is that true?
HUMANS WERE PROBABLY STILL RECOVER-ING FROM WORLD WAR II.
I don't know.
BUT IN RESPONSE...
...THE CCG FORMED A NEW ELITE SQUAD.
THE GHOULS ON THE SURFACE WERE COMPLETELY WIPED OUT.
THE ONE-EYED GHOUL...
...WAS DRIVEN UNDER-GROUND, WHERE HE BUILT A NEW COM-MUNITY.
THE 24TH WARD.
THEY'RE STILL WAITING FOR THE MOMENT TO STRIKE BACK AT THE HUMANS.
THAT'S WHAT THEY SAY, ANYWAY.

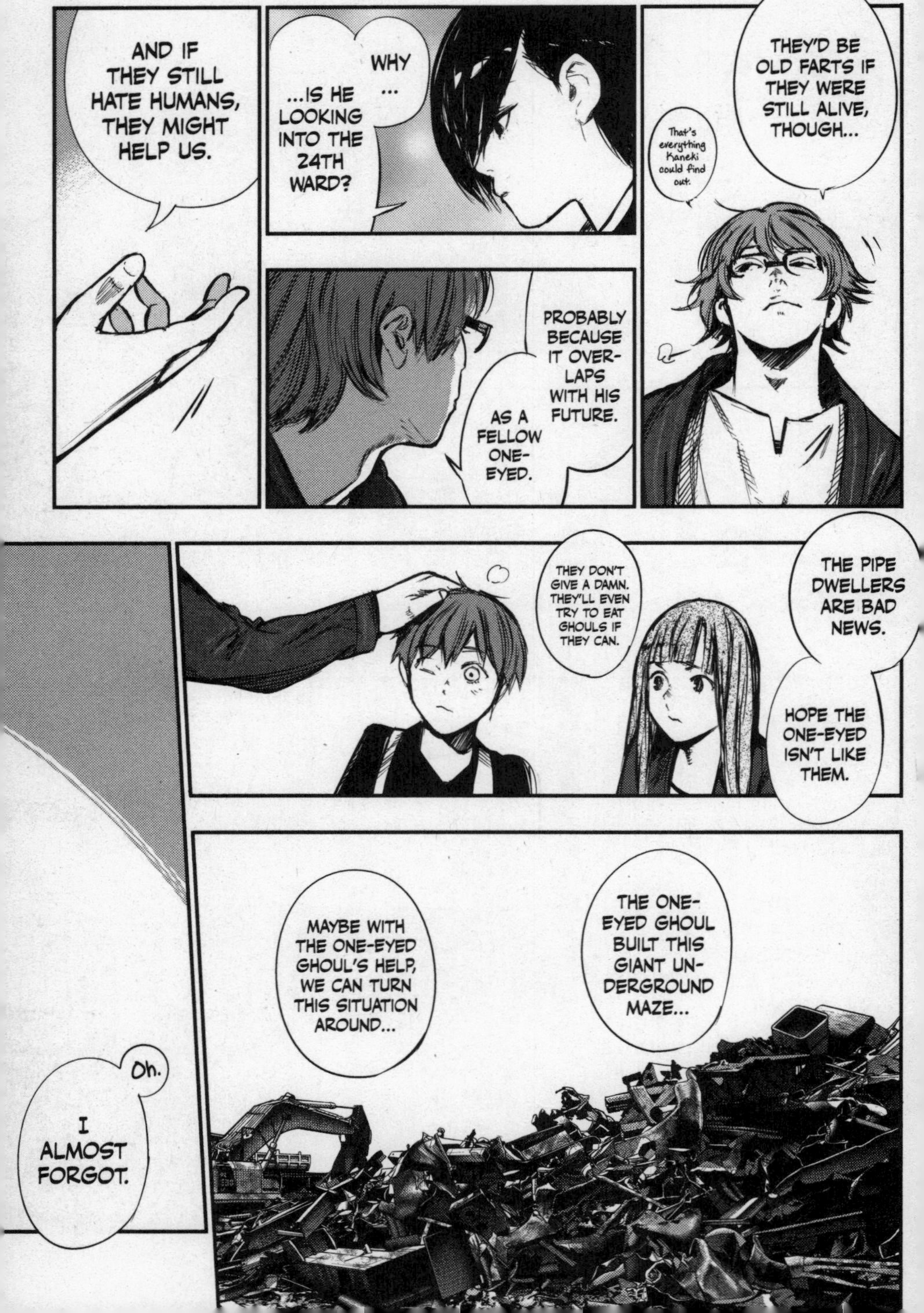
THEY'D BE OLD FARTS IF THEY WERE STILL ALIVE, THOUGH...
That's everything Kaneki could find out.
WHY ...
...IS HE LOOKING INTO THE 24TH WARD?
PROBABLY BECAUSE IT OVER-LAPS WITH HIS FUTURE.
AS A FELLOW ONE-EYED.
AND IF THEY STILL HATE HUMANS, THEY MIGHT HELP US.
THE PIPE DWELLERS ARE BAD NEWS.
THEY DON'T GIVE A DAMN. THEY'LL EVEN TRY TO EAT GHOULS IF THEY CAN.
HOPE THE ONE-EYED ISN'T LIKE THEM.
THE ONE-EYED GHOUL BUILT THIS GIANT UN-DERGROUND MAZE...
MAYBE WITH THE ONE-EYED GHOUL'S HELP, WE CAN TURN THIS SITUATION AROUND...
Oh.
I ALMOST FORGOT.

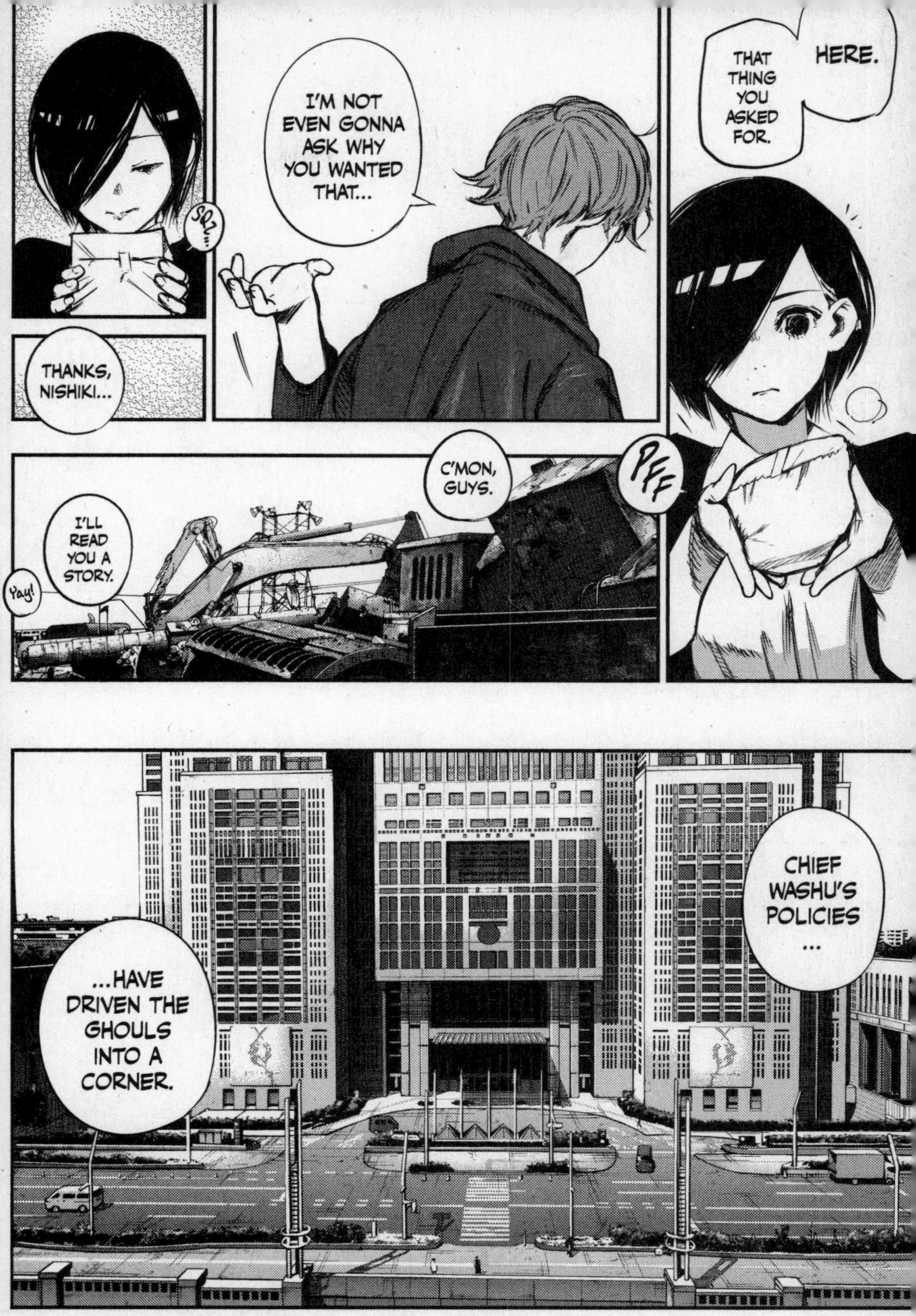
THAT THING YOU ASKED FOR.
HERE.
PFF
I'M NOT EVEN GONNA ASK WHY YOU WANTED THAT...
SQZ...
THANKS, NISHIKI...
C'MON, GUYS.
I'LL READ YOU A STORY.
Yay!
CHIEF WASHU'S POLICIES ...
...HAVE DRIVEN THE GHOULS INTO A CORNER.

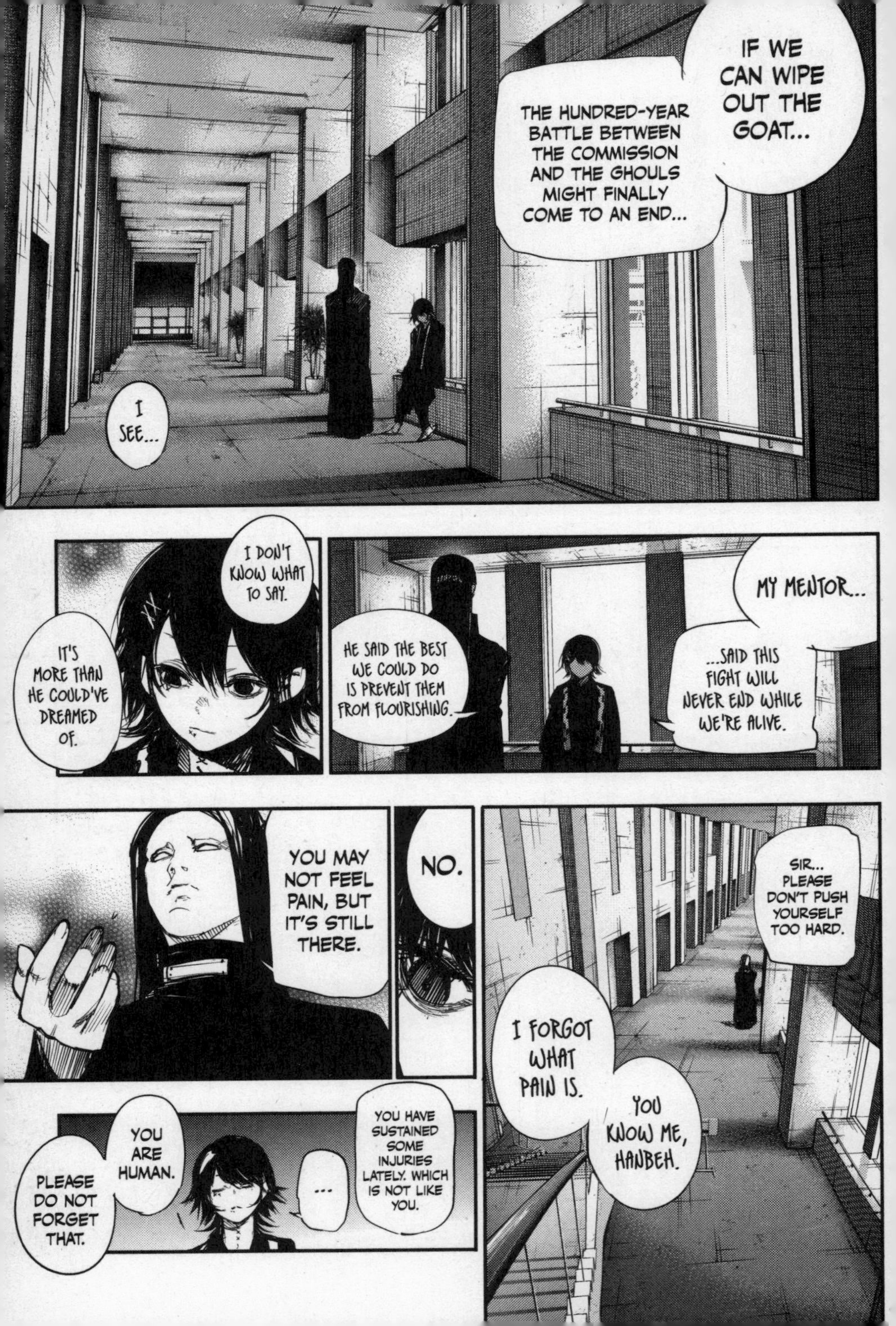
IF WE CAN WIPE OUT THE GOAT...
THE HUNDRED-YEAR BATTLE BETWEEN THE COMMISSION AND THE GHOULS MIGHT FINALLY COME TO AN END...
I SEE...
MY MENTOR...
...SAID THIS FIGHT WILL NEVER END WHILE WE'RE ALIVE.
HE SAID THE BEST WE COULD DO IS PREVENT THEM FROM FLOURISHING.
I DON'T KNOW WHAT TO SAY.
IT'S MORE THAN HE COULD'VE DREAMED OF.
SIR... PLEASE DON'T PUSH YOURSELF TOO HARD.
YOU KNOW ME, HANBEH.
I FORGOT WHAT PAIN IS.
NO.
YOU MAY NOT FEEL PAIN, BUT IT'S STILL THERE.
YOU HAVE SUSTAINED SOME INJURIES LATELY. WHICH IS NOT LIKE YOU.
...
YOU ARE HUMAN.
PLEASE DO NOT FORGET THAT.

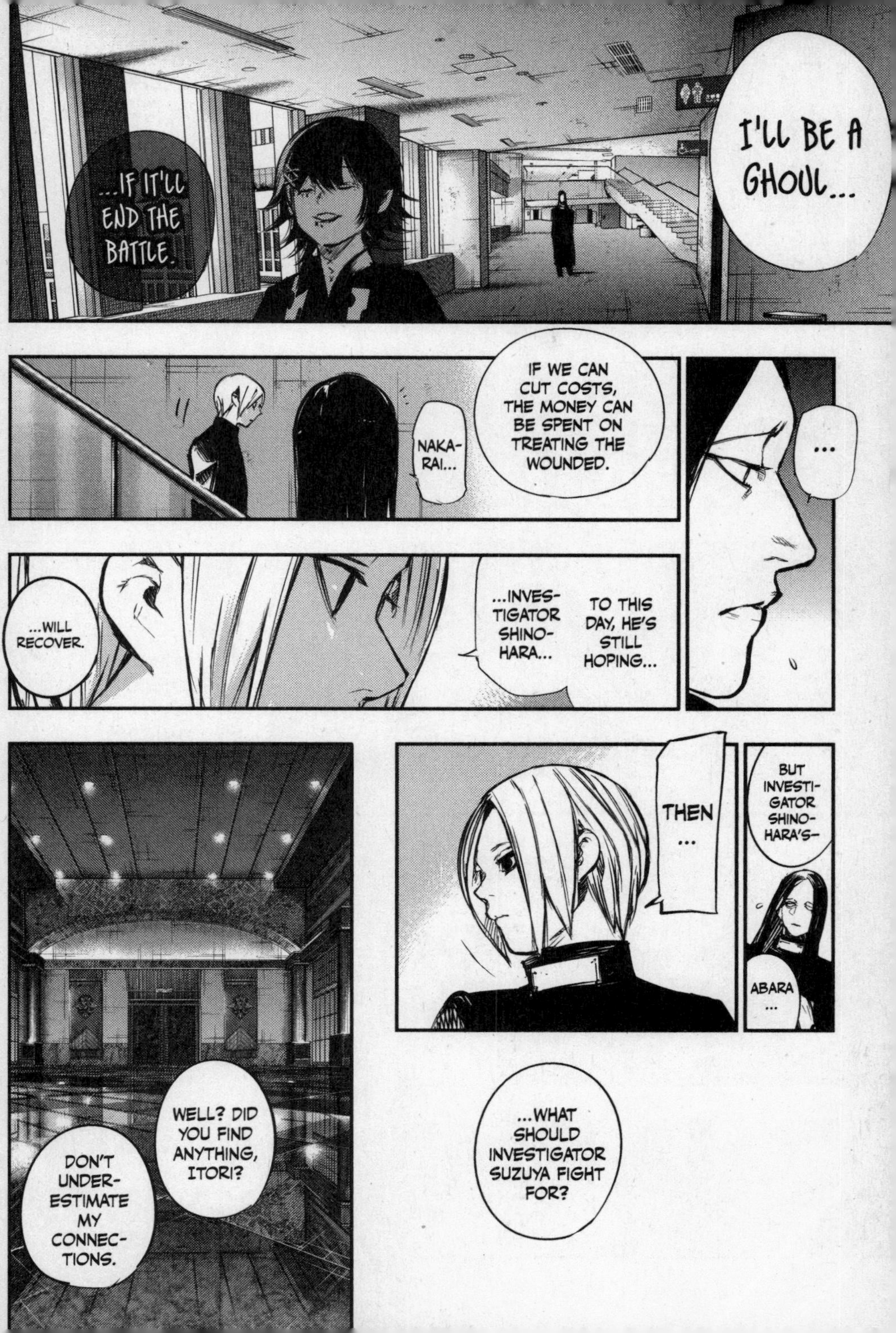
I'LL BE A GHOUL...
...IF IT'LL END THE BATTLE.
...
IF WE CAN CUT COSTS, THE MONEY CAN BE SPENT ON TREATING THE WOUNDED.
NAKA-RAI...
TO THIS DAY, HE'S STILL HOPING...
...INVES-TIGATOR SHINO-HARA...
...WILL RECOVER.
BUT INVESTI-GATOR SHINO-HARA'S-
ABARA...
THEN...
...WHAT SHOULD INVESTIGATOR SUZUYA FIGHT FOR?
WELL? DID YOU FIND ANYTHING, ITORI?
DON'T UNDER-ESTIMATE MY CONNEC-TIONS.

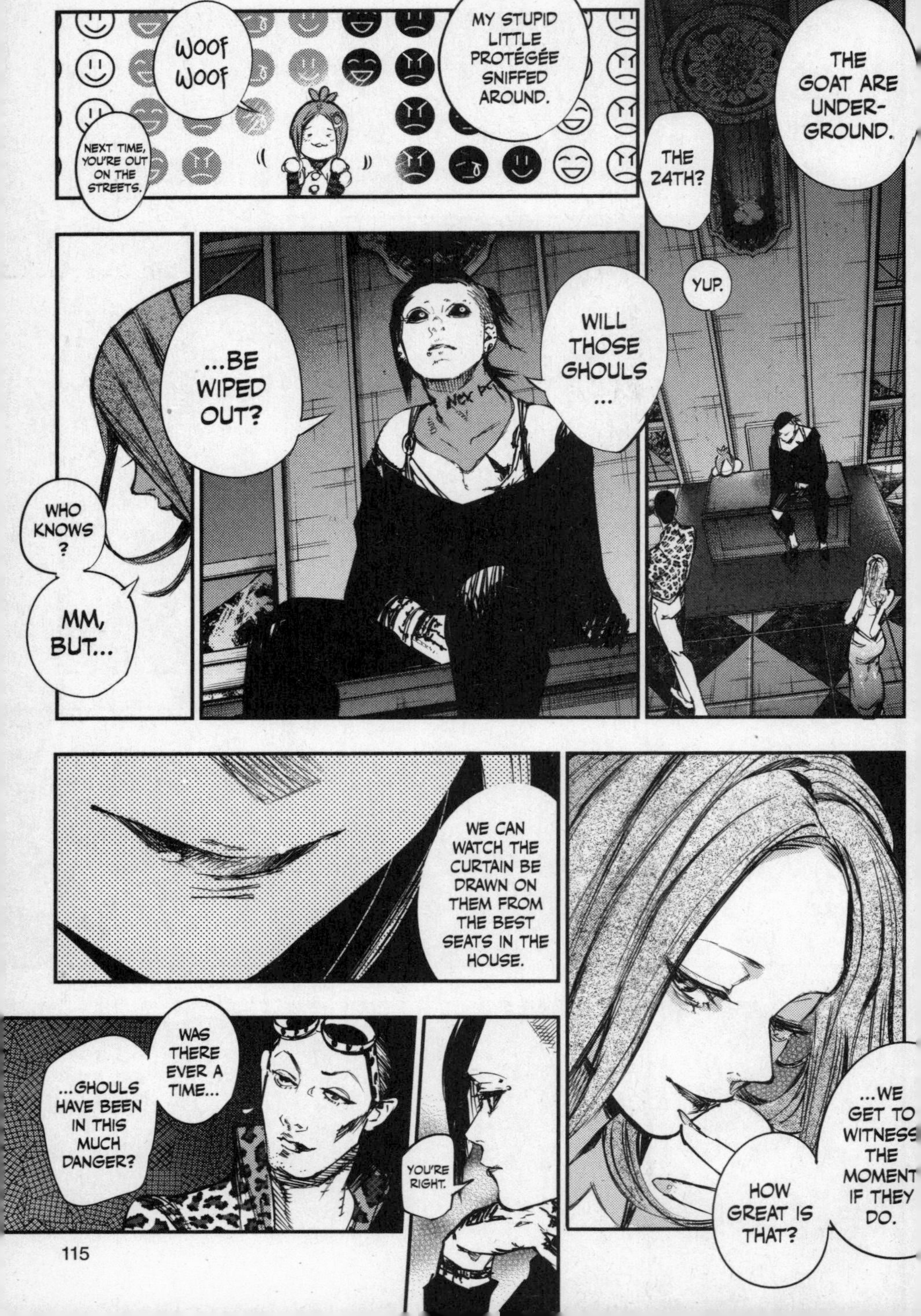
THE GOAT ARE UNDER-GROUND.
THE 24TH?
YUP.
MY STUPID LITTLE PROTÉGÉE SNIFFED AROUND.
WOOF WOOF
NEXT TIME, YOU'RE OUT ON THE STREETS.
WILL THOSE GHOULS ...
...BE WIPED OUT?
WHO KNOWS ?
MM, BUT...
...WE GET TO WITNESS THE MOMENT IF THEY DO.
HOW GREAT IS THAT?
WE CAN WATCH THE CURTAIN BE DRAWN ON THEM FROM THE BEST SEATS IN THE HOUSE.
YOU'RE RIGHT.
WAS THERE EVER A TIME...
...GHOULS HAVE BEEN IN THIS MUCH DANGER?

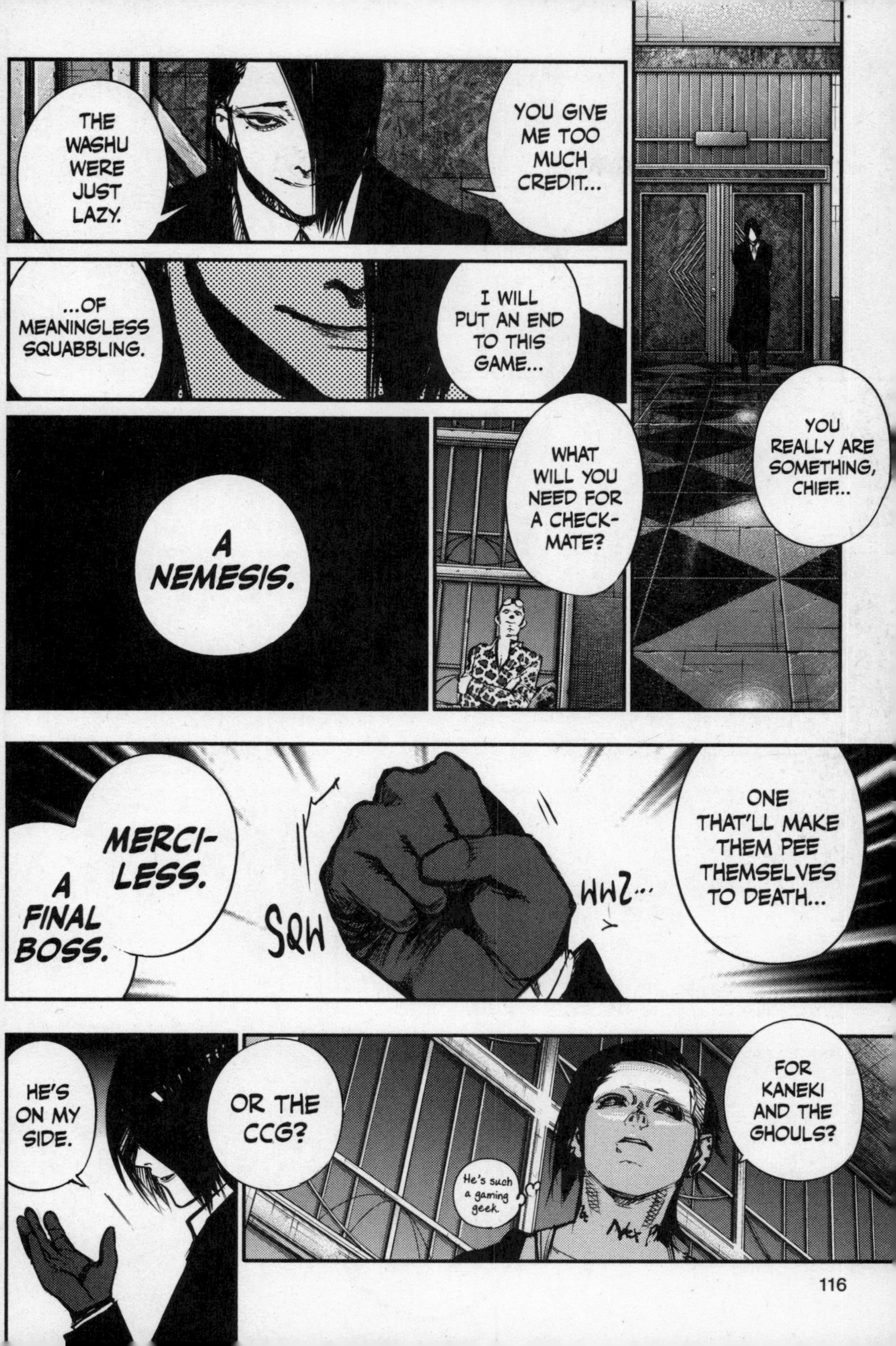
YOU REALLY ARE SOMETHING, CHIEF...
YOU GIVE ME TOO MUCH CREDIT...
THE WASHU WERE JUST LAZY.
I WILL PUT AN END TO THIS GAME...
...OF MEANINGLESS SQUABBLING.
WHAT WILL YOU NEED FOR A CHECK-MATE?
A NEMESIS.
ONE THAT'LL MAKE THEM PEE THEMSELVES TO DEATH...
WWZ...
SQW
MERCI-LESS.
A FINAL BOSS.
FOR KANEKI AND THE GHOULS?
He's such a gaming geek.
OR THE CCG?
HE'S ON MY SIDE.

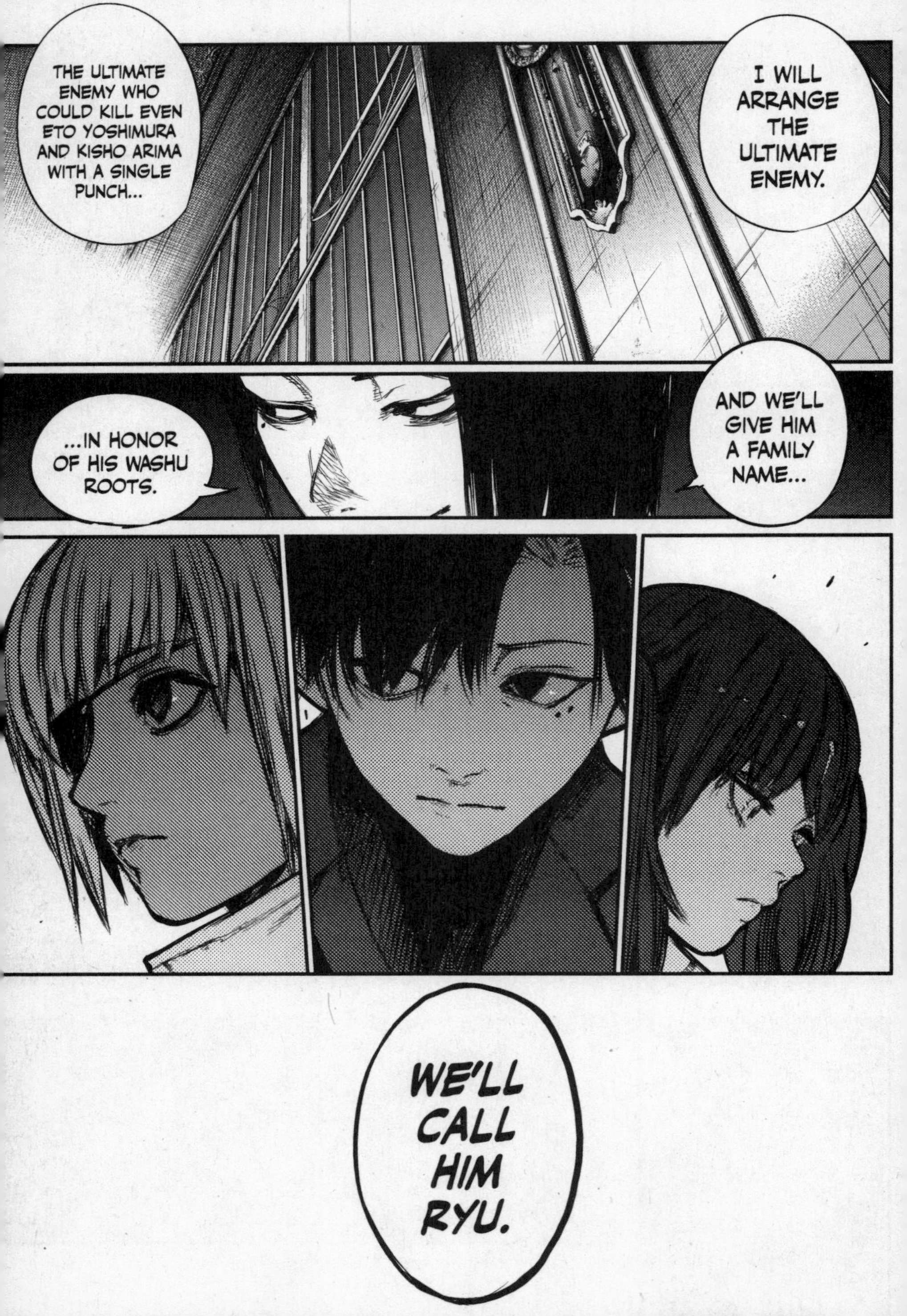
I WILL ARRANGE THE ULTIMATE ENEMY.
THE ULTIMATE ENEMY WHO COULD KILL EVEN ETO YOSHIMURA AND KISHO ARIMA WITH A SINGLE PUNCH...
AND WE'LL GIVE HIM A FAMILY NAME...
...IN HONOR OF HIS WASHU ROOTS.
WE'LL CALL HIM RYU.

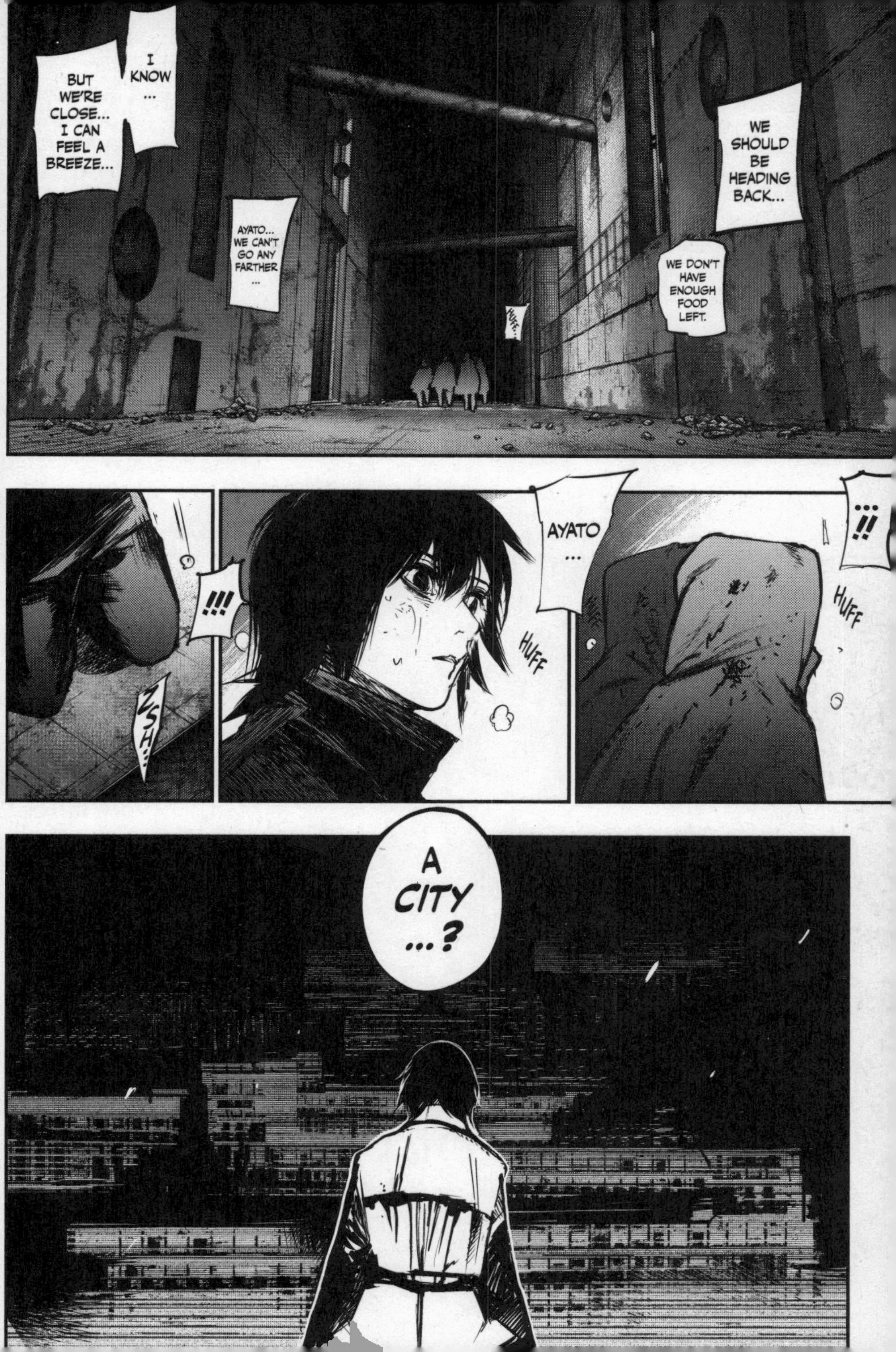
WE SHOULD BE HEADING BACK...
WE DON'T HAVE ENOUGH FOOD LEFT.
HUFF...
AYATO... WE CAN'T GO ANY FARTHER ...
I KNOW ...
BUT WE'RE CLOSE... I CAN FEEL A BREEZE...
...!!
HUFF
AYATO ...
HUFF
!!!
ZSH...
A CITY ...?

Suffering :129

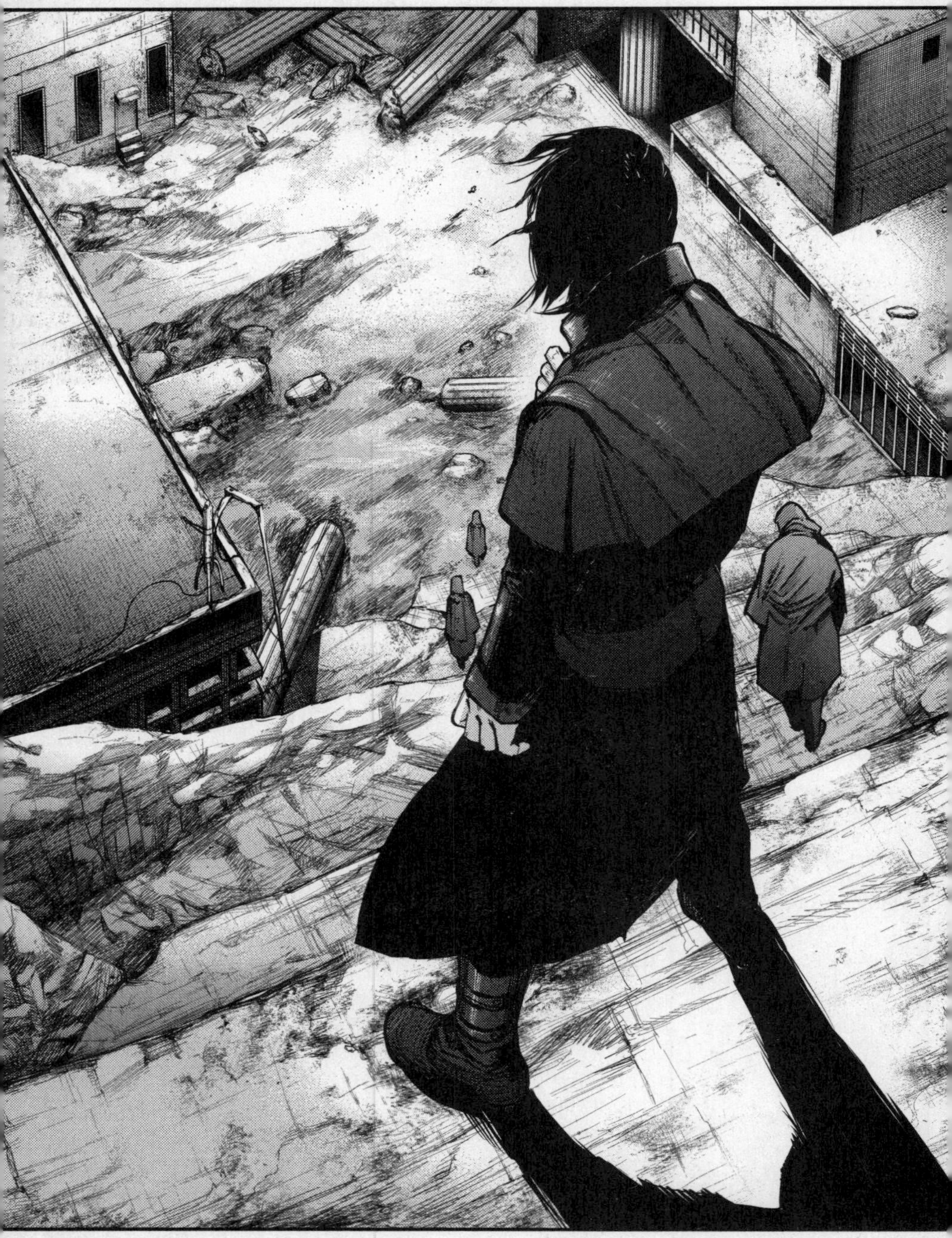

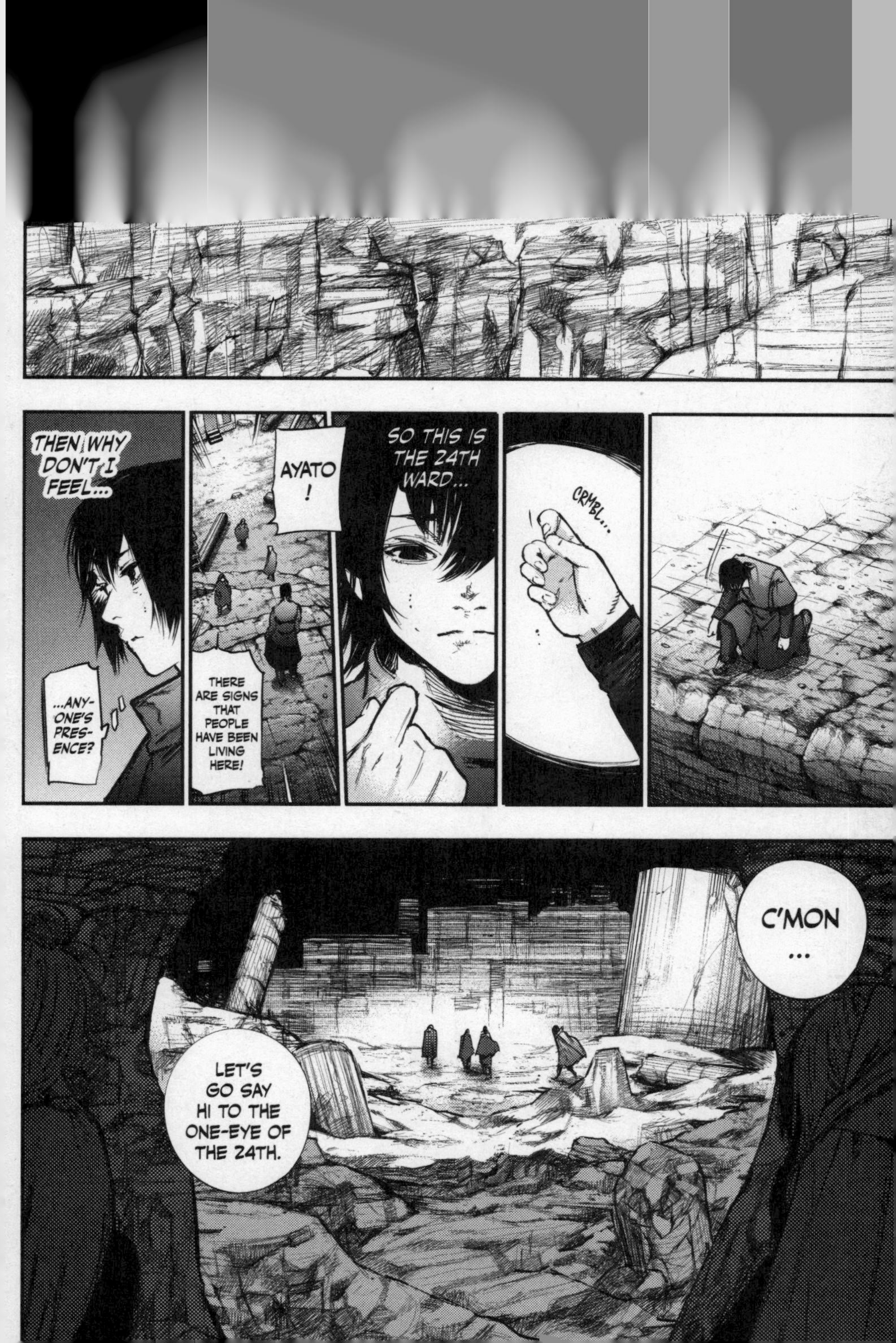
CRMBL...
SO THIS IS THE 24TH WARD...
AYATO!
THERE ARE SIGNS THAT PEOPLE HAVE BEEN LIVING HERE!
THEN WHY DON'T I FEEL...
...ANYONE'S PRESENCE?
C'MON...
LET'S GO SAY HI TO THE ONE-EYE OF THE 24TH.

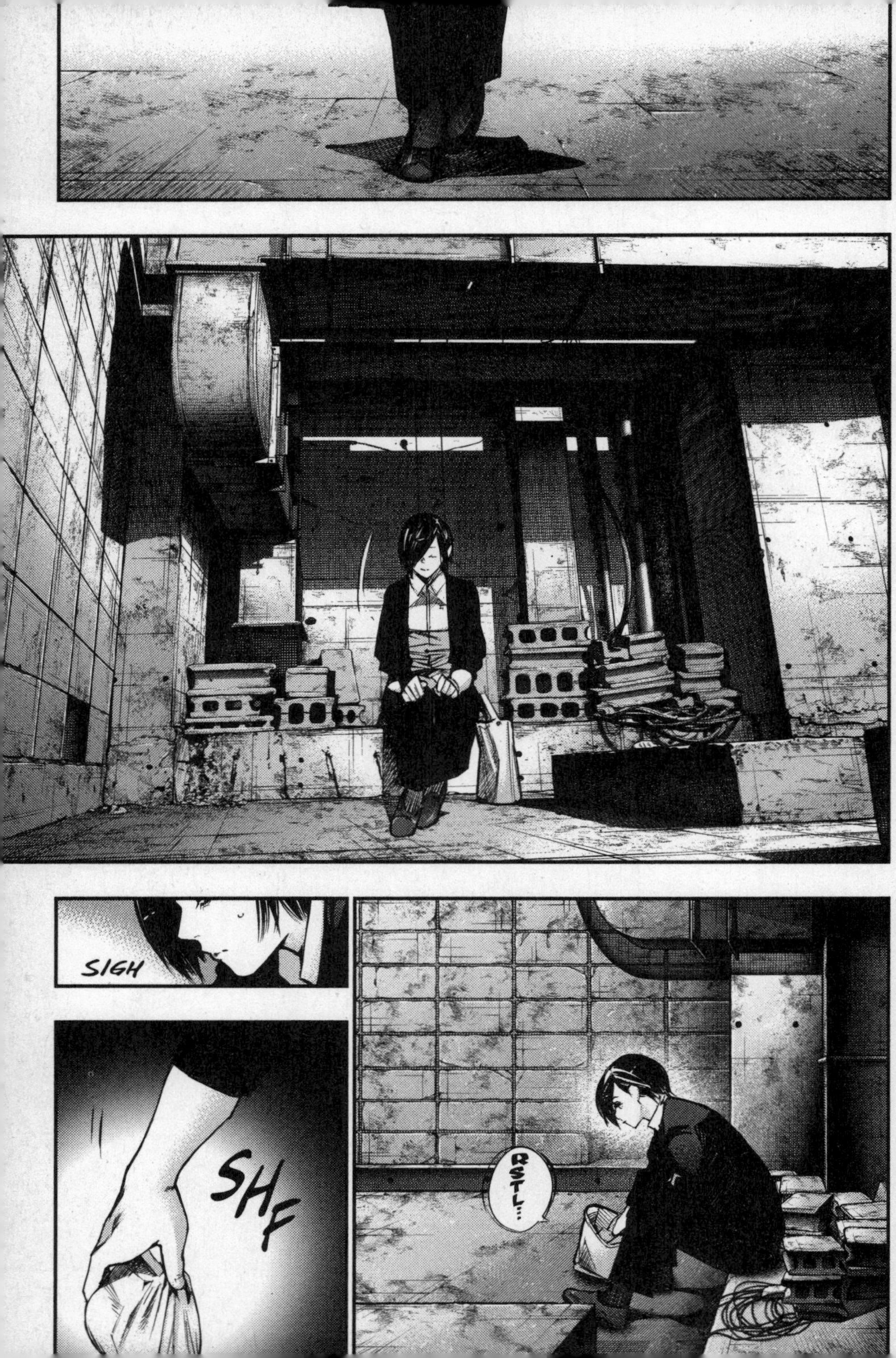
RSTL...
SIGH
SHF

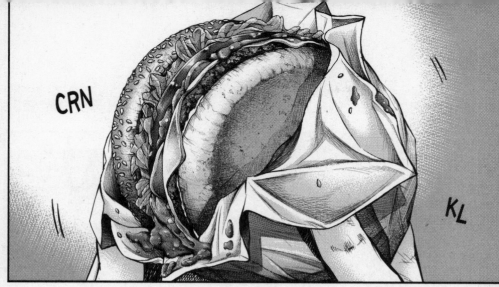

CRN

KL

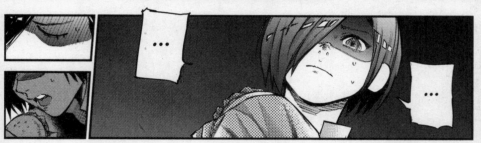

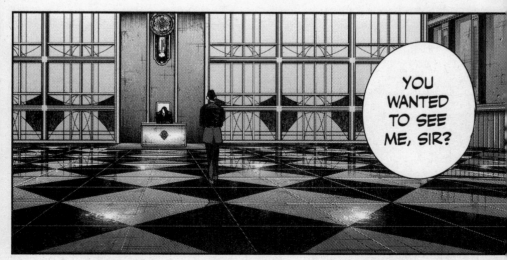

YOU WANTED TO SEE ME, SIR?

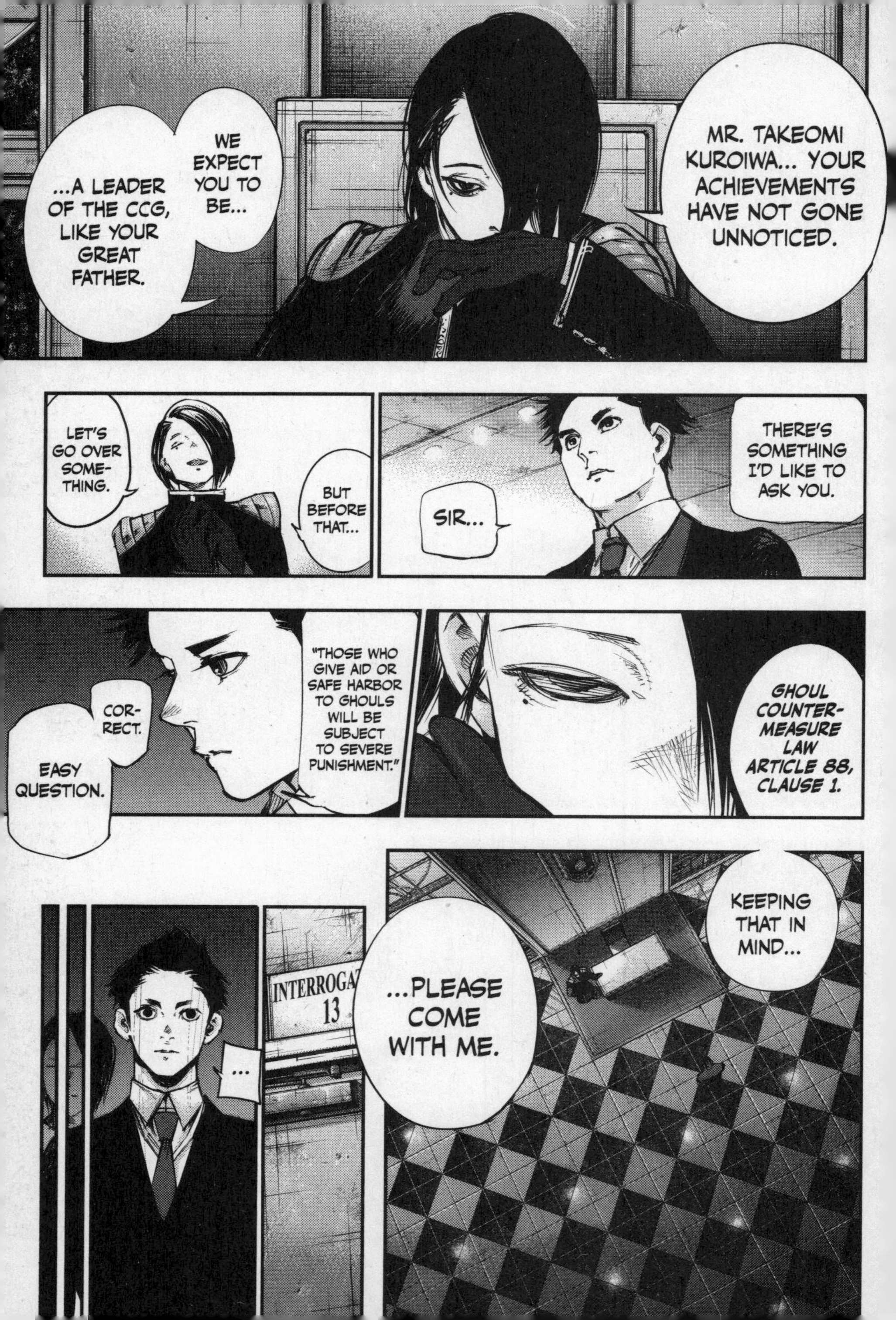
MR. TAKEOMI KUROIWA... YOUR ACHIEVEMENTS HAVE NOT GONE UNNOTICED.
WE EXPECT YOU TO BE...
...A LEADER OF THE CCG, LIKE YOUR GREAT FATHER.
THERE'S SOMETHING I'D LIKE TO ASK YOU.
SIR...
BUT BEFORE THAT...
LET'S GO OVER SOMETHING.
GHOUL COUNTERMEASURE LAW ARTICLE 88, CLAUSE 1.
"THOSE WHO GIVE AID OR SAFE HARBOR TO GHOULS WILL BE SUBJECT TO SEVERE PUNISHMENT."
CORRECT.
EASY QUESTION.
KEEPING THAT IN MIND...
...PLEASE COME WITH ME.
INTERROGA
13
...

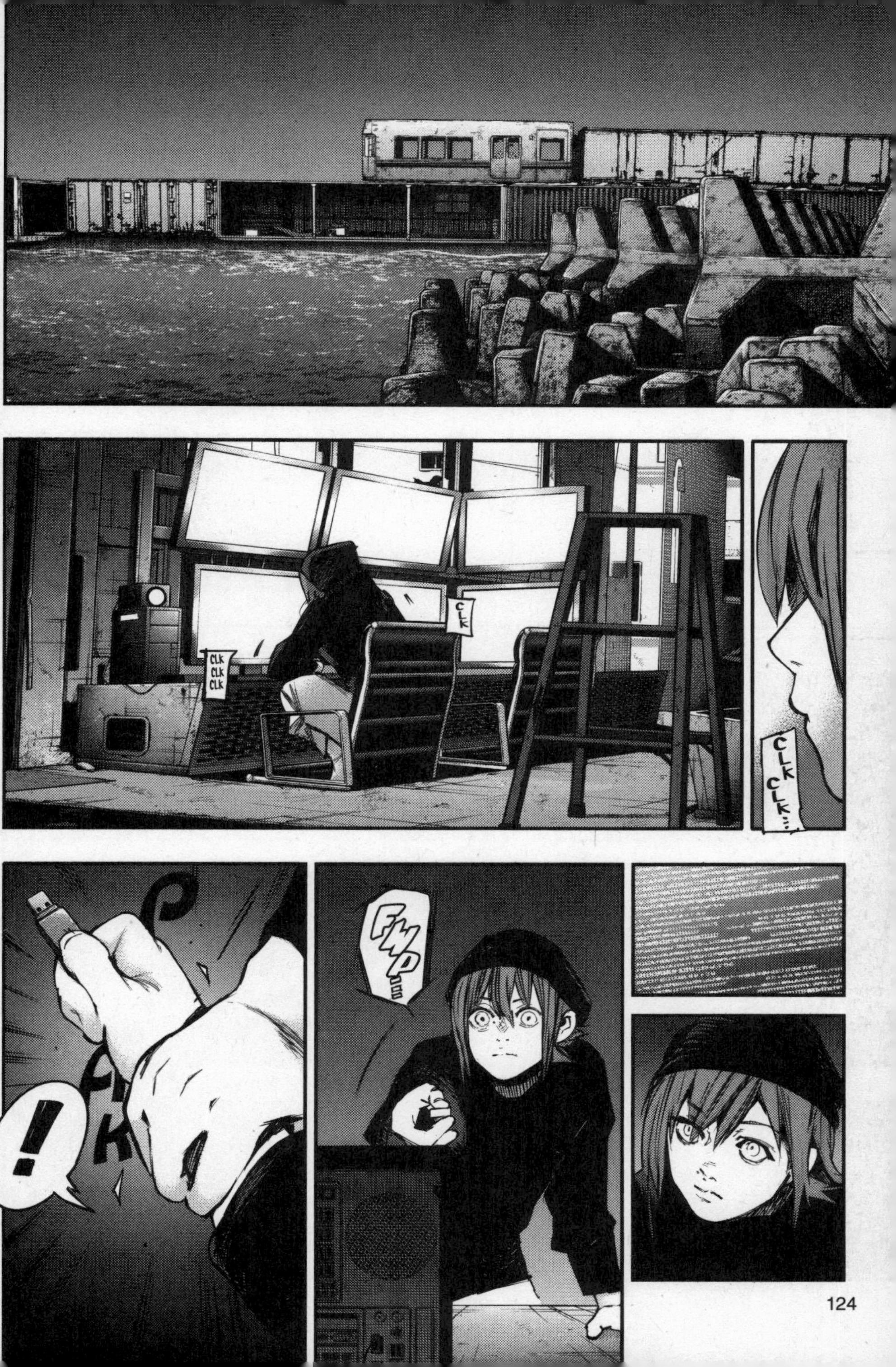
CLK CLK...
CLK
CLK CLK CLK
FWP!!
!

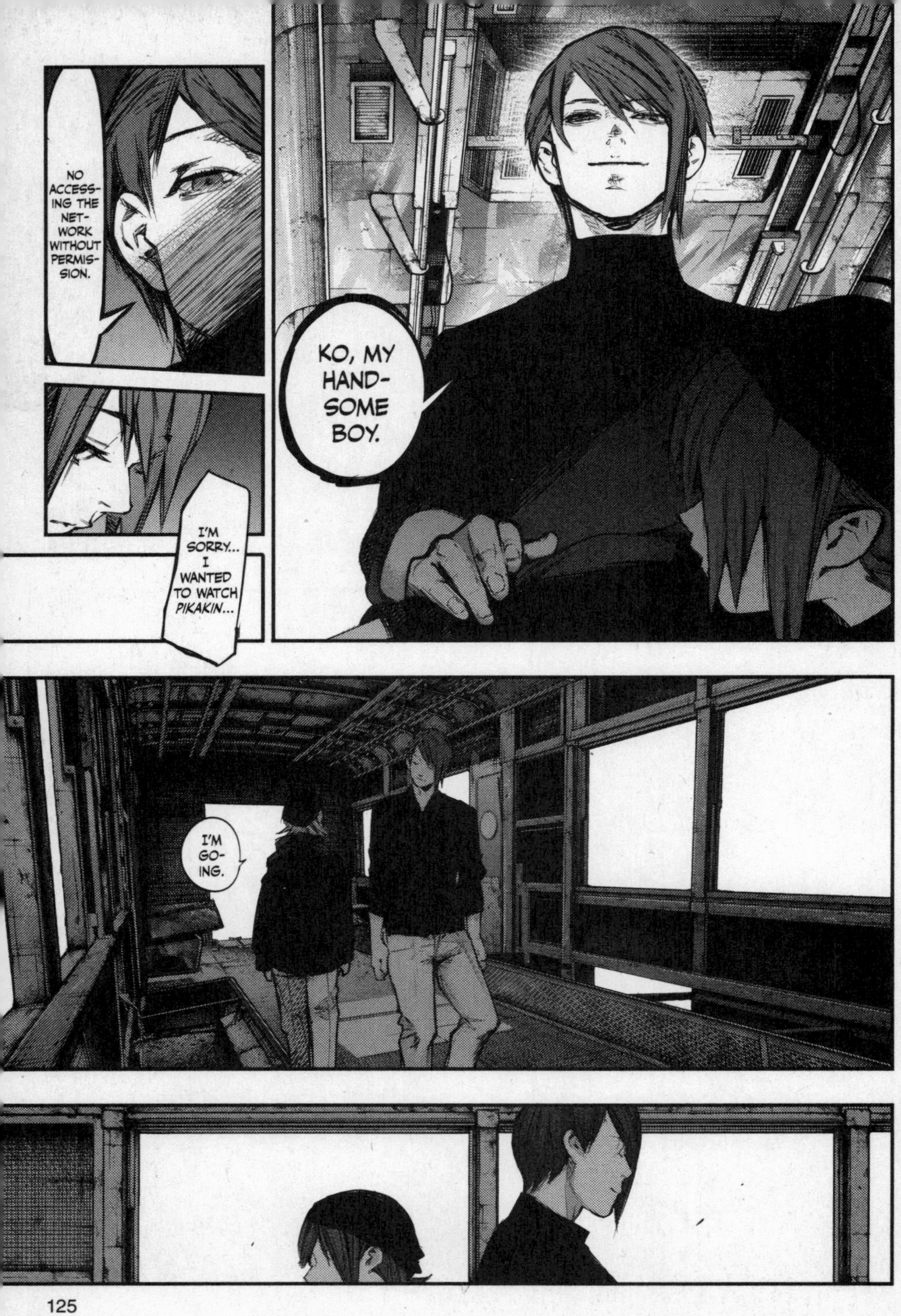
KO, MY HAND-SOME BOY.
NO ACCESS-ING THE NET-WORK WITHOUT PERMIS-SION.
I'M SORRY... I WANTED TO WATCH PIKAKIN...
I'M GO-ING.

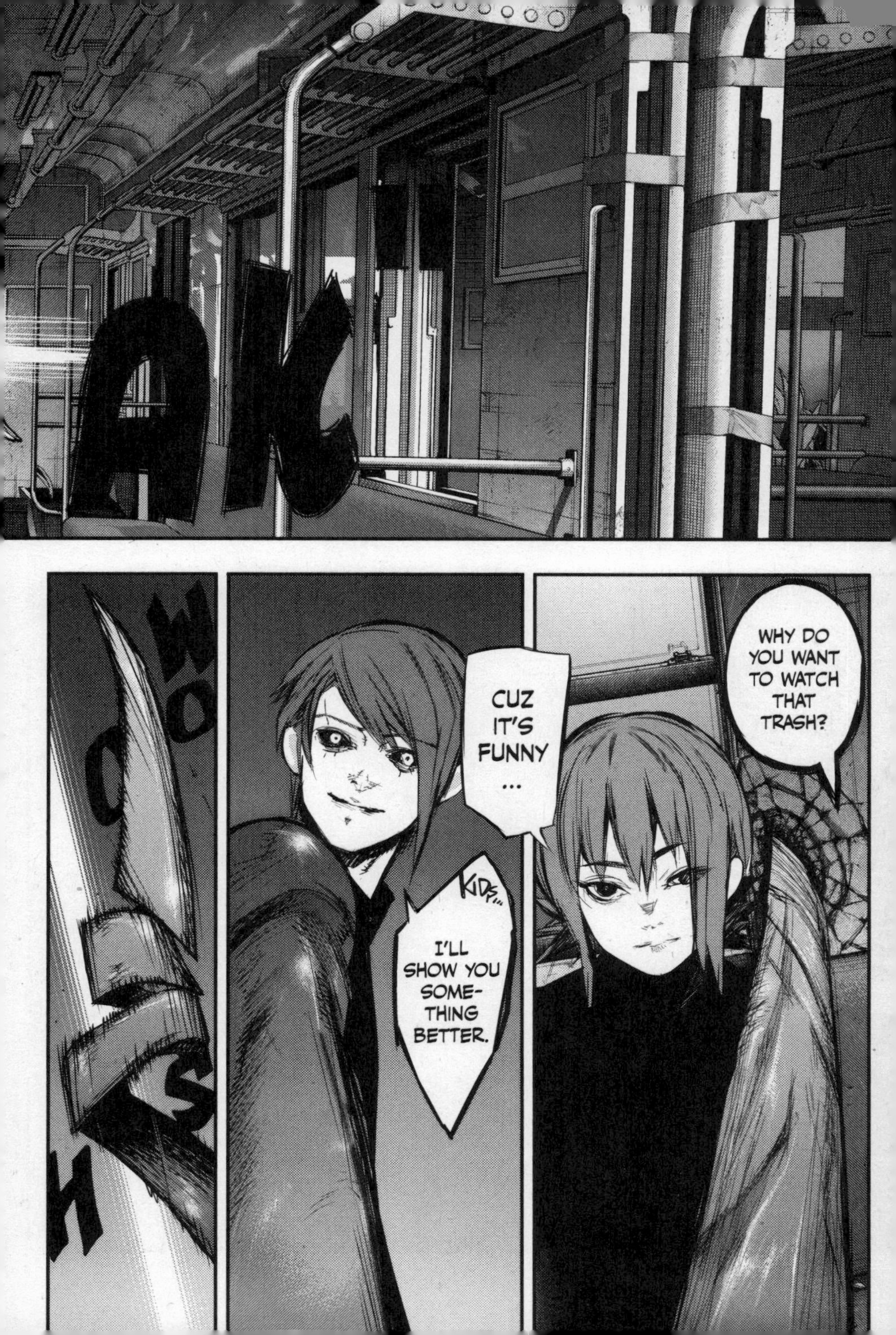
WHY DO YOU WANT TO WATCH THAT TRASH?
CUZ IT'S FUNNY ...
KIDS...
I'LL SHOW YOU SOME-THING BETTER.

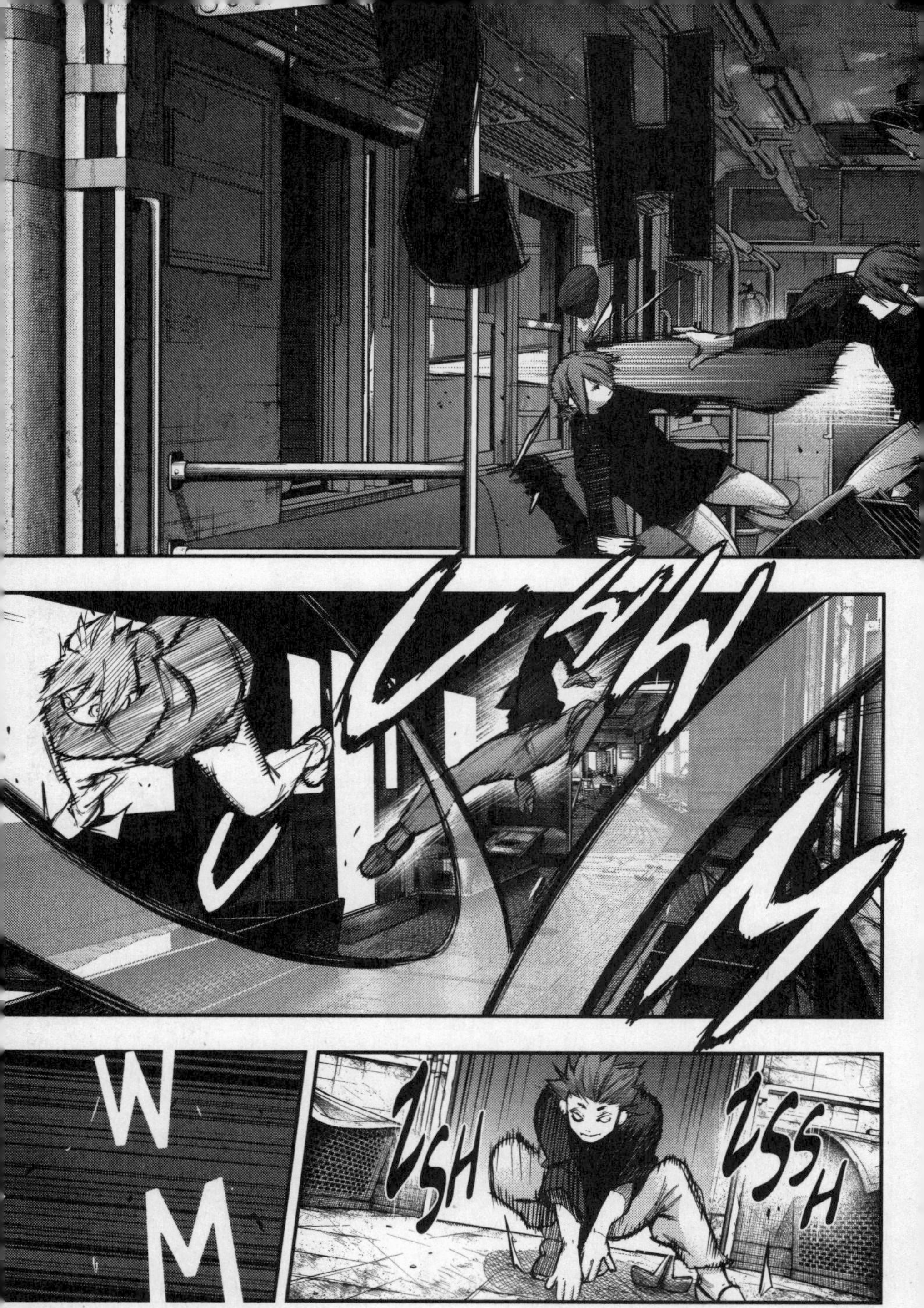
WSH
M
ZSSH
ZSH
W
M

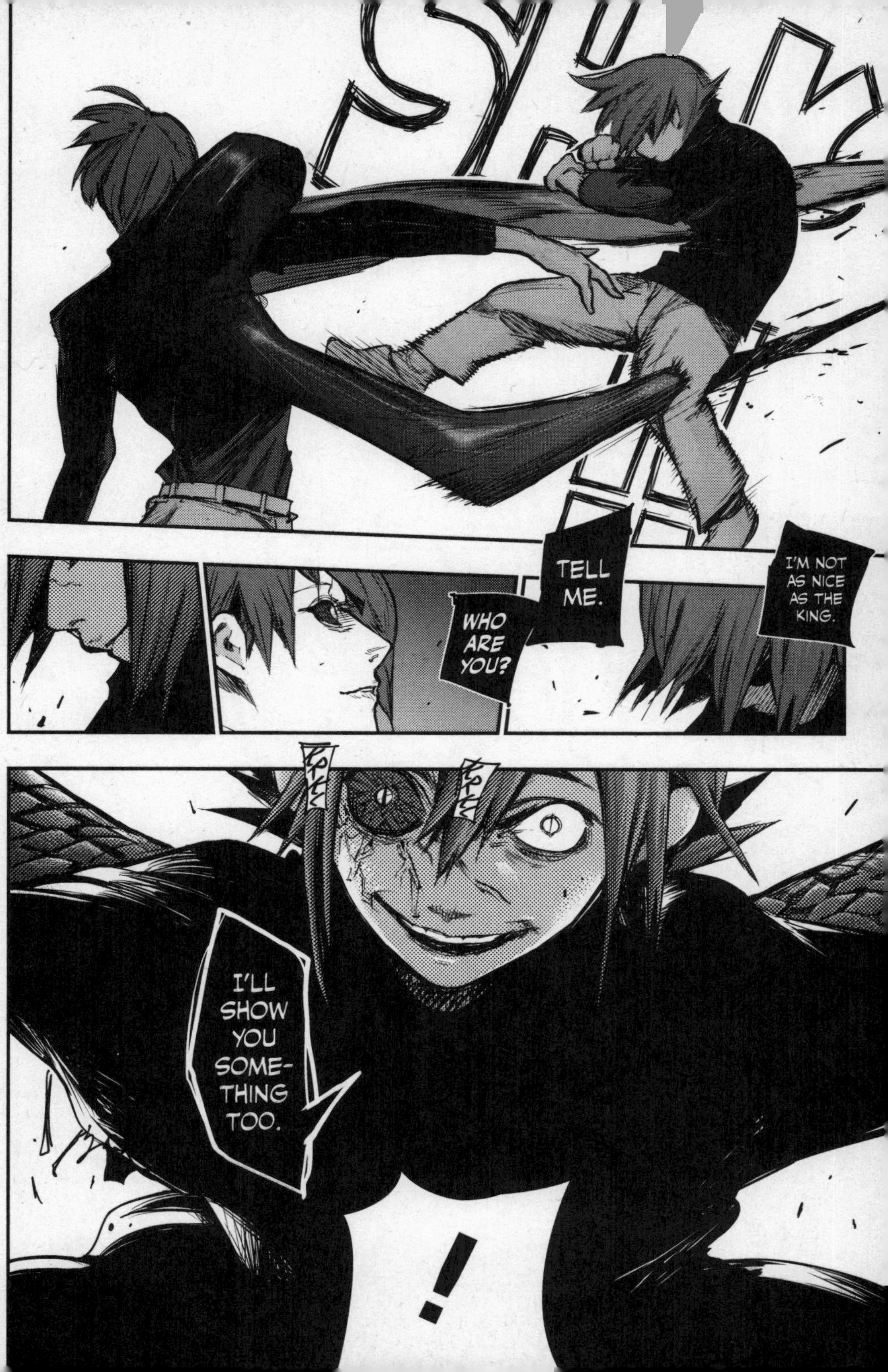
I'M NOT AS NICE AS THE KING.
TELL ME.
WHO ARE YOU?
I'LL SHOW YOU SOME-THING TOO.
!

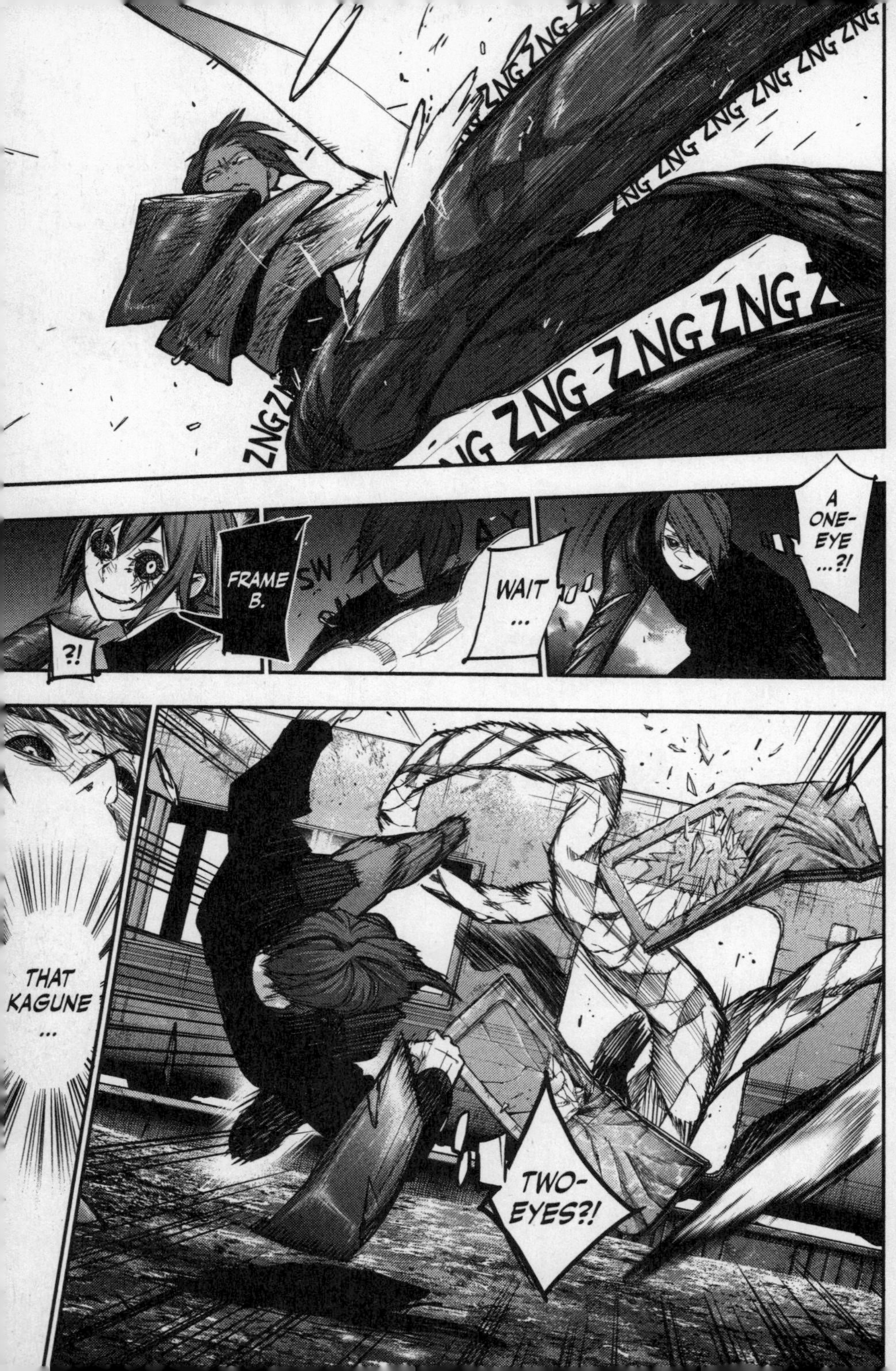
ZNG ZNG ZNG ZNG
ZNG ZNG ZNG ZNG ZNG
ZNG ZNG ZNG ZNG ZNG ZNG
ZNG ZNG
A ONE-EYE ...?!
WAIT ...
FRAME B.
?!
TWO-EYES?!
THAT KAGUNE ...

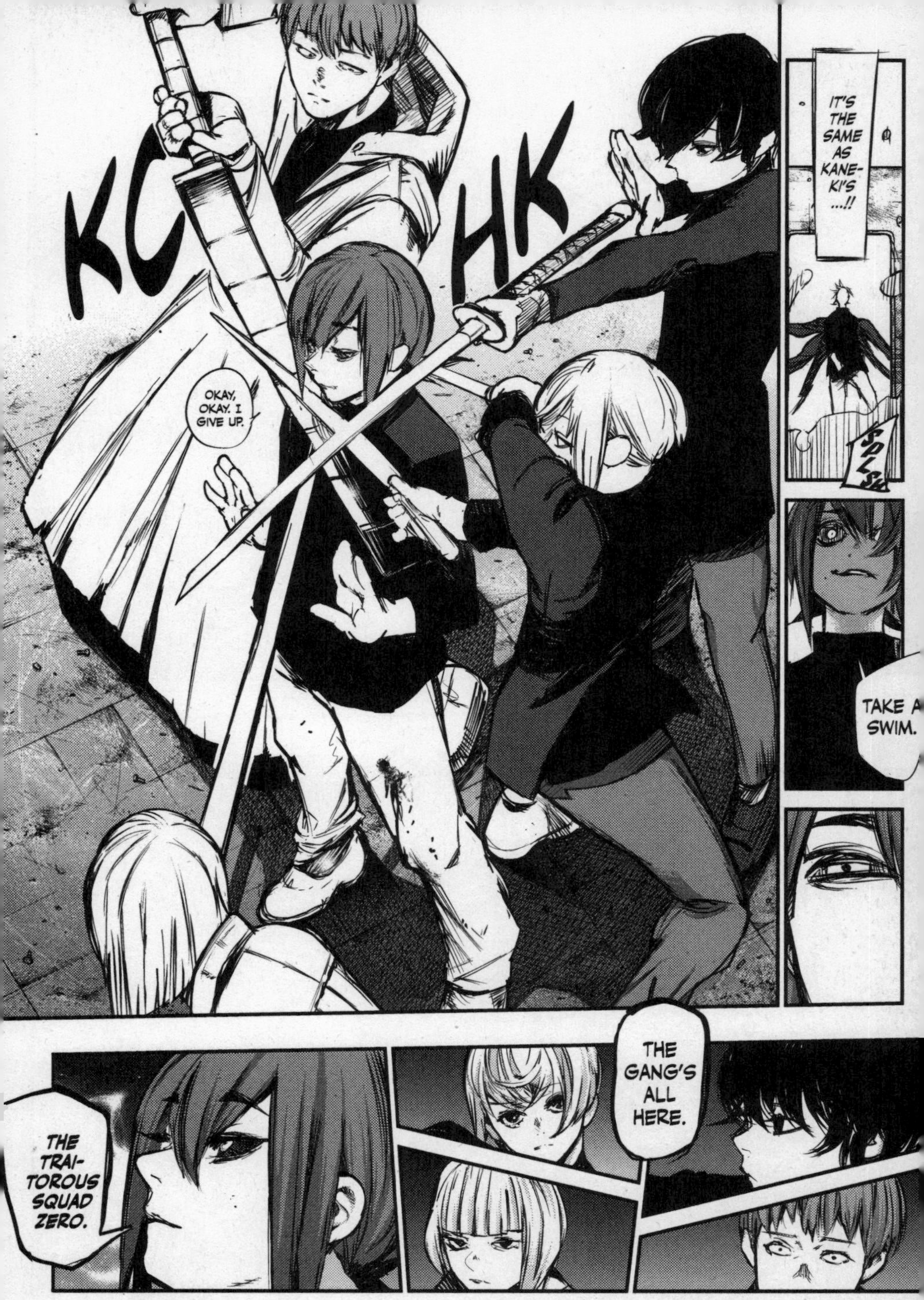
IT'S THE SAME AS KANE-KI'S ...!!
SPLSH
TAKE A SWIM.
KCHK
OKAY, OKAY. I GIVE UP.
THE GANG'S ALL HERE.
THE TRAI-TOROUS SQUAD ZERO.

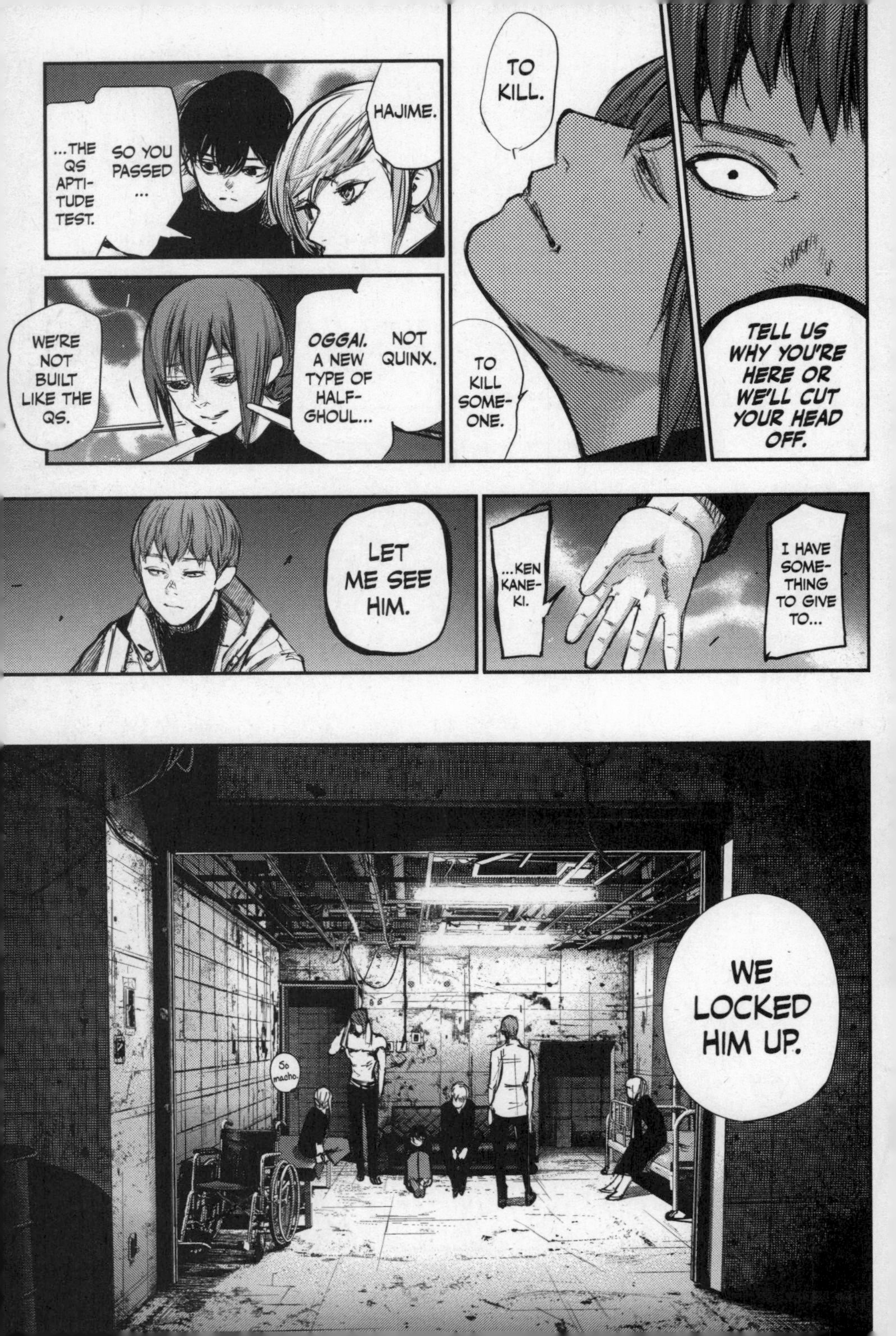
TELL US WHY YOU'RE HERE OR WE'LL CUT YOUR HEAD OFF.
TO KILL.
TO KILL SOME-ONE.
HAJIME.
SO YOU PASSED ...
...THE QS APTI-TUDE TEST.
NOT QUINX.
OGGAI. A NEW TYPE OF HALF-GHOUL...
WE'RE NOT BUILT LIKE THE QS.
I HAVE SOME-THING TO GIVE TO...
...KEN KANE-KI.
LET ME SEE HIM.
WE LOCKED HIM UP.
So macho.

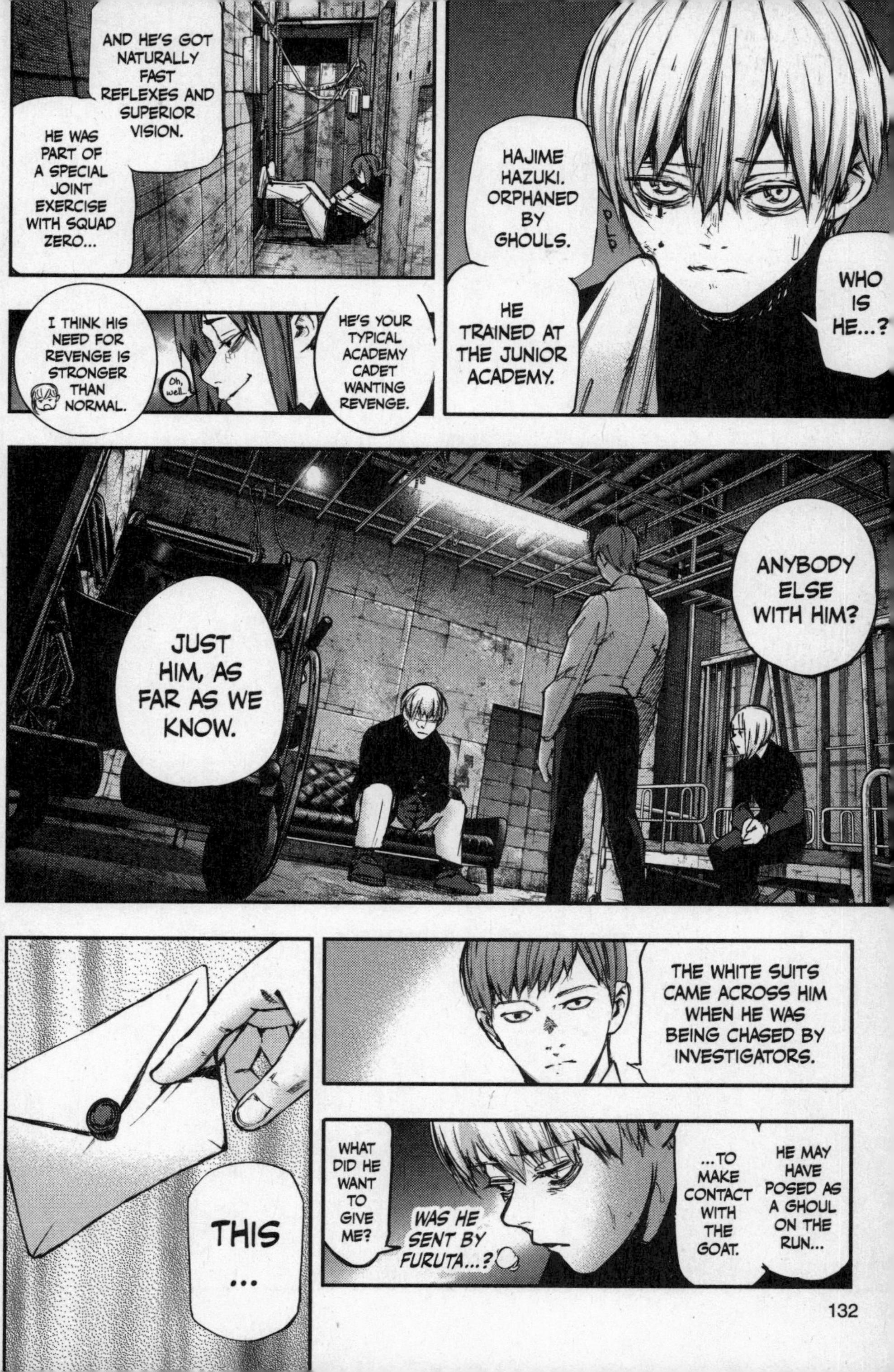
WHO IS HE...?
HAJIME HAZUKI. ORPHANED BY GHOULS.
HE TRAINED AT THE JUNIOR ACADEMY.
AND HE'S GOT NATURALLY FAST REFLEXES AND SUPERIOR VISION.
HE WAS PART OF A SPECIAL JOINT EXERCISE WITH SQUAD ZERO...
HE'S YOUR TYPICAL ACADEMY CADET WANTING REVENGE.
Oh, well...
I THINK HIS NEED FOR REVENGE IS STRONGER THAN NORMAL.
ANYBODY ELSE WITH HIM?
JUST HIM, AS FAR AS WE KNOW.
THE WHITE SUITS CAME ACROSS HIM WHEN HE WAS BEING CHASED BY INVESTIGATORS.
HE MAY HAVE POSED AS A GHOUL ON THE RUN...
...TO MAKE CONTACT WITH THE GOAT.
WAS HE SENT BY FURUTA...?
WHAT DID HE WANT TO GIVE ME?
THIS ...

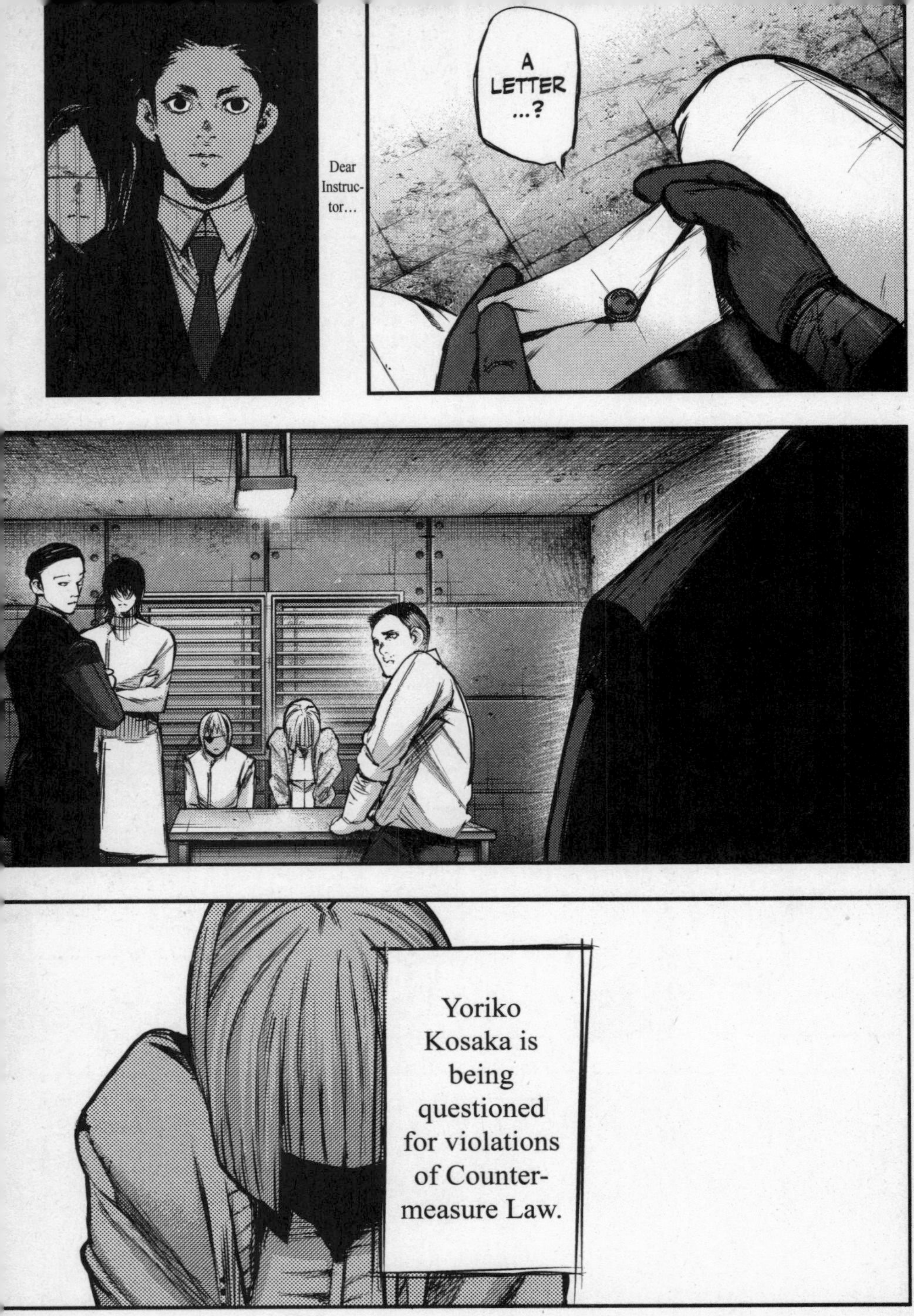
A LETTER ...?
Dear Instructor...
Yoriko Kosaka is being questioned for violations of Countermeasure Law.

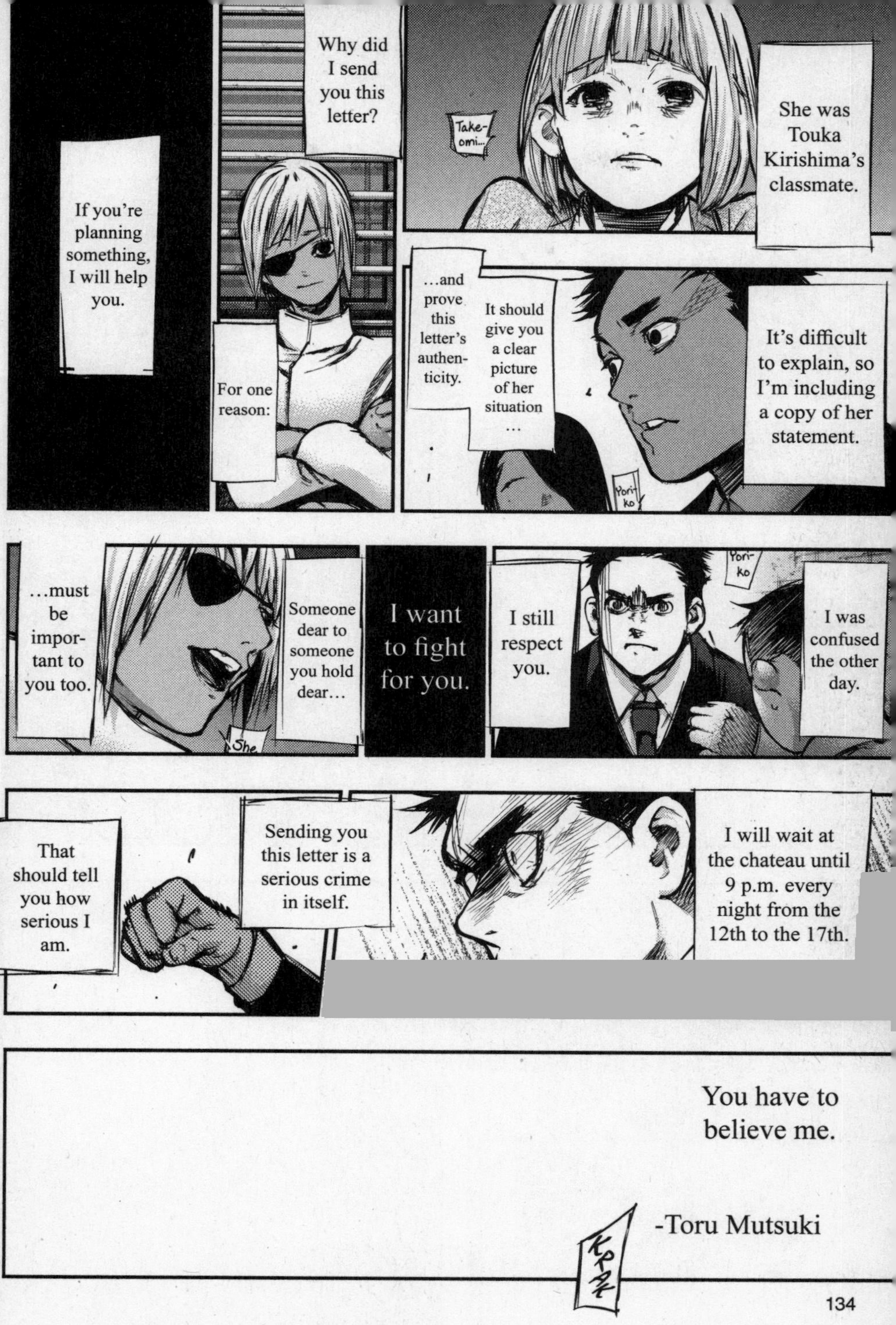
She was Touka Kirishima's classmate.
Take-omi...
It's difficult to explain, so I'm including a copy of her statement.
It should give you a clear picture of her situation …
…and prove this letter's authenticity.
Yori-ko
Why did I send you this letter?
For one reason:
If you're planning something, I will help you.
I was confused the other day.
Yori-ko
I still respect you.
I want to fight for you.
Someone dear to someone you hold dear…
…must be important to you too.
She
I will wait at the chateau until 9 p.m. every night from the 12th to the 17th.
Sending you this letter is a serious crime in itself.
That should tell you how serious I am.
You have to believe me.
-Toru Mutsuki
KRAK

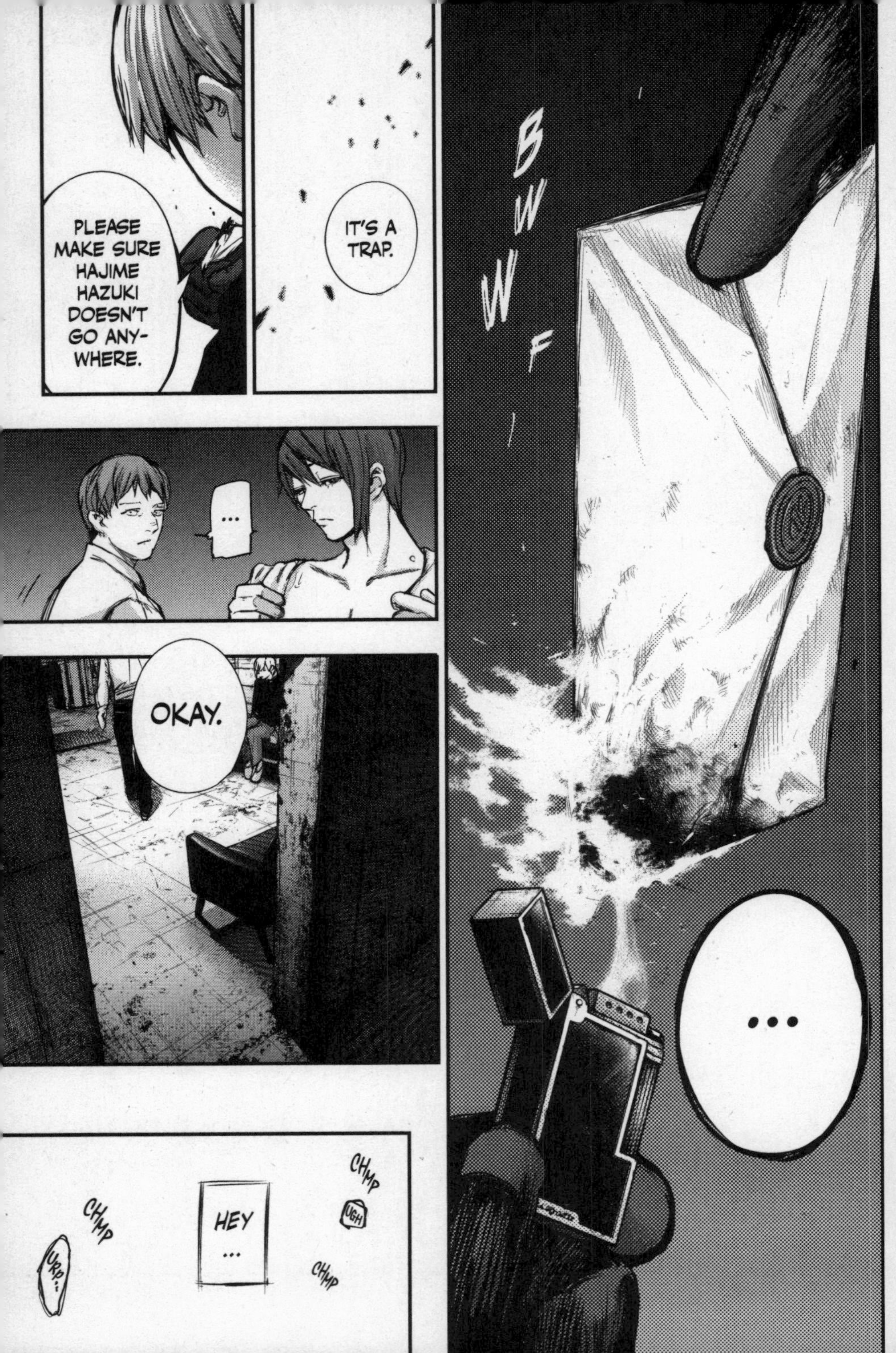
BWWF
...
IT'S A TRAP.
PLEASE MAKE SURE HAJIME HAZUKI DOESN'T GO ANYWHERE.
...
OKAY.
CHMP
UGH
HEY ...
CHMP
CHMP
URP...

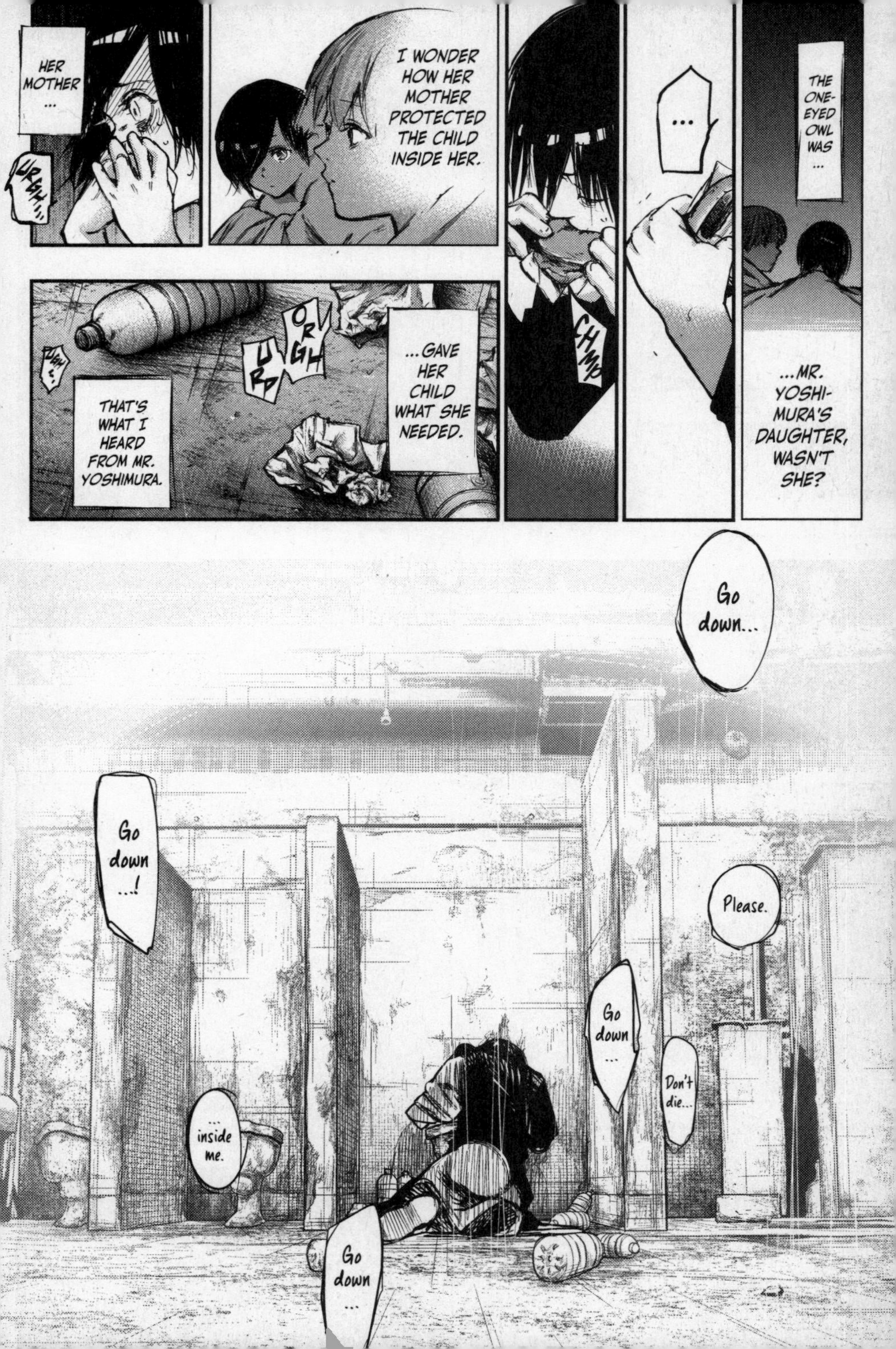
THE ONE-EYED OWL WAS ...
...MR. YOSHIMURA'S DAUGHTER, WASN'T SHE?
...
CHMP
I WONDER HOW HER MOTHER PROTECTED THE CHILD INSIDE HER.
HER MOTHER ...
URGH...
...GAVE HER CHILD WHAT SHE NEEDED.
ORGH
URP
THAT'S WHAT I HEARD FROM MR. YOSHIMURA.
Go down...
Please.
Don't die...
Go down ...
Go down ...!
... inside me.
Go down ...

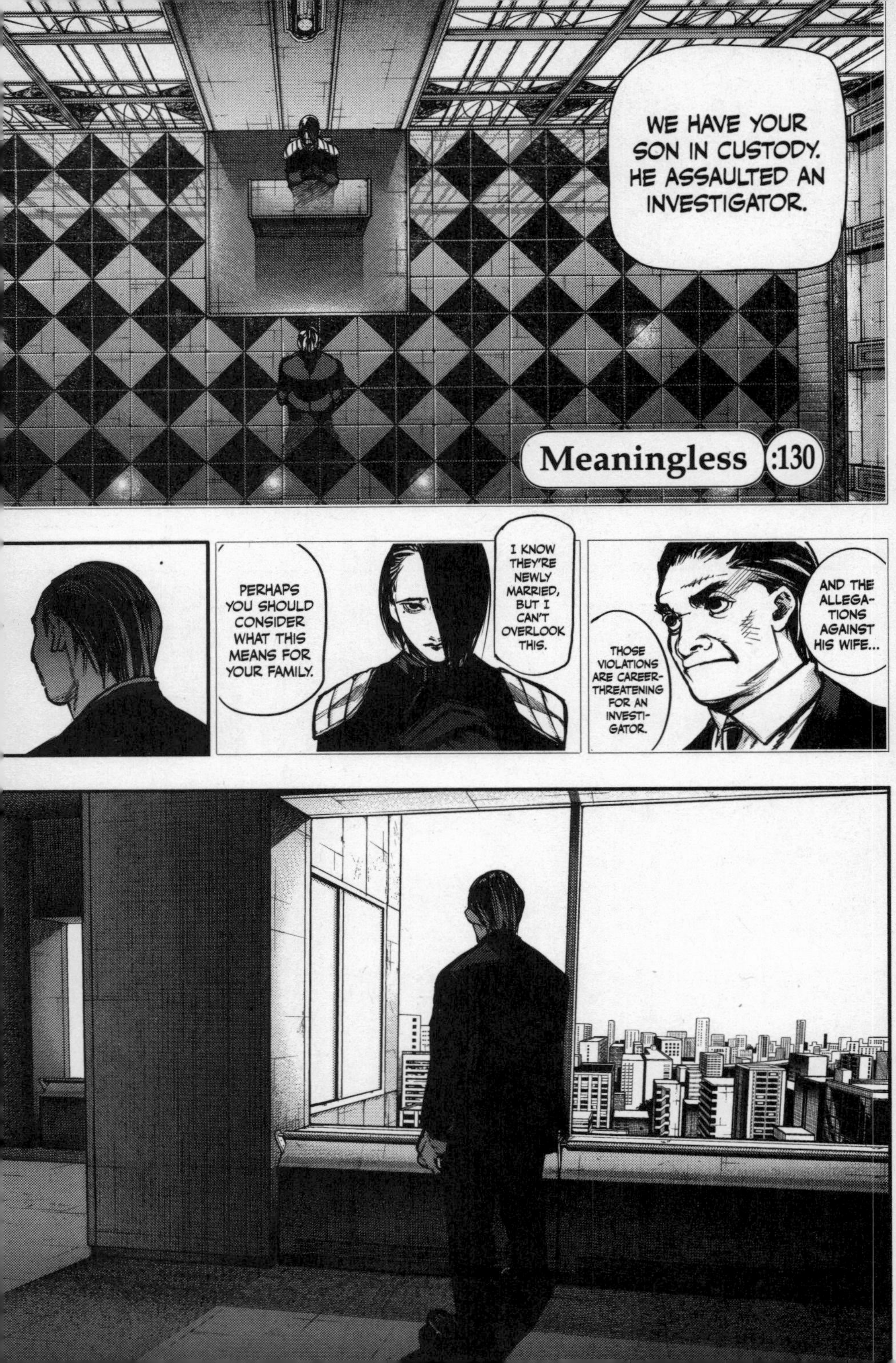
WE HAVE YOUR SON IN CUSTODY. HE ASSAULTED AN INVESTIGATOR.
Meaningless :130
AND THE ALLEGATIONS AGAINST HIS WIFE...
THOSE VIOLATIONS ARE CAREER-THREATENING FOR AN INVESTIGATOR.
I KNOW THEY'RE NEWLY MARRIED, BUT I CAN'T OVERLOOK THIS.
PERHAPS YOU SHOULD CONSIDER WHAT THIS MEANS FOR YOUR FAMILY.

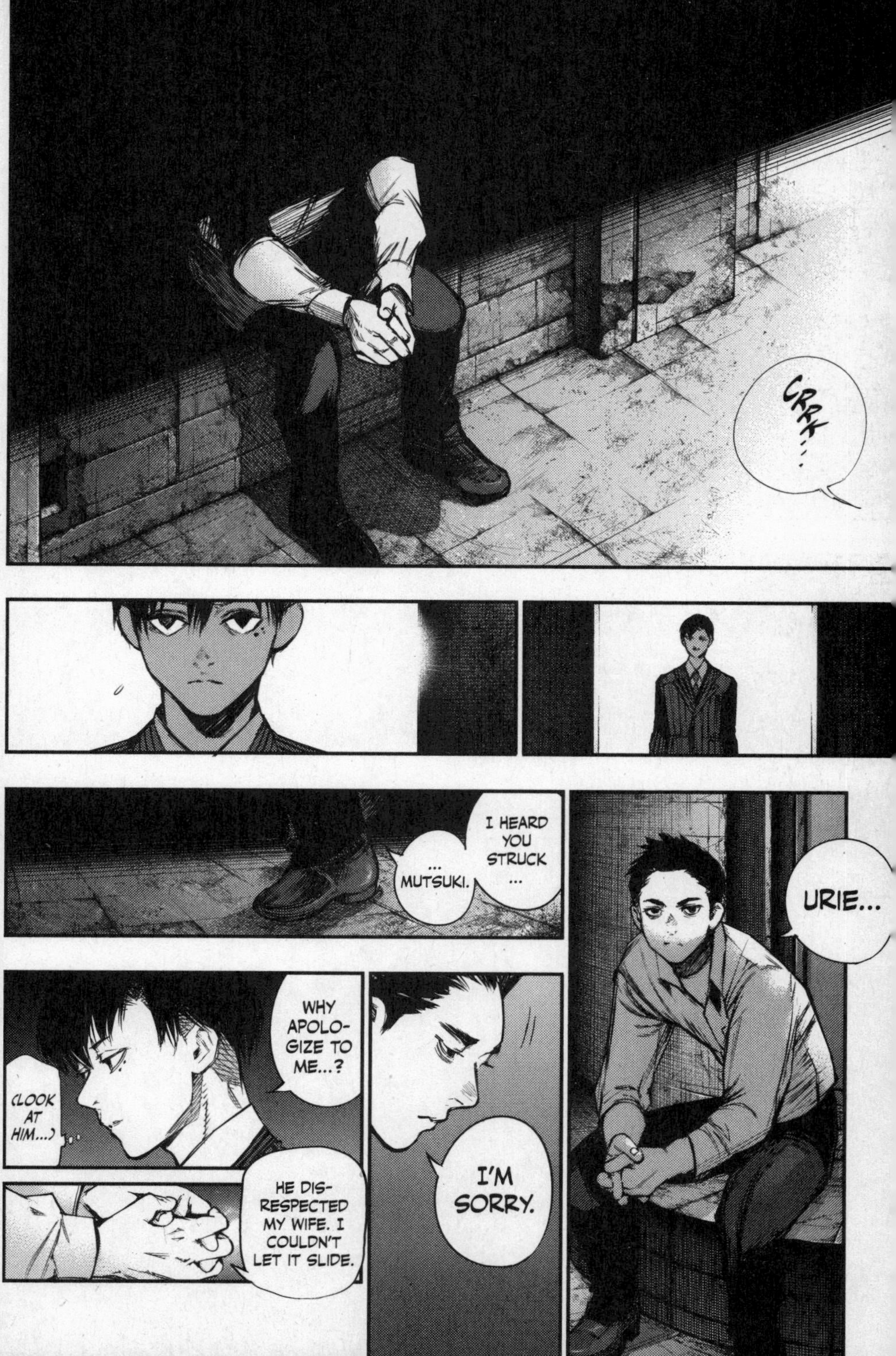
CRRK...
URIE...
I HEARD YOU STRUCK ...
... MUTSUKI.
I'M SORRY.
WHY APOLOGIZE TO ME...?
(LOOK AT HIM...)
HE DISRESPECTED MY WIFE. I COULDN'T LET IT SLIDE.

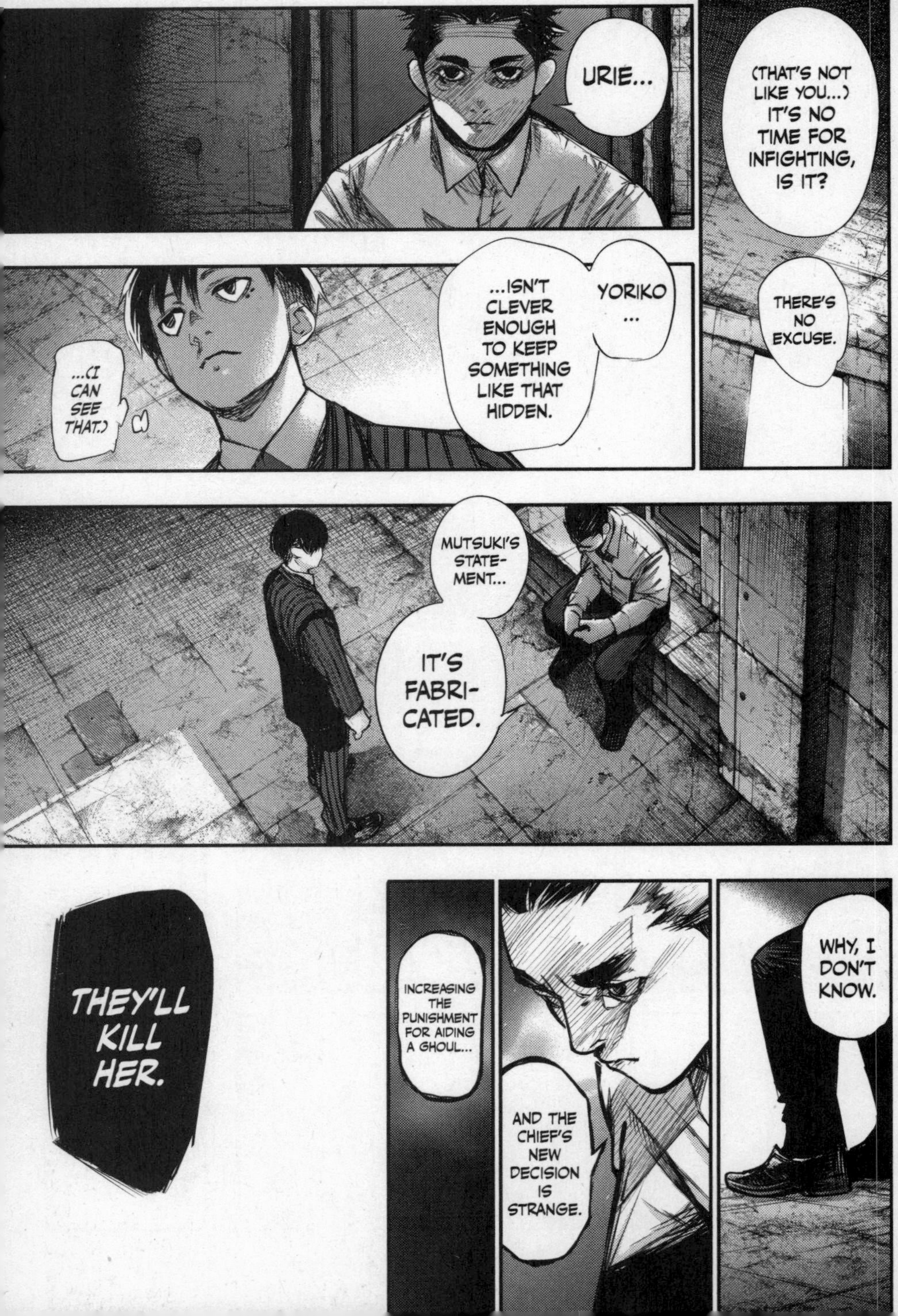
(THAT'S NOT LIKE YOU...) IT'S NO TIME FOR INFIGHTING, IS IT?
THERE'S NO EXCUSE.
URIE...
YORIKO ...
...ISN'T CLEVER ENOUGH TO KEEP SOMETHING LIKE THAT HIDDEN.
...(I CAN SEE THAT.)
MUTSUKI'S STATEMENT...
IT'S FABRICATED.
WHY, I DON'T KNOW.
INCREASING THE PUNISHMENT FOR AIDING A GHOUL...
AND THE CHIEF'S NEW DECISION IS STRANGE.
THEY'LL KILL HER.

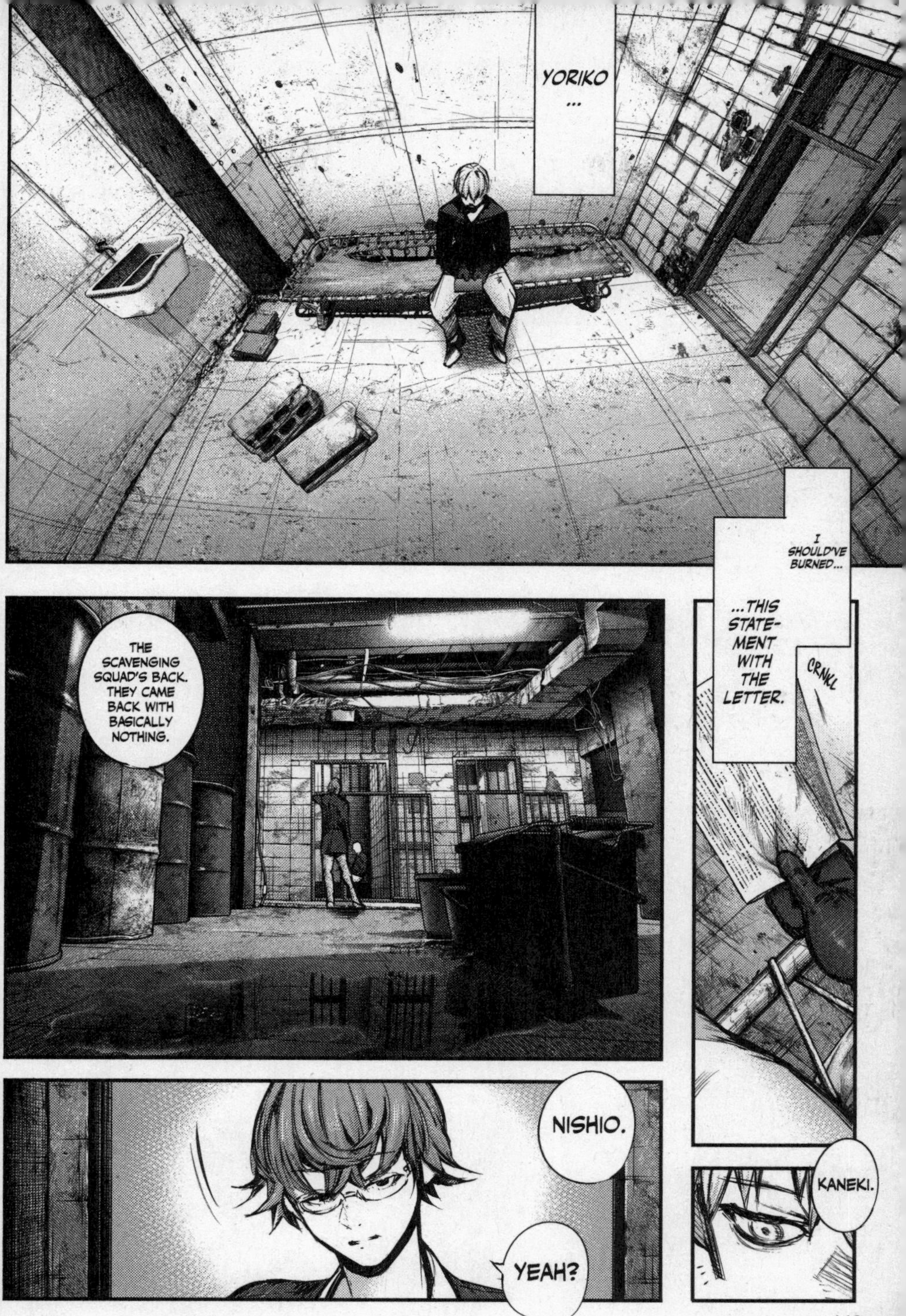
YORIKO
...
I SHOULD'VE BURNED...
...THIS STATEMENT WITH THE LETTER.
CRNKL
THE SCAVENGING SQUAD'S BACK. THEY CAME BACK WITH BASICALLY NOTHING.
KANEKI.
NISHIO.
YEAH?

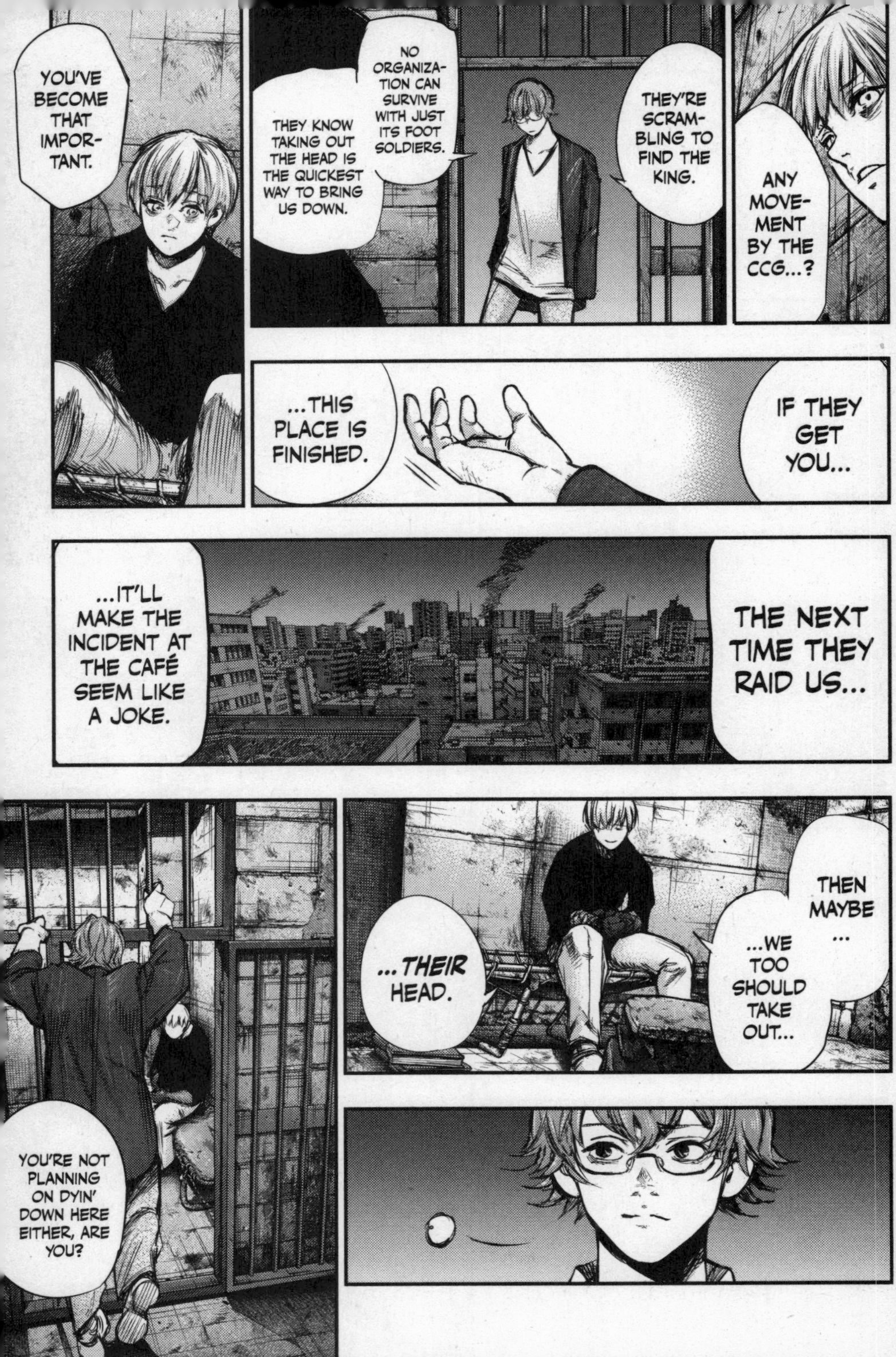
ANY MOVEMENT BY THE CCG...?
THEY'RE SCRAMBLING TO FIND THE KING.
NO ORGANIZATION CAN SURVIVE WITH JUST ITS FOOT SOLDIERS.
THEY KNOW TAKING OUT THE HEAD IS THE QUICKEST WAY TO BRING US DOWN.
IF THEY GET YOU...
...THIS PLACE IS FINISHED.
YOU'VE BECOME THAT IMPORTANT.
THE NEXT TIME THEY RAID US...
...IT'LL MAKE THE INCIDENT AT THE CAFÉ SEEM LIKE A JOKE.
THEN MAYBE...
...WE TOO SHOULD TAKE OUT...
...THEIR HEAD.
YOU'RE NOT PLANNING ON DYIN' DOWN HERE EITHER, ARE YOU?

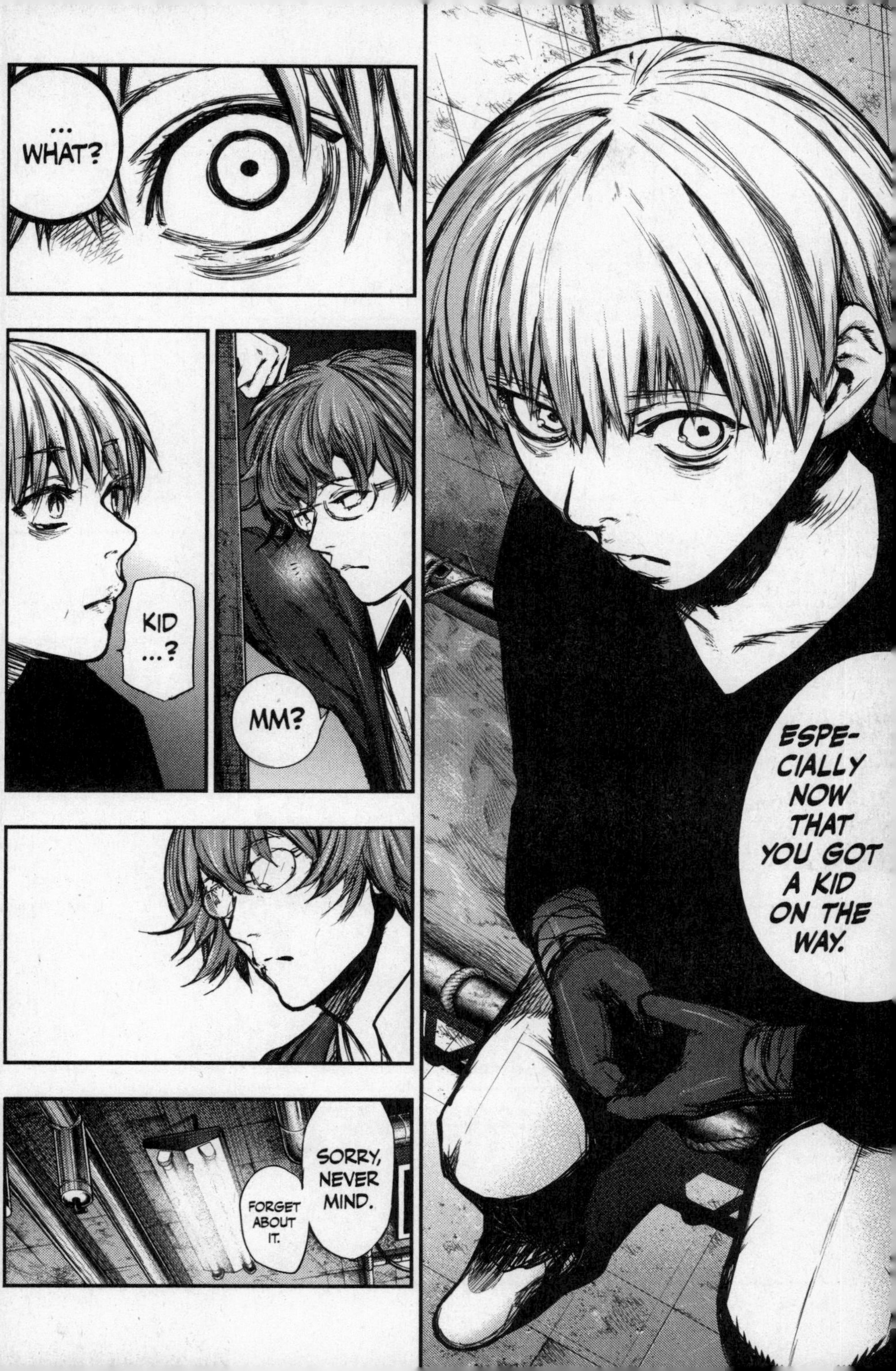
ESPE-CIALLY NOW THAT YOU GOT A KID ON THE WAY.
... WHAT?
MM?
KID ...?
SORRY, NEVER MIND.
FORGET ABOUT IT.

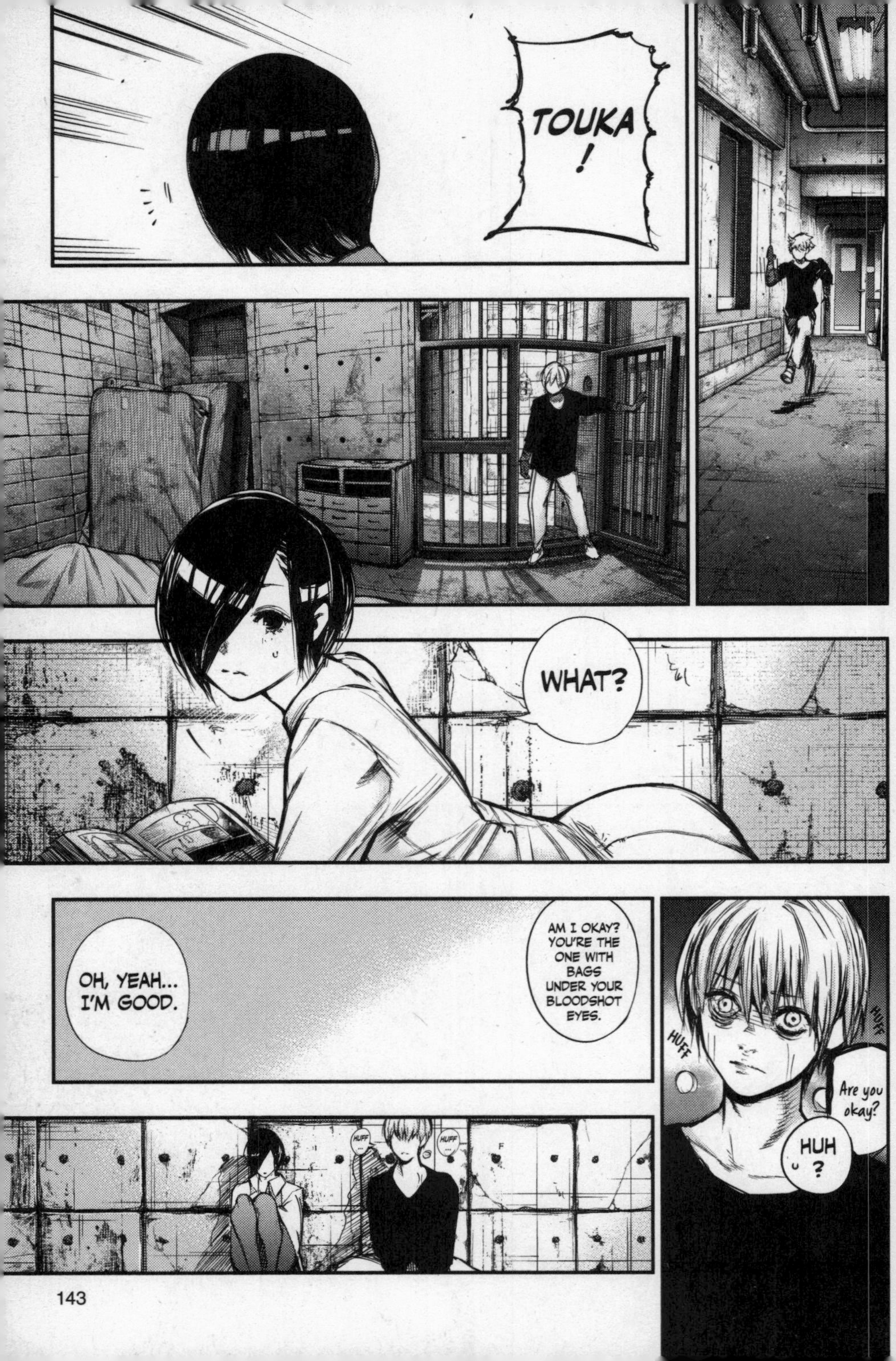
TOUKA!
WHAT?
HUFF
HUFF
Are you okay?
HUH?
AM I OKAY? YOU'RE THE ONE WITH BAGS UNDER YOUR BLOODSHOT EYES.
OH, YEAH... I'M GOOD.
HUFF...
HUFF...

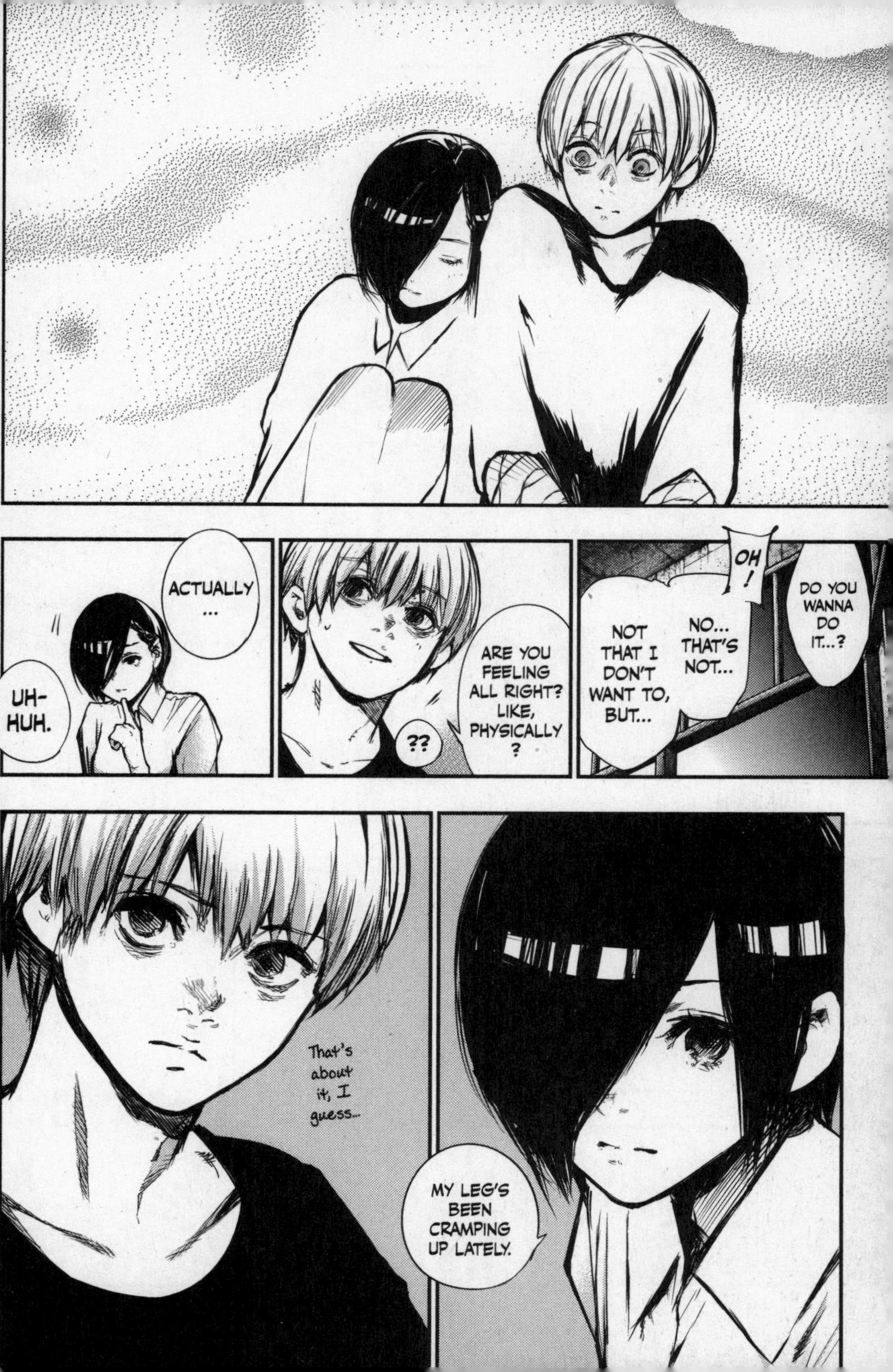
DO YOU WANNA DO IT...?
OH!
NO... THAT'S NOT...
NOT THAT I DON'T WANT TO, BUT...
ARE YOU FEELING ALL RIGHT? LIKE, PHYSICALLY?
??
ACTUALLY...
UH-HUH.
MY LEG'S BEEN CRAMPING UP LATELY.
That's about it, I guess...

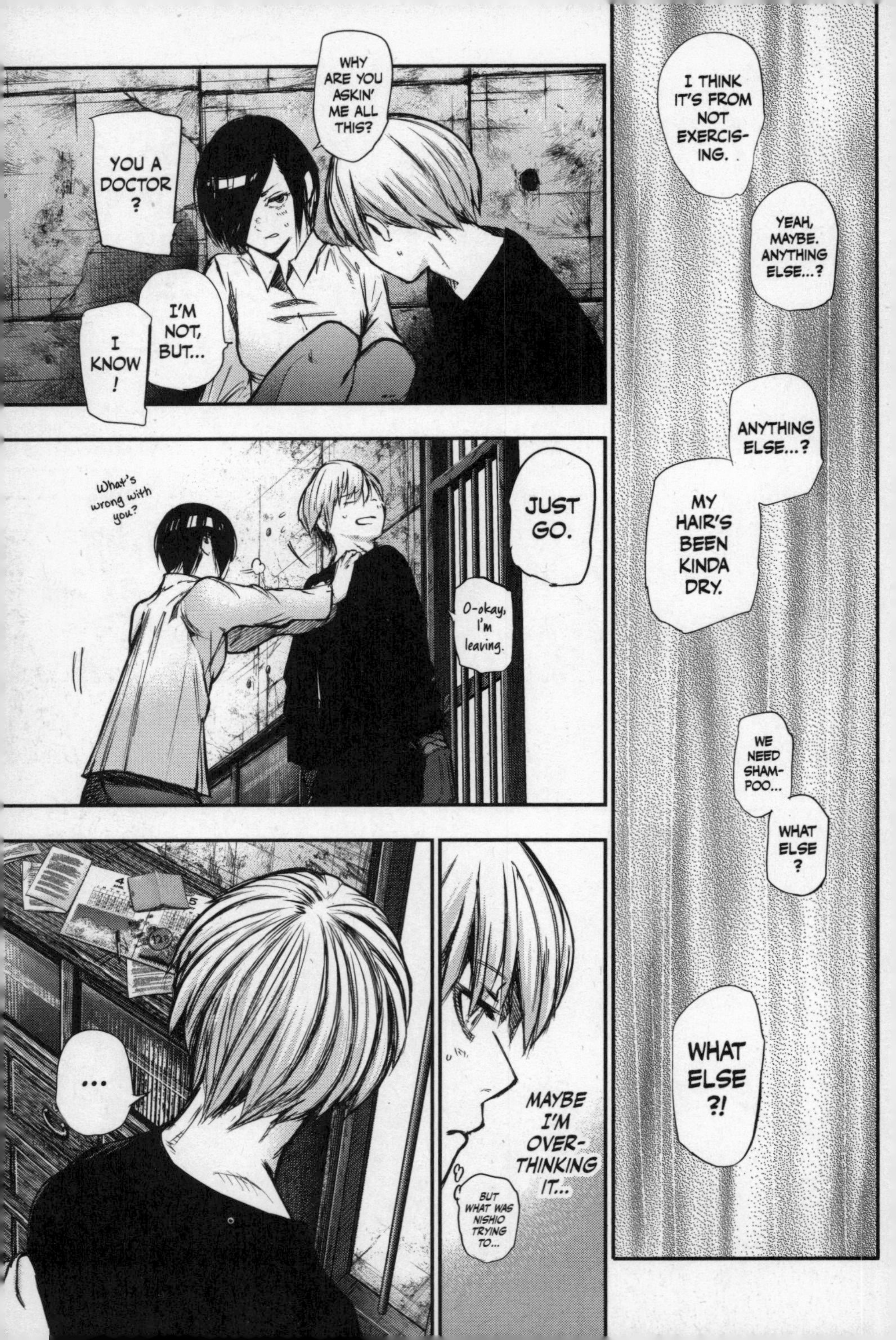
I THINK IT'S FROM NOT EXERCIS-ING.
YEAH, MAYBE. ANYTHING ELSE...?
ANYTHING ELSE...?
MY HAIR'S BEEN KINDA DRY.
WE NEED SHAM-POO...
WHAT ELSE?
WHAT ELSE?!
WHY ARE YOU ASKIN' ME ALL THIS?
YOU A DOCTOR?
I'M NOT, BUT...
I KNOW!
JUST GO.
O-okay, I'm leaving.
What's wrong with you?
MAYBE I'M OVER-THINKING IT...
BUT WHAT WAS NISHIO TRYING TO...
...

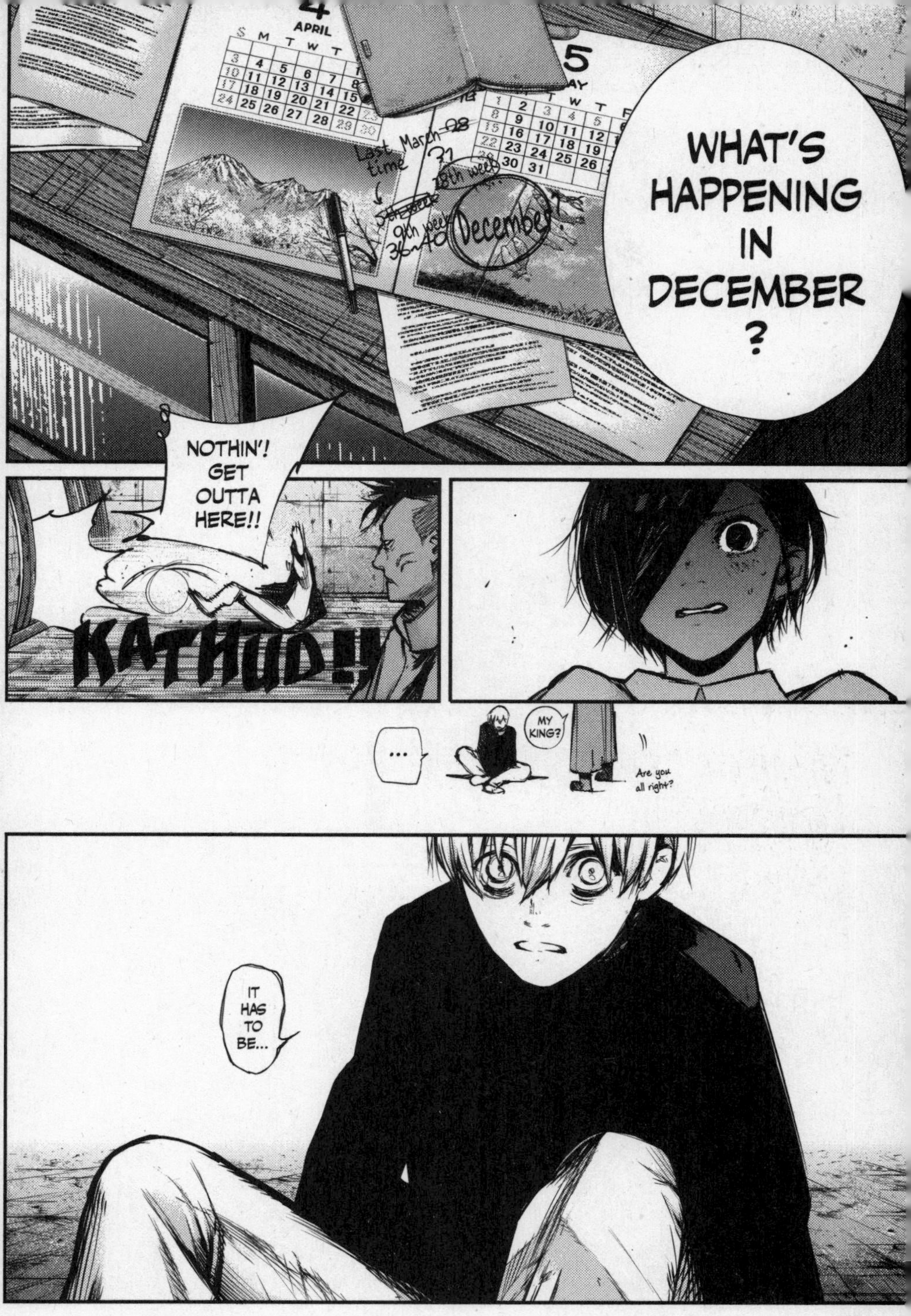
WHAT'S HAPPENING IN DECEMBER?
NOTHIN'! GET OUTTA HERE!!
KATHUD!!
Are you all right?
MY KING?
...
IT HAS TO BE...

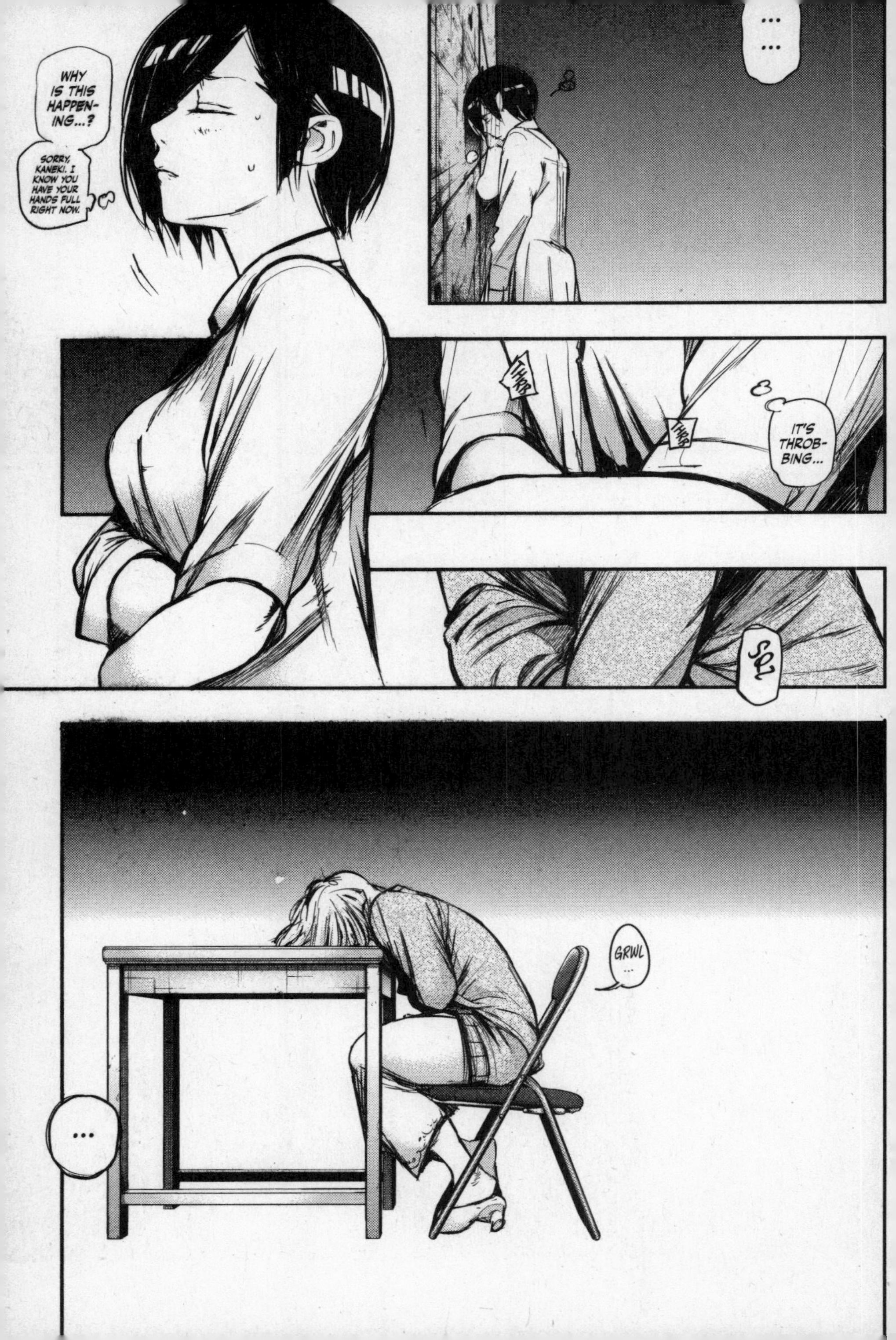
...
...
THRB
THRB
IT'S THROBBING...
SQZ
WHY IS THIS HAPPENING...?
SORRY, KANEKI. I KNOW YOU HAVE YOUR HANDS FULL RIGHT NOW.
GRWL...
...

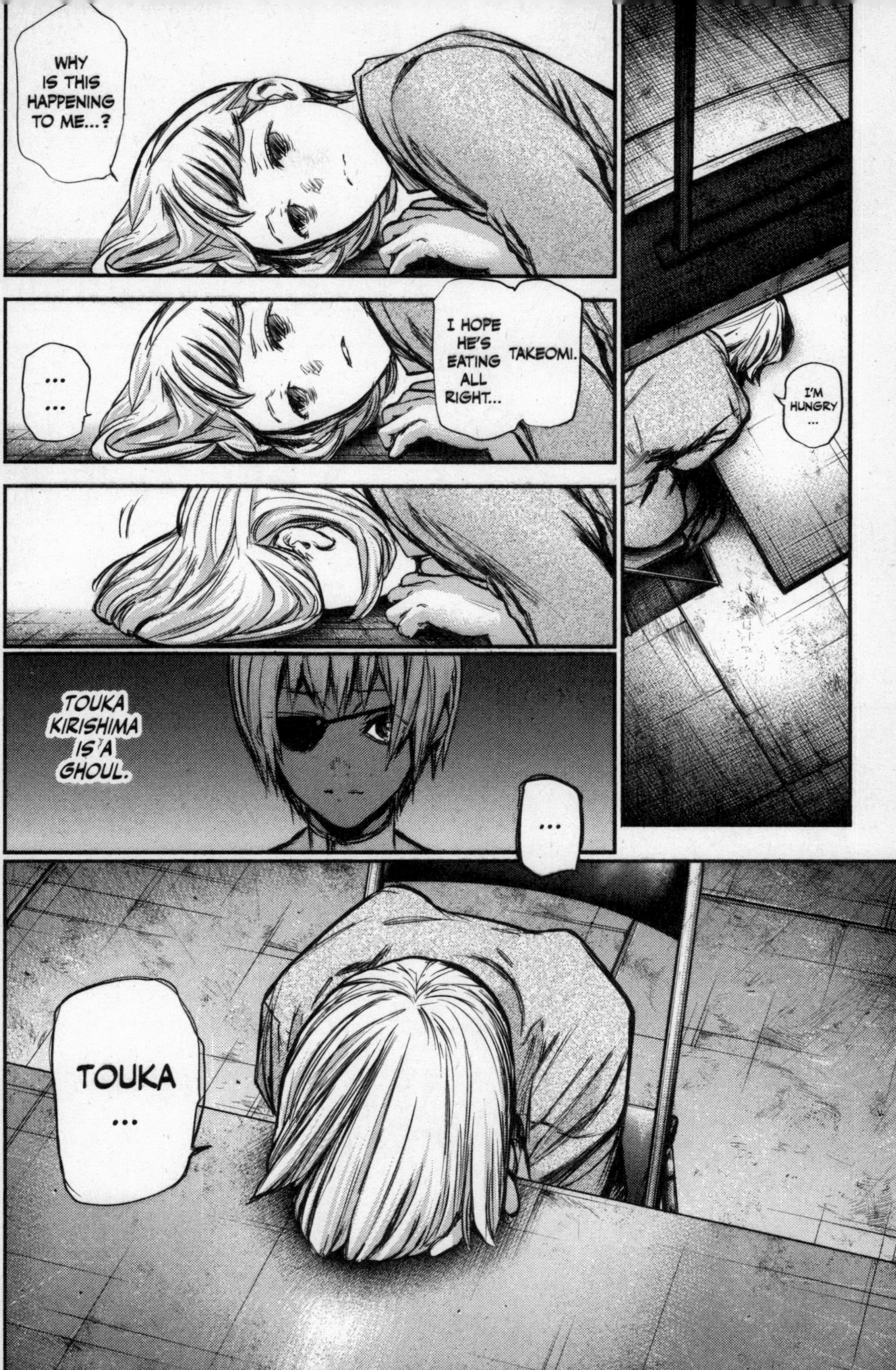
I'M HUNGRY ...
WHY IS THIS HAPPENING TO ME...?
I HOPE HE'S EATING ALL RIGHT... TAKEOMI.
... ...
...
TOUKA KIRISHIMA IS A GHOUL.
TOUKA ...

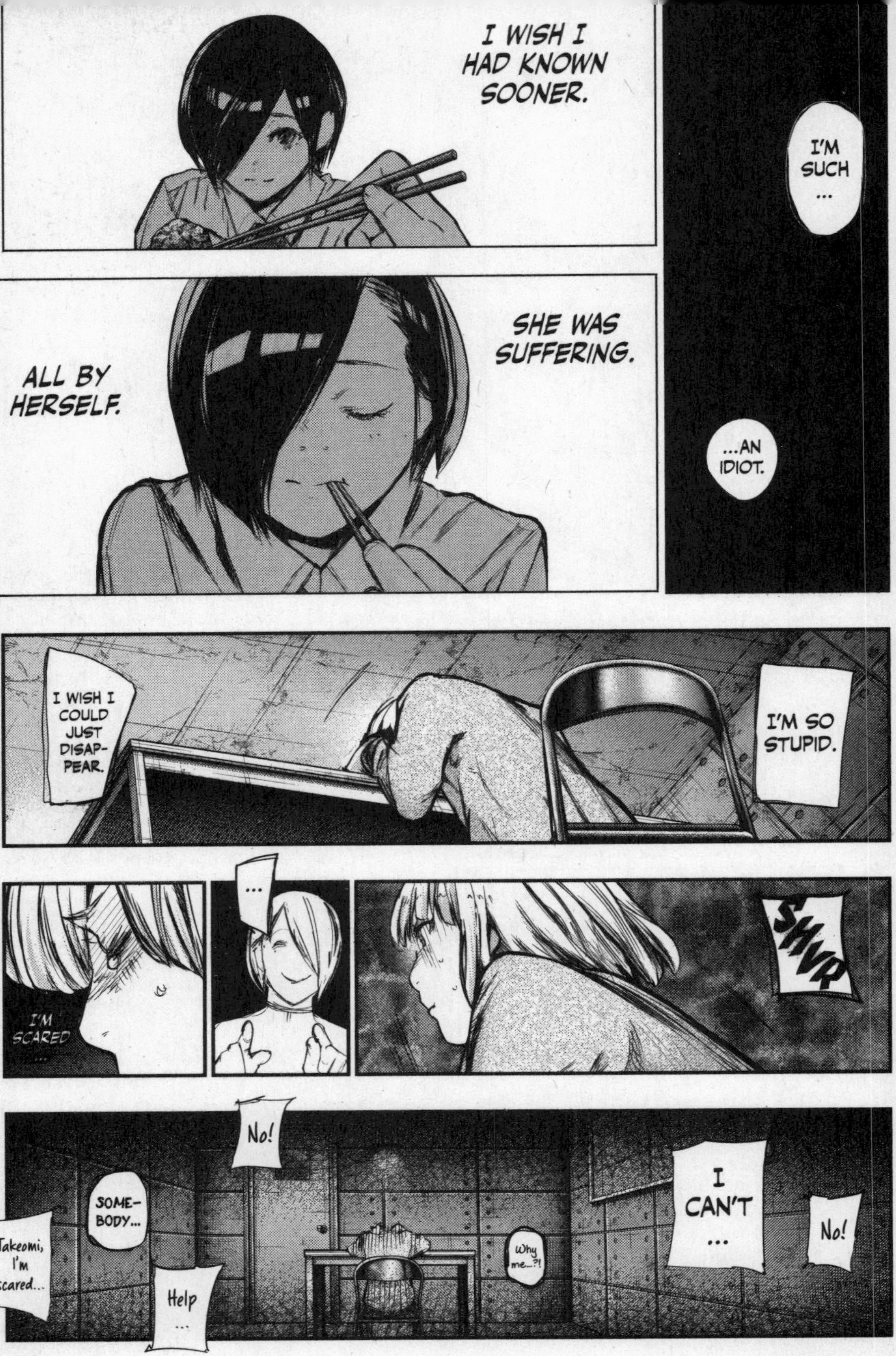

I'M SUCH ...
...AN IDIOT.
I WISH I HAD KNOWN SOONER.
SHE WAS SUFFERING.
ALL BY HERSELF.
I'M SO STUPID.
I WISH I COULD JUST DISAPPEAR.
SHVR
...
I'M SCARED ...
No!
I CAN'T ...
Why me...?!
No!
SOMEBODY...
Help ...
Takeomi, I'm scared...

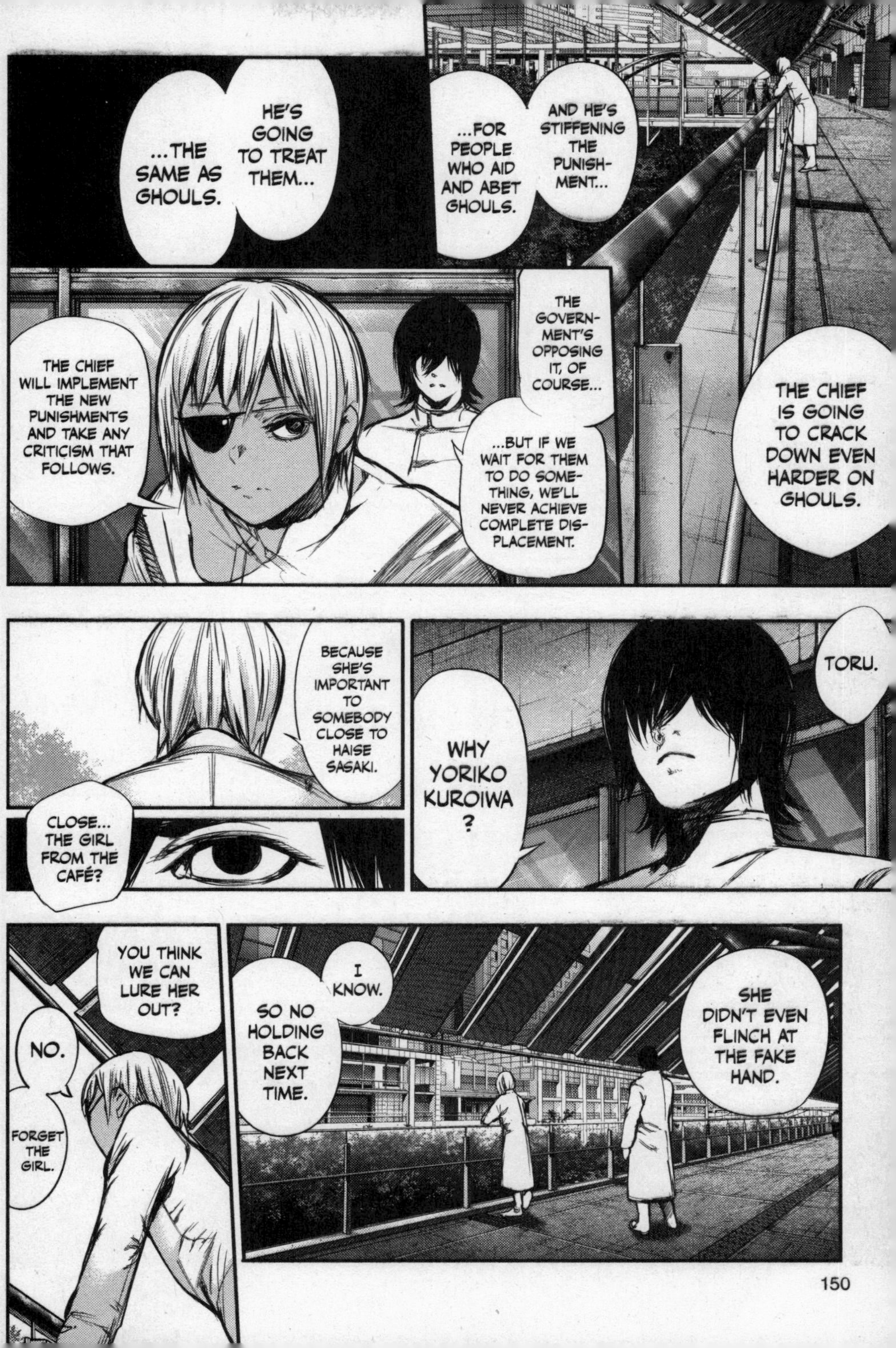
AND HE'S STIFFENING THE PUNISHMENT...
...FOR PEOPLE WHO AID AND ABET GHOULS.
HE'S GOING TO TREAT THEM...
...THE SAME AS GHOULS.
THE CHIEF IS GOING TO CRACK DOWN EVEN HARDER ON GHOULS.
THE GOVERNMENT'S OPPOSING IT, OF COURSE...
...BUT IF WE WAIT FOR THEM TO DO SOMETHING, WE'LL NEVER ACHIEVE COMPLETE DISPLACEMENT.
THE CHIEF WILL IMPLEMENT THE NEW PUNISHMENTS AND TAKE ANY CRITICISM THAT FOLLOWS.
TORU.
WHY YORIKO KUROIWA?
BECAUSE SHE'S IMPORTANT TO SOMEBODY CLOSE TO HAISE SASAKI.
CLOSE... THE GIRL FROM THE CAFÉ?
SHE DIDN'T EVEN FLINCH AT THE FAKE HAND.
I KNOW.
SO NO HOLDING BACK NEXT TIME.
YOU THINK WE CAN LURE HER OUT?
NO.
FORGET THE GIRL.

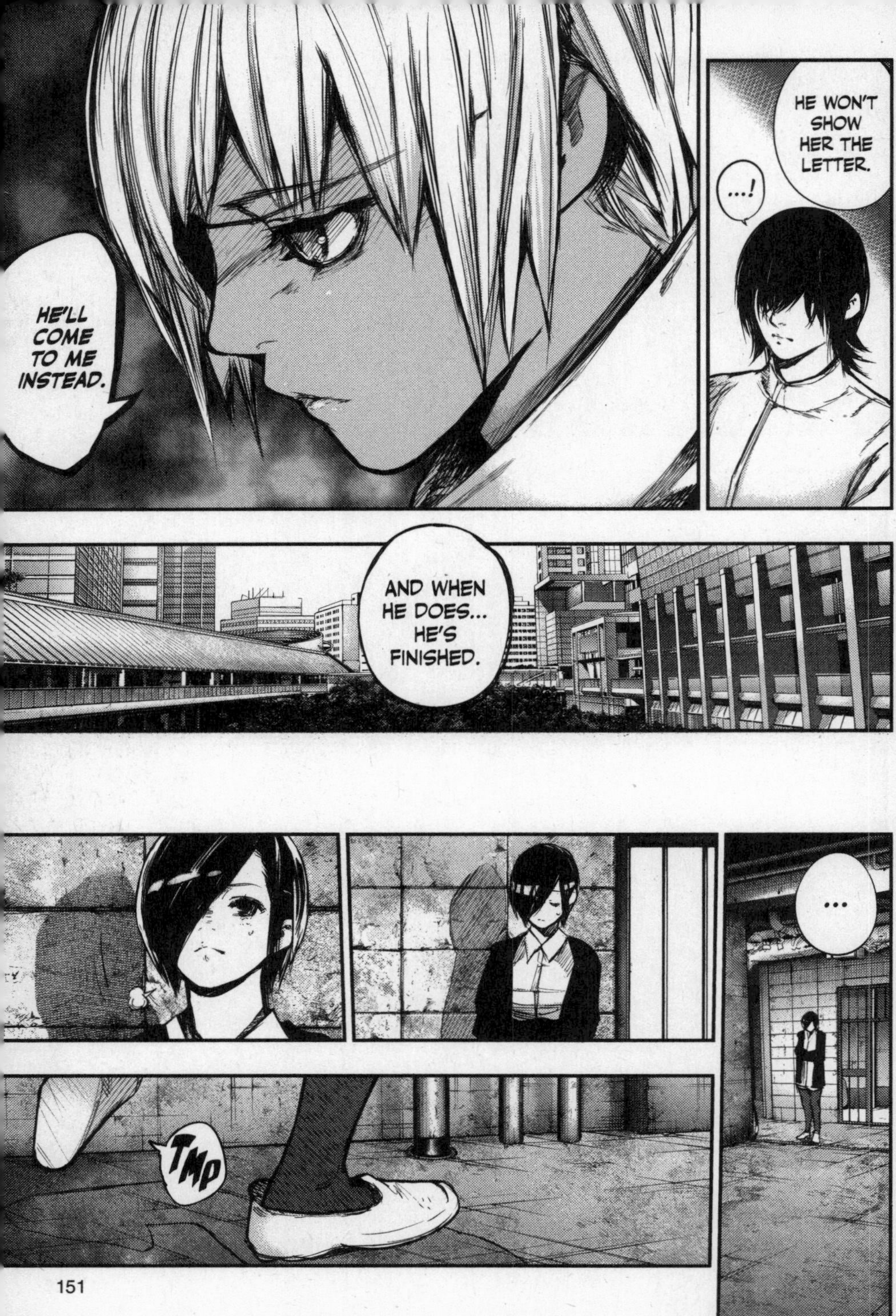
HE WON'T SHOW HER THE LETTER.
...!
HE'LL COME TO ME INSTEAD.
AND WHEN HE DOES... HE'S FINISHED.
...
TMP

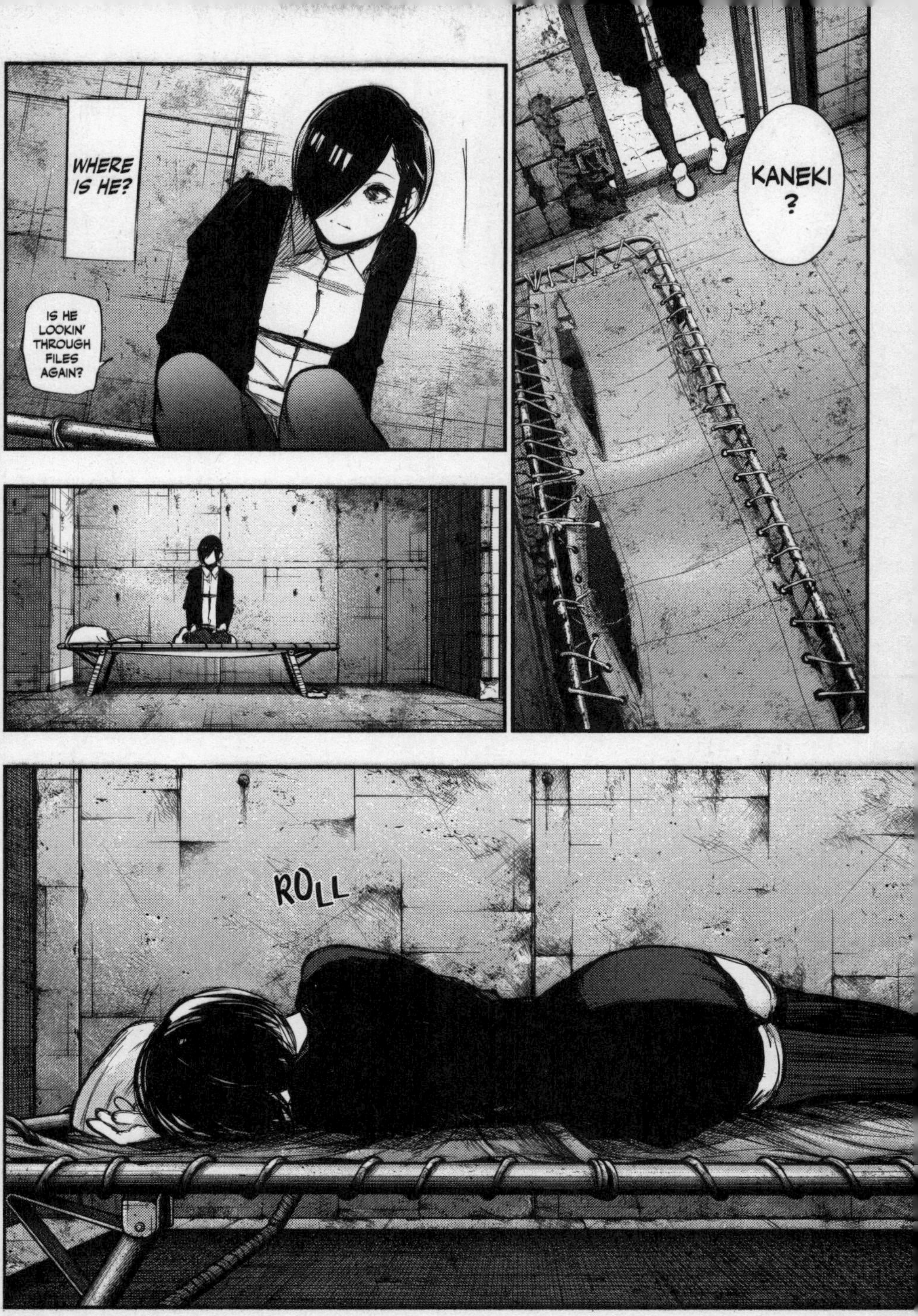
KANEKI ?
WHERE IS HE?
IS HE LOOKIN' THROUGH FILES AGAIN?
ROLL

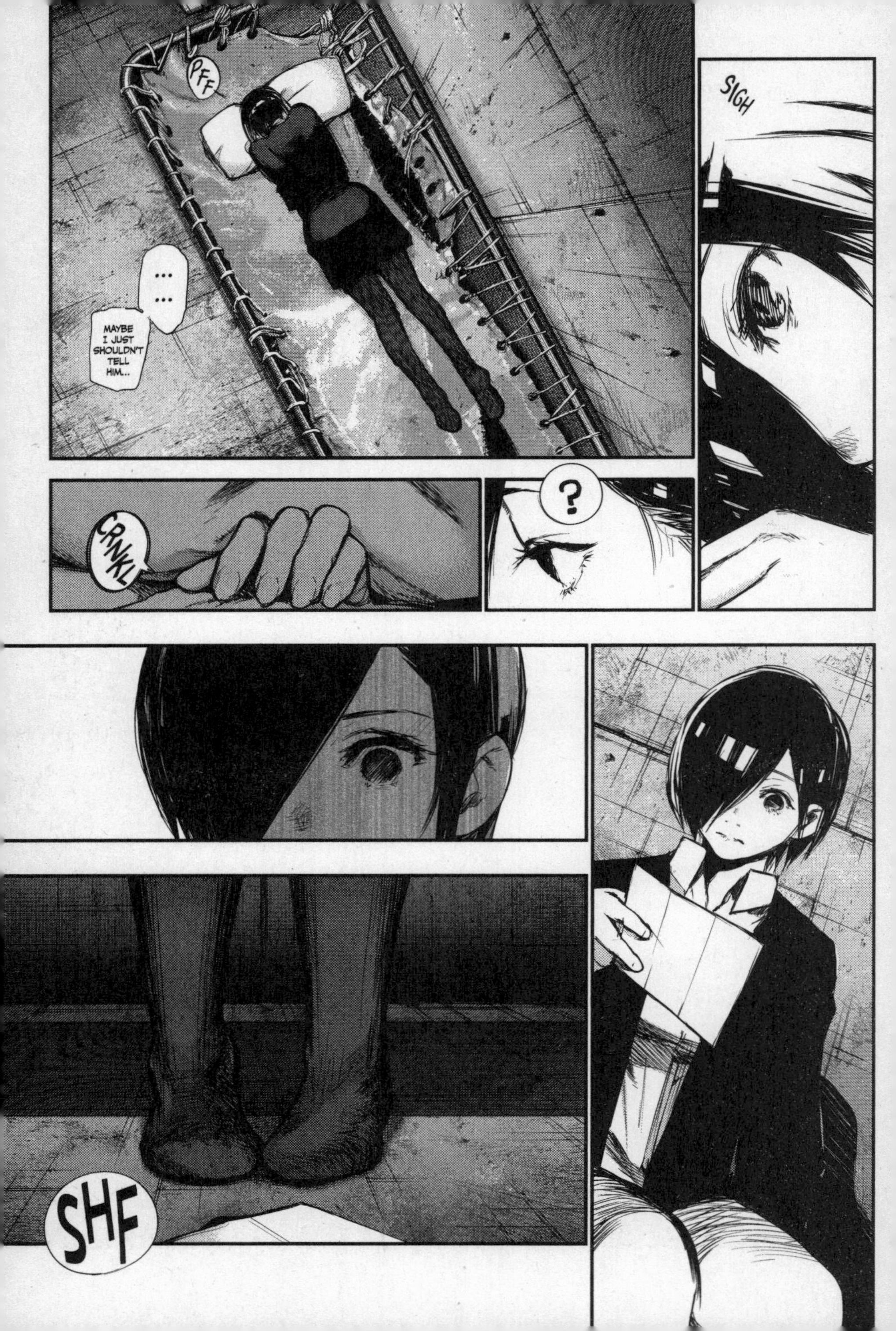
SIGH
PFF
...
...
MAYBE I JUST SHOULDN'T TELL HIM...
?
CRNKL
SHF

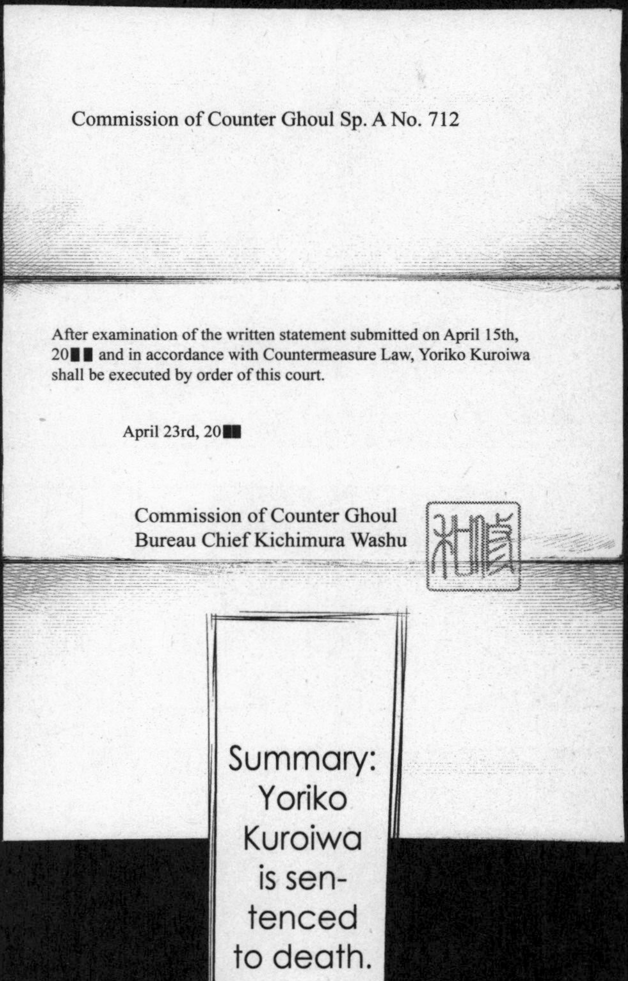
Commission of Counter Ghoul Sp. A No. 712
After examination of the written statement submitted on April 15th, 20[redacted] and in accordance with Countermeasure Law, Yoriko Kuroiwa shall be executed by order of this court.
April 23rd, 20[redacted]
Commission of Counter Ghoul
Bureau Chief Kichimura Washu
Summary: Yoriko Kuroiwa is sentenced to death.

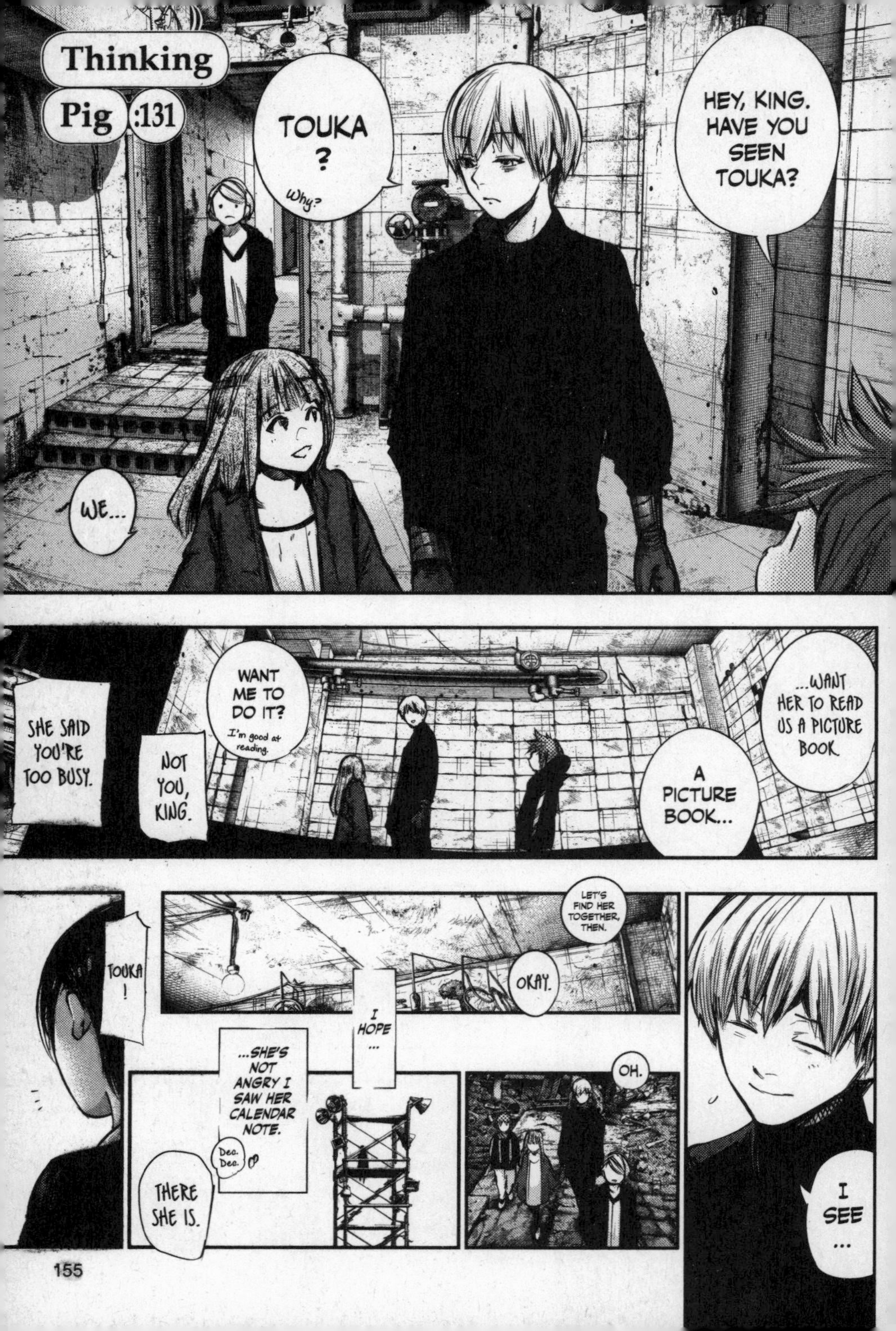

HEY, KING. HAVE YOU SEEN TOUKA?
TOUKA? Why?
Thinking Pig :131
WE...
...WANT HER TO READ US A PICTURE BOOK.
A PICTURE BOOK...
WANT ME TO DO IT? I'm good at reading.
NOT YOU, KING.
SHE SAID YOU'RE TOO BUSY.
I SEE...
LET'S FIND HER TOGETHER, THEN.
OKAY.
I HOPE...
OH.
...SHE'S NOT ANGRY I SAW HER CALENDAR NOTE.
Dec. Dec.
THERE SHE IS.
TOUKA!

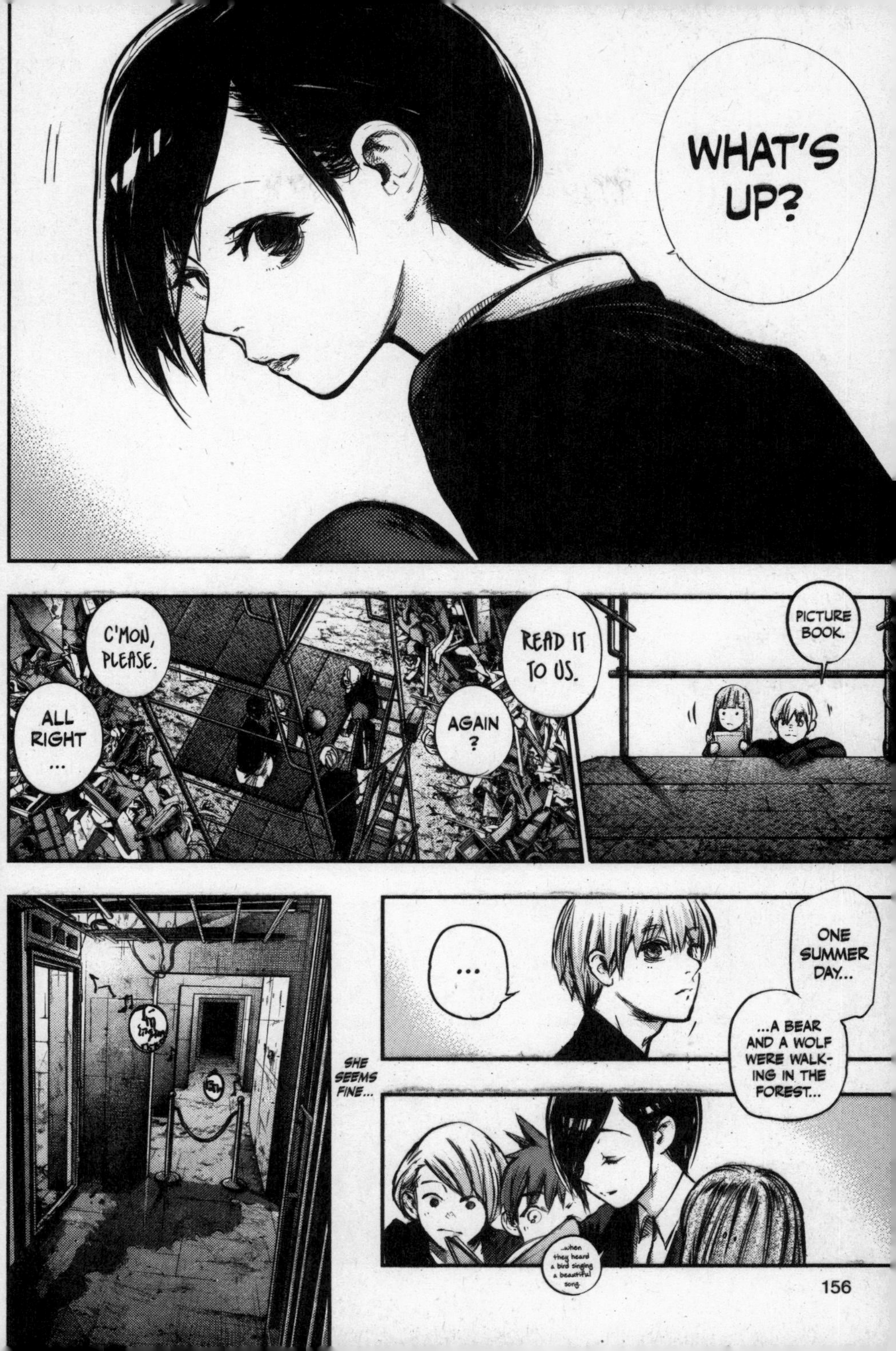
WHAT'S UP?
PICTURE BOOK.
READ IT TO US.
AGAIN?
C'MON, PLEASE.
ALL RIGHT...
ONE SUMMER DAY...
...
...A BEAR AND A WOLF WERE WALKING IN THE FOREST...
SHE SEEMS FINE...
...when they heard a bird singing a beautiful song.

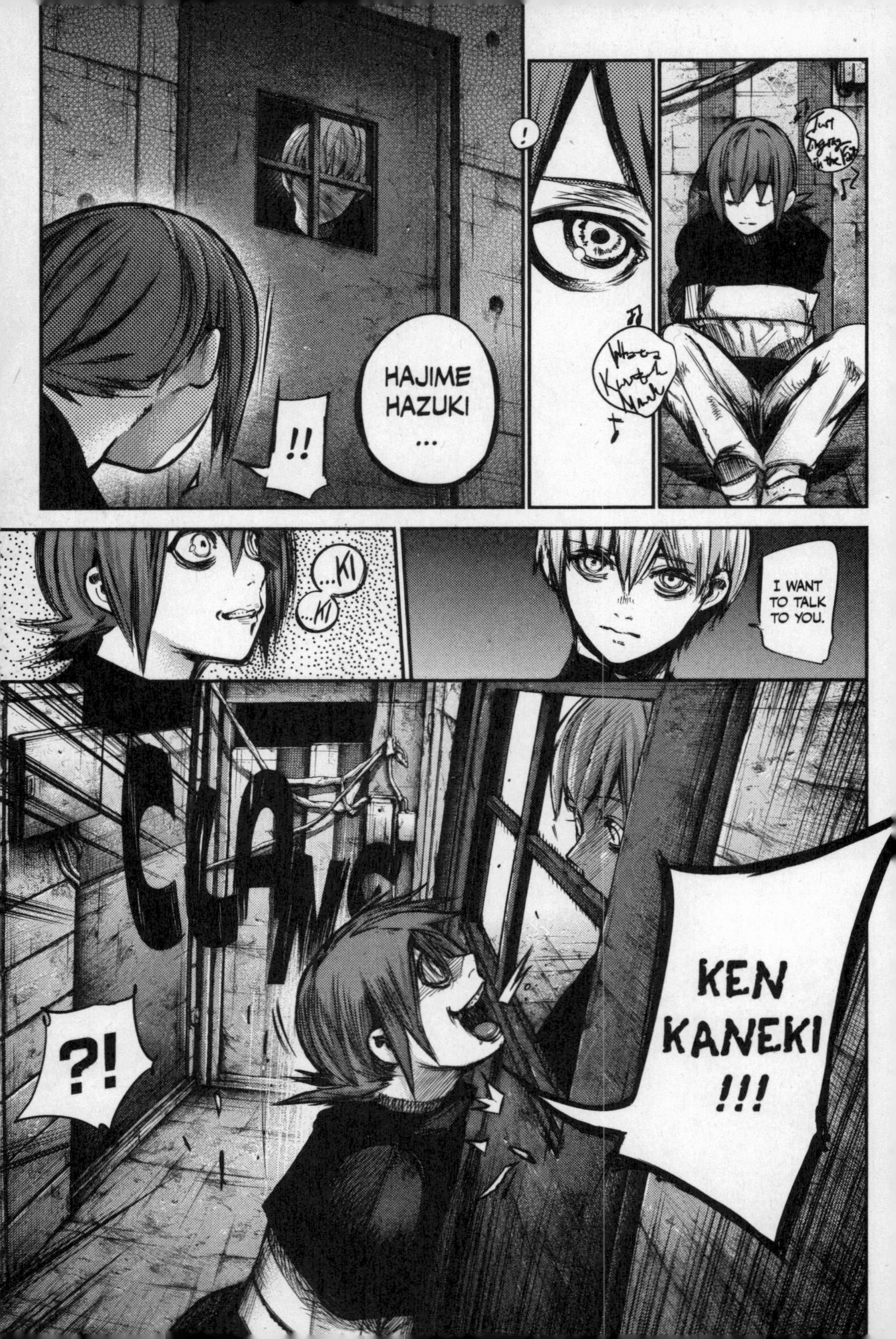
!
HAJIME HAZUKI ...
!!
I WANT TO TALK TO YOU.
...KI ...KI
KEN KANEKI !!!
?!
CLANG

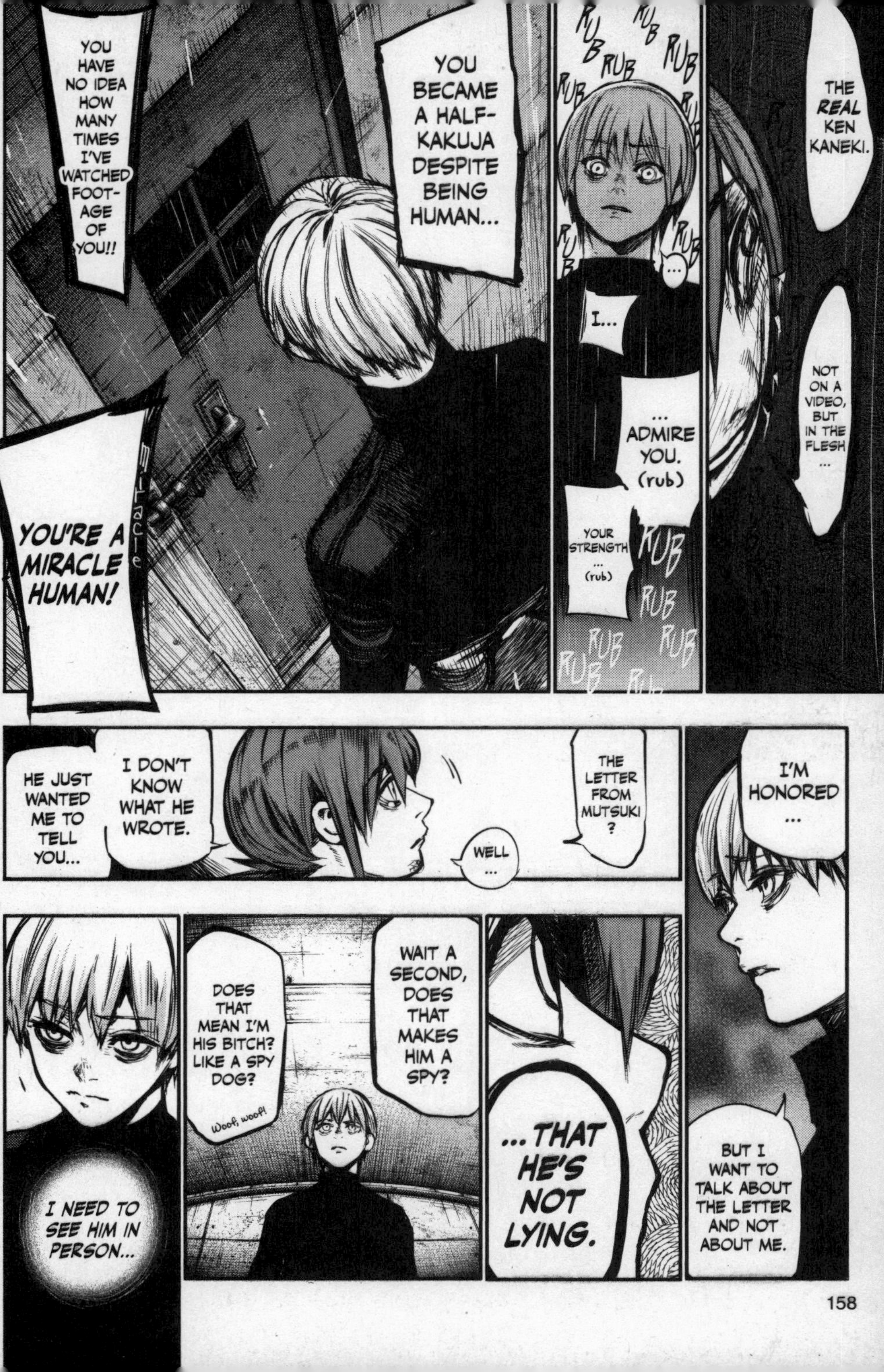
THE REAL KEN KANEKI.
NOT ON A VIDEO, BUT IN THE FLESH...
RUB RUB RUB RUB RUB RUB RUB
...
I...
... ADMIRE YOU. (rub)
YOUR STRENGTH ... (rub)
RUB RUB RUB RUB RUB
YOU BECAME A HALF-KAKUJA DESPITE BEING HUMAN...
YOU HAVE NO IDEA HOW MANY TIMES I'VE WATCHED FOOTAGE OF YOU!!
YOU'RE A MIRACLE HUMAN!
Miracle
I'M HONORED...
BUT I WANT TO TALK ABOUT THE LETTER AND NOT ABOUT ME.
THE LETTER FROM MUTSUKI?
WELL...
I DON'T KNOW WHAT HE WROTE.
HE JUST WANTED ME TO TELL YOU...
...THAT HE'S NOT LYING.
WAIT A SECOND, DOES THAT MAKES HIM A SPY?
DOES THAT MEAN I'M HIS BITCH? LIKE A SPY DOG?
Woof, woof!
I NEED TO SEE HIM IN PERSON...

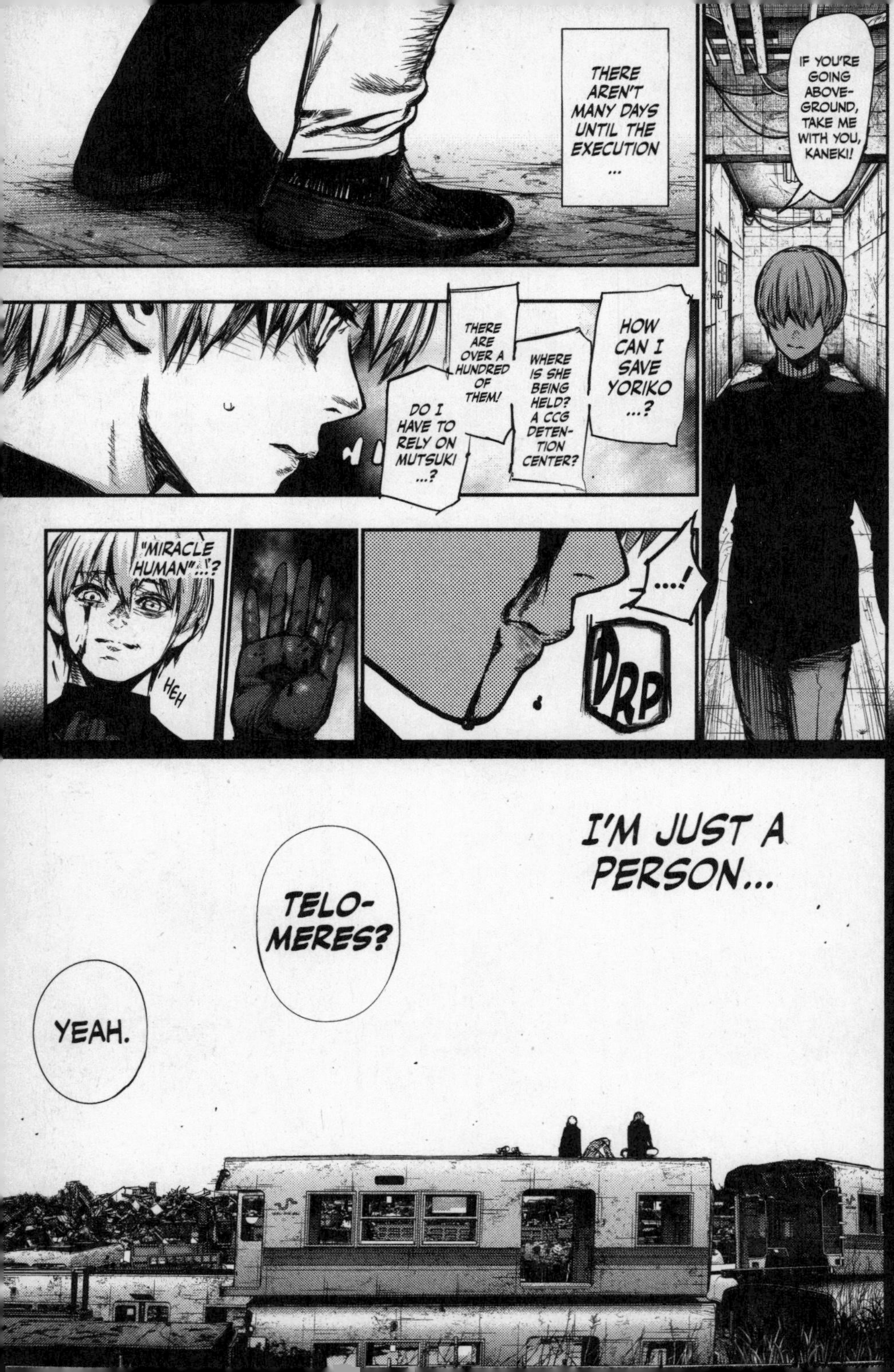
IF YOU'RE GOING ABOVE-GROUND, TAKE ME WITH YOU, KANEKI!
THERE AREN'T MANY DAYS UNTIL THE EXECUTION ...
HOW CAN I SAVE YORIKO ...?
WHERE IS SHE BEING HELD? A CCG DETEN-TION CENTER?
THERE ARE OVER A HUNDRED OF THEM!
DO I HAVE TO RELY ON MUTSUKI ...?
...!
DRP
"MIRACLE HUMAN"...!?
HEH
I'M JUST A PERSON...
TELO-MERES?
YEAH.

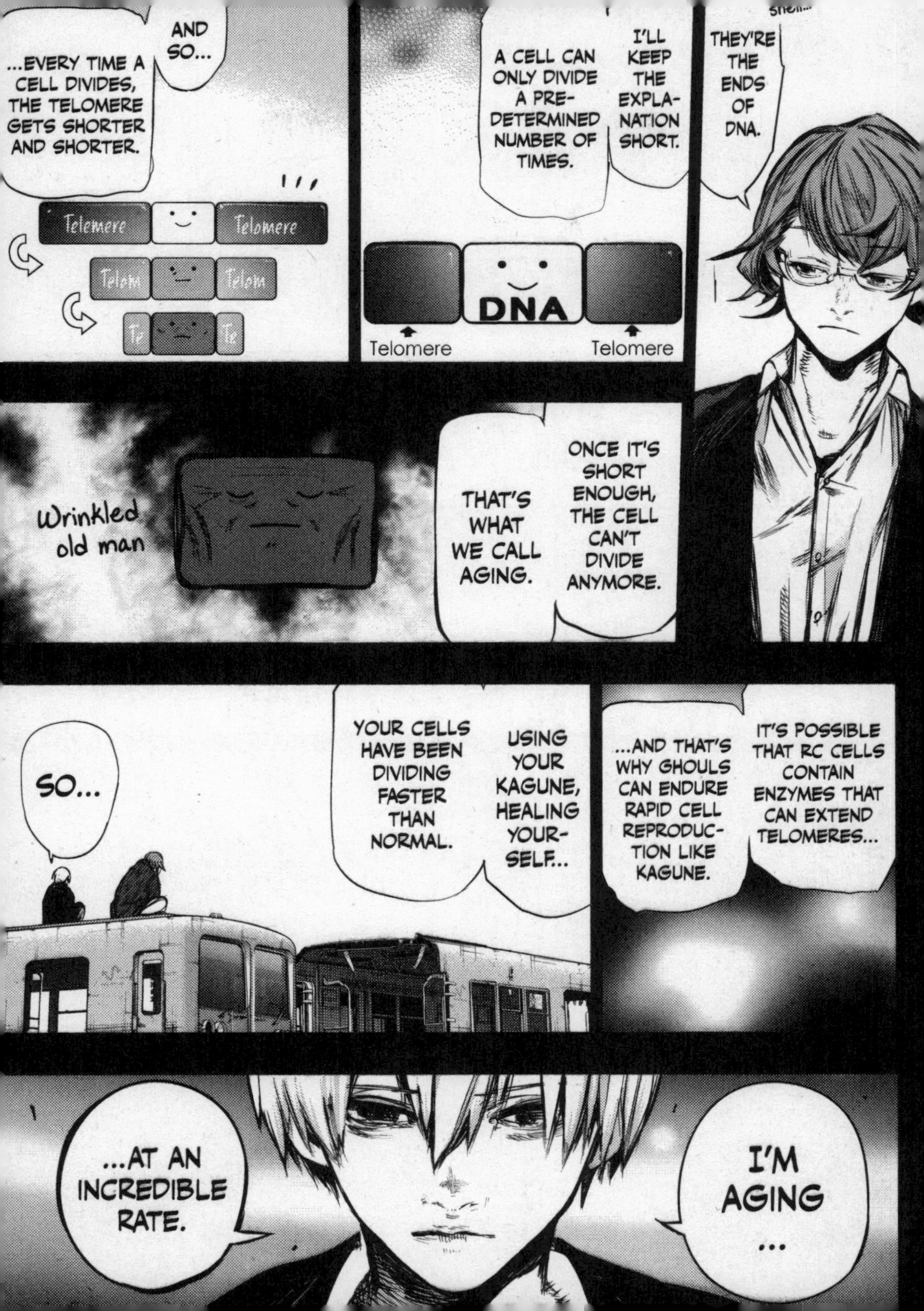
THEY'RE THE ENDS OF DNA.
I'LL KEEP THE EXPLANATION SHORT.
A CELL CAN ONLY DIVIDE A PRE-DETERMINED NUMBER OF TIMES.
DNA
Telomere
Telomere
AND SO...
...EVERY TIME A CELL DIVIDES, THE TELOMERE GETS SHORTER AND SHORTER.
Telomere
Telomere
Telom
Telom
Te
Te
ONCE IT'S SHORT ENOUGH, THE CELL CAN'T DIVIDE ANYMORE.
THAT'S WHAT WE CALL AGING.
Wrinkled old man
IT'S POSSIBLE THAT RC CELLS CONTAIN ENZYMES THAT CAN EXTEND TELOMERES...
...AND THAT'S WHY GHOULS CAN ENDURE RAPID CELL REPRODUCTION LIKE KAGUNE.
USING YOUR KAGUNE, HEALING YOURSELF...
YOUR CELLS HAVE BEEN DIVIDING FASTER THAN NORMAL.
SO...
I'M AGING...
...AT AN INCREDIBLE RATE.

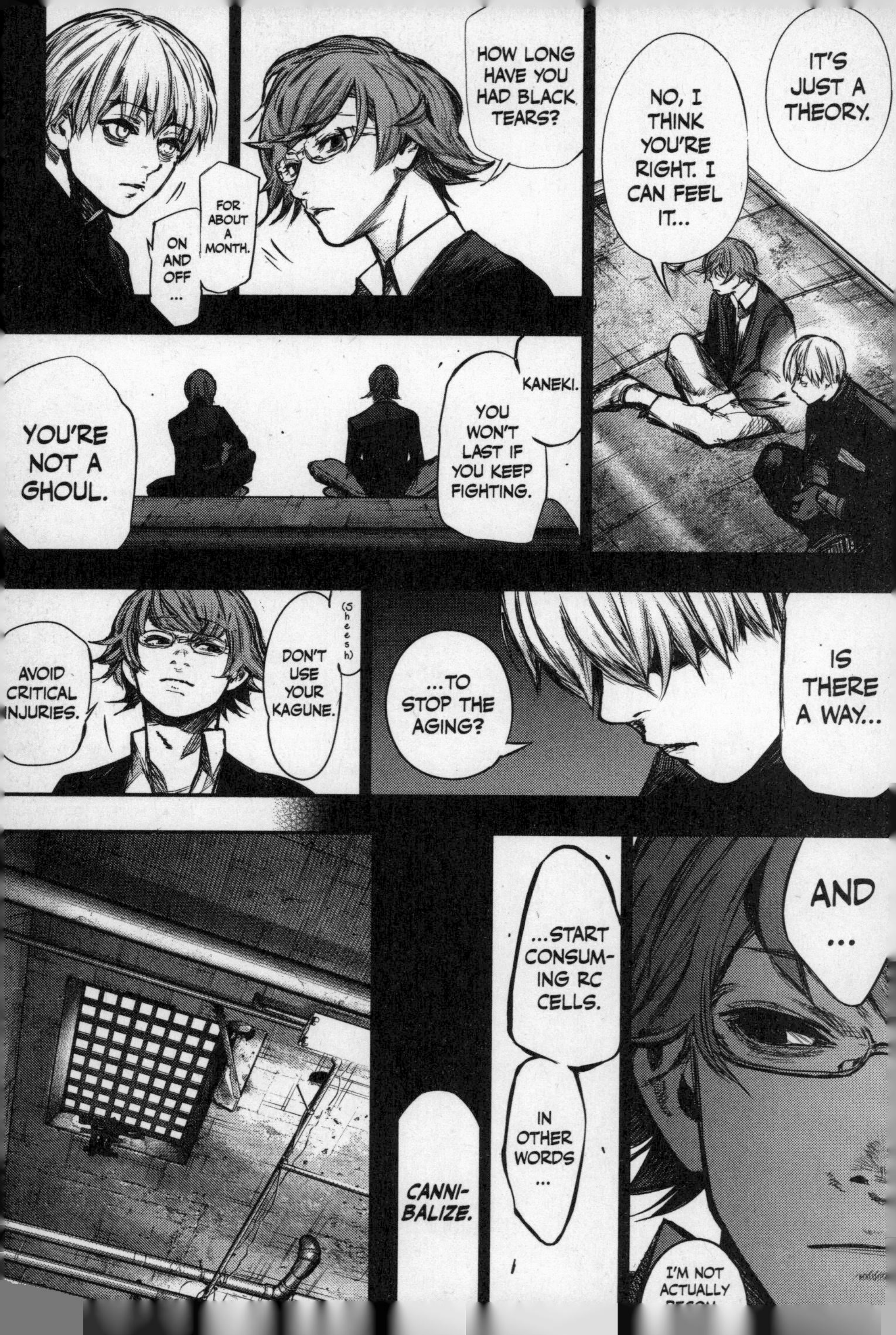
IT'S JUST A THEORY.
NO, I THINK YOU'RE RIGHT. I CAN FEEL IT...
HOW LONG HAVE YOU HAD BLACK TEARS?
FOR ABOUT A MONTH.
ON AND OFF ...
KANEKI.
YOU WON'T LAST IF YOU KEEP FIGHTING.
YOU'RE NOT A GHOUL.
IS THERE A WAY...
...TO STOP THE AGING?
(Sheesh)
DON'T USE YOUR KAGUNE.
AVOID CRITICAL INJURIES.
AND ...
I'M NOT ACTUALLY
...START CONSUMING RC CELLS.
IN OTHER WORDS ...
CANNI-BALIZE.

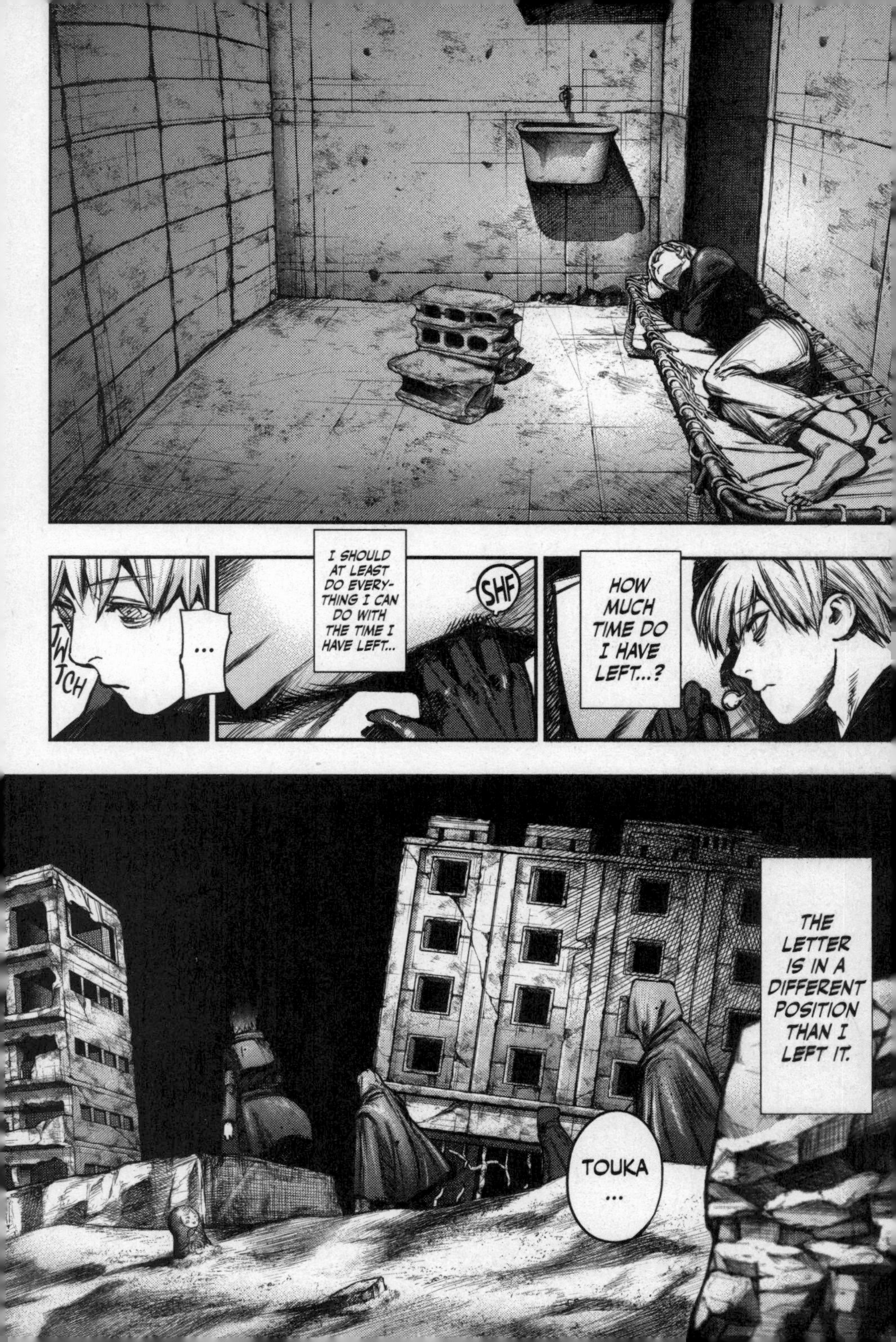
HOW MUCH TIME DO I HAVE LEFT...?
SHF
I SHOULD AT LEAST DO EVERYTHING I CAN DO WITH THE TIME I HAVE LEFT...
...
TWITCH
THE LETTER IS IN A DIFFERENT POSITION THAN I LEFT IT.
TOUKA ...

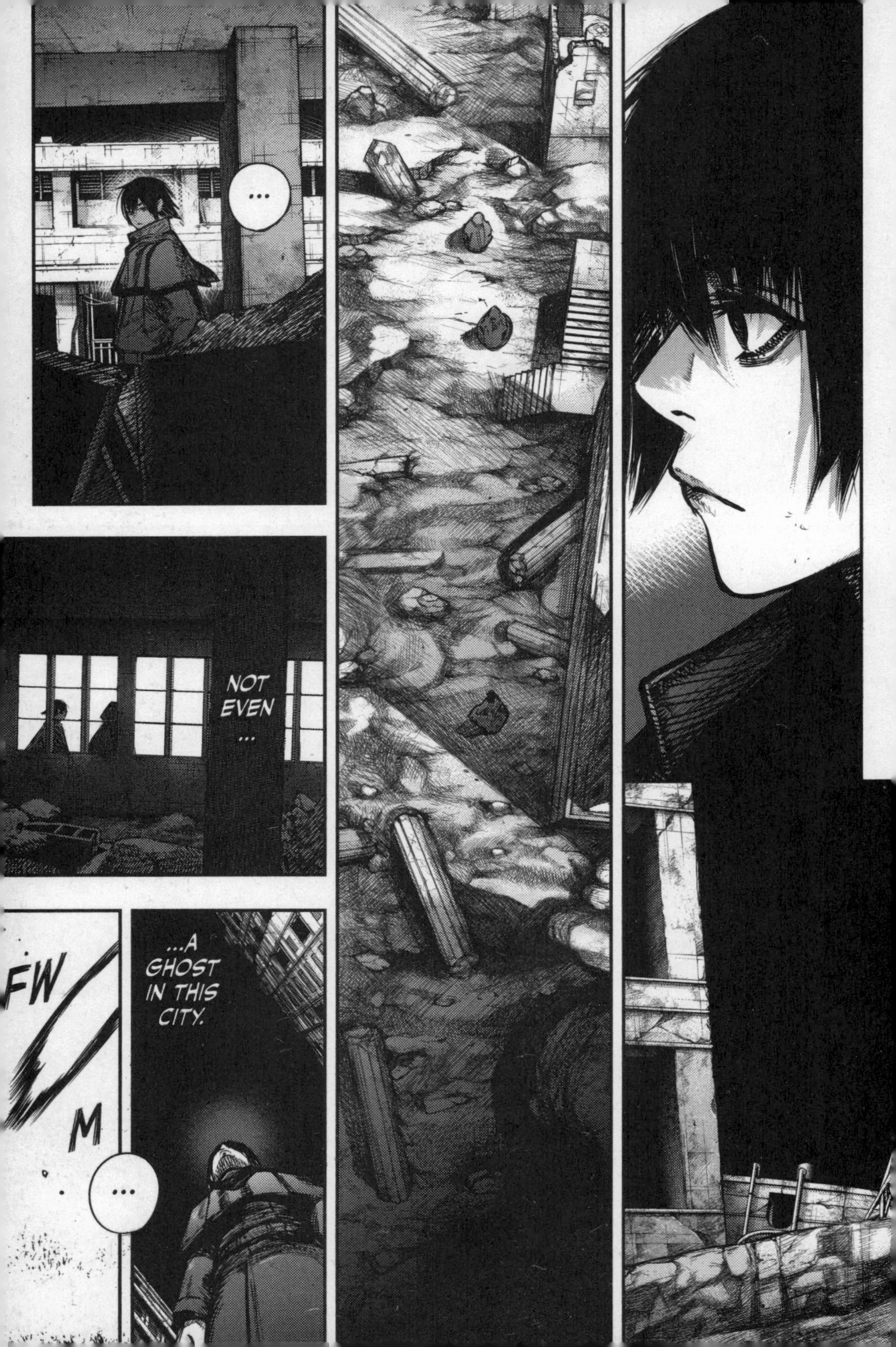
...
NOT EVEN ...
...A GHOST IN THIS CITY.
...
FWM

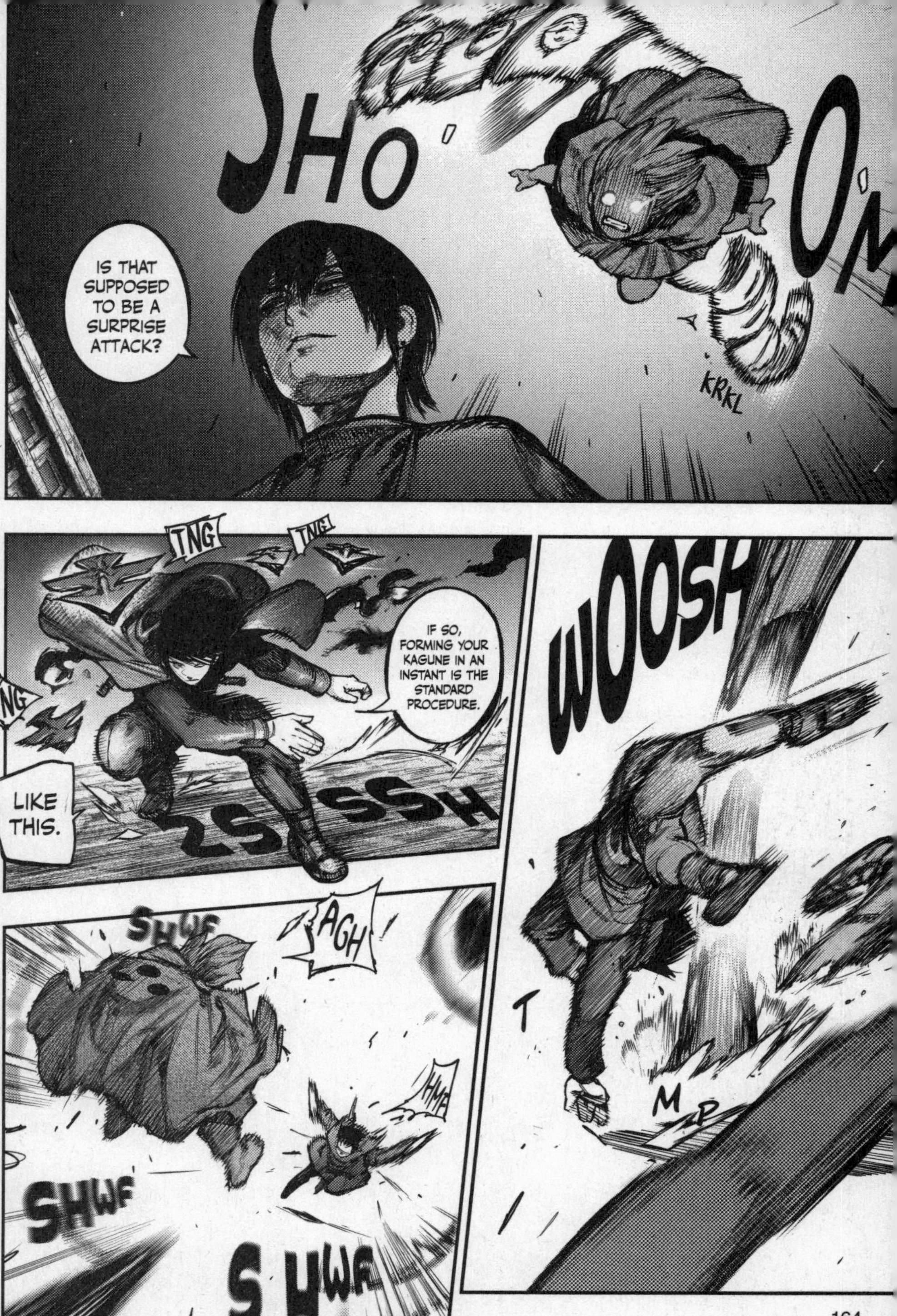

SHO'OM
IS THAT SUPPOSED TO BE A SURPRISE ATTACK?
KRKL
WOOSH
T
M
P
TNG
TNG
IF SO, FORMING YOUR KAGUNE IN AN INSTANT IS THE STANDARD PROCEDURE.
TNG
LIKE THIS.
SSSH
AGH
SHWF
HMA
SHWF
SHWA

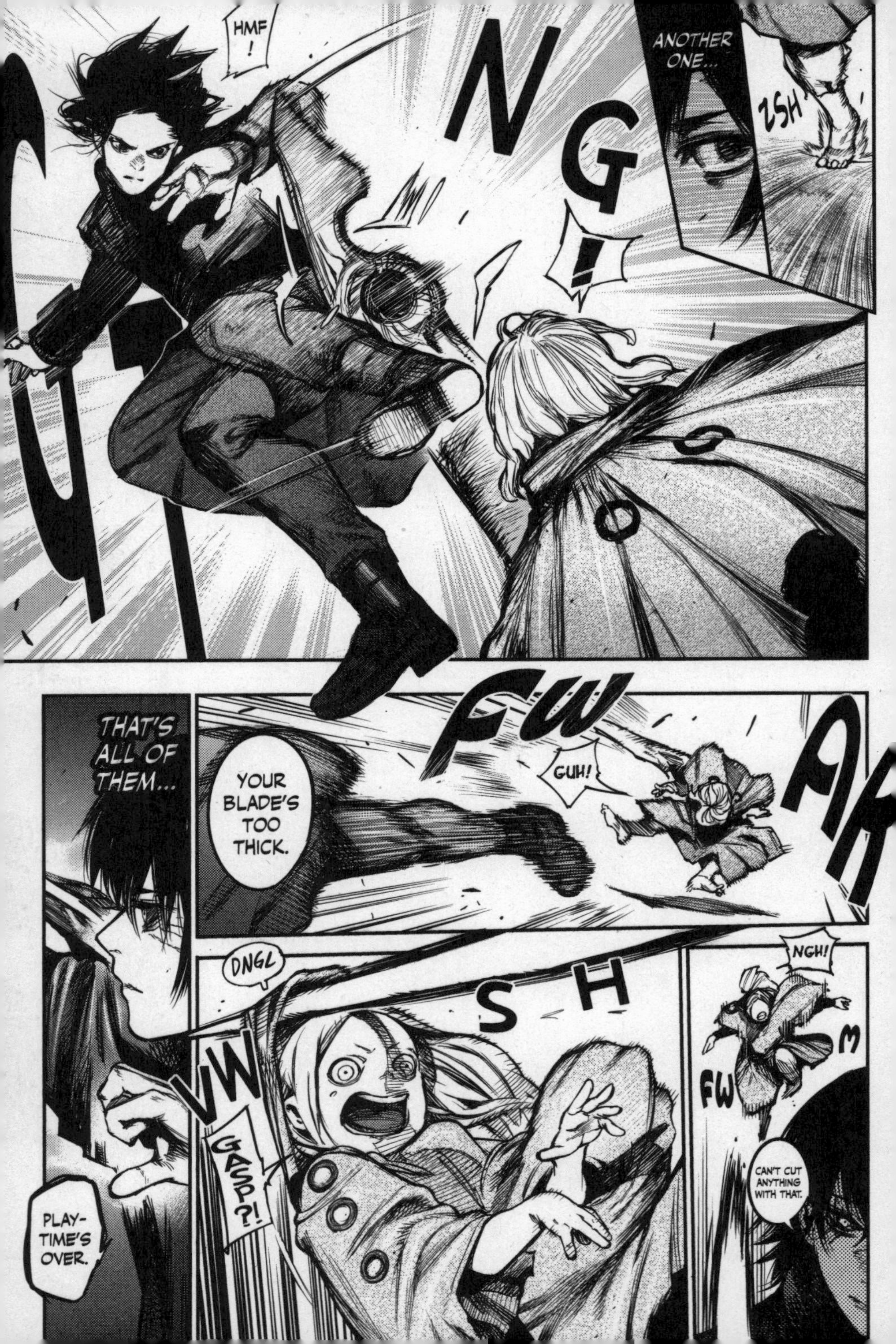
ANOTHER ONE...
ZSH
NG!
HMF!
FW
AK
GUH!
YOUR BLADE'S TOO THICK.
NGH!
FW
M
CAN'T CUT ANYTHING WITH THAT.
DNGL
S H
VW
GASP?!
THAT'S ALL OF THEM...
PLAY-TIME'S OVER.

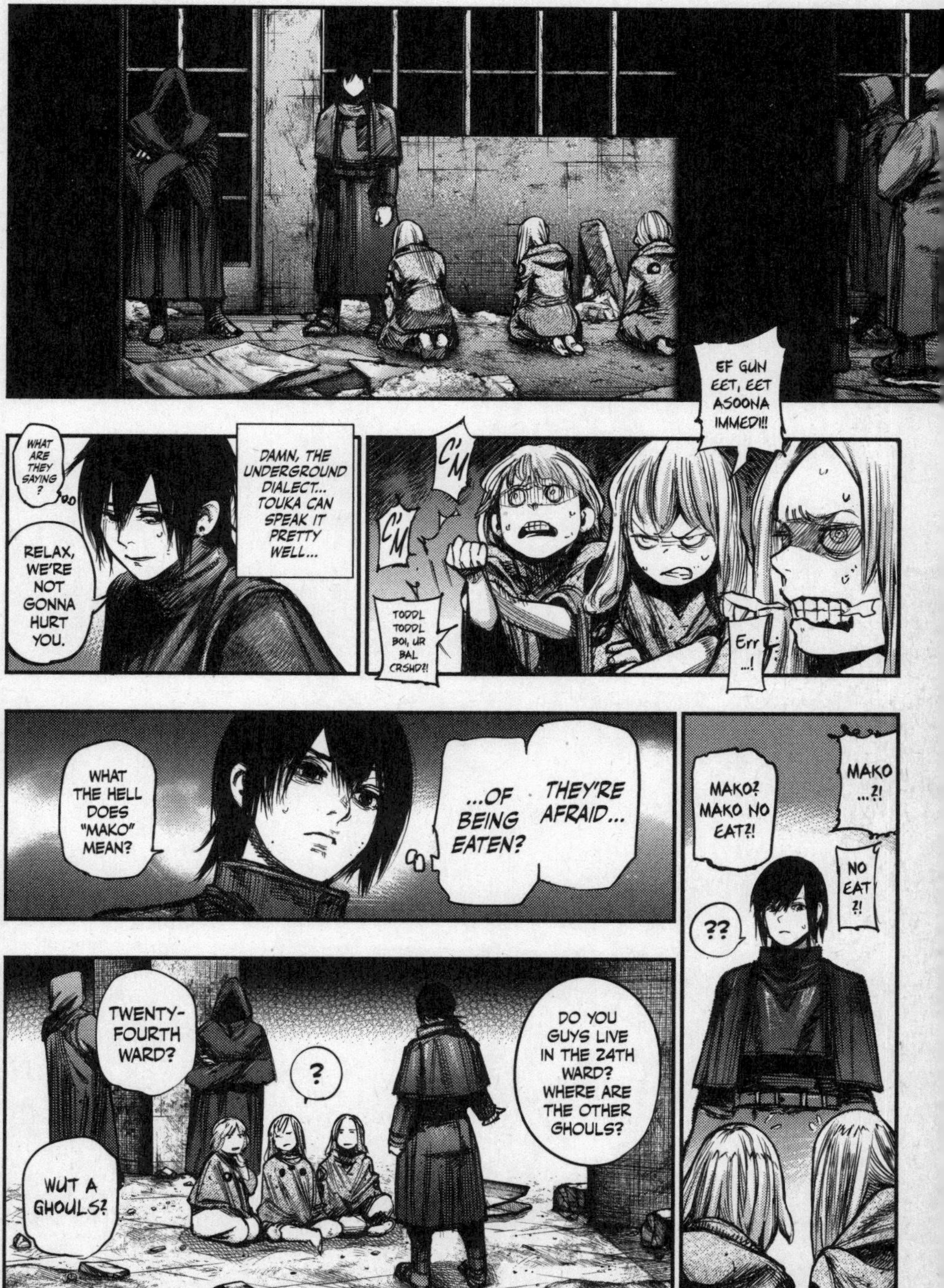
EF GUN EET, EET ASOONA IMMEDI!!!
C'M
C'M
Err ...!
TODDL TODDL BOI, UR BAL CRSHD?!
DAMN, THE UNDERGROUND DIALECT... TOUKA CAN SPEAK IT PRETTY WELL...
WHAT ARE THEY SAYING?
RELAX, WE'RE NOT GONNA HURT YOU.
MAKO ...?!
MAKO? MAKO NO EAT?!
NO EAT?!
??
THEY'RE AFRAID...
...OF BEING EATEN?
WHAT THE HELL DOES "MAKO" MEAN?
DO YOU GUYS LIVE IN THE 24TH WARD? WHERE ARE THE OTHER GHOULS?
?
TWENTY-FOURTH WARD?
WUT A GHOULS?

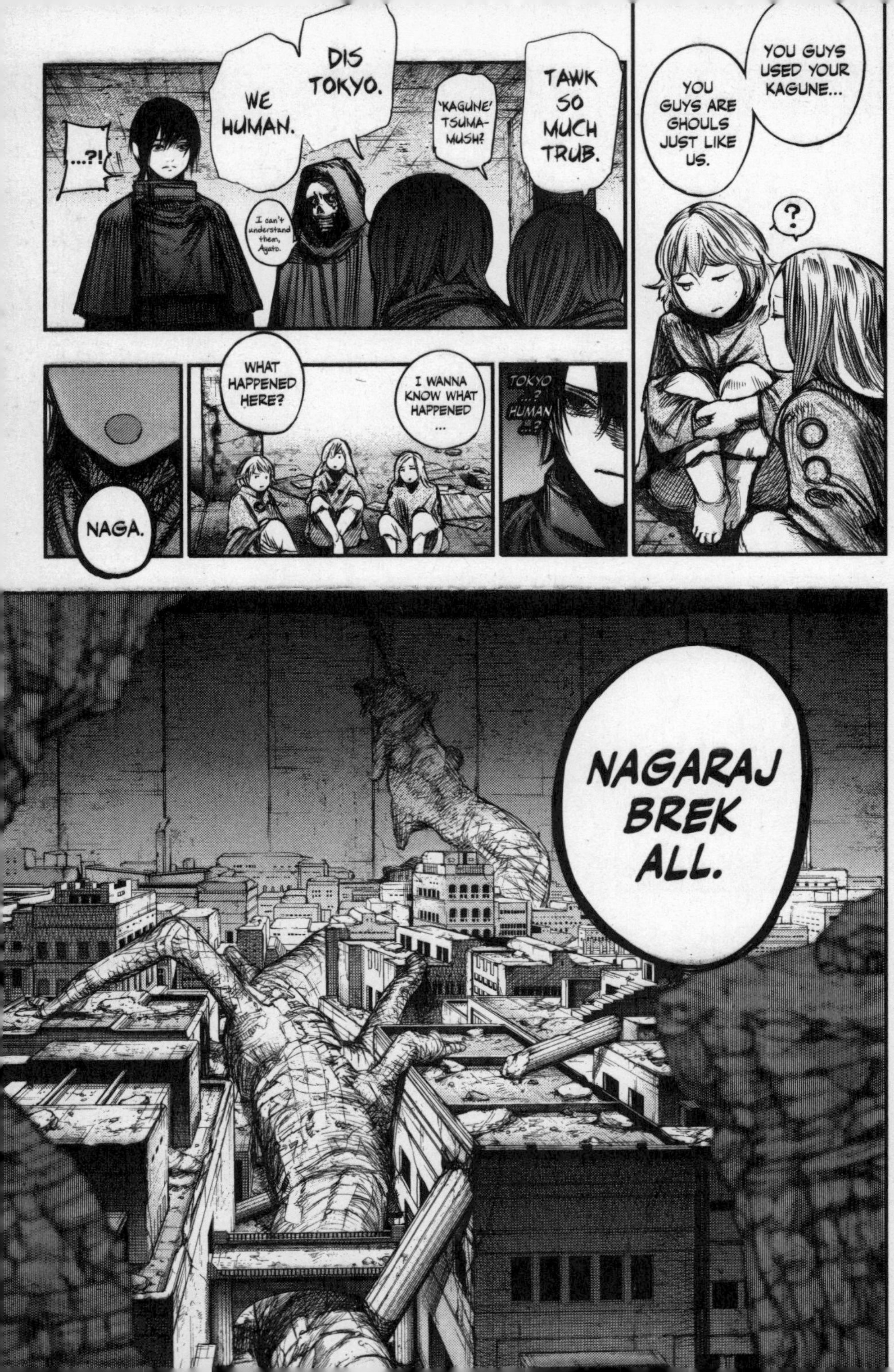
YOU GUYS USED YOUR KAGUNE...
YOU GUYS ARE GHOULS JUST LIKE US.
?
TAWK SO MUCH TRUB.
'KAGUNE' TSUMA-MUSH?
DIS TOKYO.
WE HUMAN.
I can't understand them, Ayato.
...?!
TOKYO ...? HUMAN ...?
I WANNA KNOW WHAT HAPPENED ...
WHAT HAPPENED HERE?
NAGA.
NAGARAJ BREK ALL.

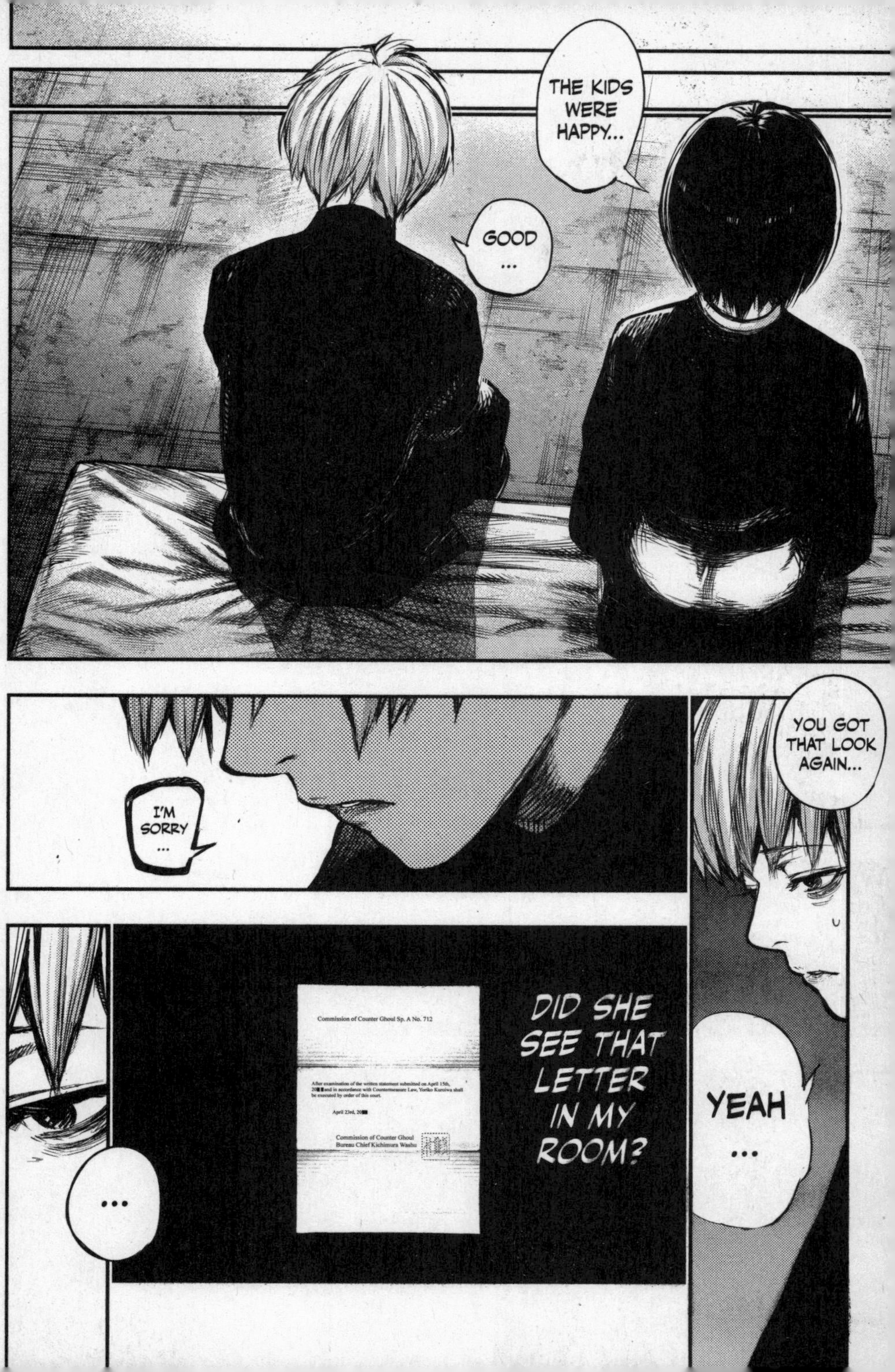
THE KIDS WERE HAPPY...
GOOD ...
YOU GOT THAT LOOK AGAIN...
YEAH ...
I'M SORRY ...
DID SHE SEE THAT LETTER IN MY ROOM?
Commission of Counter Ghoul Sp. A No. 712
After examination of the written statement submitted on April 15th, 20[redacted] and in accordance with Countermeasure Law, Yoriko Kuroiwa shall be executed by order of this court.
April 23rd, 20[redacted]
Commission of Counter Ghoul
Bureau Chief Kichimura Washu
...

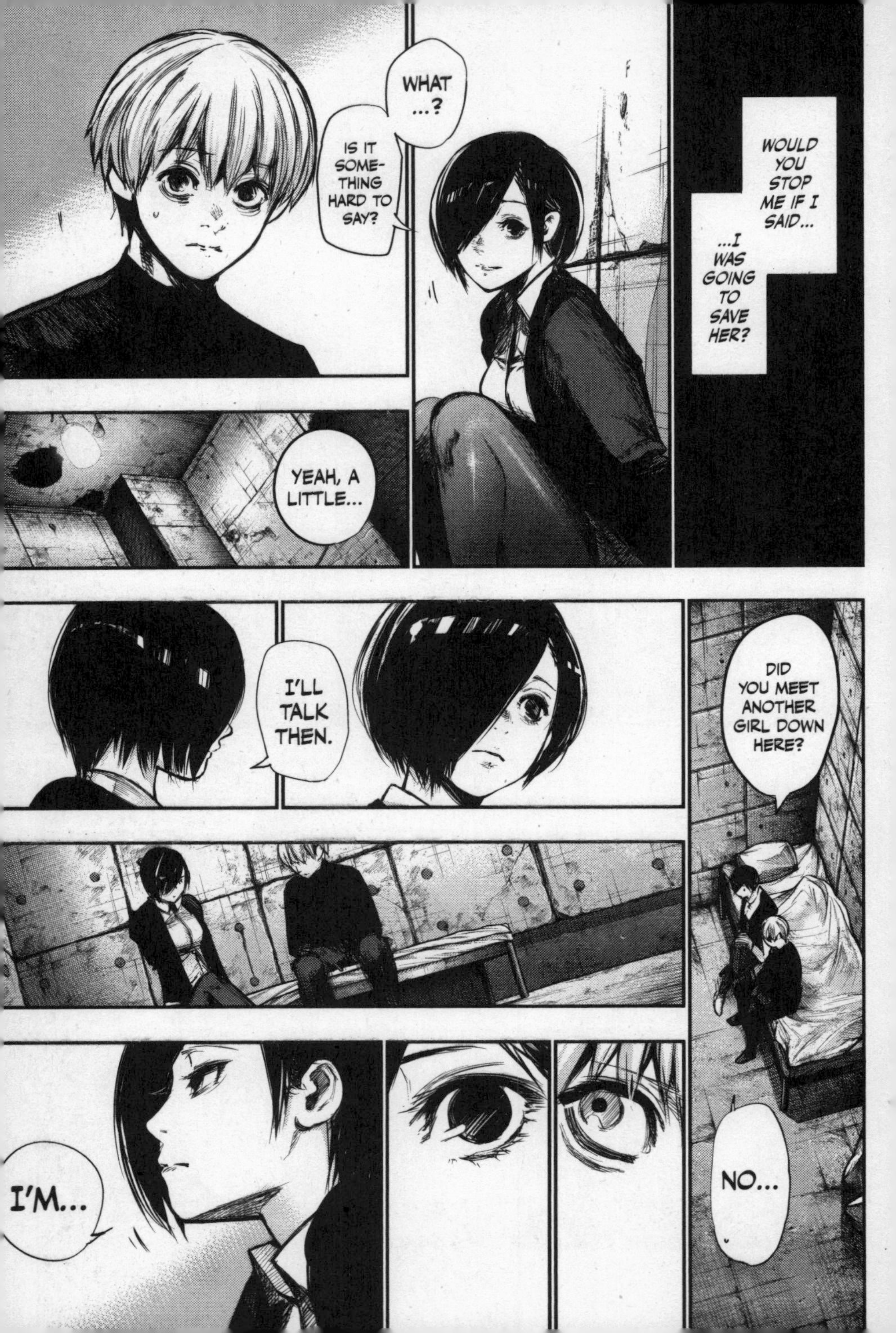
WOULD YOU STOP ME IF I SAID...
...I WAS GOING TO SAVE HER?
WHAT ...?
IS IT SOME-THING HARD TO SAY?
YEAH, A LITTLE...
DID YOU MEET ANOTHER GIRL DOWN HERE?
NO...
I'LL TALK THEN.
I'M...

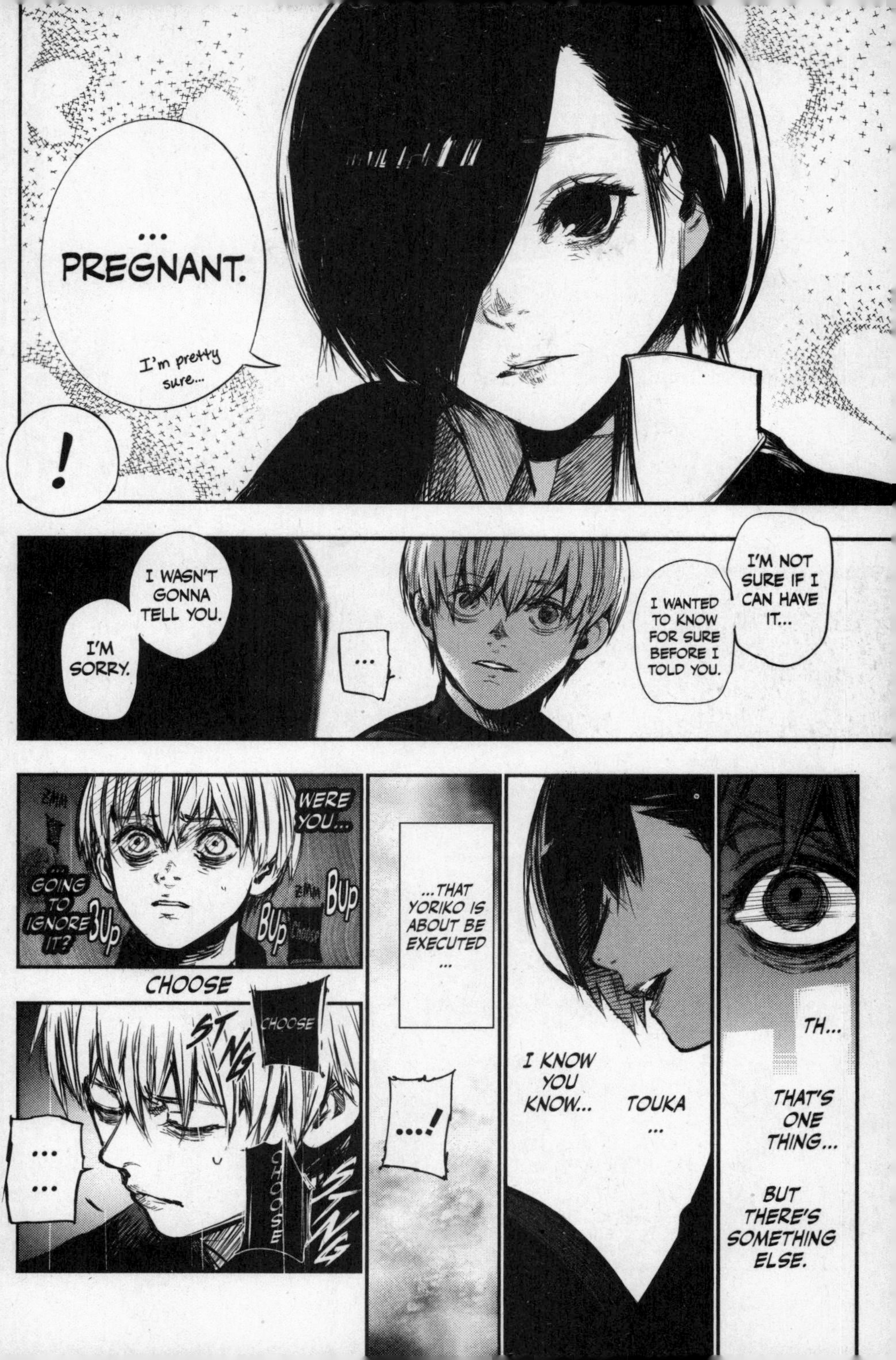
... PREGNANT.
I'm pretty sure...
!
I'M NOT SURE IF I CAN HAVE IT...
I WANTED TO KNOW FOR SURE BEFORE I TOLD YOU.
...
I WASN'T GONNA TELL YOU.
I'M SORRY.
TH...
THAT'S ONE THING...
BUT THERE'S SOMETHING ELSE.
TOUKA ...
I KNOW YOU KNOW...
...THAT YORIKO IS ABOUT BE EXECUTED ...
...!
WERE YOU...
GOING TO IGNORE IT?
BUp
BUp
BUp
CHOOSE
CHOOSE
STING
CHOOSE
STING
...
...

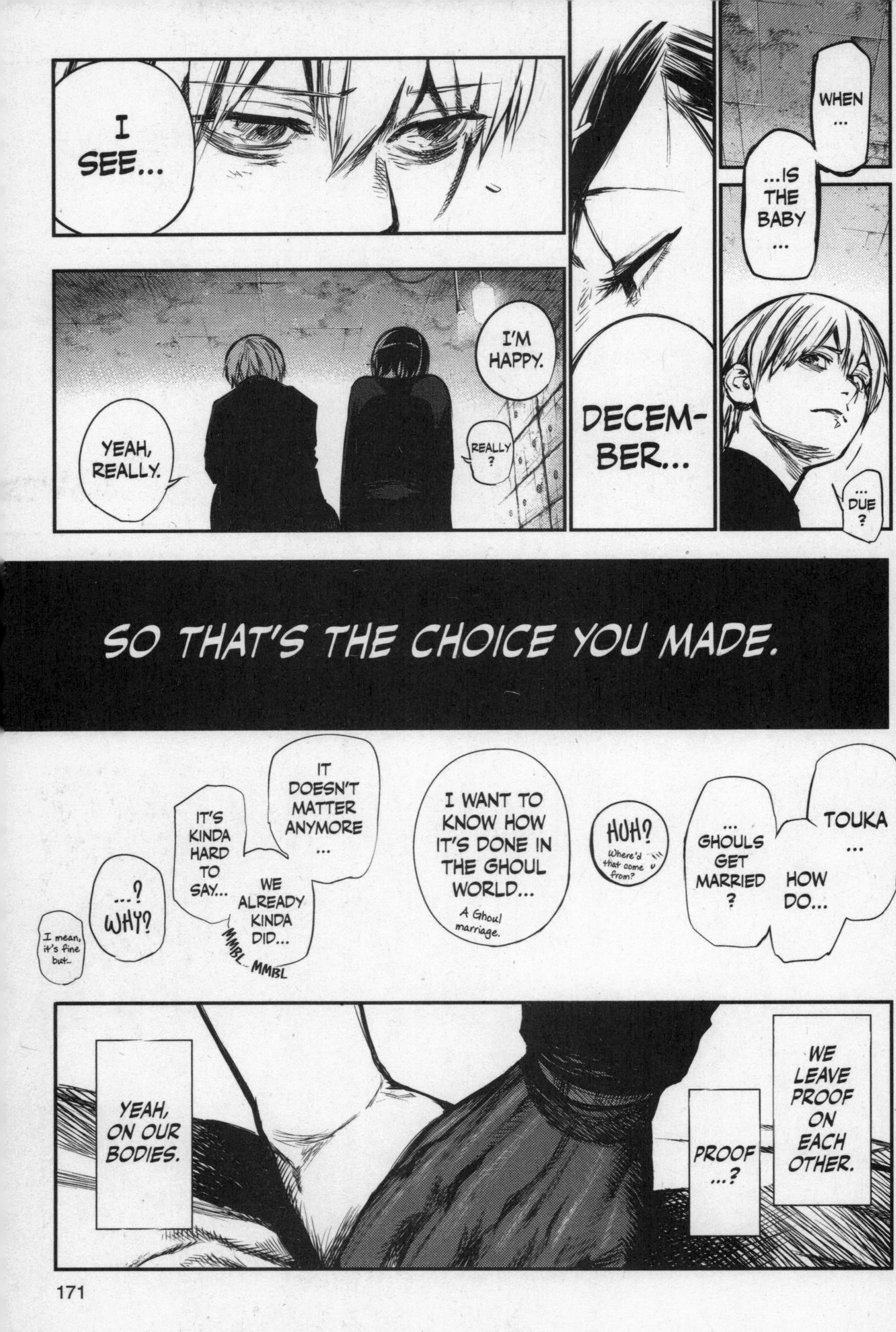
WHEN ...
...IS THE BABY ...
... DUE ?
DECEMBER...
I SEE...
I'M HAPPY.
REALLY ?
YEAH, REALLY.
SO THAT'S THE CHOICE YOU MADE.
TOUKA ...
HOW DO...
... GHOULS GET MARRIED ?
HUH?
Where'd that come from?
I WANT TO KNOW HOW IT'S DONE IN THE GHOUL WORLD...
A Ghoul marriage.
IT DOESN'T MATTER ANYMORE ...
IT'S KINDA HARD TO SAY...
WE ALREADY KINDA DID...
MMBL MMBL
...? WHY?
I mean, it's fine but...
WE LEAVE PROOF ON EACH OTHER.
PROOF ...?
YEAH, ON OUR BODIES.

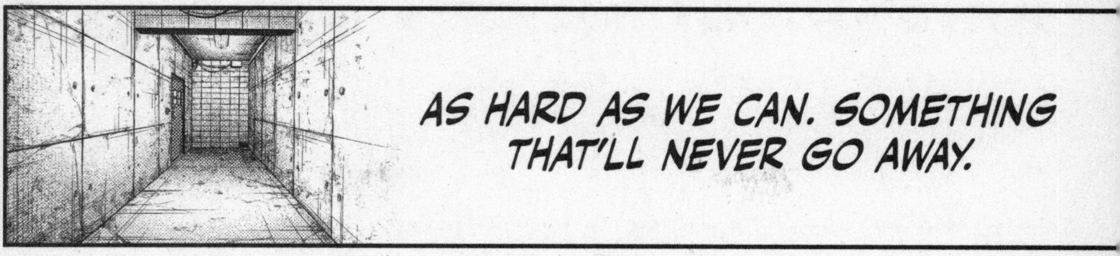
AS HARD AS WE CAN. SOMETHING THAT'LL NEVER GO AWAY.

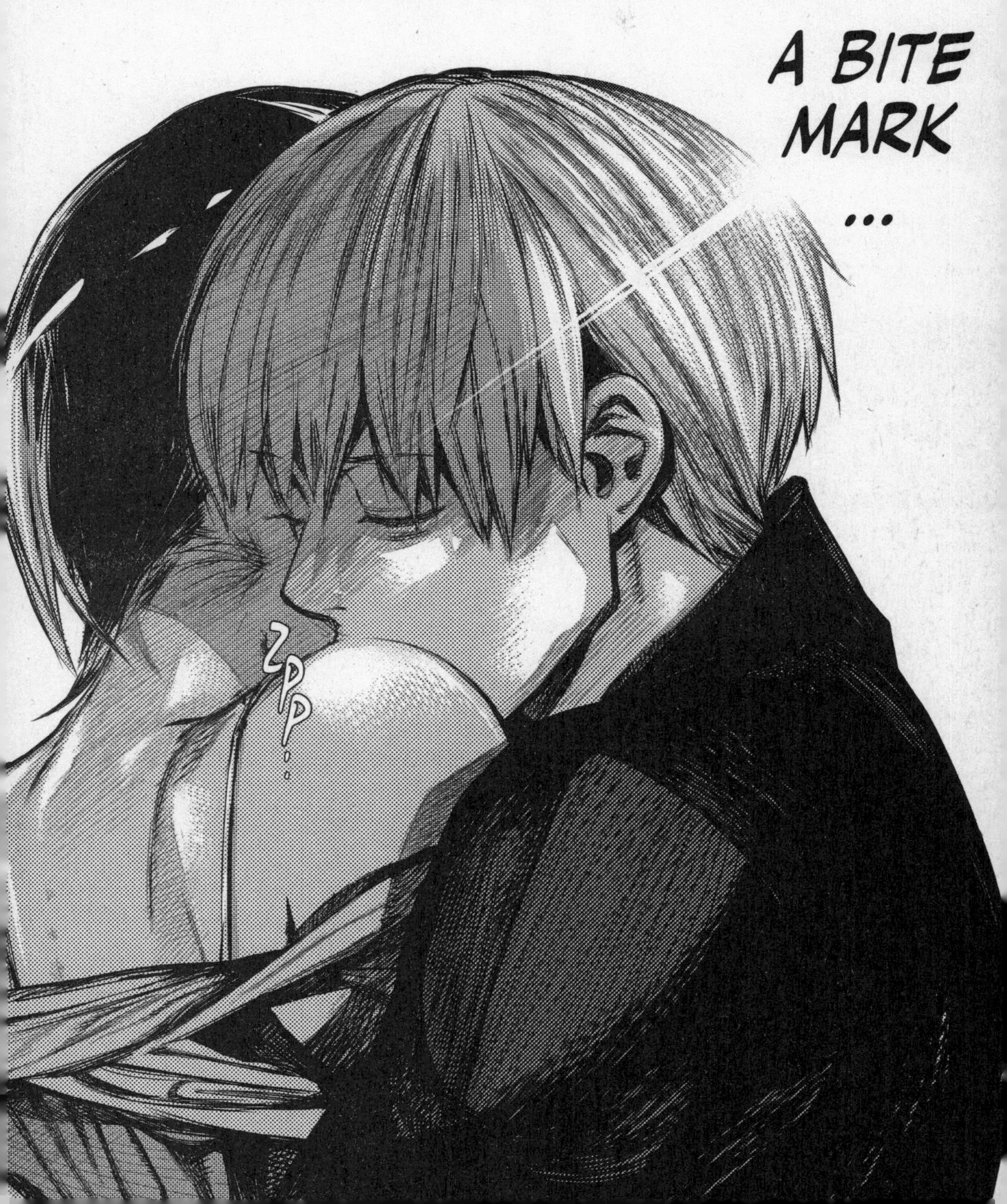
A BITE MARK
...
ZPP...

Double Meaning :132

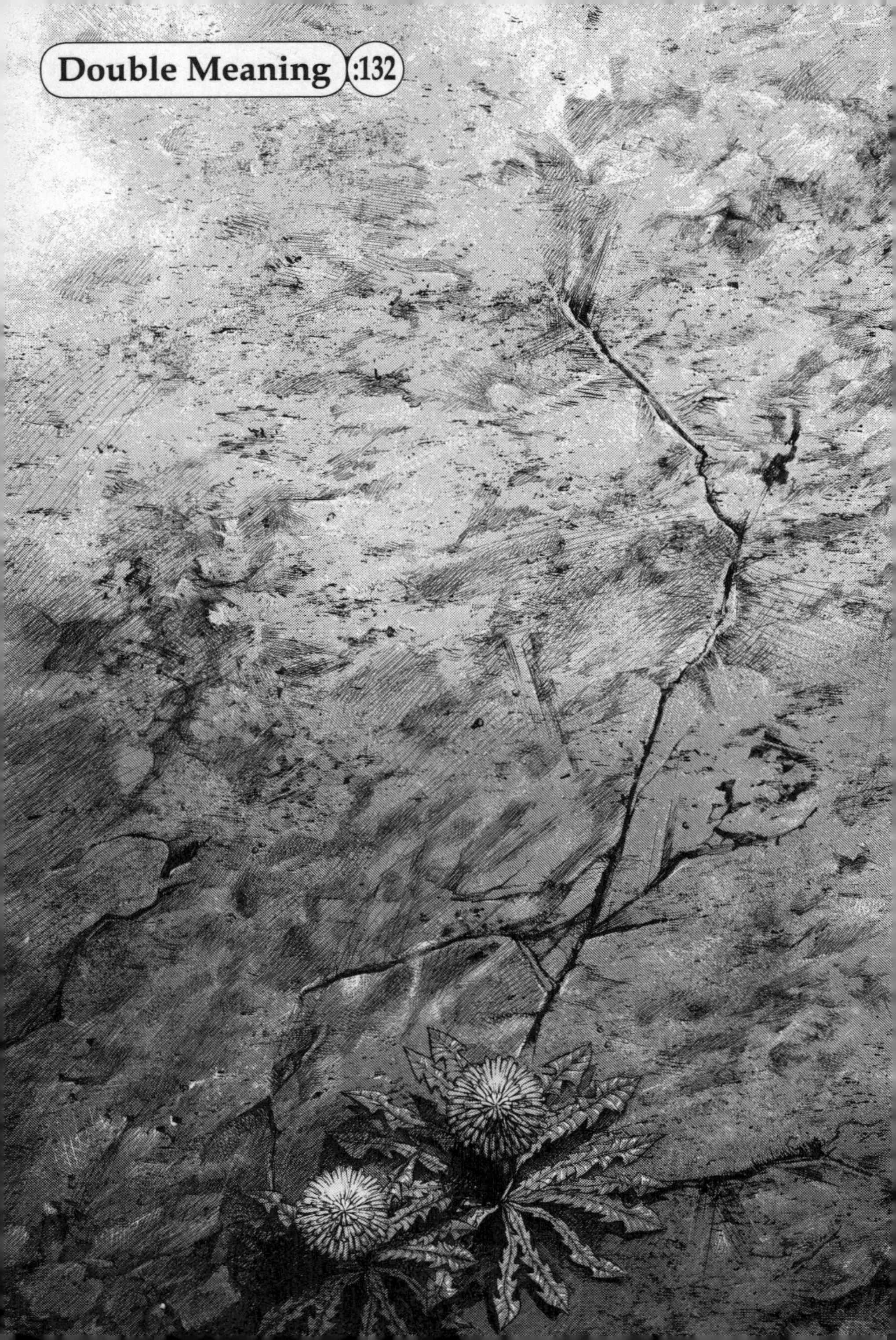

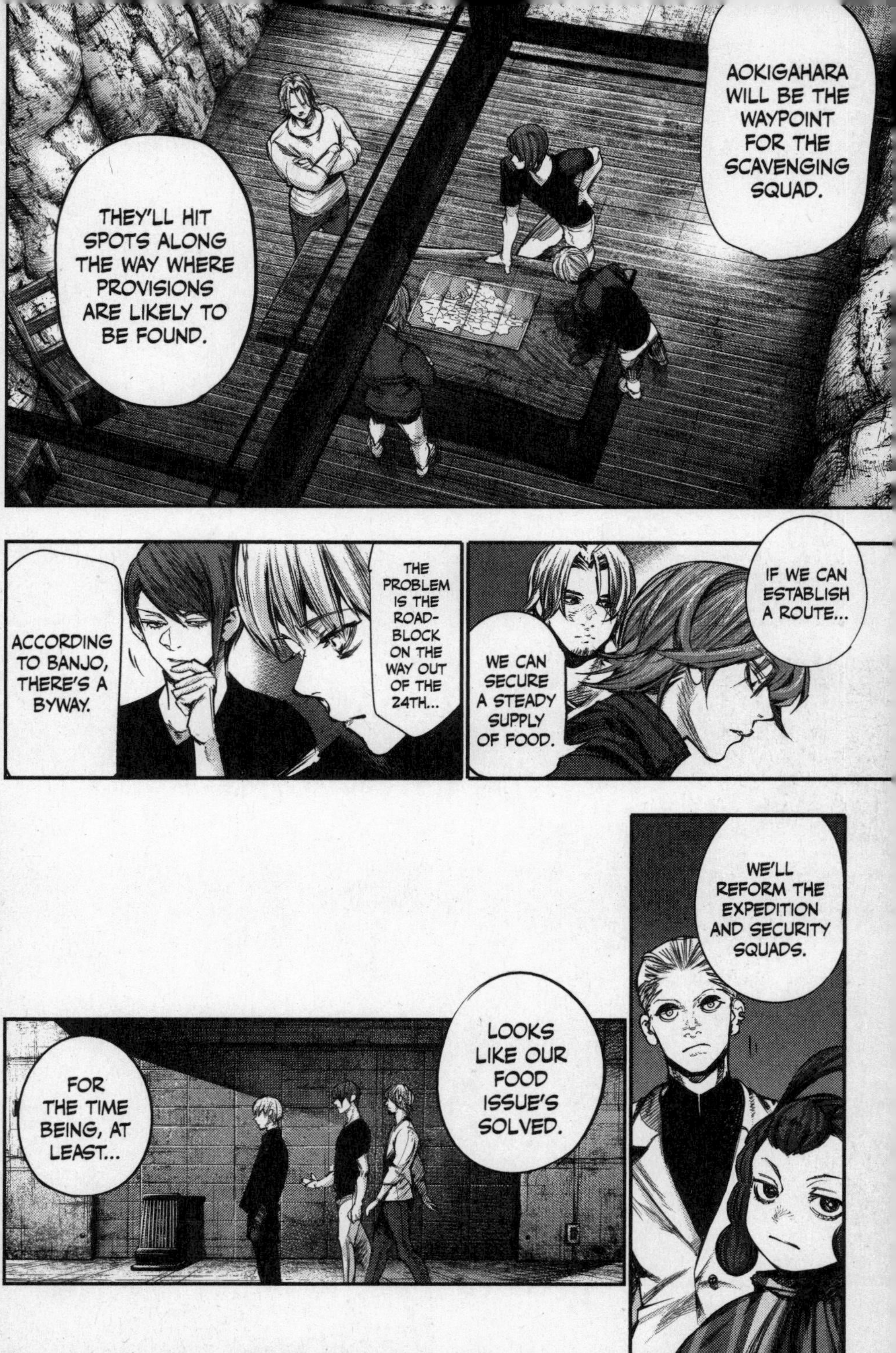

AOKIGAHARA WILL BE THE WAYPOINT FOR THE SCAVENGING SQUAD.
THEY'LL HIT SPOTS ALONG THE WAY WHERE PROVISIONS ARE LIKELY TO BE FOUND.
IF WE CAN ESTABLISH A ROUTE...
WE CAN SECURE A STEADY SUPPLY OF FOOD.
THE PROBLEM IS THE ROAD-BLOCK ON THE WAY OUT OF THE 24TH...
ACCORDING TO BANJO, THERE'S A BYWAY.
WE'LL REFORM THE EXPEDITION AND SECURITY SQUADS.
LOOKS LIKE OUR FOOD ISSUE'S SOLVED.
FOR THE TIME BEING, AT LEAST...

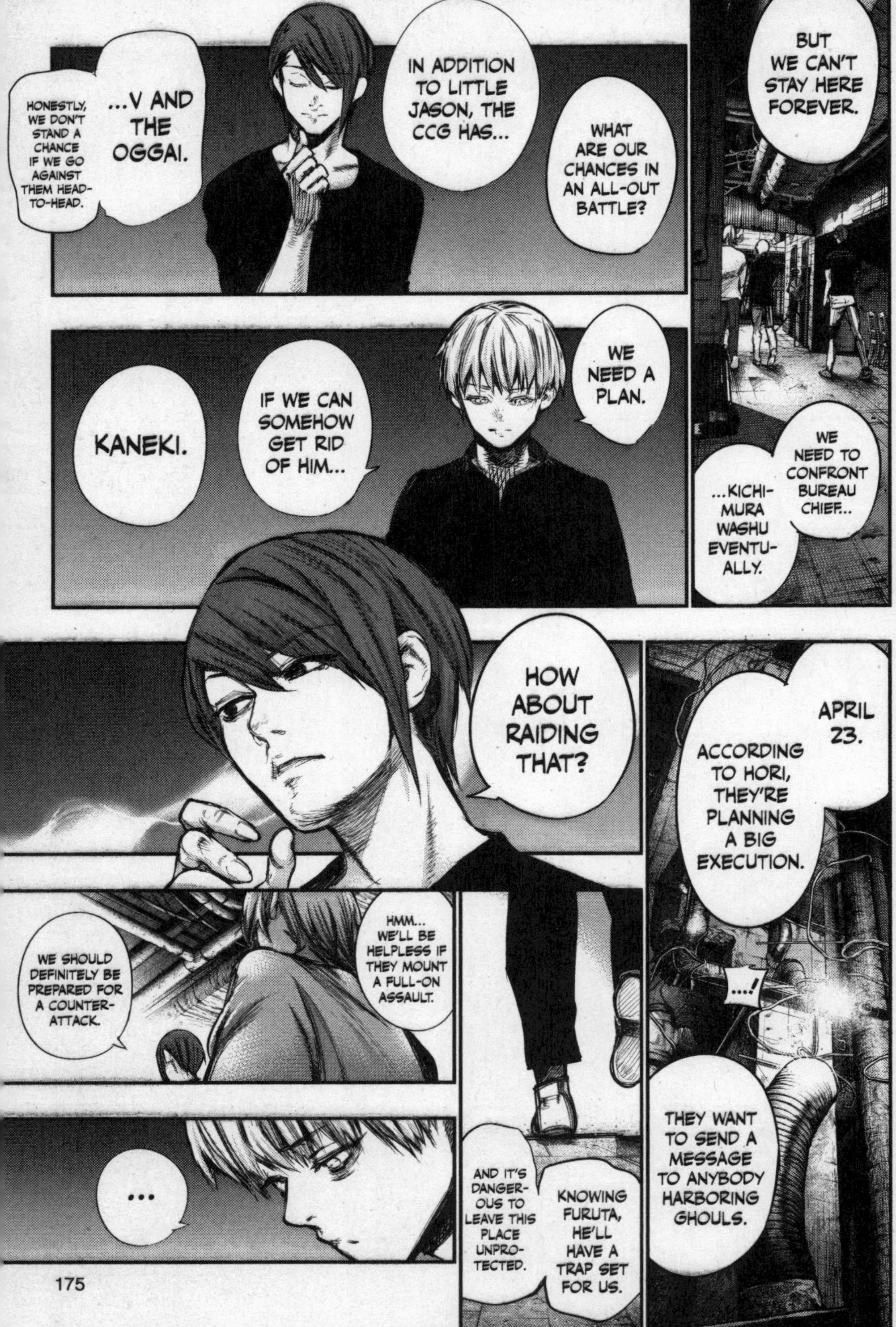
BUT WE CAN'T STAY HERE FOREVER.
WE NEED TO CONFRONT BUREAU CHIEF...
...KICHIMURA WASHU EVENTUALLY.
WHAT ARE OUR CHANCES IN AN ALL-OUT BATTLE?
IN ADDITION TO LITTLE JASON, THE CCG HAS...
...V AND THE OGGAI.
HONESTLY, WE DON'T STAND A CHANCE IF WE GO AGAINST THEM HEAD-TO-HEAD.
WE NEED A PLAN.
IF WE CAN SOMEHOW GET RID OF HIM...
KANEKI.
APRIL 23.
ACCORDING TO HORI, THEY'RE PLANNING A BIG EXECUTION.
...!
THEY WANT TO SEND A MESSAGE TO ANYBODY HARBORING GHOULS.
HOW ABOUT RAIDING THAT?
KNOWING FURUTA, HE'LL HAVE A TRAP SET FOR US.
AND IT'S DANGEROUS TO LEAVE THIS PLACE UNPROTECTED.
HMM... WE'LL BE HELPLESS IF THEY MOUNT A FULL-ON ASSAULT.
WE SHOULD DEFINITELY BE PREPARED FOR A COUNTER-ATTACK.
...

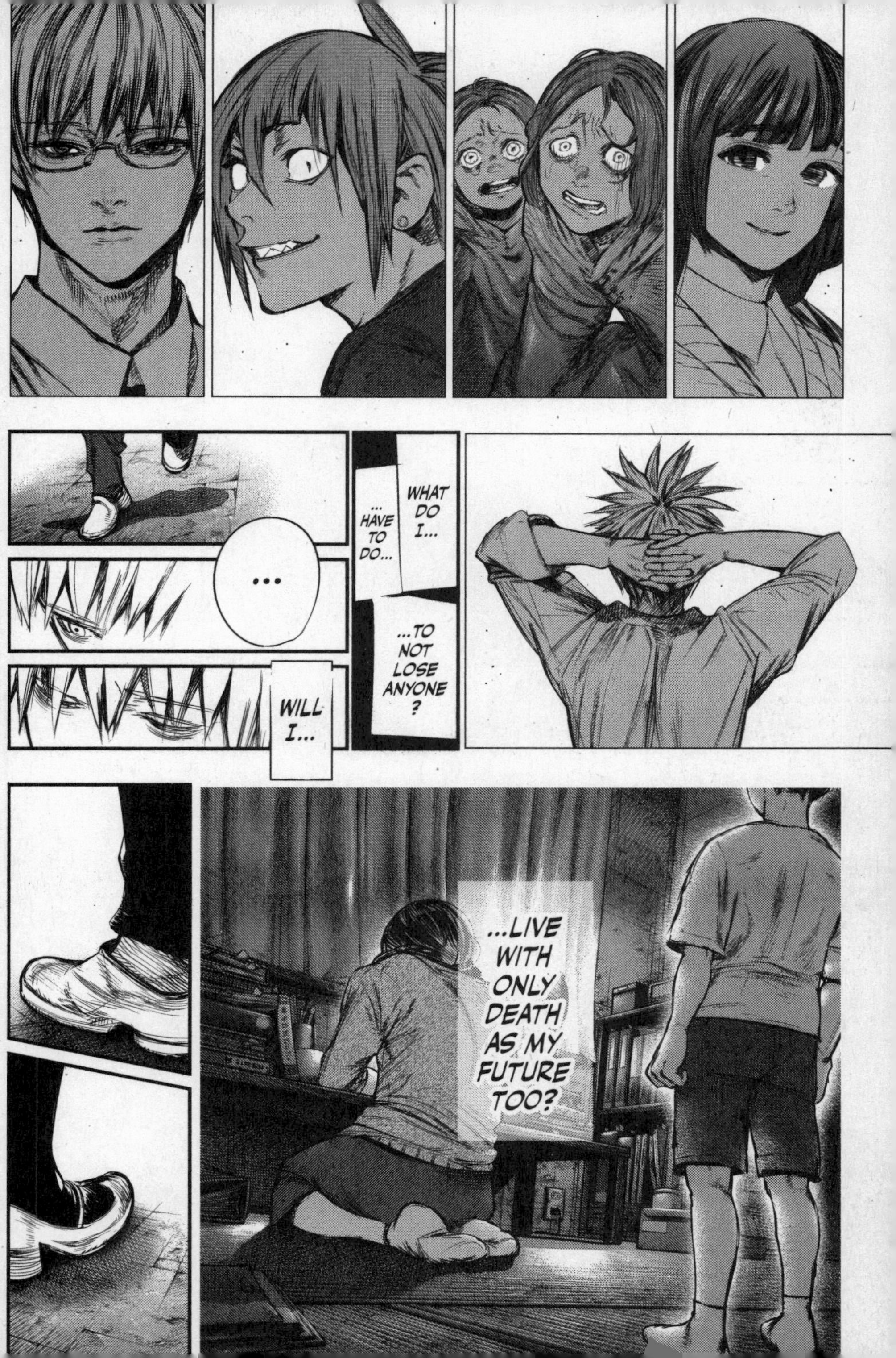
WHAT DO I...
...HAVE TO DO...
...TO NOT LOSE ANYONE?
...
WILL I...
...LIVE WITH ONLY DEATH AS MY FUTURE TOO?

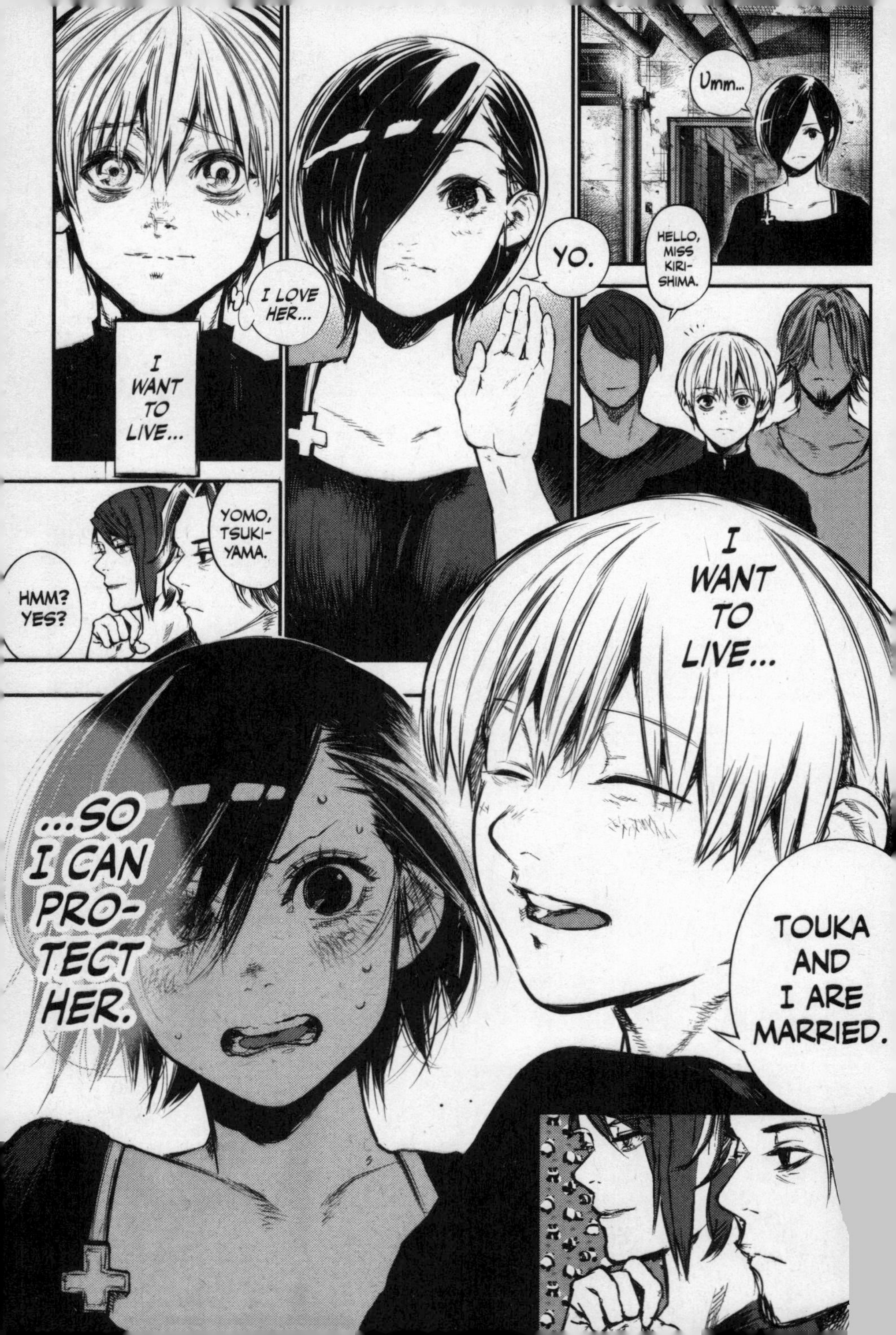
Umm...
HELLO, MISS KIRI-SHIMA.
YO.
I LOVE HER...
I WANT TO LIVE...
YOMO, TSUKI-YAMA.
HMM? YES?
I WANT TO LIVE...
TOUKA AND I ARE MARRIED.
...SO I CAN PRO-TECT HER.

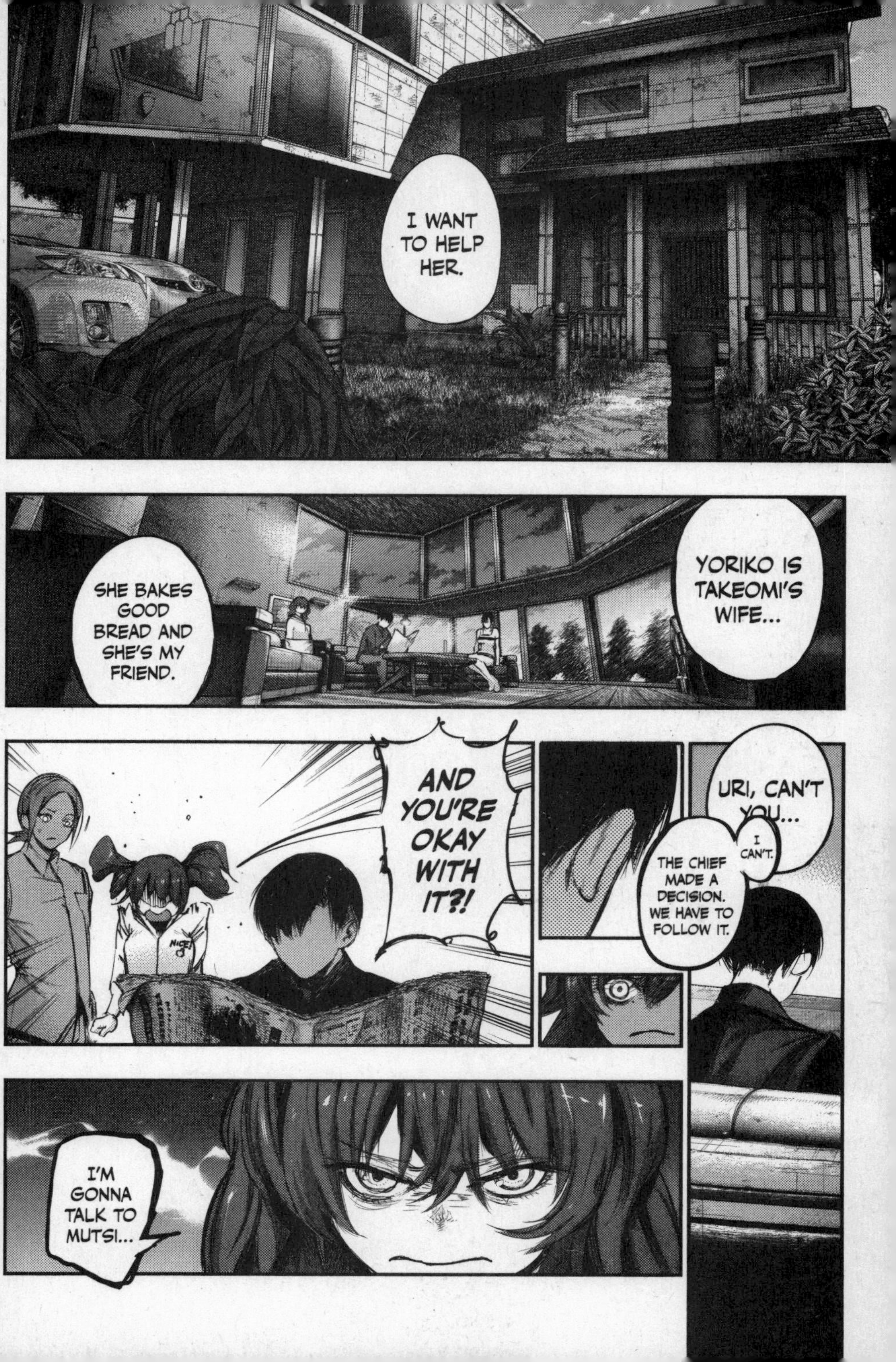
I WANT TO HELP HER.
YORIKO IS TAKEOMI'S WIFE...
SHE BAKES GOOD BREAD AND SHE'S MY FRIEND.
URI, CAN'T YOU...
I CAN'T.
THE CHIEF MADE A DECISION. WE HAVE TO FOLLOW IT.
AND YOU'RE OKAY WITH IT?!
I'M GONNA TALK TO MUTSI...

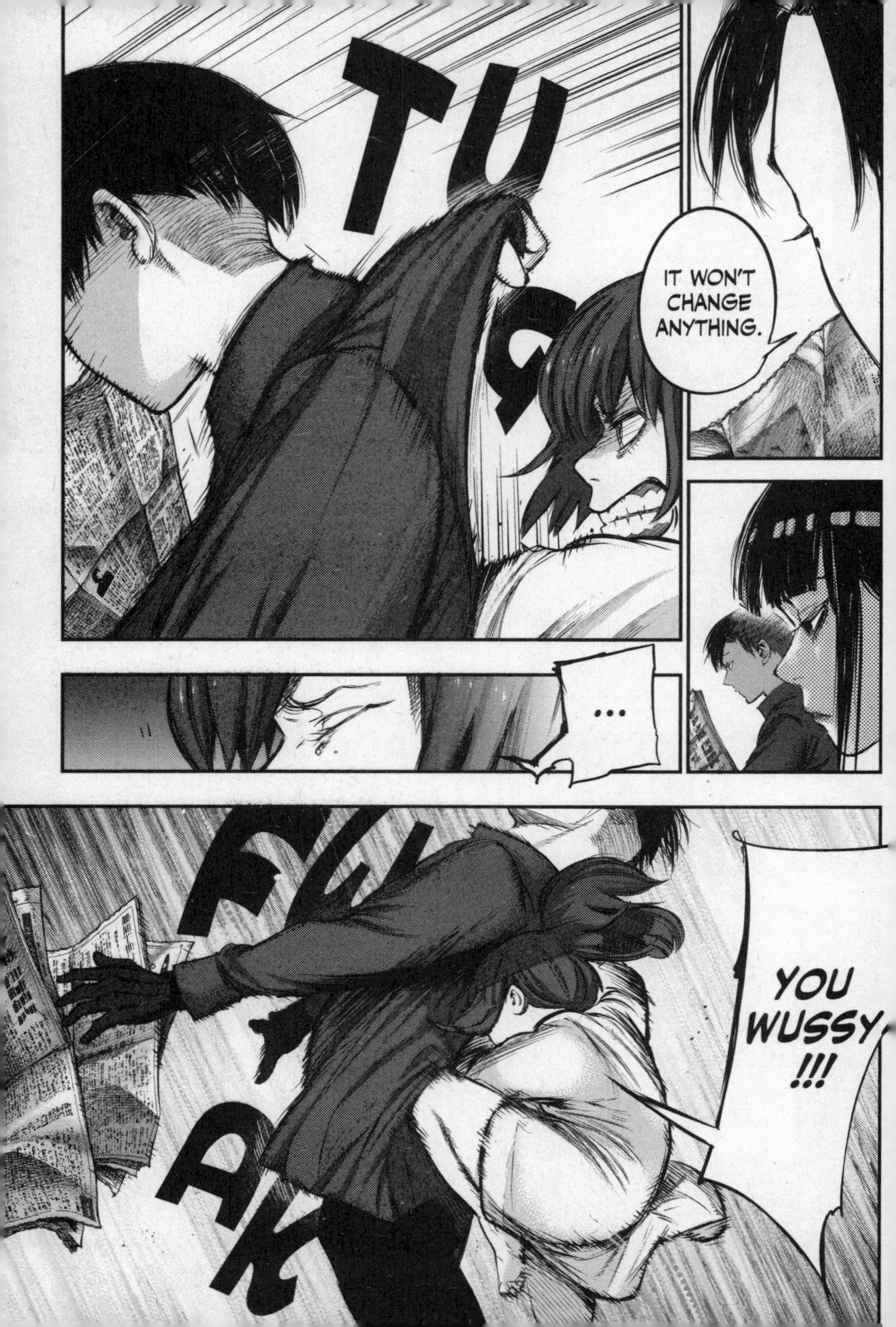
IT WON'T CHANGE ANYTHING.
TUG
...
FWAK
YOU WUSSY!!!

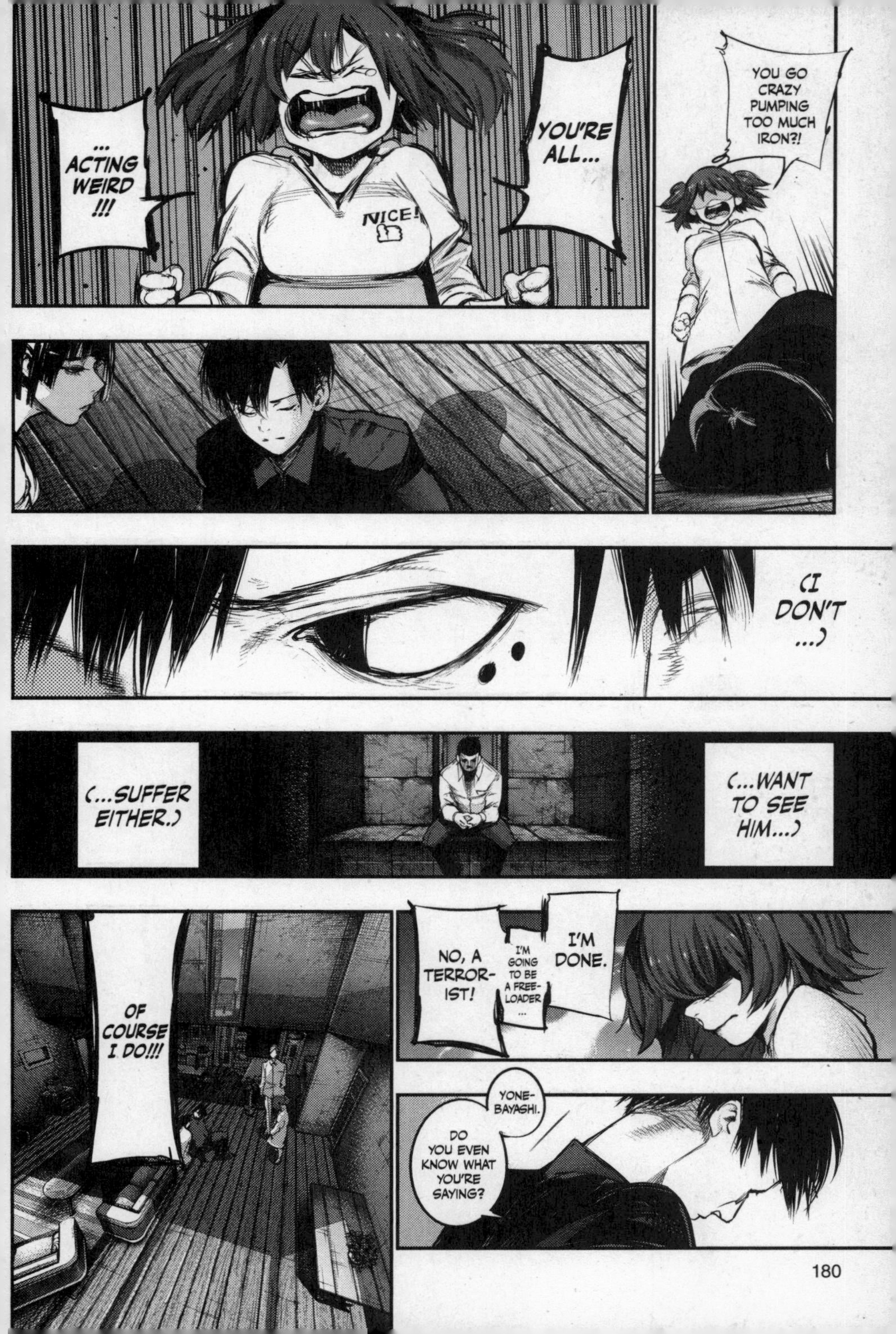
YOU GO CRAZY PUMPING TOO MUCH IRON?!
YOU'RE ALL...
... ACTING WEIRD !!!
(I DON'T ...)
(...WANT TO SEE HIM...)
(...SUFFER EITHER.)
I'M DONE.
I'M GOING TO BE A FREE-LOADER ...
NO, A TERROR-IST!
YONE-BAYASHI.
DO YOU EVEN KNOW WHAT YOU'RE SAYING?
OF COURSE I DO!!!

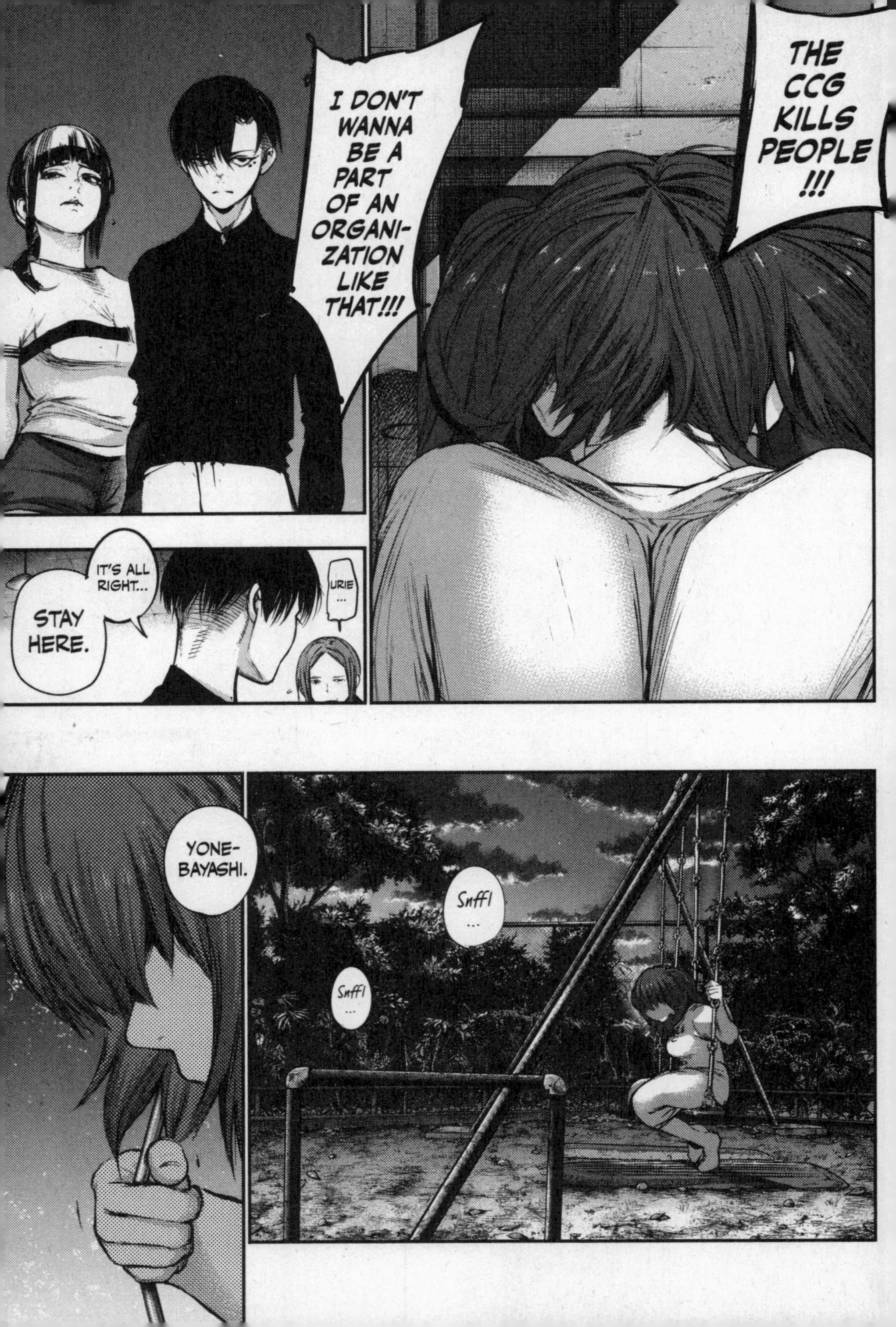
THE CCG KILLS PEOPLE!!!
I DON'T WANNA BE A PART OF AN ORGANIZATION LIKE THAT!!!
URIE ...
IT'S ALL RIGHT...
STAY HERE.
Snffl ...
Snffl ...
YONE-BAYASHI.

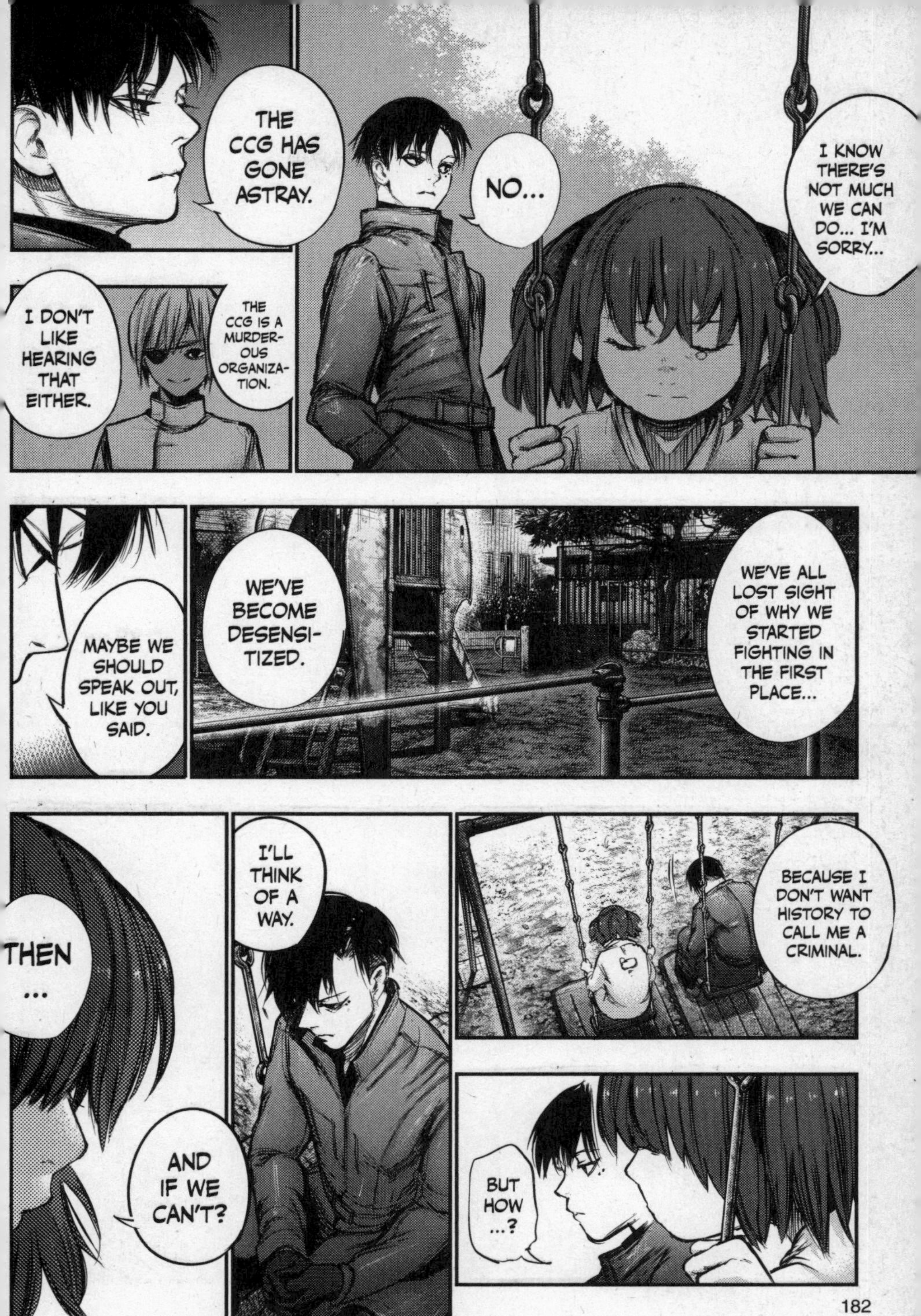
I KNOW THERE'S NOT MUCH WE CAN DO... I'M SORRY...
NO...
THE CCG HAS GONE ASTRAY.
THE CCG IS A MURDER-OUS ORGANIZA-TION.
I DON'T LIKE HEARING THAT EITHER.
WE'VE ALL LOST SIGHT OF WHY WE STARTED FIGHTING IN THE FIRST PLACE...
WE'VE BECOME DESENSI-TIZED.
MAYBE WE SHOULD SPEAK OUT, LIKE YOU SAID.
BECAUSE I DON'T WANT HISTORY TO CALL ME A CRIMINAL.
BUT HOW ...?
I'LL THINK OF A WAY.
AND IF WE CAN'T?
THEN ...

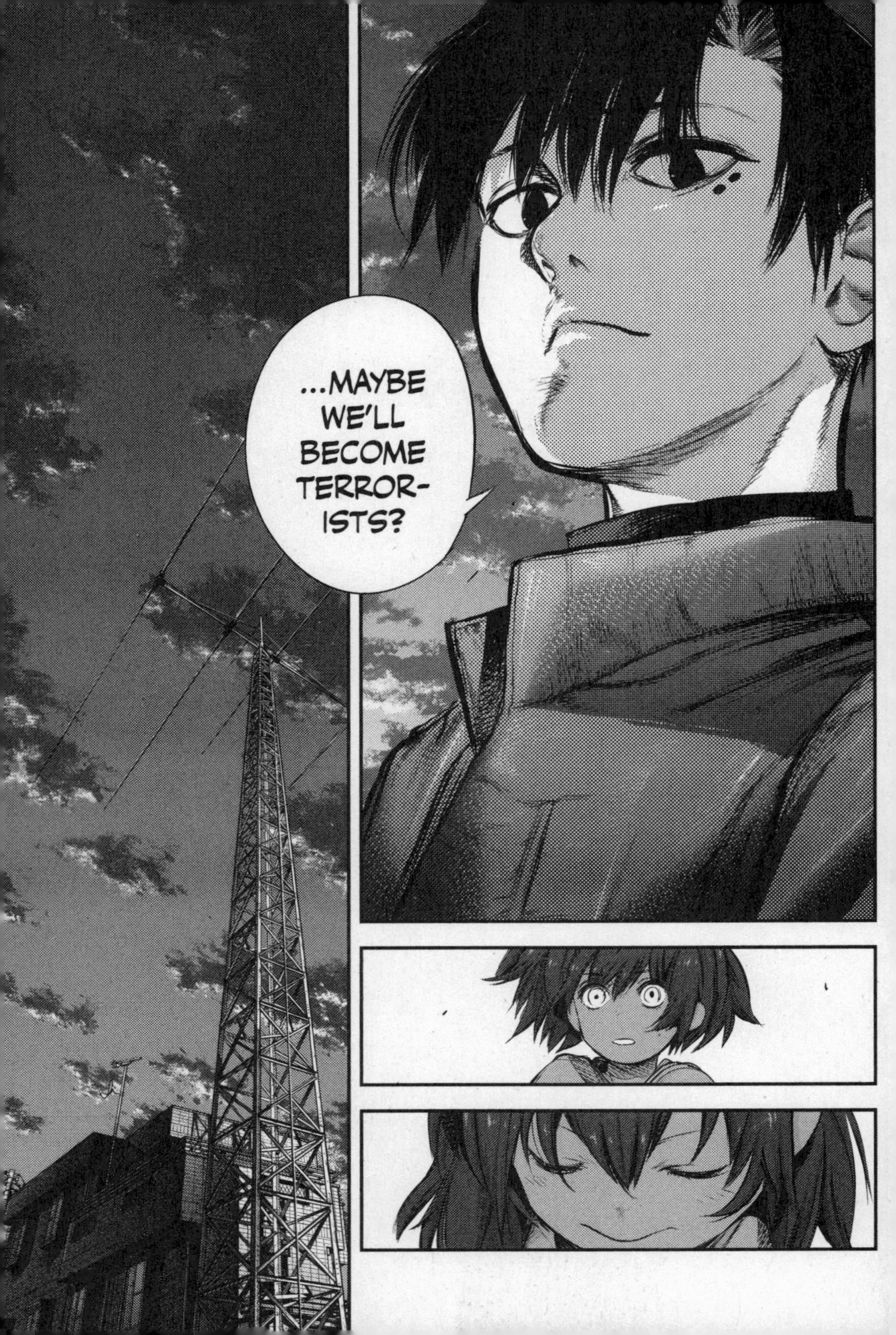
...MAYBE WE'LL BECOME TERROR-ISTS?

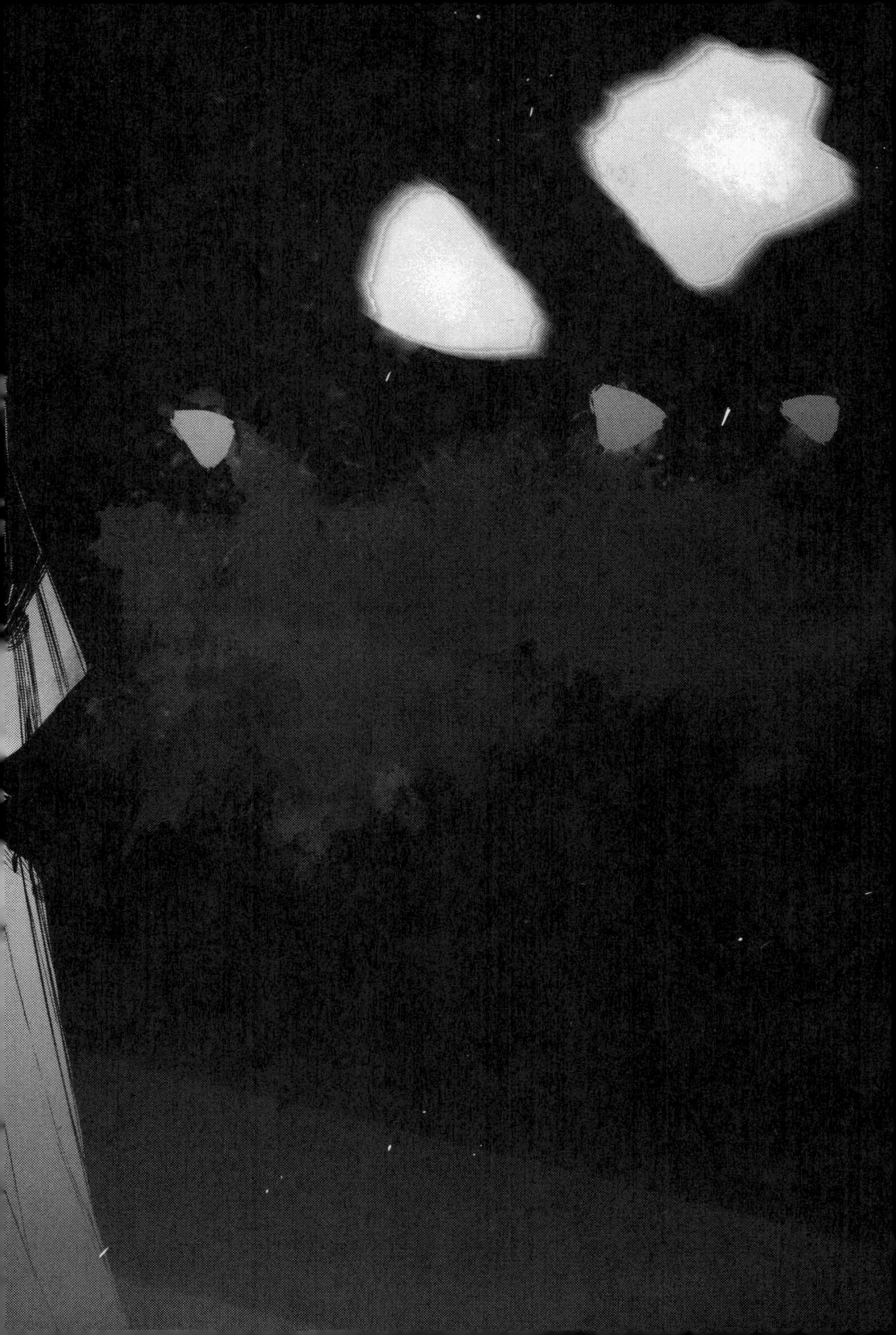

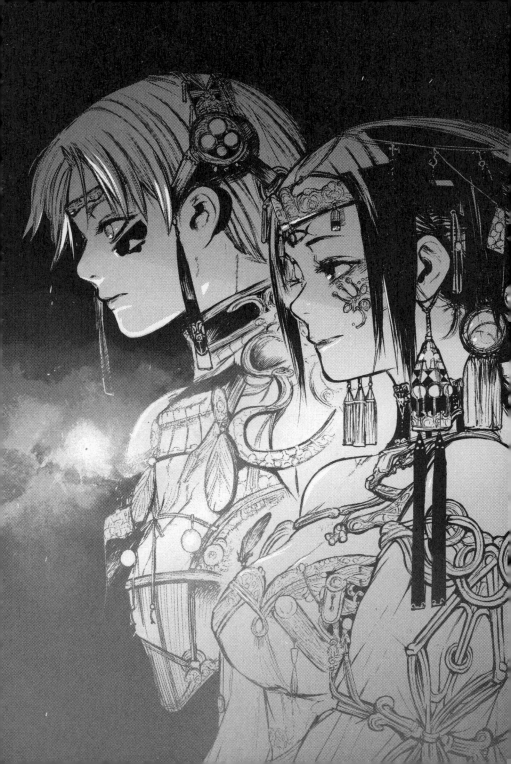

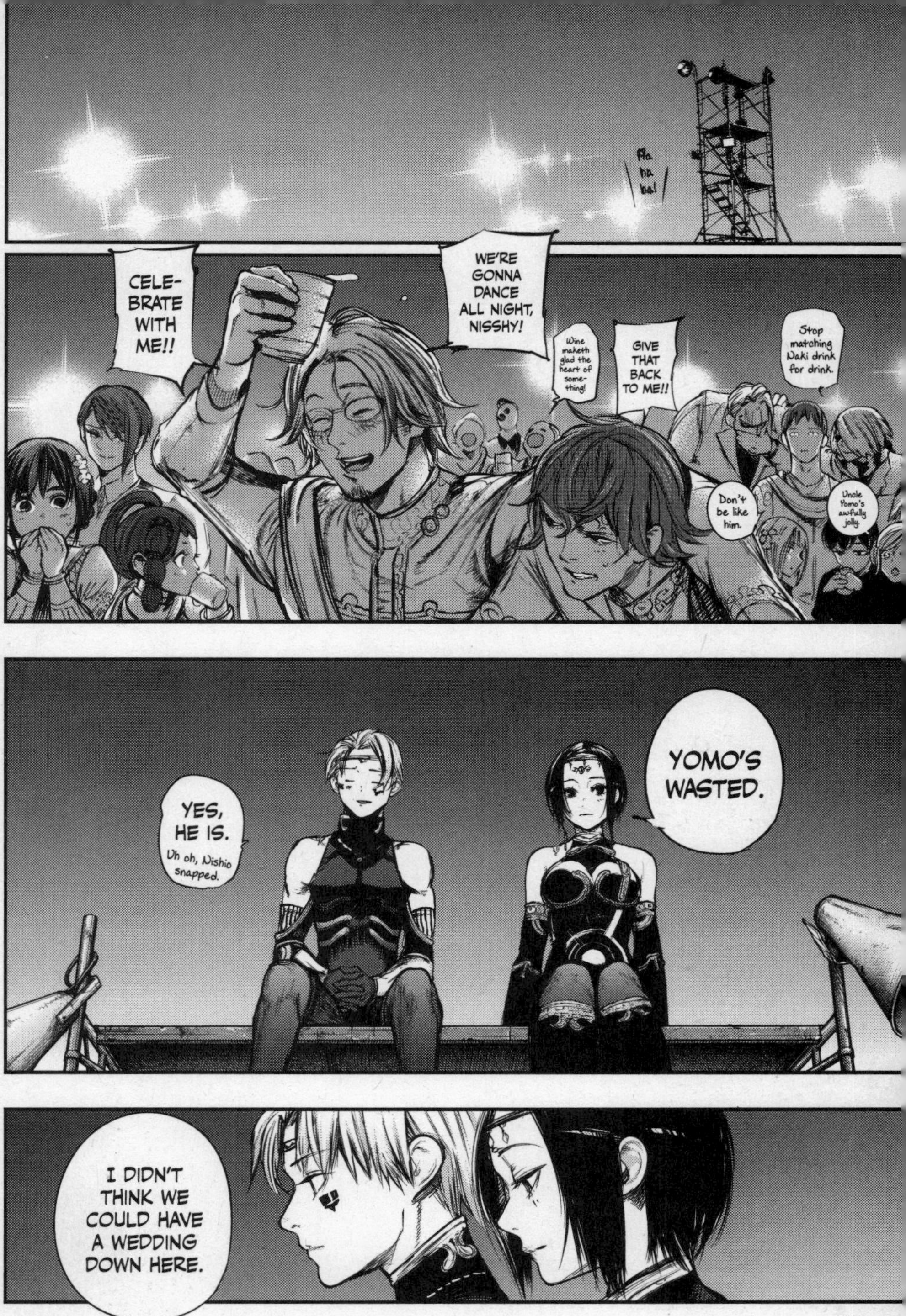
Ha ha ha!
Stop matching Naki drink for drink.
Uncle Yomo's awfully jolly.
Don't be like him.
GIVE THAT BACK TO ME!!
Wine maketh glad the heart of some-thing!
WE'RE GONNA DANCE ALL NIGHT, NISSHY!
CELE-BRATE WITH ME!!
YOMO'S WASTED.
YES, HE IS.
Uh oh, Nishio snapped.
I DIDN'T THINK WE COULD HAVE A WEDDING DOWN HERE.

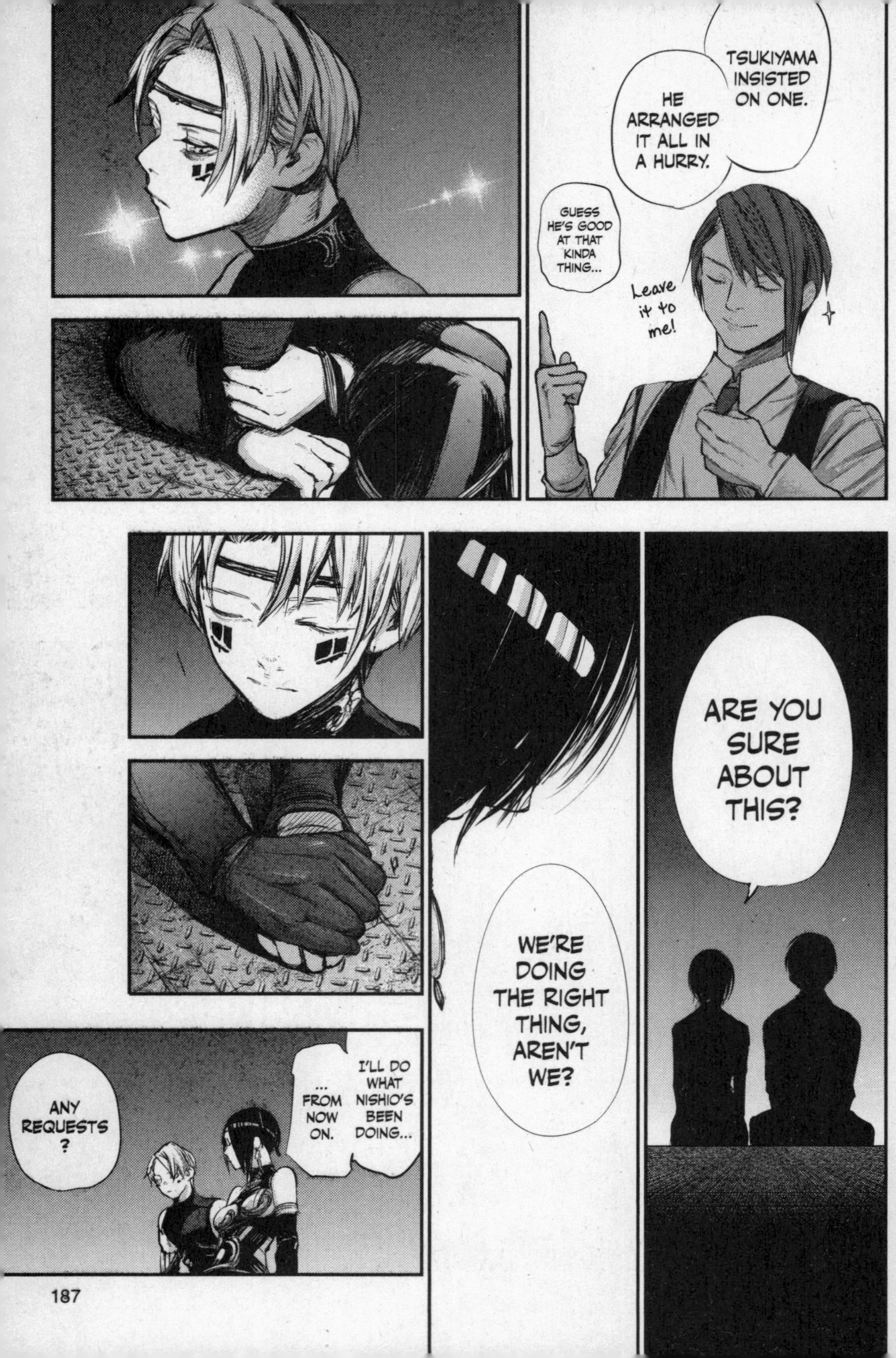
TSUKIYAMA INSISTED ON ONE.
HE ARRANGED IT ALL IN A HURRY.
GUESS HE'S GOOD AT THAT KINDA THING...
Leave it to me!
ARE YOU SURE ABOUT THIS?
WE'RE DOING THE RIGHT THING, AREN'T WE?
I'LL DO WHAT NISHIO'S BEEN DOING...
...FROM NOW ON.
ANY REQUESTS?

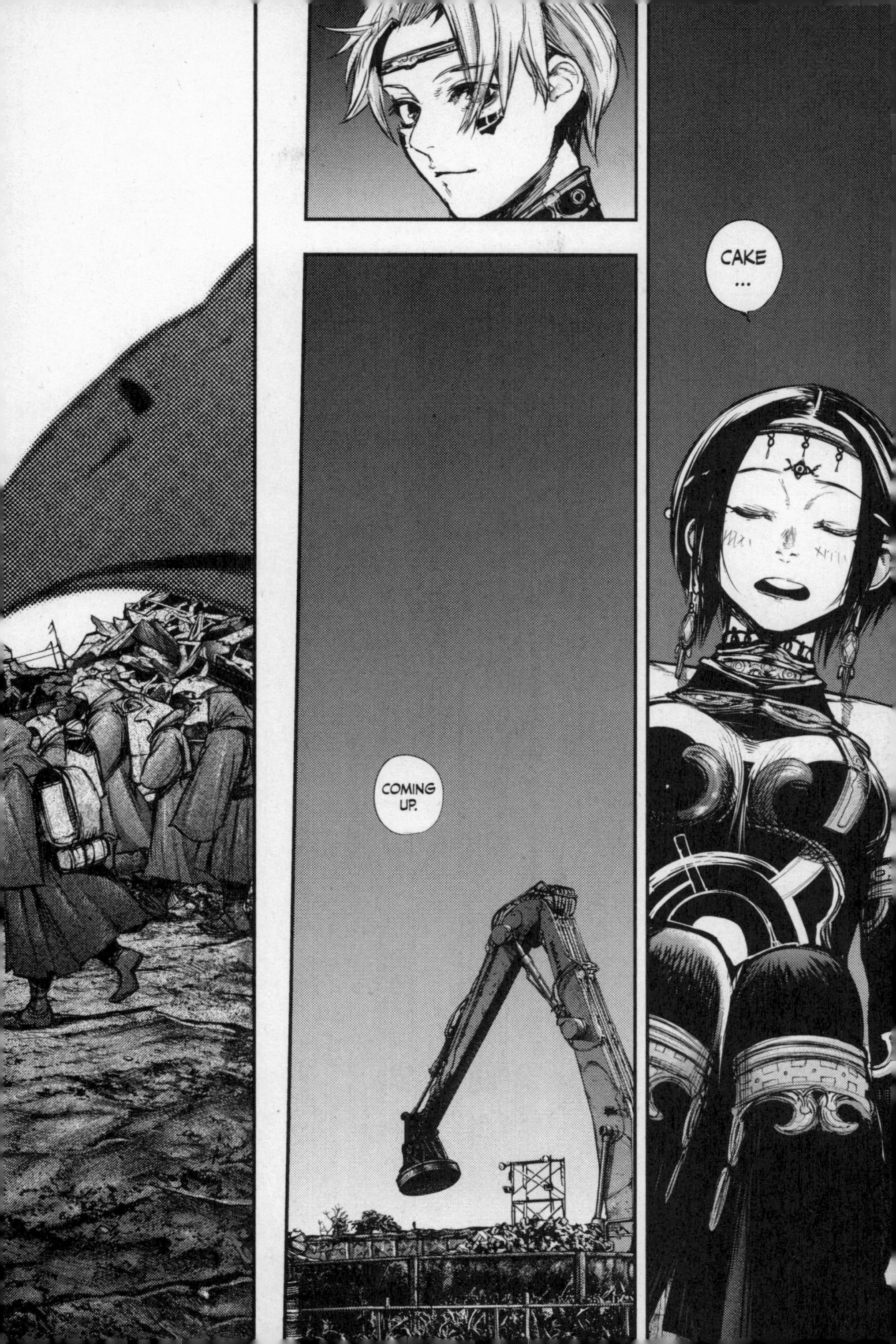
CAKE ...
COMING UP.

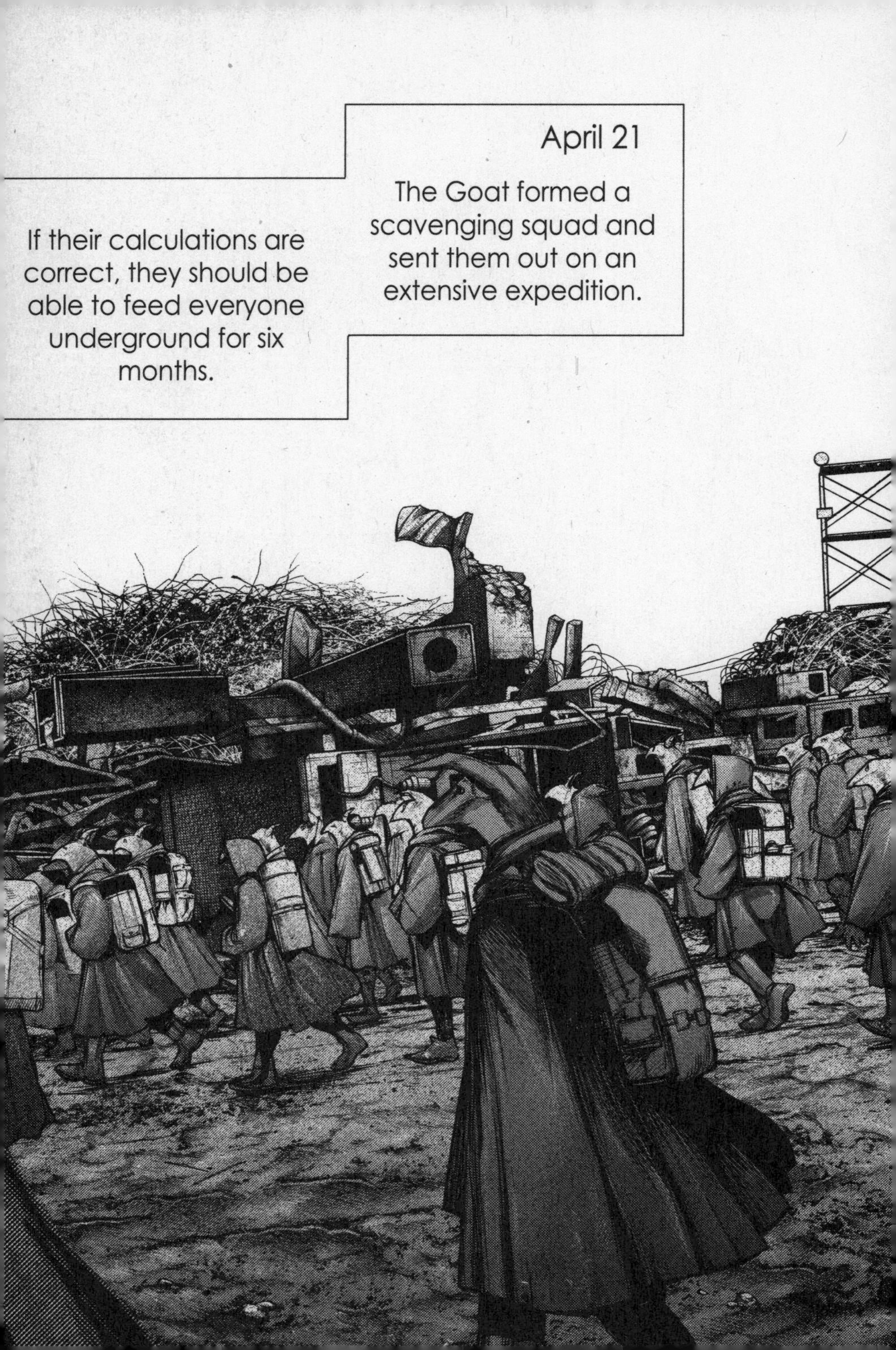
April 21
The Goat formed a scavenging squad and sent them out on an extensive expedition.
If their calculations are correct, they should be able to feed everyone underground for six months.

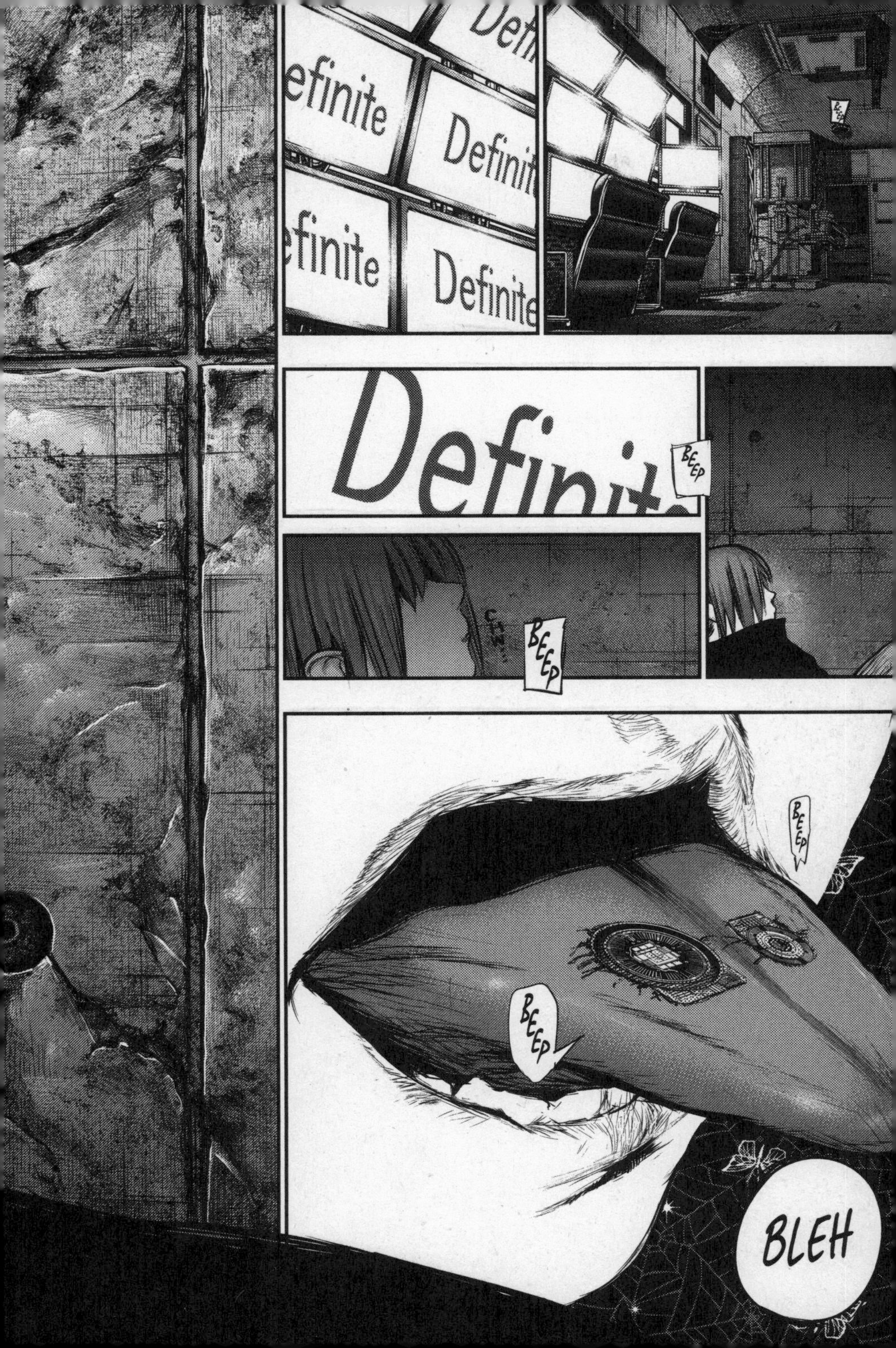

BEEP
Defi
efinite
Definit
efinite
Definite
Definit
BEEP
BEEP
BEEP
BEEP
BLEH

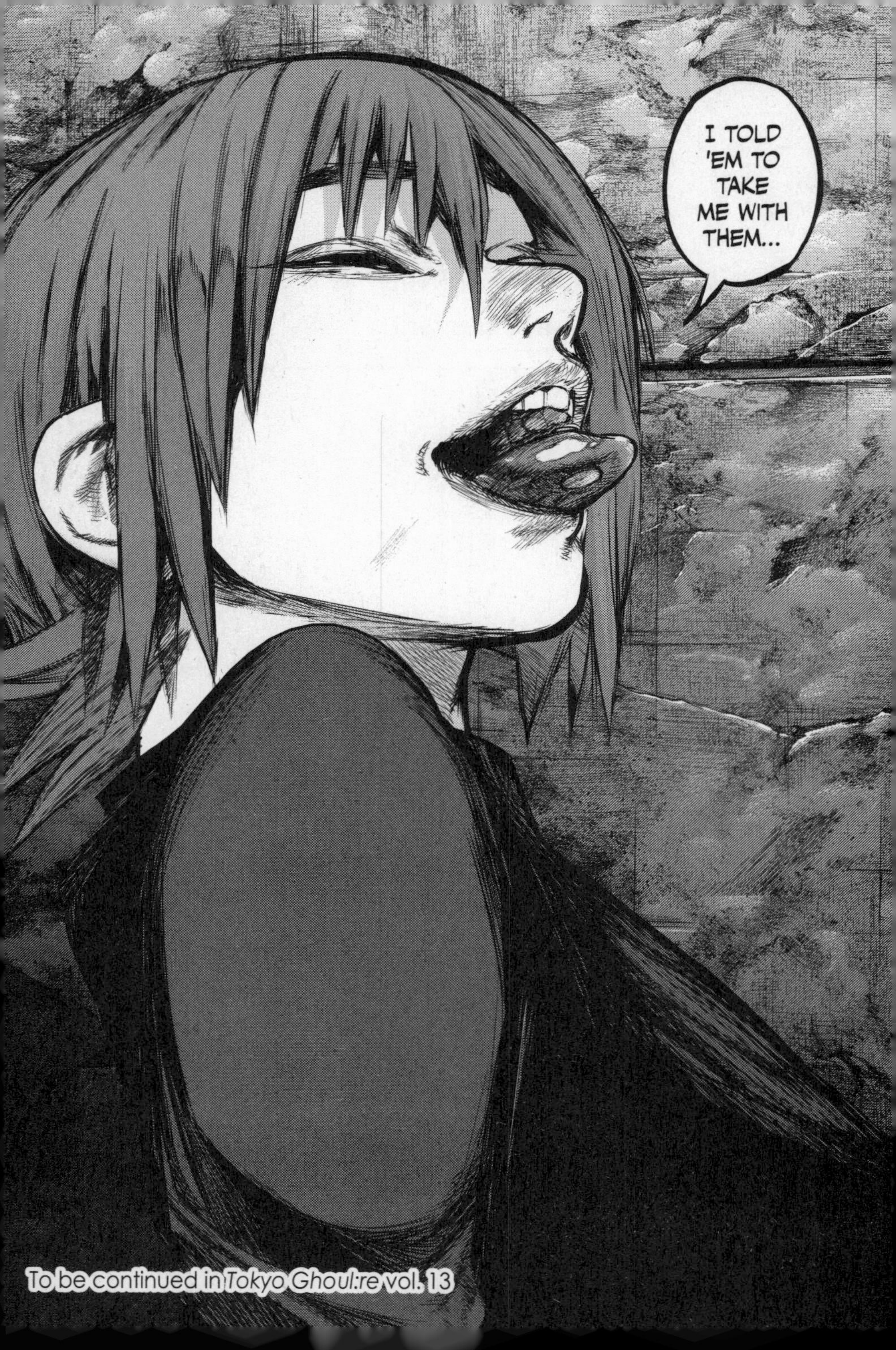
I TOLD 'EM TO TAKE ME WITH THEM...
To be continued in *Tokyo Ghoul:re* vol. 13

Weighted Mag Wristband Heated Staring Match

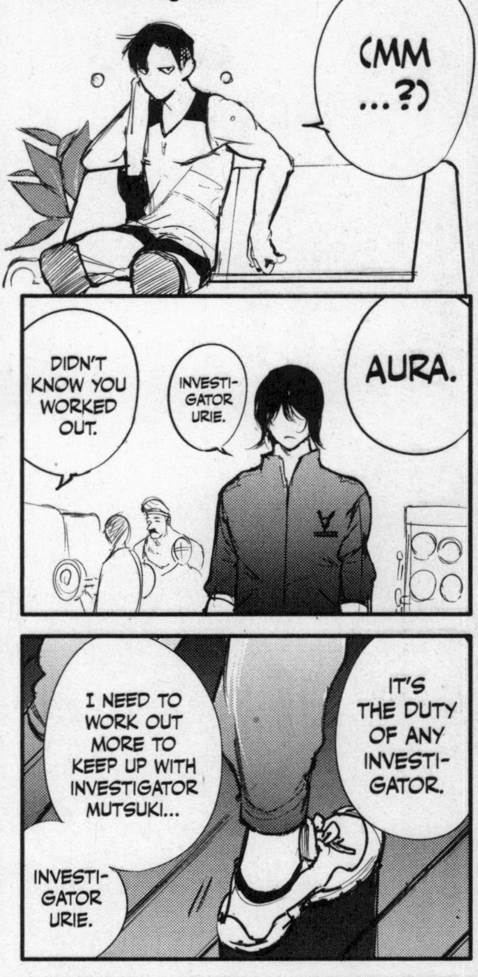
(MM ...?)
AURA.
INVESTIGATOR URIE.
DIDN'T KNOW YOU WORKED OUT.
IT'S THE DUTY OF ANY INVESTIGATOR.
I NEED TO WORK OUT MORE TO KEEP UP WITH INVESTIGATOR MUTSUKI...
INVESTIGATOR URIE.
DON'T ASSUME YOU'RE THE ONLY ONE MAGGIN', URIE.
Heh heh heh...
Heh heh...
MAGGIN' ...?

Magna Carta -Gravel Chapter-

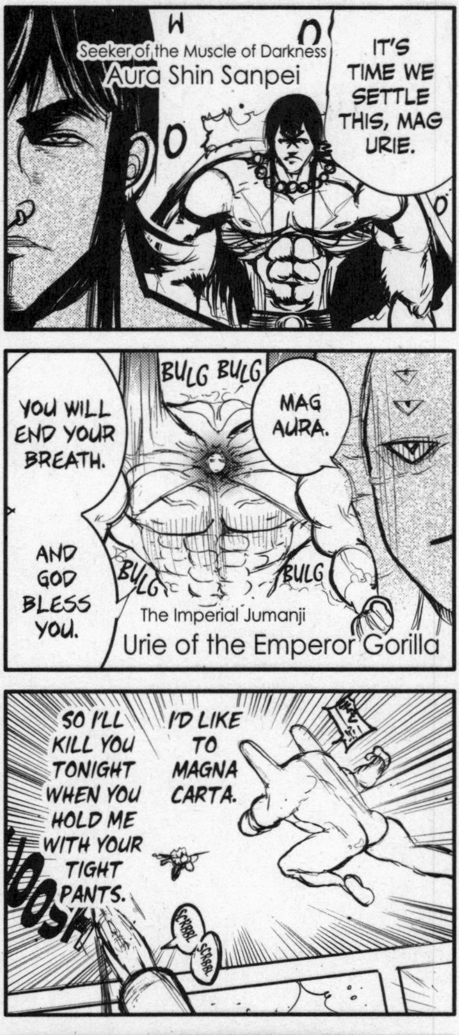
IT'S TIME WE SETTLE THIS, MAG URIE.
Seeker of the Muscle of Darkness
Aura Shin Sanpei
MAG AURA.
BULG BULG
YOU WILL END YOUR BREATH.
AND GOD BLESS YOU.
BULG
BULG
The Imperial Jumanji
Urie of the Emperor Gorilla
I'D LIKE TO MAGNA CARTA.
SO I'LL KILL YOU TONIGHT WHEN YOU HOLD ME WITH YOUR TIGHT PANTS.
SCRBBL
SCRBBL
WHAT IS THAT?
I'M GONNA SEND IT IN TO YOUNG JUMP.
SCRBBL
SCRBBL
HMM.

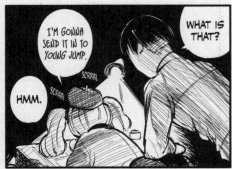

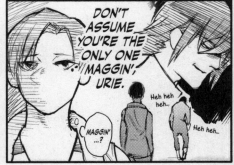

Jelly Beard

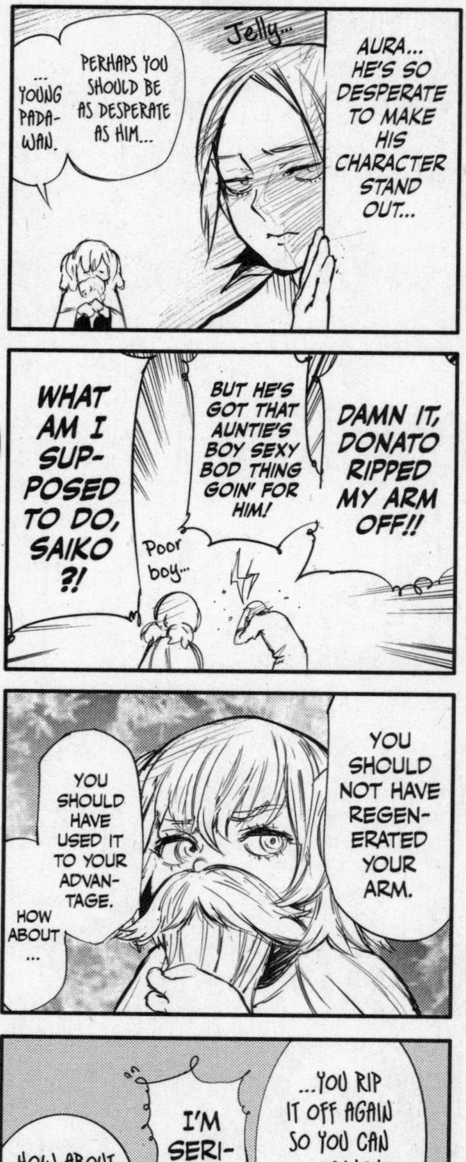
AURA... HE'S SO DESPERATE TO MAKE HIS CHARACTER STAND OUT...
Jelly...
PERHAPS YOU SHOULD BE AS DESPERATE AS HIM...
...YOUNG PADAWAN.
DAMN IT, DONATO RIPPED MY ARM OFF!!
BUT HE'S GOT THAT AUNTIE'S BOY SEXY BOD THING GOIN' FOR HIM!
WHAT AM I SUPPOSED TO DO, SAIKO?!
Poor boy...
YOU SHOULD NOT HAVE REGENERATED YOUR ARM.
YOU SHOULD HAVE USED IT TO YOUR ADVANTAGE.
HOW ABOUT...
...YOU RIP IT OFF AGAIN SO YOU CAN LAUNCH ROCKET FISTS?
VWWW
I'M SERIOUS!
HOW ABOUT ROCKET BREAD?
VWWW

Because...

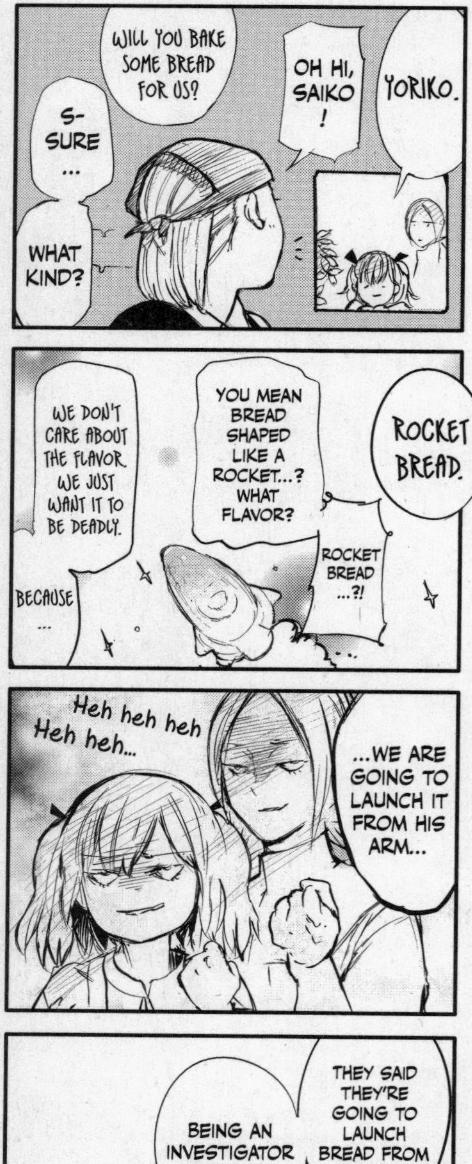
YORIKO.
OH HI, SAIKO!
WILL YOU BAKE SOME BREAD FOR US?
S-SURE...
WHAT KIND?
ROCKET BREAD.
YOU MEAN BREAD SHAPED LIKE A ROCKET...? WHAT FLAVOR?
ROCKET BREAD...?!
WE DON'T CARE ABOUT THE FLAVOR. WE JUST WANT IT TO BE DEADLY.
BECAUSE...
...WE ARE GOING TO LAUNCH IT FROM HIS ARM...
Heh heh heh Heh heh...
THEY SAID THEY'RE GOING TO LAUNCH BREAD FROM HIS ARM.
BEING AN INVESTIGATOR SEEMS FUN.

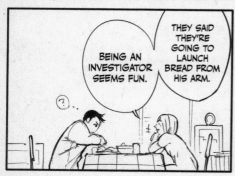

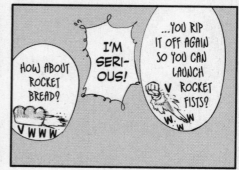

Price of Peace

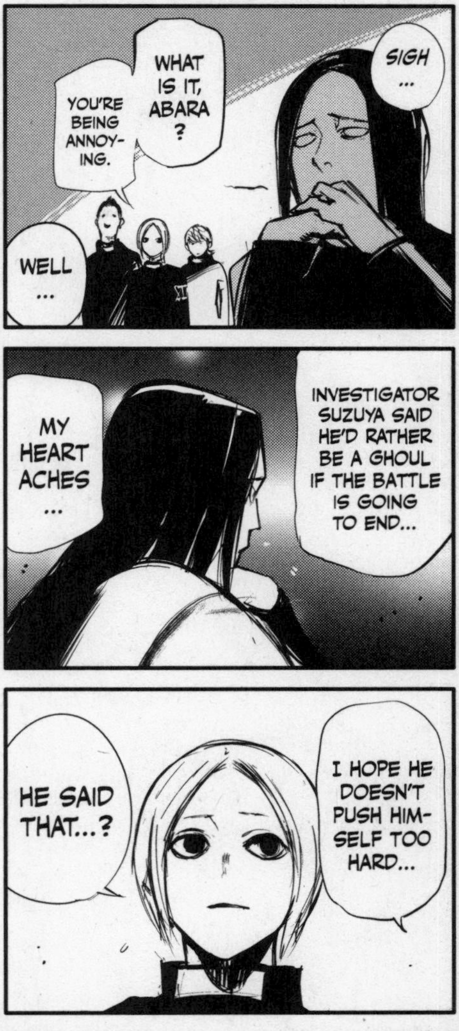
SIGH ...
WHAT IS IT, ABARA ?
YOU'RE BEING ANNOY-ING.
WELL ...
INVESTIGATOR SUZUYA SAID HE'D RATHER BE A GHOUL IF THE BATTLE IS GOING TO END...
MY HEART ACHES ...
I HOPE HE DOESN'T PUSH HIM-SELF TOO HARD...
HE SAID THAT...?
IF THE BATTLE ENDS, I COULD KILL YOU, ABARA.
ME TOO.
I WILL FIGHT UNTIL THE END AS A CHILD OF THE STARS.
MM...? MM...?

Cool

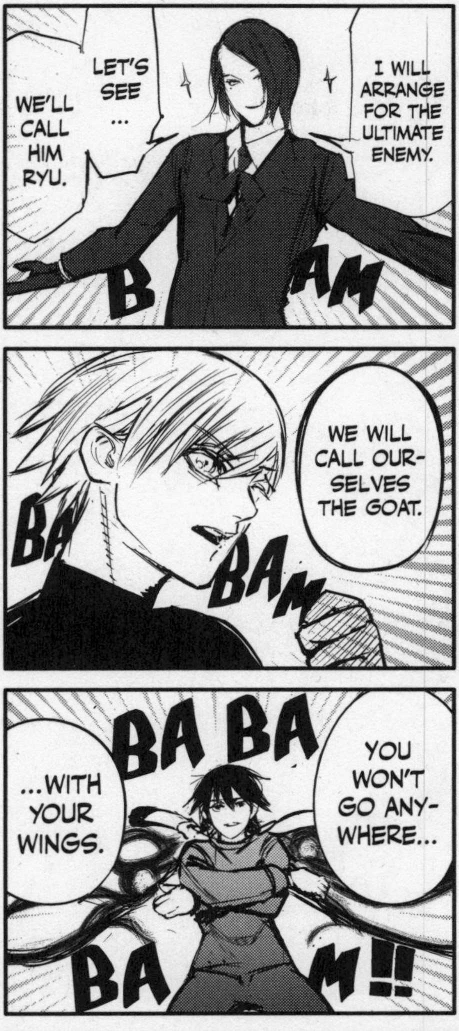
I WILL ARRANGE FOR THE ULTIMATE ENEMY.
LET'S SEE ...
WE'LL CALL HIM RYU.
BAM
WE WILL CALL OUR-SELVES THE GOAT.
BA BAM
YOU WON'T GO ANY-WHERE...
...WITH YOUR WINGS.
BA BA BA BAM!!
We have no shame!!!

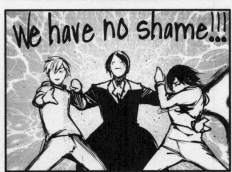

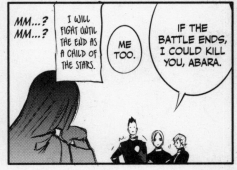

Speed comparison

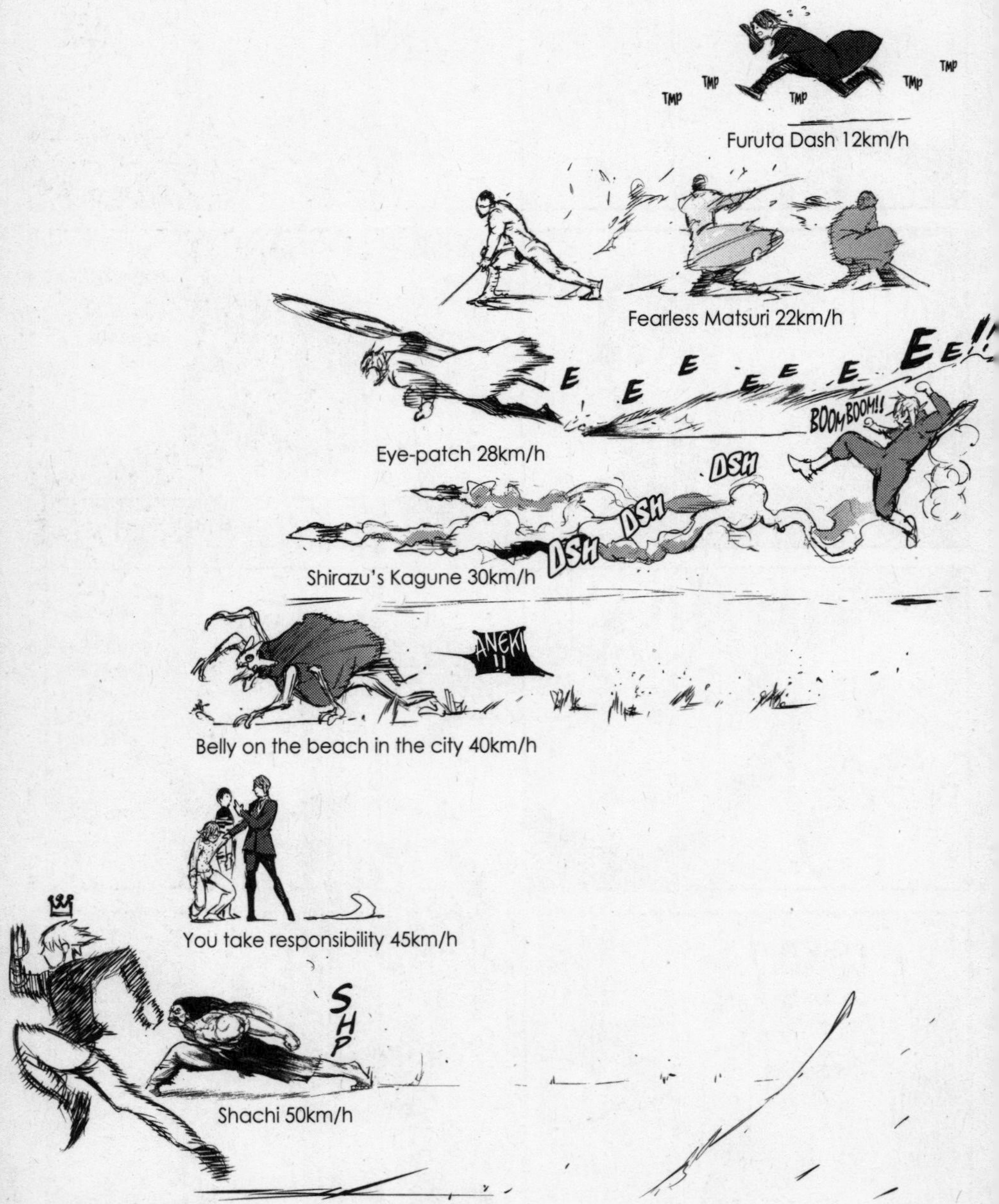
TMP TMP TMP TMP TMP
Furuta Dash 12km/h
Fearless Matsuri 22km/h
EEEEEEEEE!!
BOOM BOOM!!
Eye-patch 28km/h
DSH DSH DSH
Shirazu's Kagune 30km/h
ANEKI!!
Belly on the beach in the city 40km/h
You take responsibility 45km/h
SHP
Shachi 50km/h
King Dash 52km/h

Bigamy

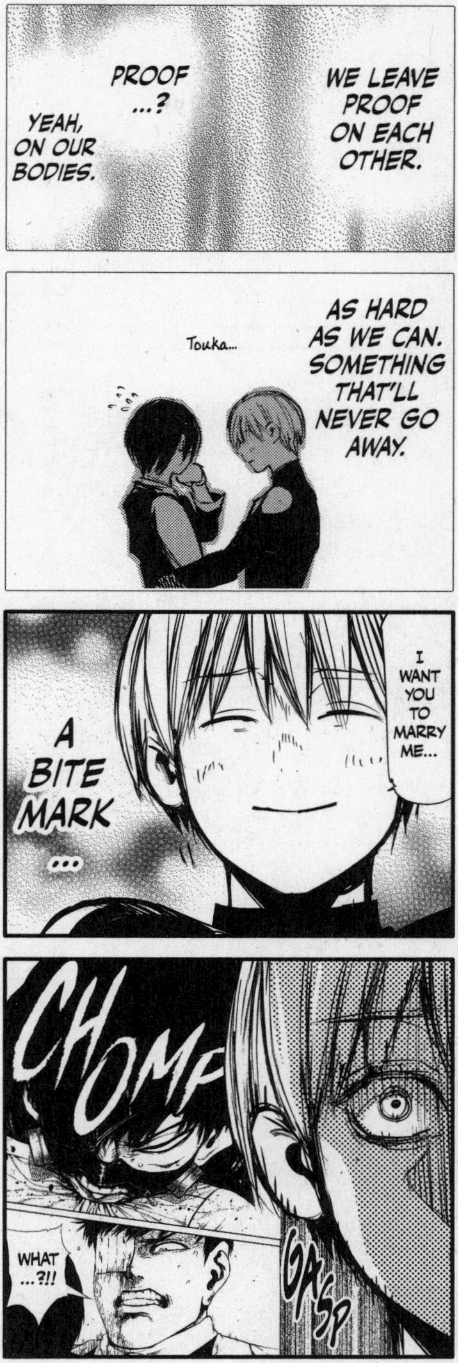
WE LEAVE PROOF ON EACH OTHER.
PROOF ...?
YEAH, ON OUR BODIES.
AS HARD AS WE CAN. SOMETHING THAT'LL NEVER GO AWAY.
Touka...
I WANT YOU TO MARRY ME...
A BITE MARK ...
CHOMP
GASP
WHAT ...?!!

Next Step

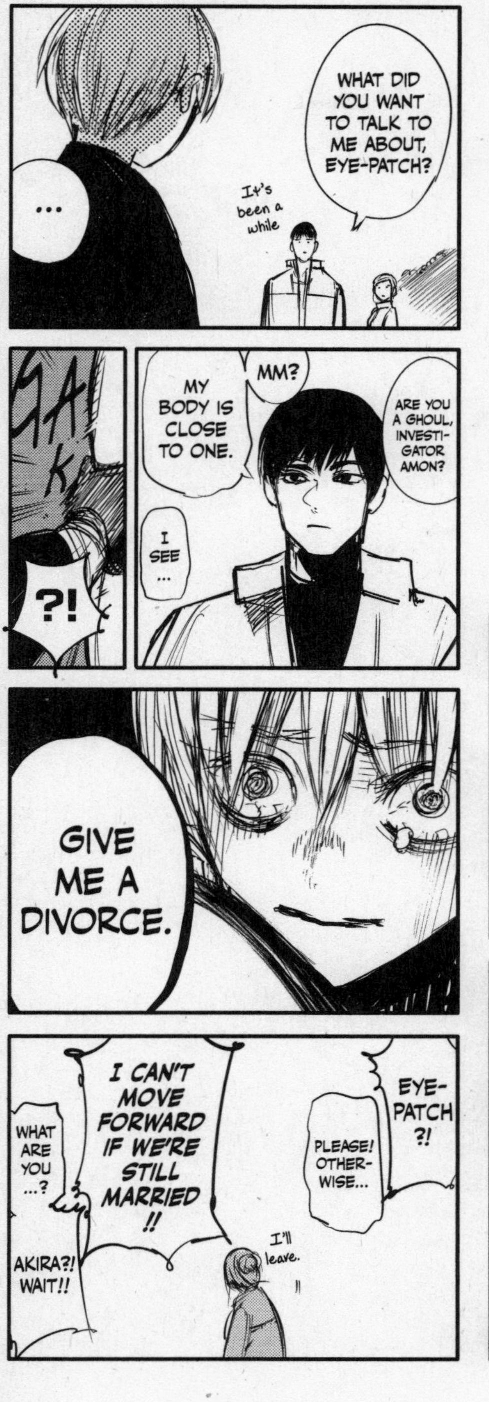
WHAT DID YOU WANT TO TALK TO ME ABOUT, EYE-PATCH?
It's been a while
...
MM?
ARE YOU A GHOUL, INVESTIGATOR AMON?
MY BODY IS CLOSE TO ONE.
I SEE ...
?!
GIVE ME A DIVORCE.
EYE-PATCH ?!
PLEASE! OTHERWISE...
I CAN'T MOVE FORWARD IF WE'RE STILL MARRIED !!
I'll leave.
WHAT ARE YOU ...?
AKIRA?! WAIT!!

You Are the Canvas

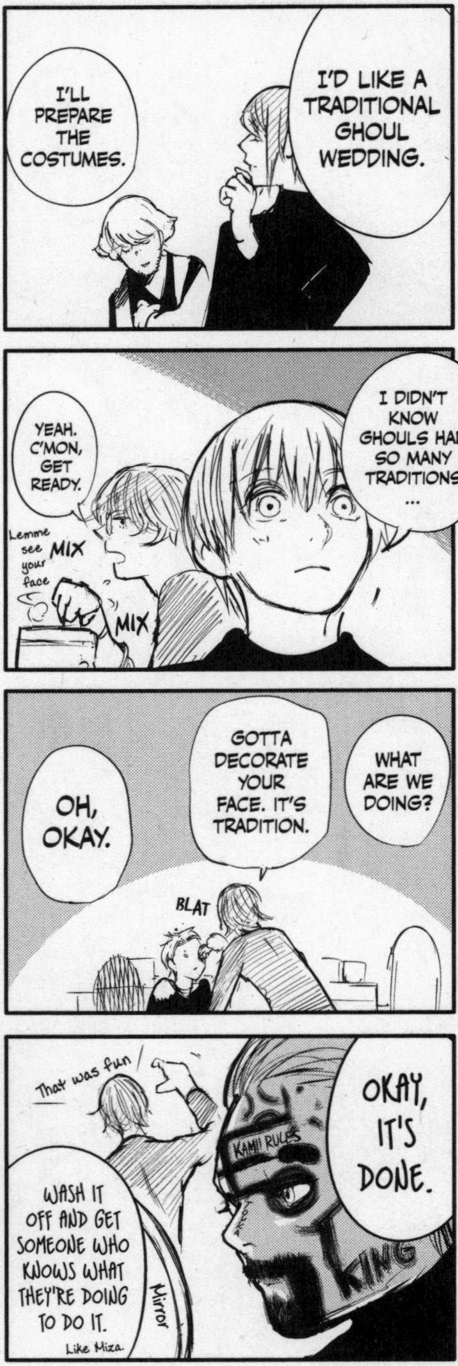
I'D LIKE A TRADITIONAL GHOUL WEDDING.
I'LL PREPARE THE COSTUMES.
I DIDN'T KNOW GHOULS HAD SO MANY TRADITIONS ...
YEAH. C'MON, GET READY.
MIX
MIX
Lemme see your face
WHAT ARE WE DOING?
GOTTA DECORATE YOUR FACE. IT'S TRADITION.
OH, OKAY.
BLAT
OKAY, IT'S DONE.
KAMII RULES
KING
That was fun
Mirror
WASH IT OFF AND GET SOMEONE WHO KNOWS WHAT THEY'RE DOING TO DO IT.
Like Miza.

Happy Till Morning

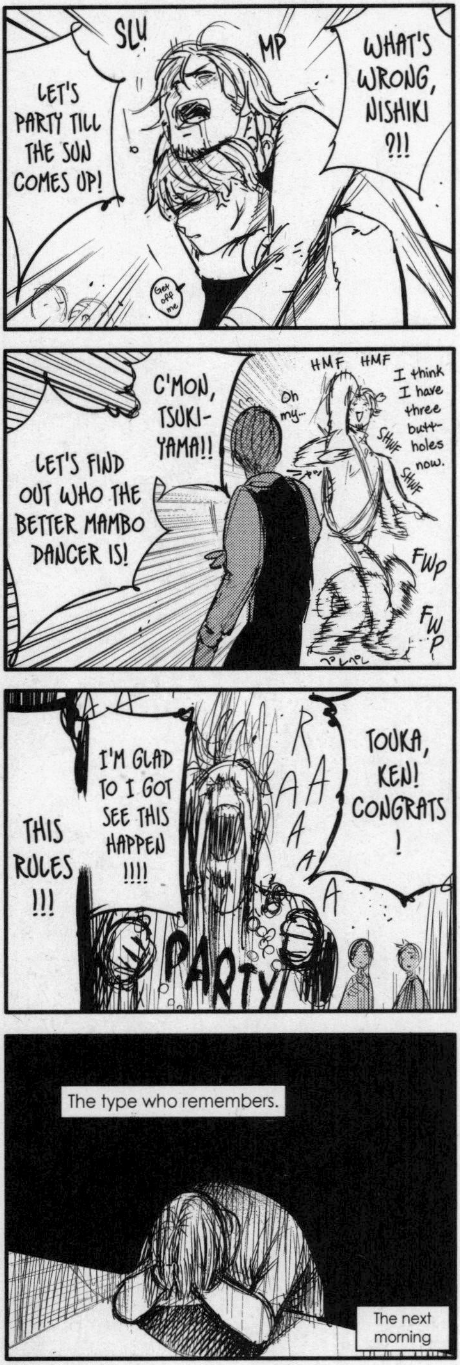
WHAT'S WRONG, NISHIKI ?!!
SLU MP
LET'S PARTY TILL THE SUN COMES UP!
Get off me
I think I have three butt-holes now.
HMF HMF
SHWF
SHWF
Oh my...
C'MON, TSUKI-YAMA!!
LET'S FIND OUT WHO THE BETTER MAMBO DANCER IS!
FWP
FWP
TOUKA, KEN! CONGRATS !
RAAAAAA
I'M GLAD TO I GOT SEE THIS HAPPEN !!!!
THIS RULES !!!
PARTY
The type who remembers.
The next morning

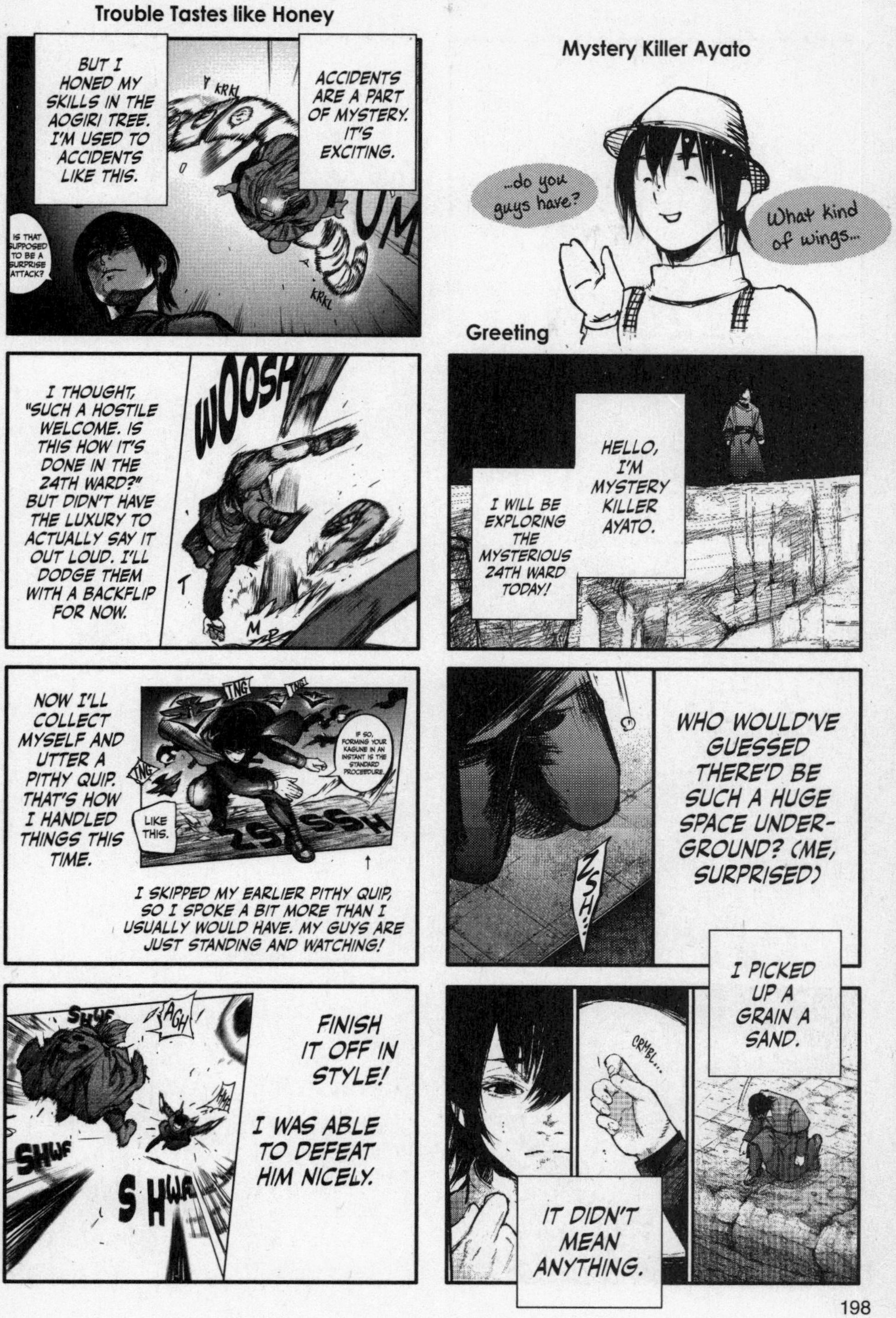
Mystery Killer Ayato
What kind of wings...
...do you guys have?
Greeting
HELLO, I'M MYSTERY KILLER AYATO.
I WILL BE EXPLORING THE MYSTERIOUS 24TH WARD TODAY!
WHO WOULD'VE GUESSED THERE'D BE SUCH A HUGE SPACE UNDER-GROUND? (ME, SURPRISED)
ZSH...
I PICKED UP A GRAIN A SAND.
CRMBL...
IT DIDN'T MEAN ANYTHING.
Trouble Tastes like Honey
ACCIDENTS ARE A PART OF MYSTERY. IT'S EXCITING.
BUT I HONED MY SKILLS IN THE AOGIRI TREE. I'M USED TO ACCIDENTS LIKE THIS.
KRKL
IS THAT SUPPOSED TO BE A SURPRISE ATTACK?
WOOSH
I THOUGHT, "SUCH A HOSTILE WELCOME. IS THIS HOW IT'S DONE IN THE 24TH WARD?" BUT DIDN'T HAVE THE LUXURY TO ACTUALLY SAY IT OUT LOUD. I'LL DODGE THEM WITH A BACKFLIP FOR NOW.
NOW I'LL COLLECT MYSELF AND UTTER A PITHY QUIP. THAT'S HOW I HANDLED THINGS THIS TIME.
TNG
IF SO, FORMING YOUR KAGUNE IN AN INSTANT IS THE STANDARD PROCEDURE.
LIKE THIS.
SSSH
I SKIPPED MY EARLIER PITHY QUIP, SO I SPOKE A BIT MORE THAN I USUALLY WOULD HAVE. MY GUYS ARE JUST STANDING AND WATCHING!
FINISH IT OFF IN STYLE!
I WAS ABLE TO DEFEAT HIM NICELY.
AGH
SHWF
SHWF

24th Ward Dialect Course

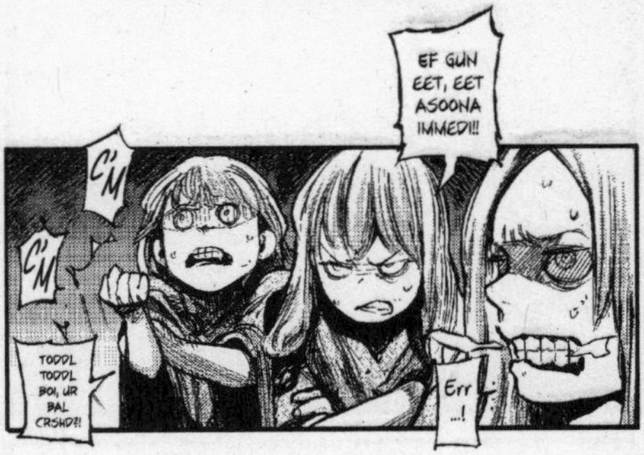
EF GUN EET, EET ASOONA IMMEDI!!
Err ...!
C'M
C'M
TODDL TODDL BOI, UR BAL CRSHD?!

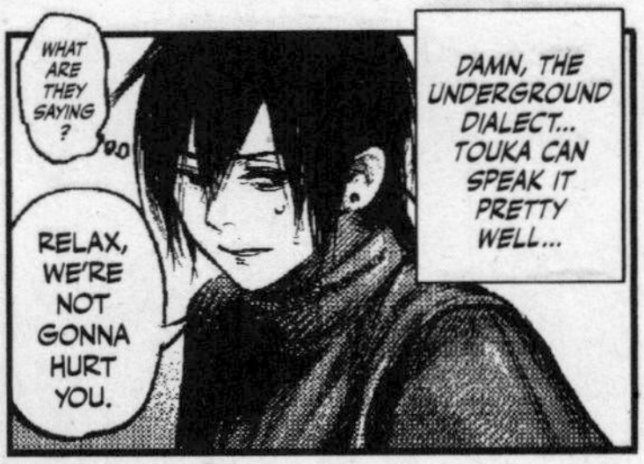
DAMN, THE UNDERGROUND DIALECT... TOUKA CAN SPEAK IT PRETTY WELL...
WHAT ARE THEY SAYING?
RELAX, WE'RE NOT GONNA HURT YOU.

■ Glossary

- **Ef:** If
- **Gun:** Going to
- **Eet:** Eat
- **Assona:** As soon as possible
- **Immedi:** Immediately (unconfirmed meaning)
- **Toddl toddl:** Insult. Treating somebody like a child
- **Boi:** You (very rude)
- **Ur:** Your
- **Bal:** Testicles
- **Crsh, Crshd:** Crush, Crushed

■ Translation

"Ef gun eet, eet asoona immedi!!"
If you're going to eat us, eat us quickly.

"Toddl toddl boi, ur bal crshd!"
You little punk, do you want your balls crushed?

Summary

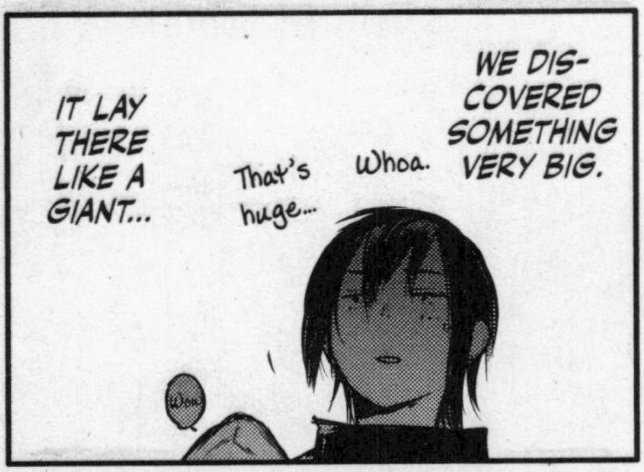
WE DISCOVERED SOMETHING VERY BIG.
Whoa.
That's huge...
IT LAY THERE LIKE A GIANT...

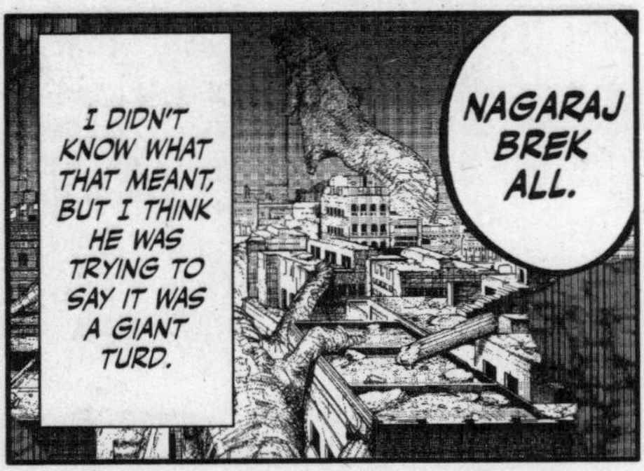
NAGARAJ BREK ALL.
I DIDN'T KNOW WHAT THAT MEANT, BUT I THINK HE WAS TRYING TO SAY IT WAS A GIANT TURD.

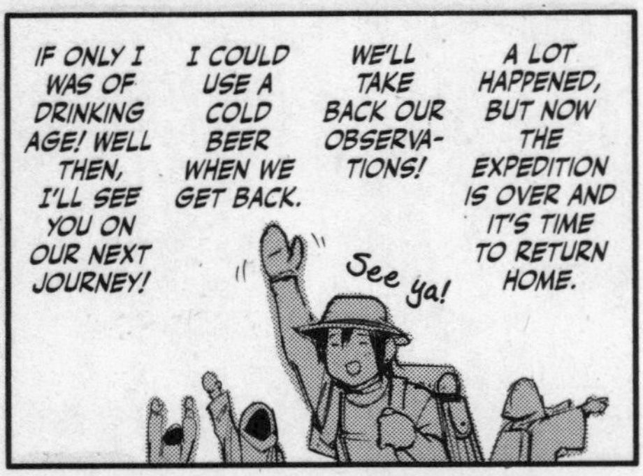
A LOT HAPPENED, BUT NOW THE EXPEDITION IS OVER AND IT'S TIME TO RETURN HOME.
WE'LL TAKE BACK OUR OBSERVATIONS!
See ya!
I COULD USE A COLD BEER WHEN WE GET BACK.
IF ONLY I WAS OF DRINKING AGE! WELL THEN, I'LL SEE YOU ON OUR NEXT JOURNEY!

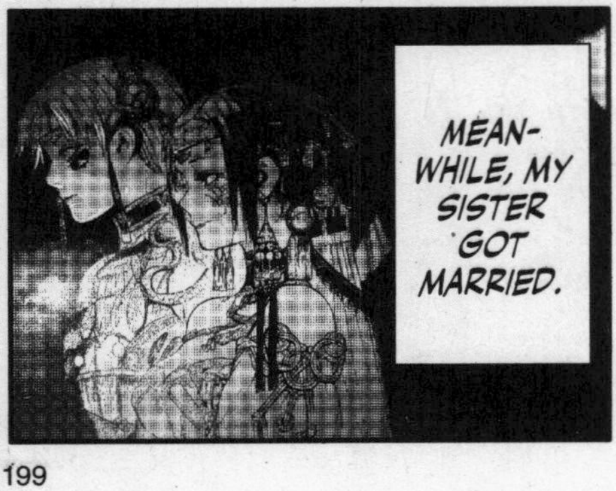
MEANWHILE, MY SISTER GOT MARRIED.

Four-Person Party

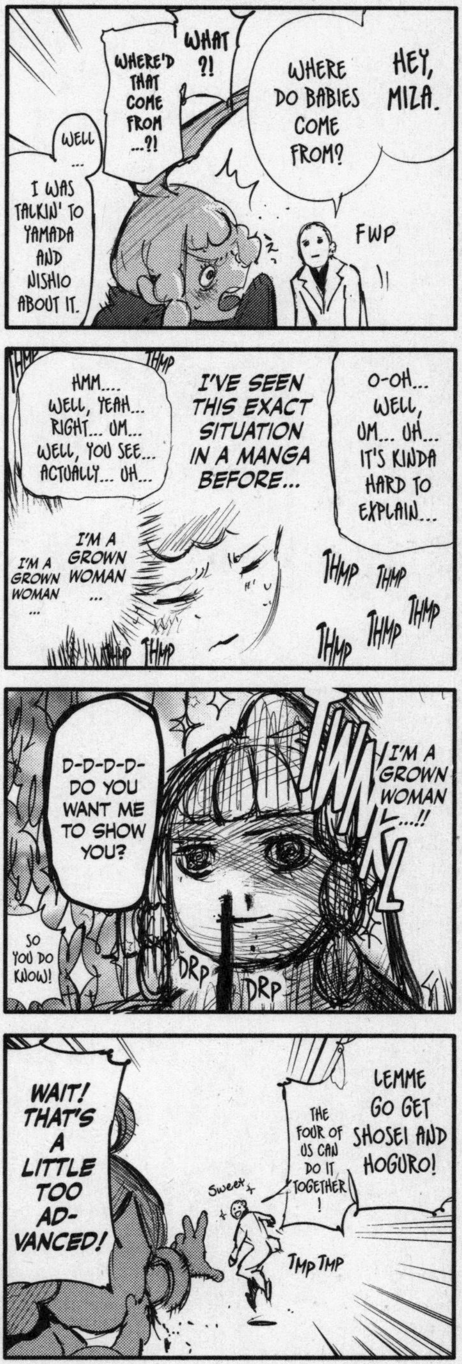
HEY, MIZA.
WHERE DO BABIES COME FROM?
WHAT ?!
WHERE'D THAT COME FROM ...?!
WELL ...
I WAS TALKIN' TO YAMADA AND NISHIO ABOUT IT.
FWP
THMP
O-OH... WELL, UM... UH... IT'S KINDA HARD TO EXPLAIN...
I'VE SEEN THIS EXACT SITUATION IN A MANGA BEFORE...
HMM.... WELL, YEAH... RIGHT... UM... WELL, YOU SEE... ACTUALLY... UH...
I'M A GROWN WOMAN ...
I'M A GROWN WOMAN ...
THMP THMP THMP THMP THMP THMP THMP
I'M A GROWN WOMAN ...!!
D-D-D-D-DO YOU WANT ME TO SHOW YOU?
SO YOU DO KNOW!
DRP DRP
LEMME GO GET SHOSEI AND HOGURO!
THE FOUR OF US CAN DO IT TOGETHER!
WAIT! THAT'S A LITTLE TOO AD-VANCED!
Sweet
TMP TMP

Clay Party

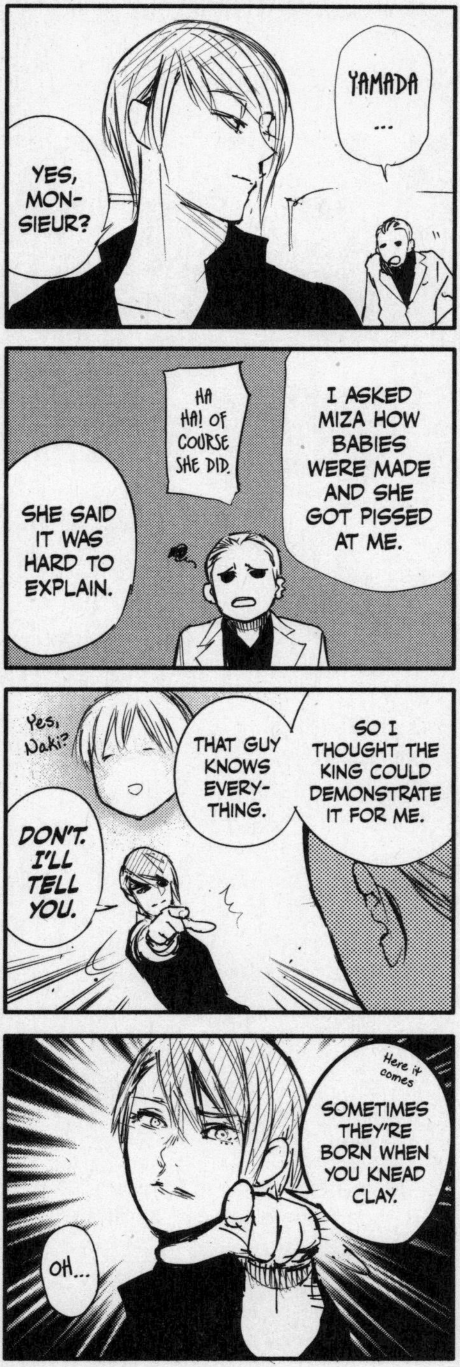
YAMADA ...
YES, MON-SIEUR?
I ASKED MIZA HOW BABIES WERE MADE AND SHE GOT PISSED AT ME.
HA HA! OF COURSE SHE DID.
SHE SAID IT WAS HARD TO EXPLAIN.
SO I THOUGHT THE KING COULD DEMONSTRATE IT FOR ME.
THAT GUY KNOWS EVERY-THING.
Yes, Naki?
DON'T. I'LL TELL YOU.
Here it comes
SOMETIMES THEY'RE BORN WHEN YOU KNEAD CLAY.
OH...

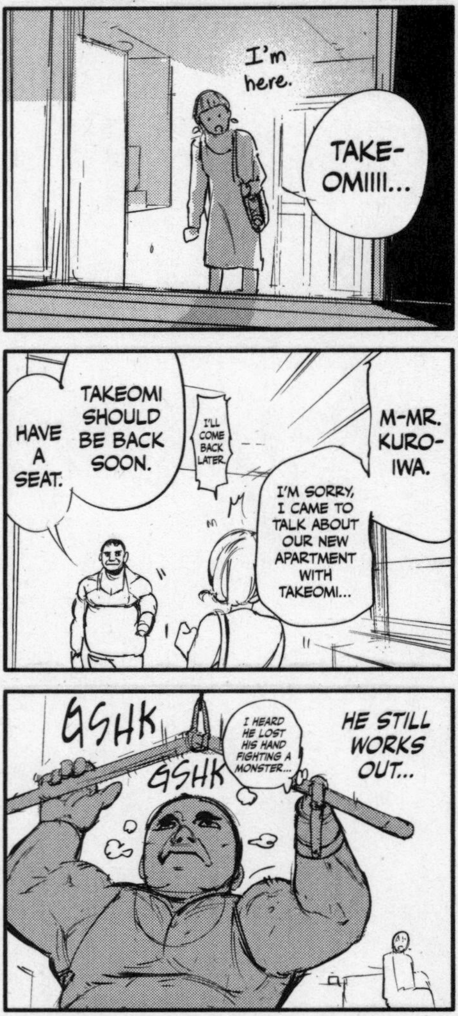
I'm here.
TAKE-OMIIII...
M-MR. KURO-IWA.
I'M SORRY, I CAME TO TALK ABOUT OUR NEW APARTMENT WITH TAKEOMI...
I'LL COME BACK LATER.
TAKEOMI SHOULD BE BACK SOON.
HAVE A SEAT.
HE STILL WORKS OUT...
I HEARD HE LOST HIS HAND FIGHTING A MONSTER...
GSHK
GSHK
IS IT TRUE HE COULD SURVIVE A FALL FROM A 20-STORY BUILDING ...?
HOW HIGH IS 20-STORY BUILDING ... 165 FEET?
...
THAT WOULD MAKE HIM A MONSTER TOO...
Waaa
Mm...
...KO

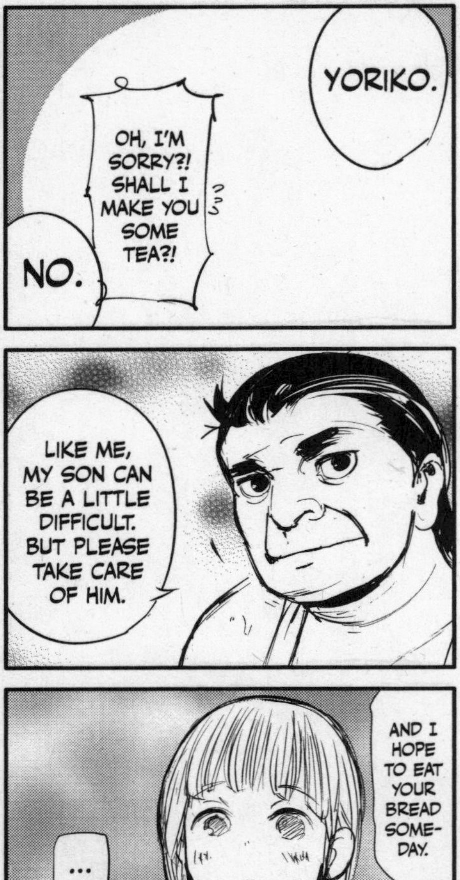
YORIKO.
OH, I'M SORRY?! SHALL I MAKE YOU SOME TEA?!
NO.
LIKE ME, MY SON CAN BE A LITTLE DIFFICULT. BUT PLEASE TAKE CARE OF HIM.
AND I HOPE TO EAT YOUR BREAD SOME-DAY.
...

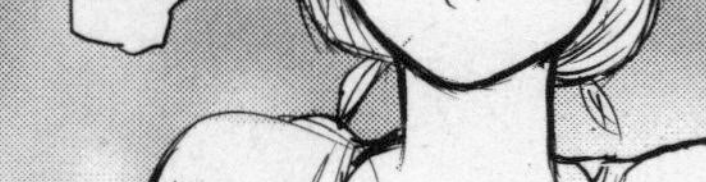
SURE ...

STAFF

Hashimoto
Kiyotaka Aihara
Akikukni Nakao
Nina
Nomaguchi
Ippo Yaguchi
Abe

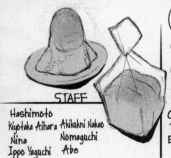

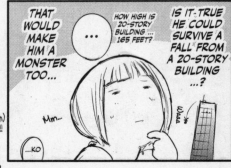

Comic Design
Hideaki Shimada (L.S.D.)
Magazine Design
Miyuki Takaoka (POCKET)
Photography
Wataru Tanaka
Comics Editor
Takehumi Ishii (Gendai Shoin)
Editor
Junpei Matsuo
Thank you!!

Volume 13 will be released October 2019.

Yoiko Kuroiwa (née Kosaka)
黒磐依子 （くろいわ よいこ）

•Age: 21 (Born 5/1) •Blood type: O •Height/weight: 157cm/50kg

High school friends with Touka Kirishima.
Enjoys cooking, especially baking bread.

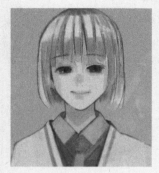

*Ages are from the start of the year.

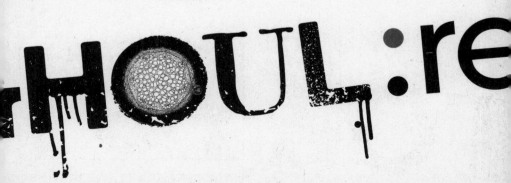

SUI ISHIDA is the author of the immensely popular *Tokyo Ghoul* and several *Tokyo Ghoul* one-shots, including one that won second place in the *Weekly Young Jump* 113th Grand Prix award in 2010. *Tokyo Ghoul:re* is the sequel to *Tokyo Ghoul*.

TOKYO

TOKYO GHOUL:re

VOLUME 12
VIZ SIGNATURE EDITION

Story and art by
SUI ISHIDA

TOKYO GHOUL:RE © 2014 by Sui Ishida
All rights reserved.
First published in Japan in 2014 by SHUEISHA Inc., Tokyo.
English translation rights arranged by SHUEISHA Inc.

Translation Joe Yamazaki
Touch-Up Art & Lettering Vanessa Satone
Design Shawn Carrico
Editor Pancha Diaz

Printed in the U.S.A.

Published by VIZ Media, LLC
P.O. Box 77010
San Francisco, CA 94107

10 9 8 7 6 5 4 3 2 1
First printing, August 2019

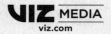
viz.com

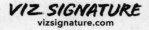
vizsignature.com

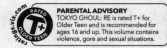

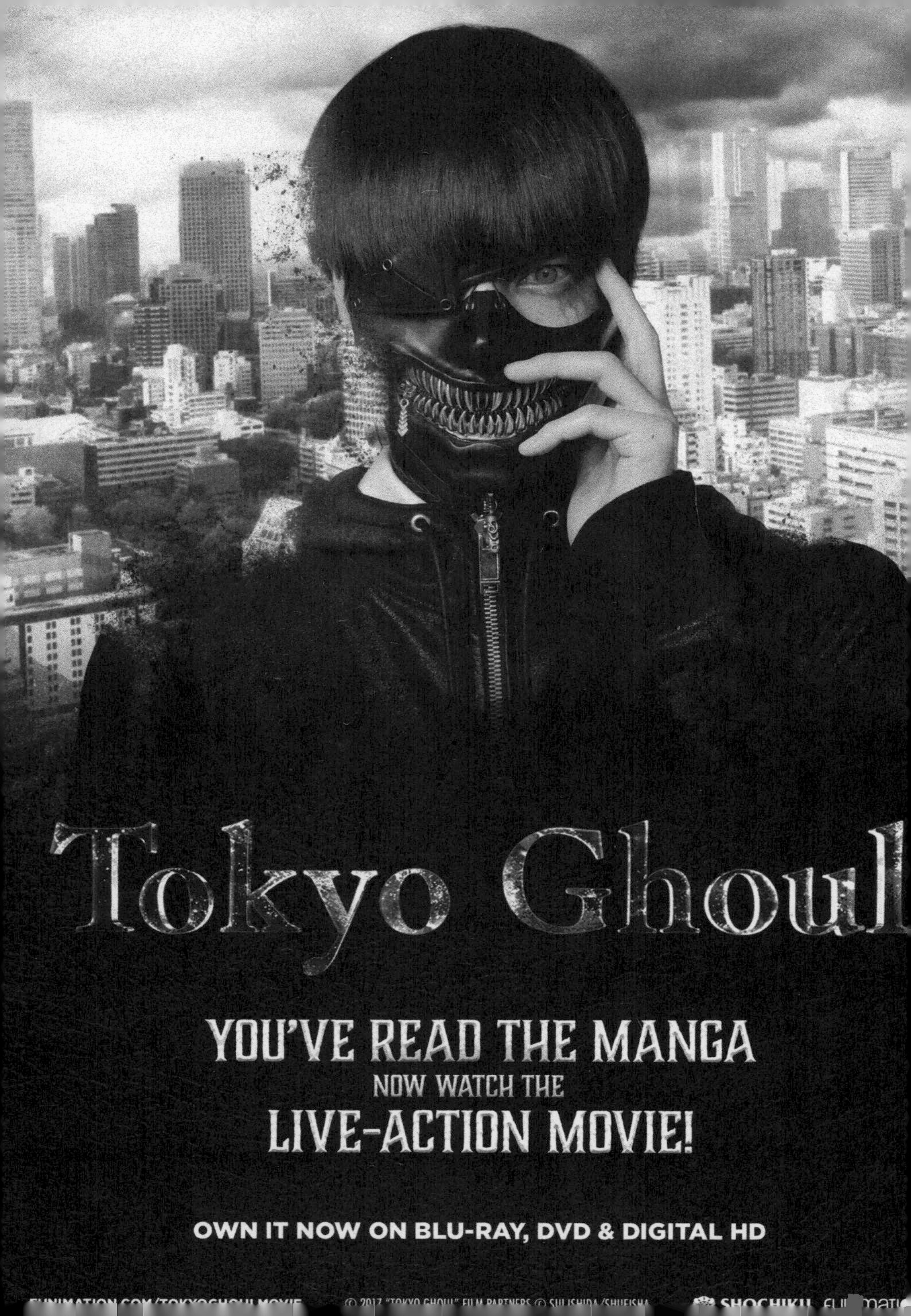

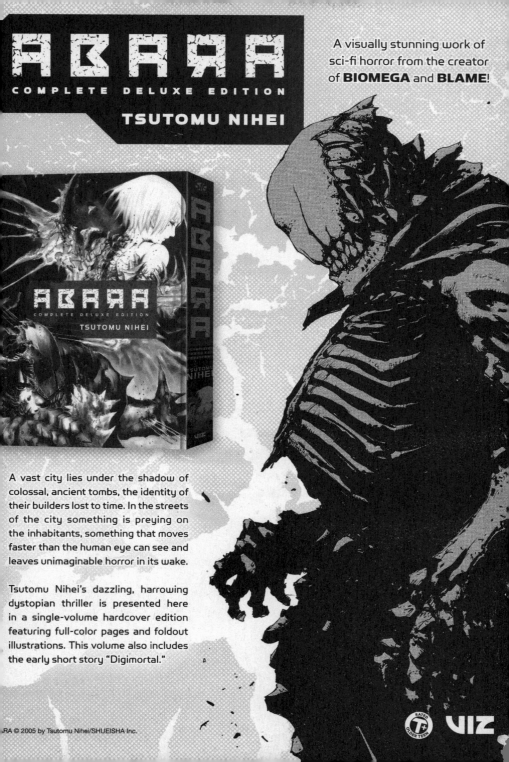

ABARA

COMPLETE DELUXE EDITION

TSUTOMU NIHEI

A visually stunning work of sci-fi horror from the creator of **BIOMEGA** and **BLAME**!

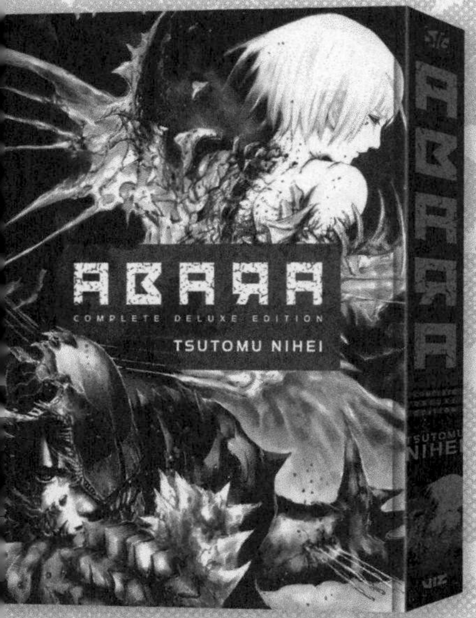
ABARA
COMPLETE DELUXE EDITION
TSUTOMU NIHEI
VIZ

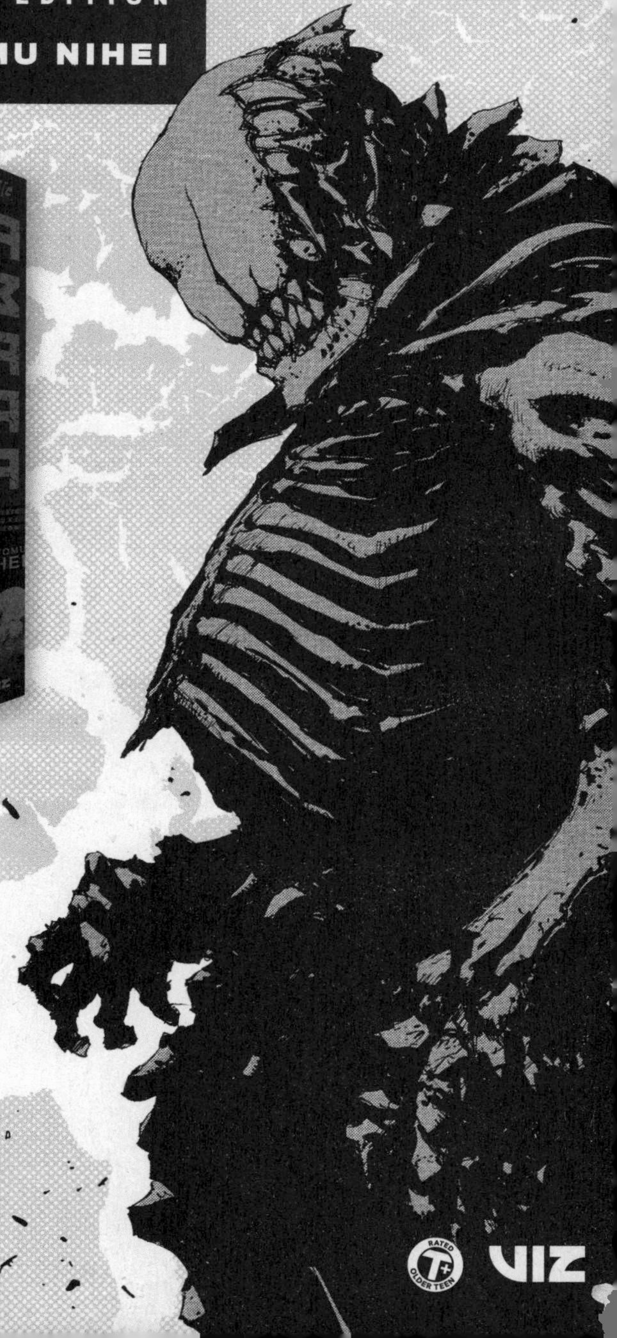

A vast city lies under the shadow of colossal, ancient tombs, the identity of their builders lost to time. In the streets of the city something is preying on the inhabitants, something that moves faster than the human eye can see and leaves unimaginable horror in its wake.

Tsutomu Nihei's dazzling, harrowing dystopian thriller is presented here in a single-volume hardcover edition featuring full-color pages and foldout illustrations. This volume also includes the early short story "Digimortal."

RATED T+ OLDER TEEN

VIZ

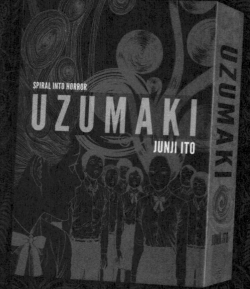

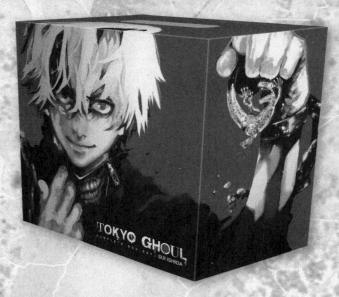

TOKYO GHOUL

C O M P L E T E   B O X   S E T   STORY AND ART BY **SUI ISHIDA**

KEN KANEKI is an ordinary college student until a violent encounter turns him into the first half-human, half-Ghoul hybrid. Trapped between two worlds, he must survive Ghoul turf wars, learn more about Ghoul society and master his new powers.

Box set collects all fourteen volumes of the original *Tokyo Ghoul* series. Includes an exclusive double-sided poster.

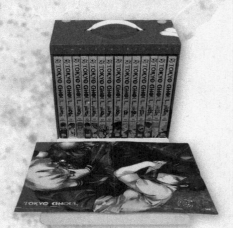

COLLECT THE COMPLETE SERIES

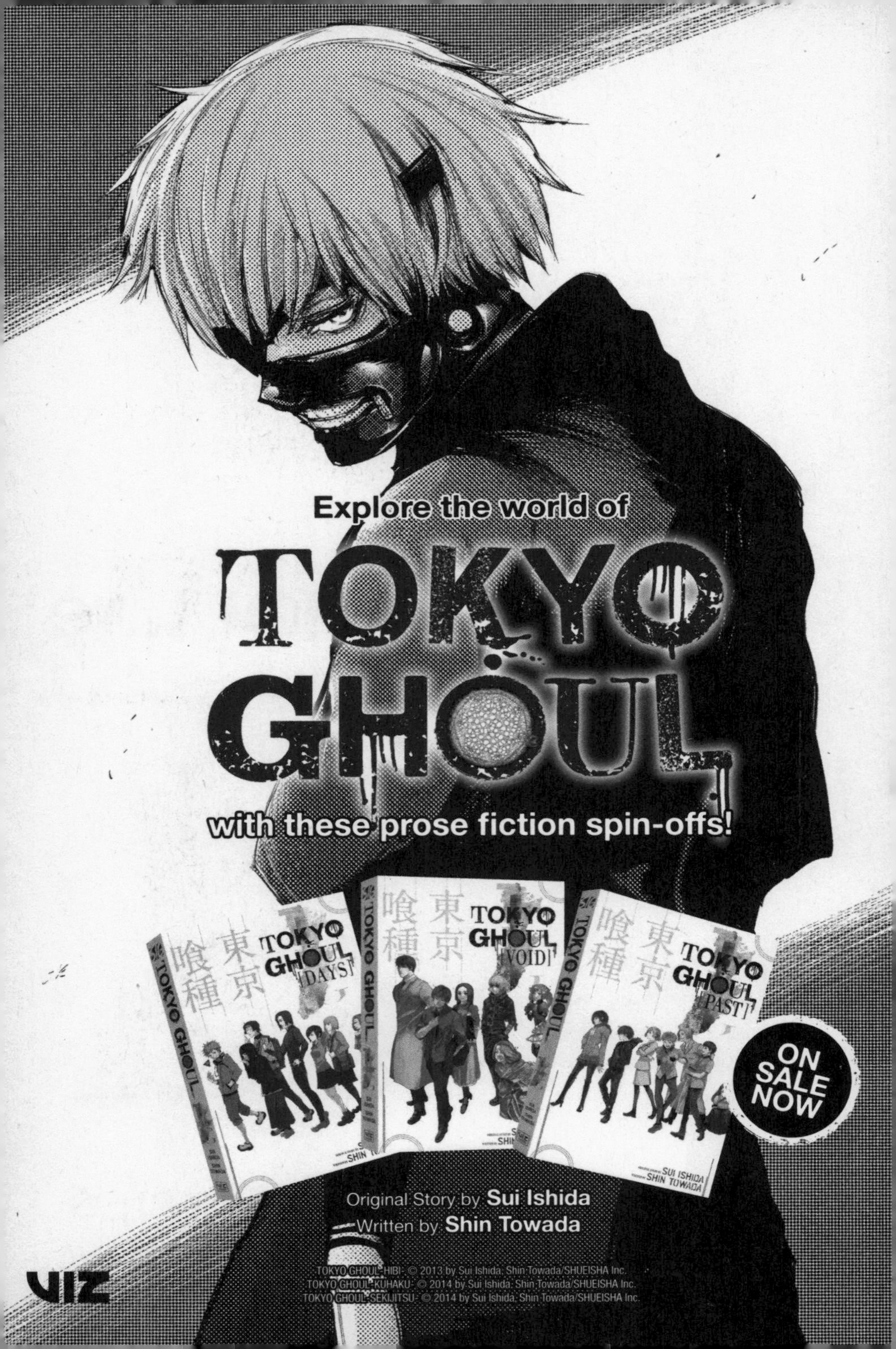
Explore the world of
TOKYO GHOUL
with these prose fiction spin-offs!
TOKYO GHOUL [DAYS]
TOKYO GHOUL [VOID]
TOKYO GHOUL [PAST]
ON SALE NOW
Original Story by Sui Ishida
Written by Shin Towada
VIZ
TOKYO GHOUL-HIBI- © 2013 by Sui Ishida, Shin Towada/SHUEISHA Inc.
TOKYO GHOUL-KUHAKU- © 2014 by Sui Ishida, Shin Towada/SHUEISHA Inc.
TOKYO GHOUL-SEKIJITSU- © 2014 by Sui Ishida, Shin Towada/SHUEISHA Inc.

TOKYO GHOUL:re

This is the last page.
TOKYO GHOUL:re reads right to left.